THE MYSTERIES OF REINCARNATION

Theosophy Trust Books

- *Theosophical Astrology*
by Helen Valborg, WQ Judge, HP Blavatsky, Raghavan Iyer
- *The Bhagavad-Gita and Notes on the Gita*
by WQ Judge, Robert Crosbie, Raghavan Iyer, HP Blavatsky
- *Theosophy ~ The Wisdom Religion*
by the Editorial Board of Theosophy Trust
- *The Gupta Vidya*, Vols. I-II-III
- *Civilization and Consciousness in the Aquarian Age*
- *The Mysteries of Karma*
- *The Mysteries of Reincarnation*
- *Self-Actualization and Spiritual Self-Regeneration*
- *Mahatma Gandhi and Buddha's Path to Enlightenment*
- *The Yoga Sutras of Patanjali*
- *Meditation and Self-Study*
- *Wisdom in Action*
- *The Dawning of Wisdom*
- *EN ESPANOL: Evolución Espiritual*
- *EM PORTUGUÊS: Evolução Espiritual:*
by Raghavan Iyer
- *The Secret Doctrine*, Vols. I and II
- *Isis Unveiled*, Vols. I and II
- *The Key to Theosophy*
- *The Voice of the Silence*
- *The Origins of Self-Consciousness in The Secret Doctrine*
- *Evolution and Intelligent Design in The Secret Doctrine*
by H.P. Blavatsky
- *The Ocean of Theosophy*
by William Q. Judge
- *Teachers of the Eternal Doctrine*, Vols. I and II
by Elton Hall
- *Symbols of the Eternal Doctrine*, Vols. I and II
by Helen Valborg
- *The Crest Jewel of Wisdom*
by Sri Shankaracharya

THE MYSTERIES OF REINCARNATION

BY

RAGHAVAN N. IYER

———

THEOSOPHY TRUST BOOKS

NORFOLK, VA

The Mysteries of Reincarnation

Copyright © June 20, 2023 by Theosophy Trust
Library of Congress Control Number: 2023910513
ISBN-13: 978-1-955958-06-6

All rights reserved. No part of this book may be used or reproduced by any means - graphic, electronic, or mechanical - including photocopying, recording, taping or by any information storage retrieval system without the written permission of the publisher, except in the case of brief quotations embodied in critical articles and reviews.

Available through Amazon.com and other retail outlets, or by visiting:
https://theosophytrust.org/theosophy-online-books.htm
Articles herein may be found at https://www.theosophytrust.org/

The nautilus image on the front cover makes special reference to a diagram on page 300, Vol. II of *The Secret Doctrine*. The discussion there involving the EVOLUTION OF ROOT RACES IN THE FOURTH ROUND says that "during that transitional period — namely, in the second half of the First Spiritual ethero-astral race — nascent mankind was devoid of the intellectual brain element. As it was on its *descending* line, and as we are parallel to it, on the *ascending*, we are, therefore devoid of the Spiritual element, which is now replaced by the intellectual. For, remember well, as we are in the *manasa* period of our cycle of races, or in the Fifth, we have, therefore, crossed the meridian point of the perfect adjustment of Spirit and Matter — or that equilibrium between brain intellect and Spiritual perception." Image creation and editing by Kirk Gradin.

Printed in the United States of America

If ye lay bound upon the wheel of change,
And no way were of breaking from the chain,
The Heart of boundless Being is a curse,
The Soul of Things fell Pain.

Ye are not bound! the Soul of Things is sweet,
The Heart of Being is celestial rest;
Stronger than woe is will: that which was Good
Doth pass to Better — Best.

I, Buddh, who wept with all my brothers' tears,
Whose heart was broken by a whole world's woe,
Laugh and am glad, for there is Liberty!
Ho! ye who suffer! know

Ye suffer from yourselves. None else compels,
None other holds you that ye live and die,
And whirl upon the wheel, and hug and kiss
Its spokes of agony,

Its tire of tears, its nave of nothingness.
Behold, I show you Truth! Lower than hell,
Higher than heaven, outside the utmost stars,
Farther than Brahm doth dwell,

Before beginning, and without an end,
As space eternal and as surety sure,
Is fixed a Power divine which moves to good,
Only its laws endure.

Edwin Arnold
The Light of Asia: Book the Eighth

CONTENTS

INTRODUCTION 1
EDITOR'S NOTE 17
THE GUPTA VIDYA ESSAYS 19
    REINCARNATION AND SILENCE 21
    DEATH AND IMMORTALITY 31
    ANAMNESIS 49
    CONTINUITY OF CONSCIOUSNESS 61
    NOETIC SELF-DETERMINATION 76
    CONTINUITY AND CHOICE 90
    SELF-TRANSFORMATION 106
APPENDIX I: FROM GOD, NATURE AND MAN ~
VOLUME I OF *THE GUPTA VIDYA* 121
    The Evolutionary Tide On Earth 123
    Transcending Ahankara 128
    That Light Which Lives In All 132
    Overcoming Alienation From The Self Of All 136
    Accessing Universal Memory 138
    The Universal Memory Of Mankind 144
    Making More Room For Others 149
    Prometheus, Christ, Are In Every Heart 152
    Assisting The Divine Evolution Of Ideas 154
    The Flame Of The *Karana* 158
APPENDIX II: FROM THE GOLDEN THREAD ~
VOLUME II OF *THE GUPTA VIDYA* 161
    Devotion And Duty 163
    The *Anahata* Vibration 166
    Renunciation And Self-Regeneration 169

The Self-Negation Of Shankaracharya 174
All Learning Is Recollection 179
The Glorious Vesture Of Immortality 182
The Inmost Sanctuary 184
Abandoning The *Antaskarana* 190
Endless Regeneration 193

APPENDIX III: FROM THE PILGRIMAGE OF HUMANITY ~ VOLUME III OF *THE GUPTA VIDYA* 195

Reincarnation And Spiritual Rebirth 197
Intensify Your Ideal Thoughts 202
The Imperishable Soul-Memory 206
Reincarnation And Cyclic Evolution 210
The Stream Of Incarnation 219
Choosing Love Of The Light 223
Strengthening Sutratman 226
Creating A Forward Impulse 230
A True Sense Of Self-Existence 233
Voluntary Reincarnation 237
Between Death And Rebirth 238

APPENDIX IV: THE AFTER-DEATH STATES 239

DIALOGUE ON THE MYSTERIES OF THE AFTER LIFE 241

On The Constitution Of The Inner Man 241

ON THE VARIOUS POST MORTEM STATES 256

The Physical and the Spiritual Man 256
On Eternal Reward and Punishment, and on Nirvana 262
On the Various "Principles" in Man 268
Why Do We Not Remember Our Past Lives? 272
On Individuality and Personality 277
On the Reward and Punishment of the Ego**(4)** 280

ON THE KAMA-LOKA AND DEVACHAN 286
   On the Fate of the Lower "Principles" 286
   Why Theosophists Do Not Believe in the Return of Pure "Spirits" .. 288
   A Few Words about the Skandhas 294
   On Post Mortem and Post-Natal Consciousness 297
   What Is Really Meant by Annihilation 302
   Definite Words for Definite Things 308
DIALOGUES BETWEEN THE TWO EDITORS 314
   On Astral Bodies, Or Doppelgangers 314
WHY DO WE ALL FEAR DEATH? 318
LIFE AND DEATH ~ A Conversation Between a Great Eastern Teacher, H. P. B., Colonel Olcott and an Indian Reported by H. P. Blavatsky 324

APPENDIX V: OTHER SOURCES 337
   On The Mysteries Of Reincarnation ~ Periodical Re-Births 339
   The Beacon Light Of The Unknown 343
   Things Common To Christianity And Theosophy 348
   Every Cell And Organ Has Memory 352
   On The Higher Mind, Kama-Loka And The Astral Light 360
   The Cyclic Pilgrimage Of The Monad 365
   Genius And Reincarnation 367
   "Isis Unveiled" And The "Theosophist" On Reincarnation 375
   Karma Requires Reincarnation 381
   Kriyashakti And Reincarnation 384
   Reincarnation And Self-Transformation 389
INDEX 395

INTRODUCTION

When one hears of reincarnation, one's mind might go back to the 1960's when "flower power" groups formed transient communes and indulged in various New Age ideas, including a rather superficial understanding of Eastern philosophy, including karma and reincarnation. For many, reincarnation may have been seen as a "new" old idea from the East. Reincarnation, however, has been a part of Western philosophical thinking for as long as one can trace its history. Nor was it a new idea in the United States. Early in the eighteenth century, a young man – Founding Father, entrepreneur, scientist, and diplomat – Benjamin Franklin wrote an epitaph for himself:

> The Body of
> B. Franklyn,
> Printer,
> Like the Cover of an old Book,
> Its Contents torn out,
> And stript of its Lettering and Gilding,
> Lies here, Food for Worms.
> But the Work shall not be wholly lost:
> For it will, as he believ'd, appear once more,
> In a new and more perfect Edition,
> Corrected and amended
> By the Author.[1]

Though Franklin is being lighthearted, he seems to have known that reincarnation had been taught at least from the time of Pythagoras. Empedocles taught it, and Plato refers to it in his

---

[1] Handwritten by Franklin in 1728. This version is in the Yale University Library. Franklin wrote out this epitaph a number of times for friends over the years, apparently from memory, and these versions vary slightly in phrasing without changing the content.

dialogues. He gives a detailed allegory at the very end of his ten-book *Republic*, a story well worth considering for its ontological and psychological insights.

Although some early Church Fathers entertained the idea of reincarnation, the Church soon suppressed it, and it was largely forgotten as Christianity spread across Europe and eventually into the New World. The reason for the erasure of this timeless idea in the West is easy to find. The ancient Greeks thought of time as cyclic, repeating itself in general conditions though not, of course, in detail. This allowed for a concept of human progress – also found in Plato's writings – that suggested an ascending spiral, periods of relative enlightened human existence, followed by loss and shadow and eventual recovery and improvement.[2] The Church, however, envisaged a linear time, beginning with the creation, entering a new period with the advent of Jesus as the Christ, and culminating in the end of the world and Last Judgment. This view of time suppressed ancient teachings by replacing reincarnation with some alleged final judgement and displaced karma as a principle of balance and recompence with the idea of sin. Individuals cannot undo sin and so forgiveness must be sought, since each human being is faced with eternal heavenly bliss or endless torment in hell. Historians note that from a sociopolitical standpoint, such a dogma gives immense power to ecclesiastics who alone can forgive sin in the name of a judgmental deity and thus offer the heavenly option. All of this cripples human awareness of immortality, even making utter extinction preferable to the dire promise of the Church.

Thinkers in the East did not accept either the foreshortened view of human progress and evolution, or this linear concept of time. Such a perspective cannot accommodate the time required for immortal

---

[2] One might think of the Mycenaean period when writing was known, then lost with the collapse of civilizations in the Eastern Mediterranean, followed by the Greek recovery which included the writing from which we derive the alphabet.

souls – all human beings – to progress by self-chosen efforts along the path the leads to self-conscious immortality. They held to ancient traditions regarding the human pilgrimage spread over billions of years, and thus remained committed to a cyclic view – in varying versions – and thus did not accept either a final judgment or an eternal afterlife. Rather, like Plato, they held to the view that humanity is on a pilgrimage of ever-increasing wisdom and self-conscious realization of what is ultimately eternal and real. Indian philosophies and religions recognized from experience and thousands of years of being concerned with the nature of consciousness – something largely ignored in the West until quite recently – that the nature of the human being and therefore reincarnation are complex matters that require diligent study to discern. This book explores that rich complexity in the theosophical teachings of Prof. Iyer's *The Gupta Vidya*.

There is a universal and unavoidable human experience that every human being needs to examine and explain, and that is the experience that we are more than our growing and ageing bodies. The seventeenth century Anglican cleric and poet Thomas Traherne captured this experience poetically:

>Till I what was before all time descry,
>The world's beginning seems but vanity.
>My soul doth there long thoughts extend;
>No end
>Doth find, or being comprehend:
>Yet somewhat sees that is
>The obscure shady face
>Of endless space,
>All room within; where I
>Expect to meet eternal bliss.[3]

---

[3] Thomas Traherne, "Insatiableness," *The Element Book of Mystical Verse*, ed. Alan Jacobs (Element: Rockport, MA, 1997).

We may not have sensed this inner experience so thoughtfully, but it is there within us. We all have sensed that we are immortal and the world is eternal, or both at least reaching far before and after a single human life. Prof. R.N. Iyer provides a clear perspective on an individual's sense of himself being more than what he perceives and takes for granted:

> . . . there is that secret of his own soul which he cannot share with anyone else or even bring to the level of human speech. He knows that there is a depth and dimension to his own experience as a conscious sentient being which can participate in the transcendental wonder of the world, which can be aroused to depths and to heights and to a tremendous breadth of cosmic vision when looking at awesome vistas in nature or when surveying the great epochs of human history. But at the same time this secret cannot be conveyed. It cannot be demonstrated or fitted into the workaday categories and concepts needed to survive in a world of psychological limitation and scarcity.[4]

So why do we not take such intimations seriously? The German Idealists and English Romantic poets and philosophers did, but nineteenth century materialist science dismissed as delusional and meaningless all experience that was not based on empirical observation. Yet that very science, especially physics, has cast simplistic materialist views in doubt, recognizing that the observer plays a fundamental role in what is observed. Although some scientists maintain that consciousness is only material brain activity of an electrochemical nature, increasingly scientists are taking larger views. Without denying the functions of the brain, they hold that mind is more than that brain, and that at the death of the brain and the systems that support it, something of the mind (or consciousness) remains. Human intuitions and intimations, some of which doubtless are fancies and illusions, have to be taken seriously, because not all of them are so. Reincarnation must be considered.

---

[4] Raghavan Iyer, "Reincarnation and Silence," *The Gupta Vidya* II, 234.

The most naïve view of reincarnation is that a person dies and returns in a new incarnation as the same person. However, we know that upon dying, the physical body immediately begins a process of recycling its biochemical components. They are disbursed in nature through decomposition or cremation, and there is nothing in experience to suggest that they somehow come back together in a new life. Indeed, throughout life, cells divide, die and are shed everywhere – hence the ability to find DNA left on cups, clothing, anything touched by an individual. Clearly all this physical material does not reconstitute itself.

"But," someone might say, "the person returns in a new body." While a more interesting view, it is nonetheless inadequate. Personality is tied to both consciousness – its attitudes, beliefs, emotions, habits, memories, etc. – and to the body, which enables and limits how one moves and what one does. Immediately we see that the whole personality cannot return because those elements lacking universality are destroyed upon the death of the body. Those who claim to have past-life memories do not claim that they were the same personalities in previous lives. But what of persons? Can persons be separated from personalities?

Here is where Theosophy steps in with a firm yes and no. First, unless we understand the nature of consciousness to some degree, the answer must be no. Consciousness is comprised of fleeting thoughts dealing with daily life in the material world, most of which are immediately forgotten, but also thoughts of universal import, personal memories, convictions, and feelings, and not all of it can survive the death of the body. Secondly, the fact of karma – the reciprocity of thought and action – requires some kind of continuity across lifetimes. Hence this volume complements its companion text, *The Mysteries of Karma*. If one accepts karma as a fundamental principle that governs all of Nature, including the human being, then reincarnation must follow, since the karmic effects of any human being's thought and action in one life cannot be fully experienced in that same life – as any observer of life can readily see. There is always karma to be balanced out at a future time, unless one has learned to become "karmaless," an exalted spiritual state described, for example, in the *Bhagavad Gita*. What survives death are those aspects of the individual that are eternal, and can become consciously immortal in incarnation survive, but those aspects of the person – the purely personal, so to speak – cannot. The yes and no of Theosophy means that individuals as spiritual beings survive death to be reborn again and again but that the earthly personality – which masquerades as the real individuality – does not survive. We are much more than we may think. Shakespeare wrote:

> For what you see is but the smallest part. . . .
> But were the whole frame here,
> It is of such a spacious, lofty pitch,
> Your roof were not sufficient to contain it. . . .[5]

There are beings whose consciousness extends beyond that accessible to present day humanity. The spiral of cyclic time underlies the Theosophical view that humanity is indeed ascending toward ever greater levels of consciousness. In that progression, human beings are gradually recovering what they once knew at very early periods of evolution but lost as they assumed ever more material bodies, leaving them with vague intuitions, such as that set out in Tomas Traherne's verse.

Theosophy teaches that human beings are gods in their inmost nature, even while they have animal bodies, though of a very advanced sort. We have a higher, imperishable divine nature within, with a lower, perishable animal nature without. That immortal spark of divinity is deep within us, while we are yet mortal animal beings. In all the life forms below man, the higher principles are latent; it is only in the human being that self-consciousness is awakened, so that we can think and reflect on ourselves, our future, and the possibilities of unlimited spiritual development.

---

[5] See "Genius and Reincarnation" in this volume, page 367.

Reincarnation of the individual human being mirrors the processes of nature and of the cosmos. Humanity is on a vast pilgrimage, in which spirit descends into matter, thereby having the opportunity to consciously recognize its immortality even while its presence and efforts to do so uplift matter to eventually become self-conscious over vast periods of time. Humanity, which includes all of us presently incarnated, have – over millions of years – descended into ever denser realms of matter so that consciousness could be awakened and our immortality become conscious. Once that happens, we will have realized the maximum potential of fully developed human beings. Humanity has begun a reascent to its spiritual condition but now with ever-growing awareness of its true nature. This whole evolutionary process can be thought of as a struggle between immortality, which is spiritual, and mortality, which is material. Helena Blavatsky explains this process thoroughly in the second volume of *The Secret Doctrine*, and she gives a panoramic view of the phases of this evolution in terms of the metaphor of war:

> What was the religion of the Third and Fourth Races? In the common acceptation of the term, neither the Lemurians, not yet their progeny, the Lemuro-Atlanteans, had any, as they knew no dogma, nor had they to believe *on faith*. No sooner had the mental eye of man been opened to understanding, than the Third Race felt itself one with the ever-present as the ever to be unknown and invisible ALL, the One Universal Deity. Endowed with divine powers, and feeling in himself his *inner* God, each felt he was a Man-God in his nature, though an animal in his physical Self. The struggle between the two began from the very day they tasted of the fruit of the Tree of Wisdom; a struggle for life between the spiritual and the psychic, the psychic and the physical. Those who conquered the lower principles by obtaining mastery over the body, joined the "Sons of Light." Those who fell victims to their lower natures, became the slaves of Matter. From "Sons of Light and Wisdom: they ended by becoming "Sons of Darkness." They had fallen in the battle of

mortal life with Life immortal, and all those so fallen became the seed of the future generations of Atlanteans.[6]

Reincarnation as the taking on of a new body and life does not, therefore, apply to those aspects of the human being that are transient and subject to dissolution. Those are drawn from material Nature and return to it, being then dispersed, and recycled, but not as their formerly aggregated whole. The triad of higher principles – what we could call spirit and soul, or, in ancient philosophical language, the monad – existed before birth into this life and persists after death. Theosophy teaches that this triad exists as long as the universe does. It adds that there are plausible ideas in the Darwinian explanations of speciation and variation, but they are wholly inadequate to explain the creative potential inherent within human beings. In Prof. Iyer's words, "Without taking into account the logic of the Logos on the plane of Akasha, it is impossible to form any adequate conception of the nature of the modes of transmission of life on the physiological plane. Genetic transmission can only account for some of the variations within patterns that themselves cannot be explained by physical heredity."[7] Consciousness has its own laws of development, and reincarnation is the process of consciousness descending into ever more diverse matter, harvesting experience and awareness, until the current stage, when it begins a long ascent back to its origins with the experience and awareness it has gained.

In such a view, reincarnation is the process of growth and learning, and we engage in both by paying attention to and analyzing our ourselves and our experiences. Prof. Iyer puts the issue straightforwardly in "Reincarnation and Silence," where he says:

> "What we need is *metanoia*, a fundamental breakthrough in consciousness. Otherwise the notion of immortality avails us naught. Many Theosophists of every sort hold to reincarnation

---

[6] *The Secret Doctrine* II, 272.
[7] *The Gupta Vidya* III, essay "Kriyashakti", pg. 199.

as a dogma rather than as a basis for meditation. It cannot help unless a man can really come to see that it is a fact in Nature – a law of life in a universe of cyclic processes – and can live by that law increasingly."[8]

What is required is not belief but recognition, and that can occur only if we make the appropriate effort. We all well know that consciousness operates on many levels, both vertically and horizontally. Horizontally, we can broaden or narrow our view of ourselves and the world around us; vertically, we can focus on ourselves alone, or we can focus on our family, our community, our country, our planet, or on all life in the cosmos. We are familiar with some overriding desire or attraction which brings consciousness to a narrow focus on some one aspect of our environment – the doughnut in the pastry shop window, the good looks of some passerby, the award one wants to win, and on and on. We also know that sometimes our thoughts are fragmented, almost random, but at other times we can discern a situation more clearly when we see it in relation to ever-larger circles. We can think at times only of ourselves, and at other times, we can think more widely to include others, even the whole of humanity. The Theosophical claim to be tested by the individual is that consciousness gains ever-increasing levels of freedom when it can abide at increasingly inclusive and universal levels, but this can be demonstrated only to one who undertakes the self-training required.

Even though each person has her or his own talents, an individual cannot win a race without athletic practice or master the violin without musical training. One cannot become a quantum physicist by glancing at a few popular articles. In all such cases, years of learning and exertion are required, and unsurprisingly the same holds true in the development of higher levels of spiritual consciousness, awareness, perception and thinking. Hence Prof. Iyer's statement that we need a radical transformation of

---

[8] *The Gupta Vidya* II, essay "Reincarnation and Silence", pg. 236.

consciousness brought about by thinking deeply about what one is as an individual and what humanity is as a whole; that – in short – we need the radical transformation of *metanoia*. He said:

> When a person discards dogmas and starts with the standpoint of genuine unknowingness, combined with a willingness to learn, he has taken a stand that is truly individual, yet within the context of all mankind. Then, as he works upon himself, he must find out what is unique and gives continuity to himself. At the same time, further growth in this quest will only be possible when he can truly dissolve the sense of separateness between himself and other beings. When the barriers fall away, his love can become almost limitless in scope. He can feel the pain in every human heart and enjoy the world through the eyes of every human being. Clearly, this cannot be done by a person except at some specific level and cannot be done totally within any short-term curve of growth.[9]

In order to understand reincarnation at some fundamental level, each individual has to deeply reflect on that aspect of himself or herself that remains unchanged throughout life to gain awareness of one's immortal nature, and simultaneously, reflect on the whole of humanity and Nature. One can begin by clearly seeing the obvious but often ignored fact of our utter interdependence on others and the world. At some level, we are aware that what we eat, what we wear – generally, every aspect of our lives – depends on the labor of others. We cannot live in isolation from others for long, just as we could not do so prenatally and at the time of our birth. There is a fundamental truth about the unity of life that is reflected in this total interdependence. And we know we must come to some level of understanding of ourselves as individuals in order to be a functioning part of the human race. This double development – the growth of the individual and the increasing recognition of the unity of interdependent life – suggests a deep responsibility in the vast

---

[9] Ibid., page 235.

scheme of the universe. If one is part of the whole – and one is such a part – then one shares in the destiny of the whole; as a self-reflective part, we share in responsibility for the whole.

Thus, although it is true we are born alone – and we each must die alone – it is also true that we come into this life each time in the company of others, those of our cohort with whom we will become friends, and with whom we share certain traits, habits and attitudes, the results of our individual and collective past karma. Hence the distinctive qualities of the various generations. The same is true in an analogous way with respect to the members of our individual family trees. Put in simple terms, reincarnation is the process of learning, and karma provides the opportunities to learn. We incarnate in the ways we do for the ultimate purpose of learning who and what we are as individuals who are an inseverable part of a unified whole.

Once reincarnation is seriously considered, everything associated with the one-life idea has to be set aside. Death is no longer deemed the end of life for an individual, and birth is not its beginning. Now death is seen as a phased transition of ongoing – indeed, endless – life. This movement from what we call life to life has been deeply explored by ancient traditions and some contemporary scientists. At the time of death, what dies and what does not? What happens during the transition to the next life? As physical incarnation ceases, the now disembodied entity enters the period between incarnations. The so-called *Egyptian Book of the Dead* symbolically and allegorically depicts the weighing of the deceased individual's heart against a feather. The spiritual purity of the individual determines whether the heart is lighter or heavier than the feather, and the results determine the fate of the surviving aspects of the deceased. The Tibetan doctrine of the *bardo* or transition between incarnated lives provides an account of the phases the disembodied entity passes through between births. Prof. Iyer recounts the first and crucial part of this process:

> Soon after the actual withdrawal from the physical body, the 'soul,' – a term derived from the Greeks, the Kwan Yin in every

man in Tibetan tradition, the Voice of the Spirit or Conscience, the Great Word, the Great Sound of the *Adi Buddha* – this 'soul,' as we call it, this self-consciousness in us, becomes capable when physical life is discarded of perceiving, though only for a very short time, the pure body of *Dharmakaya*. Simply because of the first separation of consciousness from physical embodiment, the soul begins to have a glimmer of total undifferentiated consciousness, in the form of a vision of pure, clear, colorless light. But this is a tremendous thing for us to contemplate. We are not prepared for it before we die, and therefore it may not mean anything to us unless we begin to meditate upon it now. But if it happens, and we cannot make anything of it, and we fall into some kind of swoon or stupor before this ineffable light, then we are no better off for having had a foretaste or a vision of this great experience which is perfected by the enlightened ones who remain immortal.[10]

Here we see the meaning of the assertion by Socrates that, whether we realize it or not, all life is a preparation for death. If, during life, an individual did not recognize the unity of all lives and the illusory nature of the personal 'I,' she or he cannot, at the moment of death, face the "pure, clear, colorless light" of undifferentiated consciousness; instead, he or she will simply pass out. What then follows are lesser lights, which may attract or repel the soul, peaceful or wrathful deities that are in fact only elements of one's lower nature, and those attractions and repulsions determine what are termed by Buddhist philosophers the *skandhas* – elements of embodied existence – of the next incarnation. The preparation for death by purifying one's nature is, therefore, also the preparation for future life and lives.

In Theosophy, the death of the body is only the first step in the process called dying. The remaining transient aspects of the previously incarnated being are recycled in various ways. The

---

[10] *The Gupta Vidya* II, "Death and Immortality," p. 246.

invisible frame upon which the body was developed will dissolve, but the time it takes for that process depends upon how strongly the thirst for incarnated existence (*tanha*) has suffused it. The stronger the attraction of such embodiment, the longer the time for its dissolution. The life force that pervades all life returns to its origins, the whole stream of the force; the desire that bound one to bodily existence fades away with the invisible form. That part of *manas* – called in Theosophy the "higher *Manas*" – remains with the immortal monad, and all that was transient and merely personal – centered in the earth-bound lower *manas* – enters a compensatory state known as *devachan*, a pleasant, dreamlike condition that lasts until the soul emerges to take on a new incarnation. Being itself an illusory state, *devachan* does nothing to help the soul realize its true nature, though it provides a beneficent and well-earned rest between incarnations.

Prof. Iyer explains the inner meaning of the movement from life to life toward self-conscious immortality in these terms:

> For the personal consciousness there can be no immortality, while for the indwelling soul, for the individual ray of the overbrooding *Atman,* immortality is a fact. For the mediating mind of the middle, immortality has to be won, to be earned, and is neither a gift nor a fact. The mind must progressively detach itself from its external vestures, like a musician who goes beyond worship of his instrument or of his fingers moving on the instrument or of his own self-image, and is merged into something beyond all recorded music, into a reverence for the inaudible music of the spheres. Until a man can do this self-consciously as a soul (and he cannot do it without pain and thoroughness if he is to be honest with himself), immortality for him will be merely a compensatory myth. It will not carry that conviction with which alone he could lighten the loads of others and, through eyes of love, make many lives more meaningful.[11]

---

[11] *The Gupta Vidya* II, "Reincarnation and Silence," p. 237.

Reincarnation ultimately leads to human perfection, a state of wisdom and knowledge virtually unimaginable to us. It is full consciousness of what one is as an immortal monad unified with the whole of life. There are innumerable beings who have achieved this perfection – they have been called Mahatmas, Bodhisattvas, Buddhas, Christs, and many other names; from this Brotherhood of Bodhisattvas the world's great spiritual teachers and reformers have come. Besides those who choose to incarnate in what they know is our illusory world, they also work behind the scenes of Nature to watch over and aid, so far as karma allows, the evolution of humanity and all sentient creatures.

These great beings have reached the highest state of human perfection, but were once human beings like all of us, have reached a degree of self-realization that allows them to transcend *devachan* entirely and chose the time, place and manner of their next incarnation. At the highest level, they recognize the colorless light and, rather than swooning, consciously immerse their being in its Being. Such perfected beings have consciously chosen to follow the Bodhisattva Path of selfless service to all that lives.[12] Theosophy teaches that the narrow path to what Plato called the Good, the True and the Beautiful – which are one seen under three aspects – is the path to the One Life. It is the gradual awakening to true Self-realization, which is nothing less than that One Life, presently reflected in all the forms of embodiment. A jar of water taken from the ocean seems to be separate water, distinct from the ocean. But the separateness is only the glass of the jar, and the separateness of the water is an illusion. Pour the water back into the ocean and the separateness disappears, for it was only apparent because of the jar.

Removing the limitations of consciousness – imposed by past karma and our mistaken conviction that the embodied existence we

---

[12] This path is set out in *The Voice of the Silence*, the essential guide to anyone who wishes to tread the way to conscious immortality.

experience in this life is all there is – requires continuous effort. This effort, like athletic training, involves mental diet and moral practice. The diet consists of the thoughts we dwell on, those we acknowledge and bypass, and withdrawing consciousness from distractions that bind us to illusion. Essential to practice is rigorous regular self-examination of our thoughts, actions and reactions, acknowledging those unworthy of us as immortal souls but without dwelling on them or wallowing in self-pity or condemnation. *The Voice of the Silence*, a devotional book given to all students of the Wisdom Religion in the East, teaches us that practice begins with a fundamental reorientation of our lives away from personal ambition, success, and endless searching for happiness. Rather, we orient ourselves to the welfare of humanity – both visible and invisible (those not at this time incarnated) – and understand ourselves to be an inseverable part of it. *The Voice* says,

> To live to benefit mankind is the first step. To practice the six glorious virtues is the second.[13]

The question of what we are living for – and who we are living for – is thus asked at the beginning of the Path that leads to consciously realized immortality. And it is asked again and again along that Path. The "six glorious virtues" are the *pāramitās* – love, harmony in word and deed, patience in everything, focus on nothing but Truth, meditation, and wisdom and insight. Like the question, the virtues are engaged repeatedly at every level of understanding as the Path unfolds before one. Undertaking this journey consciously means undertaking it for all humanity and, indeed, the whole of life.

Hence there is a choice to be made, a pivotal choice that will determine what the individual will accomplish. Like all such fundamental choices, this one is not made at a specific time in the future but is prepared for by being made all along the way to that future. One may aim for *nirvana*, escape from the ongoing round of

---

[13] *The Voice of the Silence*, Theosophy Company, Los Angeles, 1928, p. 36.

reincarnations into a state of perfect bliss beyond the turbulent world. This requires great effort and is certainly a noble goal, but for Theosophy, it is, as one great being put it, "exalted selfishness." Though unspeakably blissful, one would be cut off from the rest of humanity and the world, unable to help others in any way, thus enwrapped in the very subtlest sense of 'I'.

The second alternative is that of the Bodhisattva, a being who also labors on the Path to its end, but rejects *nirvana* in order to remain connected to humanity and the world and help all to the same goal. Such have been called saviors of the world, and some are recognized in the various religions, but there are legions who work for humanity unrecognized. Every human being has the potential to do what the Bodhisattva does, though it takes lifetimes of deliberate effort to achieve it.

This is the joy of reincarnation – knowing that one life does not reveal everything that each of us can be, that the horizon of human development is vast beyond imagining, and that we can reach it together with the rest of humanity – if we try. Though Benjamin Franklin may have written his epitaph light-heartedly, he wisely caught a central message of reincarnation – that our lives are amended by ourselves for a better, more universal, enlightened future. The reader will find in this book a sweeping survey of reincarnation, detailed analyses of its many dimensions, and help in gaining ever greater consciousness of what and who each of us is, individually and together as One Life.

Elton Hall Ithaca, NY
June 20, 2023

EDITOR'S NOTE

This work is modeled after two of our previous books, entitled *Consciousness and Civilization in the Aquarian Age* and *The Mysteries of Karma*. All of these books replicate the same structure as Prof. R.N. Iyer's 3-volume book, *The Gupta Vidya*, with the primary essays coming first, followed by several appendices containing important supplementary materials.

Like the previous two books in this series, all of the essays in the first chapter, The Gupta Vidya Essays, and the quotations in the first three appendices, were first published in Prof. Iyer's magnificent three-volume work entitled *The Gupta Vidya*,[14] also published by Theosophy Trust Books. The first seven essays in the first chapter form the groundwork for Prof. Iyer's teachings on Reincarnation, while the first three appendices contain extensive quotations found elsewhere in the three volumes of *The Gupta Vidya* - "supporting documents" - that amplify and extend the ideas in the essays in the first chapter. The quotations in Appendices I-II-III are quite comprehensive; i.e., they comprise all of the most significant mentions of 'reincarnation' in other places of the three volumes. Appendix IV deals with the "after-death states", and Appendix V is comprised of a wide variety of writings from theosophical literature on the subject at hand, the "mysteries of reincarnation".

Theosophy Trust is again deeply grateful to Prof. Elton A. Hall for his insightful Introduction, and to Kirk Gradin of Santa Barbara for his talented work on the cover graphic, so suggestive of the difficult teachings from *The Secret Doctrine* regarding the evolution of the human race.

All of the articles and readings in this work can be found in digital format on the Theosophy Trust website at:

https://www.theosophytrust.org/RNI-article.

Editor, Theosophy Trust Books

---

[14] Page references to *The Gupta Vidya* are to the paperback version available from Amazon.com.

THE GUPTA VIDYA ESSAYS

REINCARNATION AND SILENCE

Every man's soul has by the law of his birth been a spectator of eternal truth, or it would never have passed into this our mortal frame, yet still it is no easy matter for all to be reminded of their past by their present existence.

                                                            Plato

While we may know about the long and complex history of the doctrine of reincarnation, the crisis of our time is such that the response of thinking men and women is and should be, "How does it help me? What difference could it make to my life?" In the *Bhagavad Gita* Lord Krishna, speaking as the Logos in the cosmos, but also as the hidden god in every man, makes a supreme, unqualified affirmation. Like similar utterances in the great scriptures of the world, the words of Krishna have a ring of self-certification. He simply affirms for all men that there is an inexhaustible, inconsumable, incorruptible, indestructible, beginningless and endless spirit that is the sovereign ruler within the temple of the human body. Yet the same Krishna, having made this affirmation, ends his speech by asking Arjuna to recognize the honest position of the finite mind of the ordinary man by saying, "The antenatal state of beings is unknown; the middle state is evident; and their state after death is not to be discovered."

Any human being must recognize that, in so far as his mind is a bundle of borrowed conceptions — because he has grown up conditioned and circumscribed by the limiting factors of heredity, family, education and the social environment — he cannot do any more at first than come with pain to the point of declaring with profound honesty, "I really do not know. I do not know about evil. I have no idea of many things that happened to me earlier in this life. I have no idea of what will happen to me tomorrow, next year, let alone after the moment of death." This could give integrity to the quest. At the same time, when a human being begins at the level of categories and concepts, he also knows that there is something unspoken about his particular life — his tears, his thoughts, his deepest feelings, his loves and longings, his failures and frustrations, his invisible, hidden determination to hold fast in times of trial, to triumph over obstacles that seem forbidding. Beyond all of these there is that secret of his own soul which he cannot share with anyone else or even bring to the level of human speech. He knows that there is a depth and dimension to his own experience as a conscious sentient being which can participate in the transcendental wonder of the world, which can be aroused to depths and to heights and to a tremendous breadth of cosmic vision when looking at awesome vistas in nature or when surveying the great epochs of human history. But at the same time this secret cannot be conveyed. It cannot be demonstrated or fitted into the workaday categories and concepts needed to survive in a world of psychological limitation and scarcity.

The problem is one of translation. Seen philosophically, if we assume that there is something prior to be translated into something else that is shareable, it is a problem of self-discovery. It involves integrating the potential, intermittently intimated in our consciousness, with the actual which is a story that could be streamlined and which any Hollywood scriptwriter could convert into a celluloid version, a banal sequence of scenes. There must be something between our inchoate intuition of the inexhaustible and our painful recognition of the factuality of the temporally finite sequence that seems to string these events together. Memories clutter the mind. We look back with regrets or look forward with hopes, with longings that may be vain and ineffectual or may be impossible to share with anyone else.

What is self-validating for a Krishna or for the immortal spirit of man can only become a supreme and total fact for a human being when he has begun to strip away the layers and vestures of consciousness through which he is bound. In a Wordsworthian sense, every child is crowned by the aura of the divine, and has in his eyes some recognition of having lived before, some glint of an ancient wisdom distilled into the very essence of his response to the furniture of the world. Yet every human being, growing out of the child-state, loses those intimations. How are we to recover them compatibly with the integrity and self-consciousness that we must bring to every level and aspect of our human experience? This necessitates further work upon the whole of one's nature. Where we do not know, we may discard the dogmas that claim to know. There are those which insist that man is merely a fortuitous concurrence of atoms — in the name of a science which would be disowned by the greatest, most agnostic and creative scientific thinkers. There is the dogma derived from religion that man is a soul created by an anthropomorphic being at a certain point of time and consigned to eternal hell or heaven, and there are other corruptions of thought such as transmigration into animal form.

When a person discards dogmas and starts with the standpoint of genuine unknowingness, combined with a willingness to learn, he has taken a stand that is truly individual, yet within the context of all mankind. Then, as he works upon himself, he must find out what is unique and gives continuity to himself. At the same time, further growth in this quest will only be possible when he can truly dissolve the sense of separateness between himself and other beings. When the barriers fall away, his love can become almost limitless in scope. He can feel the pain in every human heart and enjoy the world through the eyes of every human being. Clearly, this cannot be done by a person except at some specific level and cannot be done totally within any short-term curve of growth. We would need a number of births to attain that degree of universalization wherein we could merge the universal and the individual and also maintain stasis throughout the different levels on which we have to communicate with widening or narrowing circles of human beings. In that sense, what is self-validating at one level could only become wholly valid and be a fully embodied truth when one's whole life revolves around it.

Many an unlettered man, in the words of the poet, is a mute, inglorious Milton, unknown, unnoticed by other men, and, like Markham's man with a hoe, conveys through his eyes the sad awareness that this is an old story that includes all beings and will persist far into the future. For the pseudo-sophisticated intellectual classes to see as much would be extremely difficult. People for whom there is very little else can sustain the awareness of some fundamental truth. To be able to do this self-consciously within a process of growth is extraordinarily elusive for a man burdened with the mental complexities of contemporary civilization, because he cannot ascend to universal brotherhood except very partially, intermittently and, alas, defensively.

To make reincarnation a vital truth in one's personal life is to treat each day as an incarnation, to greet every person as an immortal soul, inwardly and in silence, and to empathize with every human failure as a limitation — an effect with causes — comparable to all other limitations. It is the ability to see, even in the longing of the person who is almost totally lost, that spark of the Divine which could eventually be fanned into the flame of the cosmic and compassionate fire of wisdom of the Buddhas and Bodhisattvas. It is an old tradition in the East that those who truly know of the immortality of the soul can only say, "Thus have I heard."

Why is there no immortality for what we call the 'personality,' the particular mask that we wear, through which we appear to other people to be someone with a name and a form, a recognizable identity? However glorious the aggrandizement of personal selfhood may seem in a Nietzschean sense, it is still something that limits and is limited, and hence must participate in finitude and mortality. To wish immortality for that which is visibly mortal, for a mind which is like a cobweb of confusing conceptions, is at best a compensatory illusion. Ultimately, it is a sign of weakness. But the Great Teachers did not come to tell man what he already knows — that there are limitations. They came to tell him that beyond these limitations he could be free. Buddha declared: "Know ye who suffer, ye suffer from yourselves. None else compels that ye are caught in this Wheel of Life." When Jesus spoke of the weakness of the flesh, he also intimated that the spirit is free, that it is the source of will, and that when it is truly willing, it is immortally free.

It is only by reinforcing a weaker side of our own nature that we could project from a limited view of ourselves a confused picture of personal immortality. Despite all the self-advertisements of the age, hardly any man can do full justice to himself. A man who is loudly making the case for himself is all too often belittling himself. Even the finest self-images have some illusion built into them, and to extrapolate them into the future and into the past is to limit oneself unduly. The notion of personal immortality becomes extremely degrading in a universe of law, where everything experienced by consciousness is connected, in the course of time, with everything that follows it. If a person, early or late in life, uses the doctrine of rebirth, or some notion of personal immortality, as a crutch to cling to, physical death may well be succeeded by a dreamy state of illusory happiness after a period of purgatorial separation from all the excrescences of the life just lived. Then he will have to come back, and alas, in so doing, as Plato suggests in the Myth of Er, he may choose the very opposite of what he seeks. A person who mistakes the external tokens of the good, the true and the beautiful for the transcendental *Agathon* may well find himself drawn, even propelled, into an environment where he is punished by getting what he wants.

What we need is *metanoia*, a fundamental breakthrough in consciousness. Otherwise the notion of immortality avails us naught. Many Theosophists of every sort hold to reincarnation as a dogma rather than as a basis for meditation. It cannot help unless a man can really come to see that it is a fact in Nature — a law of life in a universe of cyclic processes — and can live by that law increasingly. He can recognize mistakes, and through repeated self-correction, open new vistas. He may make existential affirmations of perfectibility — which must be on behalf of all if they are to be authentic — and give everyone he meets something of the taste of true optimism in regard to the future. Unless a person can do these things, even if he speaks the language of *impersonal* immortality, still it would be nothing but a projection of a personal conception of immortality.

The teaching of the Mahatmas is utterly uncompromising on such matters. For the personal consciousness there can be no immortality, while for the indwelling soul, for the individual ray of the overbrooding *Atman,* immortality is a fact. For the mediating mind of the middle, immortality has to be won, to be earned, and is neither a gift nor a fact. The mind must progressively detach itself from its external vestures, like a musician who goes beyond worship of his instrument or of his fingers moving on the instrument or of his own self-image, and is merged into something beyond all recorded music, into a reverence for the inaudible music of the spheres. Until a man can do this self-consciously as a soul (and he cannot do it without pain and thoroughness if he is to be honest with himself), immortality for him will be merely a compensatory myth. It will not carry that conviction with which alone he could lighten the loads of others and, through eyes of love, make many lives more meaningful.

If we trace the English term 'soul' to its Greek antecedents and equivalents, we soon find a wide variety of meanings. Even before the time of Socrates, many accretions and materializations had already gathered around the concept. It was compared to the wind. It was also supposed to mean 'that which breathes,' 'that which is alive.' And it was given many other meanings and often couched in metaphorical terms through analogy with sparks and a central fire. It became crucially significant for Plato to enrich the notion of 'soul' and to give it an existentially human meaning to do with the very act of search, the very desire to know the good, the hunger to make distinctions — not only between the good and the bad but between the good and the attractive, not only between the true and the false but between the true and the plausible. The desire to make noetic discriminations becomes the basis for a functional definition of the soul. Plato taught that, metaphysically, the soul may be seen either as perpetual motion or as a self-moving agent. In one passage he refers to a particular kind of motion which is not visible in the material realm but may be properly ascribed to the hidden Logos, the invisible deity. Elsewhere, what he identifies as the soul is connected with volition. What would it avail a man who uses the word in a Socratic sense but does not come to terms with his own will-problem, or worse still, becomes identified intellectually with his weak-willed self?

Language is very important here. The prolonged abuse of the term 'soul' in the Middle Ages resulted from a decisive shift in meaning. An active agent was replaced by something passive, something created. In a corruption of the Socratic-Platonic meaning, the 'soul' became merely something acted upon, a passive agent receiving reward or punishment. The term 'soul' almost became unusable, so that in the Renaissance humanists had to assert the dignity and divinity of man in ways that did not involve them once again in the debased coinage of the terminology of the past. In the twentieth century the term 'self' is coming into wide circulation, recovering some of the dignity of the classical conception of the soul.

A person brought up in a corrupt language system could receive tremendous help by borrowing a term from Sanskrit and trying to recognize its open texture. The compassionate Teachers of the Theosophical Movement chose to introduce from that sacred language terms like *Manas* — the root of the word 'man,' from *man*, 'to think' — into the languages of the West. When Emerson eulogizes "man thinking" he is using two English words in a manner that confirms exactly the full glory of the idea of *Manas*. Yet we also know that both the words 'man' and 'thinking' can be so degraded in everyday usage that they do not convey the glory of manhood implied by *Manas*. The term *Manas* in Sanskrit means not only 'to think,' but also 'to ideate,' 'to contemplate.' To contemplate in this classical sense is to create, to sustain a continuous and controlled act of creative imagination enveloping more and more of the whole, while retaining that core of individuality which signifies responsibility for the consequences of all thoughts, all feelings, all words, and all acts. This is a kingly conception.

It is often advantageous for a person to go outside his particular prison-house of debased language and explore classical concepts. As we grow in our awareness, we may make the beautiful discovery that even in the accents of common speech there are echoes of those pristine meanings. The literal meaning of words is less important than the tone of voice in which we use them. It is possible for a man in the street to say to another, "Hi, man" with unconscious contempt, and for a traveller in the Sierras to say, "Hi, man," in a manner that expresses genuine fellow-feeling. Miranda in *The Tempest*, seeing human beings for the first time, exclaims:

> O, wonder!
>
> How many goodly creatures are there here!
>
> How beauteous mankind is! O brave new world,
>
> That has such people in't!

Every word has a depth and beauty of feeling that makes ordinary English words rise like wingèd skylarks into the universal empyrean — generous, cosmic and free. Beyond all languages and concepts, the very act of articulation is of immense importance.

Perhaps the most beautiful passage on the subject of reincarnation is to be found in *The Human Situation* by Macneile Dixon. This great lover of the literatures of the world, of Plato and Shakespeare, dared to suggest:

> What a handful of dust is man to think such thoughts! Or is he, perchance, a prince in misfortune, whose speech at times betrays his birth? I like to think that, if men are machines, they are machines of a celestial pattern, which can rise above themselves, and, to the amazement of the watching gods, acquit themselves as men. I like to think that this singular race of indomitable, philosophising, poetical beings, resolute to carry

the banner of Becoming to unimaginable heights, may be as interesting to the gods as they to us, and that they will stoop to admit these creatures of promise into their divine society.

By speech a man can betray his divine birth, and just as this is true of speech in its most sacred and profound sense, it is also true of human gestures. The simple mode of salutation in the immemorial land of Aryavarta is filled with this beauty. When the two hands come together, they greet another human being in the name of that which is above both, which brings the two together, and includes all others. There is something cosmic, something that has built into it a calculation of the infinite in the expedient, even in this gesture.

But what is true of gestures could be even more true of human utterance. The surest proof of the divinity and immortality of man is that through the power of sound he can create something that is truly magical. He can release vibrations that either bless or curse, heal or hinder other beings. This is determined by motivation, intensity of inmost feeling, and the degree of individual and universal self-consciousness, nurtured and strengthened through constant meditation and self-study.

Suppose one were to ask of the gods, "Give me one of two gifts for all men. Give me first that gift which will suddenly enable all men to say that they know about reincarnation and the soul, and that they believe in immortality. Second, give me that gift which enables all men to help babies to grow with a feeling of dignity, deliberation, beauty and sanctity in regard to human speech." The wise would know that the latter gift is much more valuable than the former, because mere beliefs will not save human beings even though truly philosophical reflection upon alternatives is part of the prerogative of a Manasic being, a man in Emerson's sense. These beliefs can only be made to come alive through the exercise of conscious and deliberate speech, with a delicate sensitivity for the existence of other beings, and an immense inner compassion for all that is alive. If human speech were not constantly wasted and made into something so excessive and destructive, so mean and niggardly, we would not find so much of the self-hatred, mutual distrust, pessimism and despair that characterize our lot. We would not find ourselves in a society which is free but where, alas, the loudest voice is the most feared and tends to have the widest impact.

Anyone who can existentially restore the alchemical and healing qualities of sound, speech and silence, to some limited extent, in the smallest contexts — in relations with little children, with all he encounters even in the most trivial situations — does a great deal for the Bodhisattvas. Those Illuminated Men, by their very power of thought and ceaseless ideation, continually benefit humanity by quickening any spark of authentic aspiration in every human soul into the fire which could help others to see. The truth of reincarnation requires much more than a casual scrutiny of our external lives and our spoken language. It must be pondered upon in the very silence of our souls. It is a theme for daily meditation. In the *Bhagavad Gita* Lord Krishna tells Arjuna that true wisdom is a meditation upon birth, death, decay, sickness, and error. To meditate upon each of these and all of these together is to begin to know more about the cosmic and the human significance of the truth of reincarnation.

The Gupta Vidya II, The Golden Thread

DEATH AND IMMORTALITY

> *The Soul is bound to the body by a conversion to the corporeal passions; and is again liberated by becoming impassive to the body.*
>
> *That which Nature binds, Nature also dissolves; and that which the Soul binds, the Soul likewise dissolves. Nature, indeed, bound the body to the Soul; but the Soul binds herself to the body. Nature, therefore, liberates the body from the Soul; but the Soul must liberate herself from the body.*
>
> *Hence there is a two-fold 'death'; the one, indeed, universally known, in which the body is liberated from the Soul; but the other, peculiar to philosophers, in which the Soul liberates herself from the body. Nor does the one entirely follow the other.*
>
> Plotinus

In the *Bhagavad Gita* Lord Krishna tells Arjuna that he must meditate upon birth, death, sickness, decay and error. This particular strand in the *Bhagavad Gita* is central to Buddhist thought. It is not easy for us to put ourselves in the position of a Tibetan Buddhist, to whom meditation on death is not a morbid activity, reserved for a special period in one's life, a time of deep depression owing to the fear of imminent death. It is rather part of a process of meditation which is ceaseless. To meditate on death is to meditate on life. To ask any question that is significant about the fleeting experiences that come to the ego, bringing pain as well as what appears to be happiness, to understand any of these fleeting experiences, is impossible except in the context of the total continuum. It is indeed difficult for us to understand what it means to put death in its proper place and to consider it in a wider context.

Throughout the history of European thought and of conventional Christianity, we have come to accept certain distinctions that are precious to us, a distinction between God outside the universe and the universe, between man and Nature, and ultimately between God and man. Therefore any consideration, within the context of these Western and Christian concepts of death or immortality, could only have meaning to us in terms of a relationship to be rediscovered, a lost relationship to be regained between man and God. Thus, the thought of the reabsorption of the human being into the elements of nature sounds indecent, unnatural, something that needs special explanation. We have become so identified with our own image of ourselves as detached autonomous beings — autonomous in a Cartesian sense in relation to the whole of knowledge, autonomous in a Kantian sense in relation to our moral life — that it is very difficult for us to imagine that our total standpoint is delusive, is wrong.

There is another current that has always existed as a golden stream in European thought, which is Pythagorean and Neo-Platonic and has concentrated upon a doctrine of emanations rather than a doctrine of creation. Under this scheme of things, man is intimately bound up with the universe. Man is the universe writ small. The universe is man magnified a million times. And therefore a human being only begins to be human when he understands his own relationship to Nature and the cosmos. He only begins to understand, let alone to master, the powers of Nature, when he has understood and begun to master the elements in his own nature. There is a continuous connection between man and the universe, and any conception of the divine must enter integrally into the picture that men have of the universe, and therefore it must integrally enter into one's image of oneself.

It is impossible in this view to look at Nature in a mechanistic fashion, to see it in a seventeenth-century manner. It is impossible because we are so bound up with Nature that we cannot but anthropomorphize or humanize everything in Nature. We must get rid of the great error of egoity, identification with the personal, fleeting, physical self, and begin to see that in our body, that in our personality, are material, natural elements which are the same in all beings, and in all human beings especially. We thus gain a sense of the wonder and the mystery, the glory, the grandeur, the romance, the color, of the cosmic panorama, while at the same time we need the capacity to detach ourselves from the elements of our nature and to become therapeutic in our whole approach to that nature.

This stream of thought is connected with the idea that man emanates energies, that the universe itself is a continuous stream of emanations from an unknown origin and an absolute reality, that in every emanation something is retained of the primordial origin of the emanation and something is transmitted as well, and that there is a total, ceaseless, continuous process of transformation. This idea, stressed in Pythagorean thought, is central to the Tibetan Buddhist.

If we look at the pre-Buddhist religion of the Bonpas, we find that it seems to us to be strange, primitive, terrifying in some ways, an obsession with gods and demons. But in the light of what we have just seen, it should be possible to discern that the individual belonging to the Bonpa tradition was really seeking his own way of gaining his citizenship in an apparently hostile universe. The same idea becomes richer and constructive, imbued with purpose and meaning, for the Buddhist. If we remember this central assumption, so important to understanding death and immortality in Tibetan thought, then we would readily recognize that something has gone wrong in the image of Tibet that popularly prevails in the West and in the westernized East.

A great deal has been written about the visions of the dead. There are frescoes in many Tibetan temples depicting them, sometimes in the form of bright and varied colors, which cannot have any symbolic significance to the outsider, sometimes in the form of terrifying deities stamping upon a demon and yet with a tremendous power of beneficence and redemption. When we read about these visions of the dead and about the Day of Judgment in *The Tibetan Book of the Dead*, we conjure up a picture of a people with extraordinary imagination, to whom the whole universe had a reality which we do not see or seize. Thus we miss the universal import of the teaching of death which was put in so many forms, vulgarly understood by some monks and laymen in Tibet but intuitively grasped by those who knew the purpose of this vast web of symbolism.

There is no easy way for us to meditate upon birth and death, decay, sickness and error in relation to Tibetan teaching simply by looking at a particular painting of the visions of the dead or even by reading *The Tibetan Book of the Dead*. These are no doubt useful, but what is really necessary is to get back to that central posture which Krishna enjoined upon Arjuna, to meditate upon all of these and to see them together. If it is possible to see birth and death as connected forms or phases of a single stream of consciousness, then we have to grasp the idea of a universe alive, ever-changing, conscious in a sense we cannot directly comprehend. Our consciousness is a reflected consciousness, distorted many times, distorted by particular tendencies and complexes or *samskaras*, by particular likes and dislikes, preconceptions, weaknesses of the will, by particular forms of illusion, so that it is very difficult for us to grasp directly this pure and total consciousness behind the ever-changing forms and phases assumed by a single substratum.

In Buddhist thought we are helped to begin to make the distinction by seeing that this entire universe is both *samsara* and *nirvana*. *Samsara* and *nirvana* spring from the same ultimate essence, the *Adi Buddha*, the ultimate Buddha nature; but *samsara* is the world of flux, the world of change, the world of illusion. Arising out of the sensations that we have of the very flux of *samsara*, we have *avidya*, congenital ignorance. It is more than ignorance as we normally understand it. It is not just lack of knowledge. It is a peculiar perversity of the modified consciousness available to us which prevents us from rising to the level of total universal consciousness and seeing all human and cosmic experiences as continuous events in a single stream. *Nirvana*, on the other hand, we describe by negation. *Nirvana* to us is some kind of total emptiness, nothingness; this has been the consistent interpretation of people unsympathetic to Buddhist teachings. It is very easy, of course, to conjure up a world of illusion which was manufactured by certain people because they were not able to come to terms with it, and then to suggest that they sought an escape in some imaginary and totally empty state, opposed to what we would normally call 'living,' 'becoming involved' in this world of matter. But *samsara* and *nirvana* actually refer to the two tendencies of the involvement of consciousness in form and the evolution of form to the height of consciousness, form and consciousness being differentiated only by a difference of degree and not of kind. To understand this is to see that *samsara* is ultimately the veil that is cast upon the nirvanic condition of illuminated and enlightened beings.

Even the *Nirvanee* as seen by us, the moment we personify him, the moment we separate him out from the rest of humankind as a single individual who attained to a particular state in a particular manner, immediately becomes a samsaric illusion. We then conjure up our own idealized and delusive images of enlightened, immortal individuals. So it is really important to see that if life is a continuous and total process, and if it undergoes a great variety of modes in relation to the actual forms of matter, then this consciousness in the universe must always require some form of embodiment, and therefore even the enlightened man cannot be imagined in a totally disembodied state.

There are those like the Capuchin Della Penna, who in their distorted picture of Tibetan Buddhists, give the impression of a Tibetan belief in some imaginary world of *Lha*, disembodied spirits, bodiless gods, an airy, fairy world of abstract entities, with no relationship to the universe as we know it. In 1882 *The Theosophist* published an important contribution by the Chohan Lama who was the chief of the Archive-registrars of the libraries containing manuscripts on esoteric doctrines belonging to the Dalai and Panchen Lamas of Tibet. He pointed to the distortions of the pure Tibetan teaching, and explained the basic propositions which are necessary to know before we can understand the *Lha* and so-called disembodied entities. This is why we have to grasp the statement in the *Prajnaparamita* that form and void are ultimately only aspects of each other. The moment we become aware or conscious, immediately our consciousness becomes embodied in thoughts or feelings, in images which are formal or material in relation to our actual state of awareness. In this sense, pure awareness is something that we cannot possibly visualize. All our awareness is relative to the particular plane of perception on which we function. It involves the use of organs of perception that are appropriate to this plane of perception. Now if we could see this, then we could begin to consider that the human being lives not merely in a visible, physical world but in several worlds intertwined. He is in fact constantly living in six worlds, according to the Buddhist Canon. But more important than the number, whether it be six or seven or some other, it is essential to grasp the idea that the outside world, in the context of which we become aware, is entirely relative to our organ of perception.

We are all somewhat aware of this. Phenomenalists since Berkeley have recognized how very much the existence of objects is dependent upon our perceptions of them. The same idea has been elaborated by Wittgenstein in another way — that we have no grasp of reality apart from the clusters of concepts that are bound up with our habitual usage and our language-games. Anybody who reflects for a moment could see this. We have no direct, privileged access to reality. The moment we begin to think about space or time or Nature, the moment we begin to speculate about the universe, the moment we begin to theorize about it, even when we try just to gain what appears to us to be direct awareness of a particular set of objects, we have immediately allowed to come between those apparently neutral and independent objects, in a mechanistic Cartesian universe, and ourselves as privileged spectators, the veil of concepts, the concepts which we need to produce a commonsensical map or a metaphysical map. Without these we cannot attempt to isolate particulars, let alone to apprehend them, to distinguish them, to classify them.

We need to see that each human being is continually inhabiting several universes and has available to him the various organs of awareness or perception which are appropriate to these different universes. Therefore, one could come to discern that what is life to one man on one plane of perception is death to another. In the *Gita* we have Krishna's statement that what is day to the enlightened man is night to the ordinary man, and what is night to the ordinary man is day to the sage. What is day to the ordinary man is night — the night of ignorance. To generalize the idea, what to some people are significant realities are ephemeral illusions in the eyes of others. And we are all involved in this psychological relativity. No one has a privileged position. If there were perfected men, the moment they come into a physical universe and are involved in communication with physical beings — even they cannot totally free themselves from the imprisonment that we all undergo in a physical universe. Every universe binds us.

Is it then possible, simply by grasping this idea, to conceive of the possibility of moving from one universe to another, so to speak, all within the mind, all within ourselves? Is it possible for us to study the various elements in our nature, in terms of different colors of the rainbow, in terms of different gods in Nature? Is it possible for us to see all these various facets of Nature as seemingly independent but essentially interdependent aspects of a single substratum, of a single universe? For if we can do this, then we would see that death need not be viewed as something unnatural.

It is life that seems to be unnatural. The poet Kalidasa raised this question with the help of an analogy. Why do we feel that death is unnatural and life is natural, when life is like a few drops of water in a pot. There ought to be something unnatural about this. It is this which needs explaining. And if the water is thrown back into the ocean, there is nothing unnatural about that. So death, in this view, does not require special explanation. It is life that requires explanation. Therefore we do not begin by asking why do we die. We ask why we were born. If we wish to understand what is the kind of consciousness that we are going to preserve on the eve of death, or what perhaps may be the consciousness that we will experience soon after death, we must go back to the beginning. What do we remember about our consciousness as far back as possible, near the moment of birth? What conceivably could we have felt before we were born? Now these are questions that many people would find impossible to entertain, and yet the true philosopher, the man of meditation, the man who really wishes to see life as a whole, cannot shirk them.

Buddhist philosophy explains that life in a body can be explained by the tremendous desire for bodily life that belongs to us. This we can recognize in ourselves. We can distinguish people in terms of the desire for sensation. We can distinguish the same person at different points in his life, according to the degree of his hold on life. Everything in this world of *samsara* is a conspiracy to encourage this hold on life, this hold on possessions, this hold onto the image that men form of the body, their identification with their own name and form, their *namarupa*. In this lies the seed of separateness — *ahankara*, the seed of violence — *himsa*, the seed of falsehood — *asatya*. Falsehood, violence, separateness are all rooted in the fierce craving for life, for personal existence. And when we begin to reflect upon this, we can see its significance. We can think of people who desperately wish to project their own personal existence on the stage, literal or metaphorical. We know for ourselves how very often the desire for survival or the hatred of survival is nothing but our own attitude to a continuation of our personal life. That is why, whether in the Christian or in the Buddhist tradition, all the pictures given to us of post-natal states become for us personal visions with personal prospects, awful or glorious, with immense significance for us as personalities. Whereas we are really asked by spiritual teachers to get back to the basic origin of *avidya*, or ignorance, which is *tanha*, the will to live.

This ancient Buddhist idea is not just a phrase. It is so important an aspect of this universe that Gandhi, who tried to resuscitate the teaching of Buddha, actually formulated a law. He declared that the willingness to kill is exactly in inverse proportion to the willingness to die. Some might think that there is truth in this statement, though formulated as a law it seems extravagant and pseudo-scientific. But not at all, when we grasp the idea of *tanha*, the desire for life. The greater the desire for life, the greater the craving for personal existence, the total identification of our consciousness with that which is fleeting and transitory and perishable and personal, the more intense our awareness of ourselves as separate from others, the greater is the impulse to survive, the Hobbesian fear of death which seems so crucial to all life and to all existence in society. The greater then becomes the violence, the willingness to kill, on the plane of thought or feeling as well as on the physical plane.

On the other hand, the person who does not feel so strongly, who has deliberately come to discern that this binding force which brought him into life is itself worthy of meditation and worthy of transcendence, such a man begins to loosen up this hold of his consciousness over his body and his material instruments. He then begins to see himself as others see him, as he sees a photograph of himself ten years ago, as in fact an illusory entity, a thing of no consequence or of no more consequence than any other thing. It is not necessary that he has to go from attachment to aversion. Aversion is itself a form of attachment. The man who denies loudly that he has any desire for life is deeply attached. It is not easy to master the process of getting beyond attachment and aversion, and seeing in its proper perspective the force of cohesion inherent in matter and in the forms of consciousness we consolidate. This force draws us into separative existence and engenders an ever-growing fear of death.

Death then serves simply as an opportunity to get away, temporarily, from the craving for personal existence. This force, although it seems so intense while it lasts, is still transitory. It is an interference with the pure vision of consciousness and therefore must come to an end. A great opportunity comes to each human being at the time of death. Either he sees the significance of what is happening and begins to take the first steps toward conscious immortality, or even after he has discarded the physical vesture — there are many universes and there are many vestures — he begins once again in a new form to live out his old attachments, to sublimate them, to refine and purify them. All his old loves may now become purer. They may become idealizations. But nonetheless he gets involved again in his continual craving for personal existence. And then of course his return to physical life becomes a natural thing, something involuntary to him, inevitable in Nature.

Therefore we are told that if we want to understand what happens after death, we must first grasp 'death consciousness.' What is the state of consciousness that we possess just before we die? What is the mood in which we are prepared to receive this new experience, to enter this new world? The more we have a thirst for life, the more we assume that life is natural and death unnatural, the more we are terrified of the great world of the unknown, and the more we then put up a resistance to the natural opportunities for the freeing of consciousness that are available with the discarding of the mask of the physical body.

But on the other hand, the person who has the knowledge of the *bardo* knows that he is now about to enter an intermediate state between birth and death, a period of gestation, a period in which there can be no Karma. The law of causality can operate fully only on the plane of the physical universe. A person cannot reap the results of actions generated by him in a physical body except in a physical body on the physical plane. But he is involved in a condition in which, because he has got out of the physical body or because the physical vesture has fallen away, he now has the opportunity to consider his available vestures and the other universes consubstantial with them.

These vestures have been expounded in terms of the *Trikaya* doctrine, the doctrine of the three bodies — the *Dharmakaya*, the *Sambhogakaya*, and the *Nirmanakaya*. The *Dharmakaya* is the body made up of *Dharmadhatu*, that in the universe which constitutes the undifferentiated and ultimate Buddha nature. The *Sambhogakaya* represents the manifested, the perfected, embodiment of all that exists in Nature. It is the origin of the idea of an omnipresent god, worshipped by Hindus as Vishnu, the god who pervades all things, and which in other traditions has been the subject of numerous graphic visions, vivid pictures of the perfections of Deity. The *Nirmanakaya* is that body or vesture which represents the incarnation of this ultimate substance or substratum which underlies *Dharmakaya*, and which is exhibited in its glorious universal perfection in *Sambhogakaya*. The *Nirmanakaya* vesture enables an enlightened being to project itself on a material plane. In Mahayana teaching it is suggested that we, who in physical life are bound down by it and are terrified by death, can take comfort from the fact that there is a vesture perfected by beings who are not merely able to maintain their condition of pure awareness or total enlightenment in some subtle immaterial body but are also able to materialize it, and to differentiate their embodied nature into all the beings around them, consciously and deliberately. So the mere fact of having a material body is not the obstacle, but rather attachment and identification with it.

It is possible for us to introduce into this scheme of things a dualism such as we have in orthodox Christianity, which contrasts life that is transitory with the life eternal. We could contrast physical life with pain and original sin, with 'the body of resurrection,' and then of course we get a simple dualistic scheme. Life becomes an episode not a state, unrelated to the future except through a particular mechanism such as the Day of Judgment. We are then launched into an eternity of a condition where, if we choose and we have chosen aright and repented at the right time, we shall get this body of resurrection. But in Tibet we do not have such a dualistic picture connected with the total dogmatism people bring to the idea that there is only one life, of which they have no proof — and the onus of proof is on them because the majority of humanity has thought in terms of rebirth. Even for people who think in this way, it is not easy to make the leap in imagination to a conception of innumerable universes, an endless chain of manifestation, and a continual transformation of consciousness which goes through life and beyond life, beyond what we call death, and back into incarnated life again.

Soon after the actual withdrawal from the physical body, the 'soul,' — a term derived from the Greeks, the Kwan Yin in every man in Tibetan tradition, the Voice of the Spirit or Conscience, the Great Word, the Great Sound of the *Adi Buddha* — this 'soul,' as we call it, this self-consciousness in us, becomes capable when physical life is discarded of perceiving, though only for a very short time, the pure body of *Dharmakaya*. Simply because of the first separation of consciousness from physical embodiment, the soul begins to have a glimmer of total undifferentiated consciousness, in the form of a vision of pure, clear, colorless light. But this is a tremendous thing for us to contemplate. We are not prepared for it before we die, and therefore it may not mean anything to us unless we begin to meditate upon it now. But if it happens, and we cannot make anything of it, and we fall into some kind of swoon or stupor before this ineffable light, then we are no better off for having had a foretaste or a vision of this great experience which is perfected by the enlightened ones who remain immortal.

We then enter the next state of the *bardo* where we begin to see this same total voidness or *tathata,* the *sunyata* state, the *Dharmakaya* body of the universe. But we see it through a mist, through a beautiful rainbow mist, and of course then we see many colors. We begin to dream and to experience ideal consciousness. Having failed to come to terms with total undifferentiated consciousness in its abstract, absolute manner, we now fall into a plane of consciousness where we begin to reflect upon idealized types, the archetypes of Plato. But these archetypes are connected with a personal life that is gone, so that we begin to look back without a clear awareness that we have left the physical body. Then, gradually, awareness of this grows, though one still continues to be conscious of one's personal self. Therefore all one's loves and all one's desires are in terms of the life that went before. One is in a dreamy condition, which may sound blissful by comparison with the burdens of earthly life, but is still delusive. Here is another opportunity for the person to see what has really happened, to see the unreality of it, and see once again the reality of total undifferentiated consciousness. But in fact most people cannot seize this opportunity because they are not prepared for it.

What instead happens is that they are confronted with all that they are in their personal natures. They are confronted with their natures with which they had identified themselves, and which are now exteriorized out of themselves because they imagine that they are not all the bad things that they once thought they were. Suddenly we are confronted with all the elements in our nature in the form of visions, a whole array of terrifying deities holding up to ourselves all the things which are in us. It is only if there is within us a certain weakness that we are afraid of something external. It is only when we are identified with some particular attribute which is personal and separative that we then have a certain fear of what is outside. It is a common observation that an ambitious man is the first to hold out against the ambition of another man, a proud man against the pride of another, and so on. We also know about people filled with lust who love to hold forth against lust. This is exactly what happens in the *bardo* state, only here the individual is confronted with a whole array of embodied beings, symbolized in visions for the sake of understanding. We should not anthropomorphize this condition as the literalists have done. But we are confronted with innumerable formulations of elements in our nature with which we have not come to terms, which we have not seen for what they really are in their true colors.

This great opportunity is afforded to us all. It might be called consulting the Book of Judgment, the Book of Memory. Whether we quail before this great and frightening revelation of all our personal *samskaras,* our peculiar personal and divisive tendencies, whether we are re-attracted to them and are rapidly drawn back to earthly life, or whether we are able to grasp the nirvanic (as opposed to the samsaric) stream of consciousness which enables us to see the inwardness of this great panorama — that is the choice open to us. But it cannot be made then. It has to be made during life. Herein lies the importance of considering all these teachings about death. It is only now that we have the opportunity to prepare ourselves for the appropriate state of mind before departing from the physical body, or before discarding it, which would enable us fruitfully to avail ourselves of both postnatal and post-mortem consciousness and the various phases of this intermediate state of *bardo*.

Most human beings are unable to attain the seed idea of enlightenment which is fructified in the form of an imperishable vesture by those who have fully prepared before death to enter into the state of immortality. For most people, even the seed idea of immortality cannot be grasped, and therefore they are quickly drawn to all the various *samskaras* or attributes which come back to them. There is a persisting matrix made up of all these attributes, revivified by one's own newly-formed desire or attachment. Then one begins to make one's first entry into physical life through having formed a line of attachment with particular parents. Such people dream about mating couples and get so involved with the purely physical side of life that they are very soon caught in the illusory process of birth. They cannot expect to know what birth means because they did not know what death meant.

So, this whole teaching is highly significant if we can see its practical implications and various facets. By reading *The Tibetan Book of the Dead*, or by looking at Tibetan pictures of the visions of the dead, one could accumulate a vast amount of detail about the symbolic forty-nine days of the *bardo* with all its day-to-day visions. But merely accumulating a great deal of fantastic knowledge does not add anything to our meditation on death. The moment we start with ourselves and ask not why we are afraid of death but why we hold on to life, the moment we begin to see significant connections, it will be possible for us to discern that at all times we have available to us either the standpoint of *nirvana* or the standpoint of *samsara*. If we are ready to see this, we can come to understand those who have gained or can gain immortality in this scheme of things.

Ordinarily, according to Tibetan teachings, people will not incarnate immediately. When someone has died, that person will not linger or be drawn back to earth-life except in three cases. First are those Bodhisattvas, those enlightened sages who deliberately linger, having renounced *nirvana,* to assist and help other human beings to gain the knowledge that they have of the meaning of all these states. Secondly, there are those people who die with a total obsession with one line of thinking, not necessarily bad or sinful beings, but those with an *idée fixe*. These people will also linger. They will prolong the entry into the *bardo* state, and the more they prolong it, the more difficult it will be for them to pass from the swoon into the state of awakening, into a new consciousness, and benefit front it. The third class of beings who are drawn back and hover around earth-life are those who had so intense a love — like a mother's love for children — a sense of unfulfilled or uncompleted love, or a love which, however much fulfilled, is still so powerful and so personal that it binds people and draws them back to earthly life. But even these will not appear as *bhuts* or ghosts unless they are galvanized into activity by adepts in the art of necromancy, a practice strongly condemned in pure Buddhist teaching.

Such nefarious practices do go on in the name of Buddhist tradition among several Red Cap sects, especially in places like Bhutan. They have actually been put forward as Tibetan Buddhist, in the name of scholarship, by people who have quoted supposed authorities who have never even visited Lhasa, let alone had the privilege of some kind of initiation into the pure teachings of the Panchen Lama and the Dalai Lama. It is not therefore a question of considering all the various forms which possession could take that would constitute a true understanding of the Tibetan teaching of death, let alone of immortality. That there must be such demonic usurpers is not difficult to conceive. But they are unnatural. Tibetan teachings do refer to the victims of suicides and murders, people who are in the state of swoon and could be used by other beings who function freely on subtle planes of consciousness, using subtle vestures for their own foul purpose. But this is not something that need concern us.

The crucial insight that we gain from Tibetan teaching is that immortality is not something to be achieved or won, not a prize to be awarded to a favoured few. Immortality is nothing but another aspect of mortality. Even now we either live immortally or live mortally. We either die every moment or we live and thirst, depending on whether we are focused upon the nirvanic or upon the samsaric aspect of embodied consciousness. If we are constantly able to sift the meaning of experiences and to see our formal vestures for what they are and pass from one plane of perception to another, then indeed it may be possible, when blessed with the vision of clear, pure light — the great vision of *sunyata* — to enter straightaway into that vesture which enables us to remain free from the compulsion of return to earthly life. But this cannot happen unless it flows naturally out of the line of life's meditation. It cannot happen all of a sudden. It is not some kind of special dispensation. It is itself a product of the working of Karma.

Beings who have undergone this condition of final illumination have either chosen to remain immortal but in the *Dharmakaya* vesture, unrelated to manifested beings and humanity, or they have chosen the *Nirmanakaya* vesture and deliberately chosen to enter into relationships with human beings. These *Nirmanakayas* ceaselessly point to the basic truths concerning the meaning of death and the perpetual possibility of immortality. They teach people that within themselves they are Buddhas without knowing it. Now, the *Prajnaparamita* states that the Buddhas are themselves only personifications and therefore they could become illusions for us. What is it that we are going to meditate upon when we consider the immortals? Are we going to think of them as glorified physical personalities, archangels in radiant raiment, somehow idealized and more beautiful but related to our own physical conception of physical life? Or are we going to think of them as minds, a great gathering of extraordinary and powerful minds who collectively constitute the great mind of the universe? Or are we going to look upon them simply as beings who have become aware of their true Buddha nature and have therefore become instruments for the working of consciousness, instruments that will be helpful and unifying, because that is the nature of consciousness, whereas the nature of form is divisive.

Thus the whole doctrine, even of the *Lha*, those gods seemingly tucked away in a limbo, refers to beings who not merely work in relation to the world but also by their ceaseless collective ideation maintain in the world the force of the Buddha nature. The Buddha nature is not some abstract principle. It is actually embodied in the collective consciousness of such beings perpetually in the universe. We come to see that the various phases in the process of the concretization of the universe from an absolute realm, through archetypes, through individualized forms of thought, and ultimately to material forms, that this whole process is re-enacted in the *bardo* state, between death and rebirth. A great re-enactment has taken place. Who knows what re-enactment takes place within the embryo especially during the first seven months in the mother's womb? Science and medicine know almost nothing about what happens then or why. These are the great mysteries connected with the primal facts of birth and death. If we can consider that there is available in Buddhist teaching the knowledge that there is regular re-enactment of a continuous cosmic process before the eye of the soul, then we can see that enlightenment is not the great terminus to a laborious and boring process of striving, but a ceaseless opportunity which inheres in this very world of woe and delusion, which we call *samsara*, and to which we cling like blind fools, knowing not Life and afraid of death.

Caxton Hall, London
November 1963

They who are on the summit of a mountain can see all men; in like manner they who are intelligent and free from sorrow are enabled to ascend above the paradise of the Gods; and when they there have seen the subjection of man to birth and death and the sorrows by which he is afflicted, they open the doors of the immortal.

Tched-Du Brjod-Pai Tsoms

... as 'there is more courage to accept being than non-being, life than death,' there are those among the Bodhisatwas and the Lha — 'and as rare as the flower of udambara are they to meet with' — who voluntarily relinquish the blessing of the attainment of perfect freedom, and remain in their personal selves, whether in forms visible or invisible to mortal sight — to teach and help their weaker brothers.

A Gelung Of The Inner Temple

The Gupta Vidya II, The Golden Thread

ANAMNESIS

Since, then, the soul is immortal and has been born many times, since it has seen all things both in this world and in the other, there is nothing it has not learnt. No wonder, then, that it is able to recall to mind goodness and other things, for it knew them beforehand. For, as all reality is akin and the soul has learnt all things, there is nothing to prevent a man who has recalled — or, as people say, 'learnt' — only one thing from discovering all the rest for himself, if he will pursue the search with unwearying resolution. For on this showing all inquiry or learning is nothing but recollection.

Plato

Anamnesis is true soul-memory, intermittent access to the divine wisdom within every human being as an immortal Triad. All self-conscious monads have known over countless lifetimes a vast host of subjects and objects, modes and forms, in an ever-changing universe. Assuming a complex series of roles as an essential part of the endless process of learning, the soul becomes captive recurrently to myriad forms of *maya* and *moha*, illusion and delusion. At the same time, the soul has the innate and inward capacity to cognize that it is more than any and all of these masks. As every incarnated being manifests a poor, pale caricature of himself — a small, self-limiting and inverted reflection of one's inner and divine nature — the ancient doctrine of anamnesis is vital to comprehend human nature and its hidden possibilities. Given the fundamental truth that all human beings have lived many times, initiating diverse actions in intertwined chains of causation, it necessarily follows that everyone has the moral and material environment from birth to death which is needed for self-correction and self-education. But who is it that has this need? Not the shadowy self or false egoity which merely reacts to external stimuli. Rather, there is that eye of wisdom in every person which in deep sleep is fully awake and which has a translucent awareness of self-consciousness as pure primordial light.

We witness intimations of immortality in the pristine light in the innocent eye of every baby, as well as in the wistful eye of every person near the moment of death. It seems that the individual senses that life on earth is largely an empty masquerade, full of sound and fury, signifying nothing. Nevertheless, there is a quiet joy in the recognition that one is fully capable of gaining some apprehension not only of the storied past but also of the shrouded future by a flashing perception of his unmodified, immutable divine essence. If one has earned this through a lifetime of meditation, one may attain at the moment of withdrawal from the body a healing awareness of the reality behind the dense proscenium of the earth's drama.

Soul-memory is essentially different from what is ordinarily called memory. Most of the time the mind is clouded by a chaotic association of images and ideas that impinge upon it from outside. Very few human beings, however, are in a position to make full use of the capacity for creative thinking. They simply cannot fathom what it is like to be a thinking being, to be able to deliberate calmly and to think intently on their own. Automatic cerebration is often mistaken for primary thinking. To understand this distinction, one must look at the fundamental relation between oneself as a knower and the universe as a field of knowledge. Many souls gain fleeting glimpses of the process of self-enquiry when they are stilled by the panoramic vistas of Nature, silenced by the rhythmic ocean, or alone amidst towering mountains. Through the sudden impact of intense pain and profound suffering they may be thrown back upon themselves and be compelled to ask, "What is the meaning of all of this?" "Who am I?" "Why was I born?" "When will I die?" "Can I do that which will now lend a simple credence to my life, a minimal dignity to my death?"

Pythagoras and Plato taught the Eastern doctrine of the spontaneous unfolding from within of the wisdom of the soul. Soul-wisdom transcends all formal properties and definable qualities, as suggested in the epistemology, ethics and science of action of the *Bhagavad Gita*. It is difficult for a person readily to generate and release an effortless balancing of the three dynamic qualities of Nature — *sattva, rajas* and *tamas* — or to see the entire cosmos as a radiant garment of the divine Self. He needs to ponder calmly upon the subtle properties of the *gunas*, their permutations and combinations. Sattvic knowledge helps the mind to meditate upon the primordial ocean of pure light, the bountiful sea of milk in the old Hindu myths. The entire universe is immersed in a single sweeping cosmic process. Even though we seem to see a moving panorama of configurations, colours and forms, sequentiality is illusory. Behind all passing forms there are innumerable constellations of minute, invisible and ultimately indivisible particles, whirling and revolving in harmonic modes of eternal circular motion. A person can learn to release anamnesis to make conscious and creative use of modes of motion governing the life-atoms that compose the variegated universe of his immortal and mortal vestures.

The timeless doctrine of spiritual self-knowledge in the fourth chapter of the *Bhagavad Gita* suggests that human beings are not in the false position of having to choose between perfect omniscience and total nescience. Human beings participate in an immense hinterland of differentiation of the absolute light reflected within modes of motion of matter. To grow up is to grasp that one cannot merely oscillate between extremes. Human thought too often involves the violence of false negation — leaping from one kind of situation to the exact opposite rather than seeing life as a fertile field for indefinite growth. This philosophical perspective requires us to think fundamentally in terms of the necessary relation between the knower and the known. Differences in the modalities of the knowable are no more and no less important than divergences in the perceptions and standpoints of knowers. The universe may be seen for what it is — a constellation of self-conscious beings and also a vast array of elemental centres of energy — *devas* and *devatas* all of which participate in a ceaseless cosmic dance that makes possible the sacrificial process of life for each and every single human being. If one learns that there are degrees within degrees of reflected light, then one sees the compelling need to gain the faculty of divine discrimination *(viveka)*. That is the secret heart of the teaching of the *Bhagavad Gita*.

The *Gita* is a jewelled essay in *Buddhi Yoga. Yoga* derives from the root *yog*, 'to unite', and centres upon the conscious union of the individual self and the universal Self. The trinity of Nature is the lock of magic, and the trinity of Man is the sole key, and hence the grace of the Guru. This divine union may be understood at early stages in different ways. It could be approached by a true concern for *anasakti*, selfless action and joyous service, the precise performance of duties and a sacrificial involvement in the work of the world. It may also be attempted through the highest form of *bhakti* or devotion, in concentrating and purifying one's whole being so as to radiate an unconditional, constant and consistent truth, a pure, intense and selfless feeling of love. And it must also summon forth true knowledge through altruistic meditation. *Jnana* and *dhyana* do not refer to the feeble reflections of the finite and fickle mind upon the finite and shadowy objects of an ever-evolving world, but rather point to that enigmatic process of inward knowing wherein the knower and the known become one, fused in transcendent moments of compassionate revelation. The pungent but purifying commentary by Dnyaneshvari states in myriad simple metaphors the profoundest teaching of the *Gita*. In offering numerous examples from daily life, Dnyaneshvari wants to dissolve the idea that anything or any being can be known through *a priori* categories that cut up the universe into watertight compartments and thereby limit and confine consciousness. The process of true learning merges disparate elements separated only because of the looking-glass view of the inverted self which mediates between the world and ourselves in a muddled manner. The clearest perception of *sattva* involves pure ideation.

The *Gita* presents a magnificent portrait of the man of meditation who has all his senses and organs under complete control. Whatever he does, he remains seated like one unaffected and aloof *(kutastha)*. He does not identify with any of the instruments musically necessary for the creative transformation of the cosmic process. The Religion of Responsibility is rooted in *Ṛta*, sattvic motion in unmanifested Nature, and it makes sattvic consciousness *(dharma)* accessible to imperfect individuals. A human being who valiantly journeys in consciousness behind and beyond the visible process of Nature — like a ballerina in Stravinsky's "Rite of Spring" becoming Spring itself while remaining a single character in the concordant ballet — maintains a joyous and silent awareness of the whole process while coolly functioning at various levels with deft dexterity. All human beings, insofar as they can smoothly function at diverse levels of precise control and painless transcendence, can attain to firm fixity of mind and serene steadfastness of spirit — the sacred marks of initiation through sattvic ideation in the secret heart. Sattvic knowledge is the invisible common thread transcending all apparent differences. It gives support to rhythmic activity which is simultaneously precise, liberating and intrinsically self-validating, without the creeping shadow of inconstancy.

The self of the individual who is sattvic is integrated with the Self which surveys the whole world with its congeries of forms and objects, whilst seeing all of these appearances in local time and visible space as evanescent parts of a continuous process of interconnected if conceptually discrete causes and consequences. This is like a mighty river that flows from a hidden stream issuing from a sacred source in the depths of the highest mountain ranges. Dnyaneshvari offers an apt analogy which applies both to anamnesis and to *Turiya-Sattva*. Just as when a stream becoming a river empties itself into the great ocean, so too will individual consciousness when it withdraws itself from its reflected sense of 'I-ness' within the world of insupportable illusions. When the principle of self-consciousness initiates this inner withdrawal, it quietly empties itself into the great ocean of primordial light, *Daiviprakriti*, universal and self-luminous consciousness. Yet at the same time it remains active within

Hiranyagarbha, the pristine golden egg of immortal individuality, cosmic and trans-human.

From the standpoint of the man of meditation, light and darkness are archetypal categories applicable at many levels. Philosophically and mystically, darkness at the level of inversion is chaos, and light as we understand it in nature is associated with the illumination of a field of consciousness. Psychologically, for many sad souls darkness is the deepening shadow of loneliness, and light shines as the resplendent vision of human brotherhood and the spiritual solidarity of all that lives. This can become a glorious vision of enduring hope, invulnerable faith and unwavering affirmation. Rodin's well-known simile in stone suggests that the pilgrim-soul and weary toiler is plunged in deep thought. All such persons are asking the oldest question — "Who am I?" Significant trends are emerging across the globe, and the crisis is aggravated by the breakdown of alternatives everywhere and especially in the North American continent. Light and darkness refer to every revivified conception of what is real, what is abstract and what concrete in the vast field of unilluminated objects and hazy memories, the negations and affirmations of consciousness resulting from the repeated negation of a false sense of 'I' in a fast-changing world.

The Secret Doctrine offers the ancient analogy of the Sun to the individual emerging out of the cave of *avidya* in search of Universal Good (SAT). Though difficult to exemplify, a talismanic exercise in practical instruction is conveyed. Close your eyes, and from the depths of inmost consciousness travel outward to the extremest limits in every direction. You will find equal lines or rays of perception extending evenly in all directions, so that the utmost effort of ideation will terminate in the vault of a sphere. Think of yourself as within a numinous golden egg, a divine sphere. Close your eyes, draw within, behind and beyond your own shadowy conception of yourself, behind the superficial and self-limiting images of the mind's surface, cast there by the lunar activity of the world, and eclipse your own restless lunar self.

As you withdraw behind your five senses, focus upon the point between your eyes and see that point as only a representation in the physical face of a field of consciousness where there are innumerable points, each of which is at the centre of a radiant sphere formed by a reflection of the fiery substance of the dark ocean of space.

From the standpoint of your own self-conscious ray of light, try to think outward to the extreme limits of boundless space in every direction. You will find that equal lines or rays of perception will terminate in all directions in the invisible vault of a macrocosmic sphere. The limit of the sphere will be a great circle, and the direct rays of thought in any direction must be right-line radii from a common centre in an immaterial, homogeneous medium. This is the all-embracing human conception of the manifesting aspect of the ever-hidden *Ain-Soph*, which formulates itself in the geometrical figure of a circle with elements of continuous curvature, circumference and rectilinear radii. This geometrical shape is the first recognizable link between the *Ain-Soph* and the highest intelligence of man. The rule proclaimed at the portals of the Pythagorean School and the Platonic Academy limited entry to those who had deeply reflected upon divine geometry.

According to Eastern esotericism, this great circle, which reduces to the point within the invisible boundless sphere, is Avalokiteshwara, the Logos. It is the manifested God, the Verbum of the *Gospel According to St. John,* unknown to man except through its manifested universe and the entirety of mankind. The One is intuitively known by the many, although the One is unthinkable by any mode of mere intellection. Reaching within consciousness means going behind and beyond every possible perception and conception, every possible colour and form. Form corresponds to knowledge on the lower reflected lunar plane; colour corresponds to the knower at the level of the reflected ray. The objects of knowledge are merely modifications of a single substance. These do not yield any simple triadic diagram, but involve a gradual ascent within consciousness, in a tranquil state of contemplation, towards the greatest parametric conception of the One. The Logos sleeps in the bosom of *Parabrahm* — in the Abstract Absolute — during *pralaya* or non-manifestation, just as our individual Ego is in latency during deep, dreamless sleep. We cannot cognize *Parabrahm* except as *Mulaprakriti,* the mighty expanse of undifferentiated cosmic matter. This is not merely a vesture in cosmic creation through which radiate the energy and wisdom of *Parabrahm.* It is the Divine Ground.

The Logos in its highest aspect takes no notice of history. The Logos is behind and beyond what appears important to human beings, but the Logos knows itself. That transcendent self-knowledge is the *fons et origo* of all the myriad rays of self-conscious, luminous intelligence focused at a certain level of complexity in what we call the human being, rays which, at the same time, light up the infinitude of points in space-time. As the Logos is unknown to differentiated species, and as *Parabrahm* is unknown to *Prakriti,* Eastern esotericism and the Kabbalah alike have resolved the abstract synthesis in relatively concrete images in order to bring the Logos within the range of human conception. We have images, therefore, such as that of the sun and the light, but there is freedom through concentration, abstraction and expansion, while there is bondage through consolidation, concretization and desecration. The Logos is like the sun through which light and heat radiate, but whose energy and light exist in some unknown condition in space and are diffused throughout space as visible light. If one meditates at noon on the invisible midnight sun, which sages reflect upon in a calm state of ceaseless contemplation, and if one remains still and serene, one could exercise the privilege of using the divine gift of sound. The sun itself is only the agent of the Light in *The Voice of the Silence.* This is the first triadic hypostasis. The Tetraktys is emanated by concentrating the energizing light shed by the Logos, but it subsists by itself in the Divine Darkness. A tremendous light-energy flows from the deepest thought, wherein one continuously voids every conception of the reflected ray of egoity or the individual self, all objects and universes, everything in what we call space and time.

Thus the individuating mind enters subtler dimensions, through which it can approach universal cognition in a resplendent realm of noumenal reality, opening onto a shared field of total awareness in *Mahat*, wherein the self-consciousness of divine wisdom (*Vach*) is eternally enacted by self-luminous Mahatmas, the Brotherhood of Light.

The true teaching of Brahma Vach is enshrined in the secret code language of Nature. A new mode of initiation has already begun. Invisible beings in their *mayavi rupas* cherish the teaching, but no visible beings are entirely excluded. The quintessential teaching is conveyed in so many different ways that prepare for the sacred instructions in deep sleep, even for those struggling souls who seize their last chance in this life. The more any person can maintain during waking hours the self-conscious awareness of what is known deep within — even though one cannot formulate it — the more one can hold it and see it as blasphemous to speak thoughtlessly about it. Though such persons participate in all the fickle changes of the butterfly mind, the more attentively they can preserve and retain the seminal energy of thought with a conscious continuity, the more easily will every anxiety about themselves fade into a cool state of contentment. Like a shadow following the lost and stumbling seeker of the light, a true disciple will unexpectedly encounter the forgotten wisdom, the spiritual knowledge, springing up suddenly, spontaneously, within the very depths of his being. Then he may receive the crystalline waters of life-giving wisdom through the central conduit of light-energy, symbolized in the physical body by the spinal cord. One may walk in the world with deep gratitude for the sacred privilege of being a self-conscious Manasaputra within the divine temple of the universe for the sake of shedding light upon all that lives and breathes. In seeing, one can send out beneficent rays. In hearing, one can listen beyond the cacophony of the world. Whilst one is listening constantly to the music of the spheres echoing within one's head and heart, one is able to send forth thoughts and feelings that are benevolent and unconditional, extended towards all other human minds. These thoughts could become living talismans for the men and women of tomorrow in the fields of cognition wherein the war between light and darkness, the living and the dead, is now being waged.

The Philosophy of Perfection of Krishna, the Religion of Responsibility of the Buddha and the Science of Spirituality of Shankara, constitute the Pythagorean teaching of the Aquarian Age of Universal Enlightenment. There are general and interstitial relationships between the idea of perfectibility, the idea of gaining control over the mind, and the exalted conception of knowledge set forth in the eighteenth chapter of the *Gita*. To begin to apprehend these connections, one must first heed the mantramic injunction from *The Voice of the Silence:* "Strive with thy thoughts unclean before they overpower thee." Astonishingly, there was a moment in the sixties when millions became obsessed with instant enlightenment; fortunately, this is not true at present. Few people now seriously believe that they are going to die as perfected beings in this lifetime. This does not mean that the secret doctrines of the 1975 cycle are irrelevant to the ordinary man who, without false expectations, merely wants to finish his life with a modicum of fulfilment. All such seekers can benefit immensely from calmly meditating upon the *Sthitaprajna,* the Self-Governed Sage, the Buddhas of Perfection. This is the crux of Krishna's medicinal method in the *Gita*. He presents Arjuna with the highest ideal, simultaneously shows his difficulties and offers intensive therapy and compassionate counsel. This therapeutic mode continues until the ninth chapter, where Krishna says, "Unto thee who findeth no fault I will now make known this most mysterious knowledge, coupled with a realization of it, which having known thou shalt be delivered from evil." In the eighteenth chapter he conveys the great incommunicable secret — so-called because even when communicated it resides within the code language of Buddhic consciousness. The authors of all the great spiritual teachings like the *Gita, The Voice of the Silence* and *The Crest Jewel of Wisdom* knew that there is a deep mythic sense in which the golden verses can furnish only as much as a person's state of consciousness is ready to receive.

H.P. Blavatsky dedicated *The Voice of the Silence* to the few, to those who seek to become *lanoos,* true neophytes on the Path. Like Krishna, she gave a shining portrait of the man of meditation, the Teacher of Mankind. In chosen fragments from the *Book of the Golden Precepts,* the merciful warning is sounded at the very beginning: "These instructions are for those ignorant of the dangers of the lower IDDHI." In this age the consequences of misuse of psychic powers over many lives by millions of individuals have produced a holocaust — the harvest of terrible effects. Rigid justice rules the universe. Many human beings have gaping astral wounds and fear that there is only a tenuous connecting thread between their personal consciousness and the light of the higher nature. Human beings have long misused *Kriyashakti,* the power of visualization, and *Itchashakti,* the power of desire. Above all, they have misused the antipodal powers of knowledge, *Jnanashakti,* so that there is an awful abyss between men of so-called knowledge and men of so-called power. What is common to both is that their pretensions have already gone for naught, and therefore many have begun to some extent to sense the sacred orbit of the Brotherhood of Bodhisattvas. On the global plane we also witness today the tragic phenomenon of which *The Voice of the Silence* speaks. Many human beings did not strive with their unclean hobgoblin images of a cold war. The more they feared the hobgoblin, the more they became frozen in their conception of hope. Human beings can collectively engender a gigantic, oppressive elemental, like the idea of a personal God, or the Leviathan of the State, which is kept in motion by reinforcement through fear, becoming a kind of reality and producing a paralysis of the will on the global plane.

Today, for the first time in recent decades, we live at that fortunate moment when psychopathology and sociopathology have alike become boring, throwing the individual back upon his intuitions, dreams and secret intimations. Individuals cannot suddenly create refined vestures for the highest spiritual thought-energy, but they can at least desist from self-degradation. No protection a human being can devise is more potent or powerful than the arc of light around every human form. Any individual with unwavering faith in the divine is firmly linked with the ray descending into the hollow of the heart. One can totally reduce the shadowy self to a zero. The cipher may become a circle of sweetness and a sphere of light. It is imperative to keep faith with oneself in silence and secrecy, as every telling weakens the force that is generated. Krishna says, "In whatever way men approach me, in that way do I assist them." This is offered unconditionally to all. Near the end of his instruction he says, "Act as seemeth best unto thee."

Basic honesty will go far to clean out the cobwebs of delusion and confusion so that the seeds of spiritual regeneration may be salvaged. Patience is needed together with enduring trust in the healing and nurturing processes of Nature that protect the seeds silently germinating in the soil. They cannot be pulled up and scrutinized again and again, but must be allowed to sprout in the soft light of the dawn, enriched by the radiant magnetism of universal love which maintains the whole cosmos in motion. Even a little soul-memory shows that there is no need to blame history or Nature, much less the universe, for the universe is on the side of every sincere impulse. Even the most wicked and depraved man may have some hope. Even a little daily practice delivereth a man from great risk. Even a minute grain of soul-wisdom, when patiently assimilated with a proper mental posture in relation to the sacred teachings and the sacrificial Teachers, will act as a beneficent influence and an unfailing guide to the true servant of the Masters of the Verbum. This incommunicable secret of Krishna is the sweetest and most potent gift of the divine Logos of the cosmos to the awakened humanity of today and the global civilization of tomorrow.

The Gupta Vidya II, The Golden Thread

CONTINUITY OF CONSCIOUSNESS

What does modern science know of the duration of the ages of the World, or even of the length of geological periods?

Nothing; absolutely nothing. . . . Indeed, in the Cimmerian darkness of the prehistoric ages, the explorers are lost in a labyrinth, whose great corridors are doorless, allowing no visible exit into the Archaic past. Lost in the maze of their own conflicting speculations, rejecting, as they have always done, the evidence of Eastern tradition, without any clue, or one single certain milestone to guide them, what can geologists or anthropologists do but pick up the slender thread of Ariadne. . . . They are 'prehistoric' to the naked eye of matter only. To the spiritual eagle eye of the seer and the prophet of every race, Ariadne's thread stretches beyond that 'historic period' without break or flaw, surely and steadily, into the very night of time; and the hand which holds it is too mighty to drop it, or even let it break.

The Secret Doctrine, ii 66-67

Ariadne's thread represents unbroken continuity of consciousness in the One Life. In relation to perception (*samvriti*) and knowledge (*prajna*), it stands for the principle of *Buddhi*, spiritual intuition, which by analogy and correspondence cuts through the maze of detail to the heart of the matter. Ariadne's thread is also the *sutratman*, the integrity of the immortal soul, the meta-psychological basis of individual awareness extending back over eighteen million years and serving as the storehouse of soul-memory (*anamnesis*). Through its capacity to tap *Akasha*, the universal empyrean upon which are recorded all the archetypal truths behind the mass of manifested projections, the immortal soul, by reference to its inherent wisdom, can recover the most illuminating continuity of consciousness. It can bridge apparent gaps on the physical plane — between days and nights, between seasons and years — and cross chasms between incarnations. Even more important, it can span the *pralayas*, the periods of obscuration between Races and Rounds. This timeless wisdom of the soul cannot be comprehended by the ratiocinative, rationalizing mind.

Through material evidence, sensory data and induction, it is possible to accumulate masses of information which may then be submitted to logical or methodological analysis. Thus one can infer conjectural estimates of the age of the sun and the moon, of the earth and man. But such inferences, however intriguing, shed no light upon the complex relationship between cosmic and human chronology. Even if one extends anthropological estimates of the age of man to a period of nearly twenty million years, as suggested in the late work of L.S.B. Leakey, one grasps no sense of what happened to humanity during those unchronicled years. And, seeing only fragments of the conscious life of humanity, it is nearly impossible to conceive of the humanity of the hoary past, and its vital relationship to the decisive lighting up of *Manas* over eighteen million years ago at the midpoint of the Fourth Round. With regard to more antique times and previous Rounds, empirical evidence that the physical earth and physical entities in space go back hundreds of millions of years reveals no helpful connections between all these enormously ancient relics and human evolution. In short, nearly nothing that is significant or definitive can be known about the primordial origins of conscious life through a reductionist methodology relying upon sensory evidence and inference from external shells and petrified astral deposits.

Instead of expecting such an unphilosophical methodology to assist in the recovery of universal continuity of consciousness, one must adopt a radically different approach, grounded in metaphysics. Employing a dialectical methodology analogous to the ontological process it seeks to apprehend, one must begin with persistent enquiry into the profound connection between the One and the many, the Logos and the Logoi. One must meditate upon phases of progressive manifestation, coming down from the most subjective level conceivable to the most objective visible level. This radical transformation of method requires introversion, a turning within the immortal soul. But, since external evidence is so incomplete and so inadequate to understanding millions of years of conscious life, and since at the same time it is immensely difficult to turn within, it may seem impossible to make much progress. Without seed thoughts for meditation, it may appear hopeless even to begin the enquiry. Yet, this is not true. It is merely a presumptive delusion arising from the protracted hubris of Western nations, which, out of habitual ignorance of other languages, simply have not seriously considered the calendars and chronologies of ancient Indian, Chinese and other cultures. As H.P. Blavatsky repeatedly and forcefully affirmed a century ago, one must revert to time-honoured Eastern sources even to make sense of what may be sporadically inferred from physical evidence.

Paradoxically, despite the pioneering efforts of intrepid thinkers in the latter part of the nineteenth century in philology and phonetics connected with the entire stock of Indo-European languages, there has been subsequently an enormous shrinkage of chronologies in reference to Eastern civilizations. The balance has been redressed somewhat, in reference to China, largely through the work of Joseph Needham over the past thirty years. More recently, Jawaharlal Nehru, in his remarkable *The Discovery of India*, observes that there are five times as many books on India in the London Library as on China. Many were written by nineteenth-century Englishmen who confidently explored such various topics as the early relationship between India and Mediterranean civilization, the parental connection between Sanskrit and other languages, and the suggestive similarities between the oldest forms of architecture in India and architectural forms which later became prominent in Gothic Europe and throughout the Middle East.

Whilst many of these authors were overwhelmed with admiration by what they discovered over a lifetime — when not blinded by religious bigotry — they nonetheless could not recognize the continuing relevance of the ancient Indian records. This resistance arose either because they did not have free access to them and also to accurate Brahminical explanations, or because they were obsessed by the supposed primacy of Greek civilization. Now, all of this has been exploded, and anyone with a lively sense of karma can appreciate the appropriateness of atonement for past ingratitude. When modern Europeans came in contact with the much older and essentially noble civilization of India, and found elements far more ancient than Egyptian relics, something went clearly wrong with xenophobic assumptions and even with regard to 'scholarly' dating. *The Discovery of India* invaluably demonstrates that many Europeans, even before the twentieth century, had traced the origins of major elements of Western civilization to ancient India. Despite their discomfort in proceeding to the fullest conclusions, they established the necessity of taking Eastern records seriously.

It is no wonder, then, that H.P. Blavatsky took the trouble in *The Secret Doctrine* to spell out certain details of ancient Indian and Brahminical calendars and chronologies. Before specifying exact figures, she remarked:

> The best and most complete of all such calendars, at present, as vouched for by the learned Brahmins of Southern India, is the ...Tamil calendar called the 'Tirukkanda Panchanga,' compiled, as we are told, from, and in full accordance with, secret fragments of Asuramaya's data. As Asuramâya is said to have been the greatest astronomer, so he is whispered to have also been the most powerful 'Sorcerer' of the 'WHITE ISLAND, which had become BLACK with sin,' *i.e.*, of the islands of Atlantis.... He was an Atlantean; but he was a direct descendant of the *Wise Race, the Race that never dies.* Many are the legends concerning this hero, the pupil of Surya (the Sun-God) himself, as the Indian accounts allege.
>
> *The Secret Doctrine*, ii 67

According to this calendar, 1,955,884,687 years had elapsed between the beginning of evolution on Globe A of the earth chain in the First Round and the year 1887. It also located the manvantaric period of astral evolution in the sub-human kingdoms, and distinguished it from the subsequent period after the appearance of incipient 'humanity' on the earth chain. H.P. Blavatsky cited certain puzzles connected with the internal figures in this Tamil calendar, and also contrasted it with other orthodox Hindu calendars. As she explained both here and elsewhere, these riddles develop because esoteric figures cannot be revealed outside initiation. She then proceeded to present a simpler schema computed by P. Sreenivas Row, which begins with a single mortal day and extends all the way to the Age of Brahmā. The telling significance of these figures is that they show that abundant knowledge is available, not only in the inaccessible cave libraries of the Kunlun Range, but also in calendars in common use in South India today, which could be employed as the basis of study. To understand this, one needs something more than a knowledge of mathematics: the method of analogy and correspondence.

Sanskrit and what is now called Tamil are *reliquiae* of ante-Diluvian and ante-Poseidonian languages. In them critical terms like *kalpa* and Manu have a depth of occult symbolism which can only be grasped by taking them as generic terms applicable to the large and to the small and to many diverse levels of manifestation. This plasticity of meaning affords some protection to those who made these figures available but wanted to hold back certain clues that could, in the hands of unprepared human beings, become dangerous. At the same time, because of the generic nature of these words, one can understand by analogy and correspondence that what pertains to the vast *Mahakalpa* also applies to the *kalpa* in the small. What applies to a hundred years of Brahmā applies to one day of Brahmā and also to the much smaller period of a *Mahayuga*.

All of this poses a formidable challenge to the intuition and provides a great deal of food for thought and meditation. Working by analogy and correspondence with various sets of figures, myriad applications may be made not only on the vast scale of cosmic evolution, but equally on the minute scales of days, hours and minutes. For example, H.P. Blavatsky cited the views set forth by Dr. Laycock in *Lancet* regarding the universal applicability of septenary cycles of days and weeks to all animal life, from the ovum of an insect up to man, and affecting all their vital functions, including birth, growth, maturity, disease, decay and death.

> Dr. Laycock divides life by *three great septenary periods;* the first and last, each stretching over 21 years, and the central period or prime of life lasting 28 years, or four times seven. He subdivides the first into *seven distinct stages,* and the other two into *three* minor periods, and says that 'The fundamental unit of the greater periods is *one week of seven days, each day being twelve hours';* and that 'single and compound *multiples* of this unit, determine the length of these periods by the same ratio, as multiples of the unit of twelve hours determine the lesser periods. *This law binds all periodic vital phenomena together, and links the periods observed in the lowest annulose animals, with those of man himself, the highest of the vertebrata.*' If *Science* does this, why should the latter scorn the Occult information, namely that (speaking Dr. Laycock's language) *'one week* of the manvantaric *(lunar)* fortnight, of fourteen days (or seven manus), that fortnight of twelve hours in a day representing seven periods or seven races — is now passed'? This language of science fits our doctrine admirably.
>
> Ibid., 623

Anyone who tentatively explores such mysterious connections between numbers and daily life begins to touch the Ariadne's thread of the immortal soul. Exactly how this is done and what its effect will be depends upon one's motivation and the tropism of one's soul. Some, ill at ease with the shrunken categories of modern science, yet enthralled with the sky, the planets and the galaxies, may be able to discern intuitive connections which inspire them in their dreams and activate their soul-memory. Others, who tend to think philosophically and metaphysically, may find that such enquiries arouse a hunger for meditation, which in turn helps them to see the archetypal logic of these processes. At the very least, such enquiries will yield an enormous sense of freedom from all that limits the horizons of human thought, all that constrains the reach of the human imagination. Once the imagination is freed, one can make one's own discoveries, through myth and symbol, and express them, through poetry or otherwise. The core discovery strengthened by all this enquiry is a sense of kinship, not only with all humanity and all past civilization, but also with the flora and fauna of the earth, and ultimately the living cosmos in its entirety.

The recovery of continuity of consciousness and the reawakening of soul-memory are central to *The Secret Doctrine*. These cannot emerge except through devotion and gratitude, and through preparing oneself to sit at the feet of real Gurus. Hence, H.P. Blavatsky's repeated insistence that the West must relinquish its adolescent egotism; hence, too, her constant recurrence to the figure of the Arhat, the perfected man, the Adept and Initiate. Before one can recover continuity of consciousness in the *sutratman*, one must acknowledge the existence not only of soul-memory but also of perfected sages, souls free from the illusion of time and able to witness vast periods of evolution as ordinary human beings watch moments. For the Mahatma, Ariadne's thread stretches in unbroken continuity and total wakefulness beyond the manifestation of this world and into the night of *pralaya* and beyond.

The highest ideal in the Brotherhood of Bodhisattvas is to gain a sense of continuity with the substratum of reality that persists even when there are no worlds, but only the night of nonmanifestation. By plumbing the depths of that night, even beyond the night of time, Buddhas and Bodhisattvas find a freedom and detachment that enables them to see worlds and aeons through an instantaneous flash of Buddhic light. What the perfected human being can do in fullness every human being can attempt, if he or she will practise the toughest of all kinds of mental asceticism — turning a deaf ear to the conventional unwisdom of the exoteric world whilst remaining constantly attentive to every source of potential learning. To release this oceanic sense of universal continuity, one should turn to the sky and the stars, to the poets and the prophets.

To trace Ariadne's thread across incarnations, much less *pralayas* affecting Races and Rounds, requires the tremendous courage that can come only through systematic meditation. This inner discipline is not merely one activity amongst others, capriciously undertaken. It is, rather, the basis for awakening the powers of discrimination of different levels of composition or aggregation, of reduction, reabsorption and dissolution. The mastery of these processes, which takes place within the subtle vestures and is centered on the *karana sharira*, has a direct relationship with the alternation of *manvantara* and *pralaya*. Broadly, the septenary Teachings of Gupta Vidya concerning the seven planes of matter and seven states of consciousness have a general reference to all systems within the cosmos. The Teachings also have a more specific reference to the solar system and a primary focus for humanity on this earth. Humanity, circling round the seven globes, finds itself in the Fourth Round on Globe D, the most material of the terrestrial spheres. This globe is preceded by three ethereal globes and succeeded by three globes which are also ethereal but represent a more evolved state of consciousness. In the present fourth life-wave, occupying millions upon millions of years in its circuit through the seven globes, humanity finds itself evolving through a sevenfold series of vestures that are adapted to matter as it exists in this system. Having attained self-consciousness over eighteen million years ago, in the middle of the Third Root Race, and now belonging to the Fifth Sub-Race of the Fifth Root Race, it still must experience many periods of relative activity and rest before arriving at the close of the present Round.

The most immediately relevant shift in the basis of active manifestation applicable to humanity in general is the gradual transition from the Fifth to the Sixth Sub-Races of the Fifth Root Race. Because the Law of periodicity is universal, this transition cannot take place without a pralayic dissolution of aspects of the human vestures and their subsequent remanifestation in a transformed mode. Whatever the subtle consequences of this significant change on the four lower planes, the essential locus of this transmutation is in the fifth and sixth principles of human nature — *Manas* and *Buddhi*. Hence, the meaning and magnitude of the present transformation cannot be apprehended from any standpoint bound up with the lower quaternary, but only from within the Manasic principle of self-consciousness through its meditative attunement to *Buddhi*. Otherwise, the apparent *pralaya* of contemporary civilizations, as well as the promise and potential of an incipient golden age, cannot be comprehended.

The teachings of Gupta Vidya with regard to *manvantara* and *pralaya* are meant to be studied not merely out of intellectual interest or philosophic curiosity. They are intended for those who truly seek to become *yogins*: those who, by daily meditation, daily self-study and the daily renunciation of the fruits of action, seek self-consciously to bring about profound changes in their subtle vestures consonant with the present phase of evolution. Through the spiritual discipline of concentration, they aim at making the astral form coherent, and the mind controlled. In the context of such a regenerative discipline, the radical difference between psychic action — which works at the level of the molecular and the structural — and noetic action — which works at the level of the atomic — is vital. Here the term 'atomic' refers to that which is even more rudimentary than what science calls atomic or even subatomic. This cannot be apprehended unless a person experiences self-consciously the progressive refinement of magnetism, involving sub-hierarchies of colour and sound and yielding a percipient awareness of the most minute subdivisions of various classes of elementals.

The basic distinction between the psychic and the noetic applies not only to all the elements, but also to thoughts, and indeed to everything perceptible at any level of form. Through deep meditation, one may awaken the capacity to touch that golden Buddhic potency which is in everything, and thus bring about a beneficent alchemical transubstantiation. But one must first have attained to such a degree of disinterestedness that one can consciously assist and accelerate the processes of change, quickening the process of dispersion. Through meditation one must learn to cooperate intelligently with the atomic noetic potential of the higher

Triad in a pralayic process of continuous dispersion and dissolution, refusing to allow any recoalescence of that which is dying, so as to sustain continuity of consciousness into that which is being born.

Unfortunately, through possessiveness, through enormous thirst for sensation, through reassertion of *ahankara* — the drives inherent in the Fourth Round, whose dominant principle is *kama* — most humans tend to solidify, to concretize the moribund residues of the past. This is analogous to the physical process, whereby creatures that lived in previous, more ethereal Rounds leave behind them fossils, concretized residues. If this process of consolidation applies to all the life-atoms that make up the astral form in its aspects linked to the physical body, it is also relevant to the subtler states of the astral vesture. To understand and assist the corresponding process of perpetual dissolution, or *nitya pralaya*, is to engage in a kind of letting go, that continual practice of dying which Plato depicts in *Phaedo* as central to the life of the true philosopher. Conscious and continuous dispersion of all the elements is inseparable from an equal sensitivity to constant and perpetual creation, or *nitya sarga*, the invisible creation at the primary causal level of Nature which continually maintains the universe in motion. Taken together, *nitya pralaya* and *nitya sarga* are complementary aspects of the Great Breath. Meditation upon *pralaya* and *manvantara*, dissolution and creation, is linked with mastering spiritual and mental breathing. This involves not only their rhythm but also their attunement to the subtlest level of cosmic breathing.

The profound Teaching regarding *nitya pralaya* and *nitya sarga*, like everything else connected with spiritual self-transformation and self-regeneration, cannot be consciously applied unless one learns to work in terms of cycles of seven and fourteen years. One must prepare for that stage by thinking out to the core who one is, why one is alive, what one truly wants, and what it is one is prepared to live for. This requires a careful preparation in detachment, as well as the courage to face and fully accept one's karmic responsibilities in the realm of dharma. These are the prerequisites of discipleship and practical occultism. Merely by thinking upon these ideas, individuals can tap soul-knowledge in relation to past lives, wherein this knowledge was direct and active. If a person is sufficiently compassionate, suffused with an authentic concern for the welfare of all that lives, determined to be vitally helpful to humanity in some future life — ten lives or a hundred lives from now — then he or she can sufficiently prepare for occult training by coming to understand now that which will come to one's aid at the moment of death. This self-conscious strengthening of the sutratmic thread will enhance the moment of birth in the next life, easing entry early in that life into the Bodhisattvic current.

In the nineteenth century H.P. Blavatsky sought to assure those who had retired from productive lives that even in old age they might prepare their mental luggage for the next life. Today many suffer from impetuosity rather than procrastination. Through weak wills, frustrated ambitions or fearful eschatologies, they are resolved to do everything quickly or not at all. This is mental laziness, as well as a futile attempt at moral blackmail directed against the universe. Instead of such self-destructive cowardice, one should strive to be fearless in the metaphysical imagination, and dwell on the highest conceptions. One should be ready to look up to the boundless sky whilst addressing one's obligations on earth. Holding fast to a serene rhythm of selfless devotion, one should develop an ethical sensitivity to others, whilst maintaining an alert attentiveness to one's own obligations. One must refine a sense of balance, soaring to the empyrean in meditation, whilst controlling the quotidian details of ethical involvement. Thus metaphysics and ethics may be brought together, to create a steady, strong current of fervent aspiration. Thus too, the process of dissolution is quickened, the potential for continuous creation increased. By letting go, one cooperates with nature's archetypal rhythms.

Beyond these cyclic transformations lies the Triad of absolute abstract Space, Duration and Motion, the metaphysical basis for all continuity of consciousness. All three may be seen as aspects of the

Three-in-One, expanding the conceptions of matter, time and motion into primordial substance, boundless eternity and divine thought. It is also helpful to concentrate on absolute abstract Motion as the One Life. This has a philosophical bearing upon one's notions of relative degrees of reality and unreality, of emptiness and illusion, of dependence and causality. The One Life comprises both light and electricity in all their cosmic manifestations and is equivalent to the universal soul or Anima Mundi. In Sanskrit it is the *Jivatman*, the analogue of the Platonic *nous* or mundane cosmic intelligence, absolutely free from differentiated matter and ever-designing action. Through the invocation of the *Jivatman*, the ever-pulsating life-principle, infinite and all-transcendent, Aryan philosophy addresses itself to that perpetual motion which is beyond the distinction between consciousness and unconsciousness. Only in relation to a field of manifestation, relative to *Mahat* in *manvantara* and *pralaya*, can one speak of that which is conscious, self-conscious or unconscious. So entirely does *Jivatman* transcend all human conception that it may as well be spoken of as absolute unconsciousness as absolute consciousness.

If the One Life or *Jivatman* is beyond all these distinctions, this implies that absolute and abstract continuity of consciousness has nothing to do with the purposes and processes of manifestation. It could, for example, be confusing to speak as Hegel does of the Absolute seeking to attain self-consciousness, or, in Hindu terms, of *Parabrahm* having some motive in manifestation. The notion of pure being or absolute consciousness admits of no contrast or polarity, and can participate in no relativities whatsoever. Nor can it have anything to do with the infinite extension of any attribute of finite manifestation (even so subtle an attribute of manifestation as thought, which necessarily presupposes the differentiation of a field and its perceiver). If, then, one is going to meditate upon universal life as a boundless ocean of energy without frontier or finite purpose, one must be freed of all binding conceptions and limiting teleologies, and even all thought bound up with mental instantiation in time.

One of the Rishis likened the Reality apprehended in *pralaya* to the depths of a boundless ocean of ceaseless energy.

In that fathomless divine abyss, everything is potential, but as a formless and fundamental rhythm or pulsation without reference to any worlds or to manifestation itself. It cannot be understood in relation to the absence of worlds. It is neither definable through affirmation nor through negation, neither through instantiation nor through privation. Cyclic or periodic existence, on the other hand, involves changes of form and state. Archetypally, this may be understood in terms of the potential of the seed, which gestates, then sprouts, then, as a tree with branches and limbs, bears in turn a myriad seeds. On an abstract level, this entire process contains an intrinsic reference to form and matter as it appears to minds that perceive it, and therefore, also a reference to variations of states of perceptive consciousness. These contrasts within manifested matter and consciousness are essential to cyclic existence but in no way characterize the impartite and boundless Reality beyond manifestation.

To every cycle there is a mayavic element, a veiling of that which is indestructible and entirely unaffected by transformation. The life potency that is in the seed in essence is a reflection of something on the Akashic plane unaffected by the seed's sprouting. Some beings on this plane may worry whether seeds sprout, but in terms of the essence, the sprouting is of no significance. Once this idea is grasped, one can begin to understand how it is possible, through perception of formless spiritual essences, to change one's perspective in reference to any cycle or to relate the phases of one cycle to another. One may, for example, relate the seven days of the week to the seven planets, and both to the seven phases of human life. Thus one may discern both sequence and possibility, whilst stripping certain cycles of a portion of their limitation. The ability to do this at will depends upon the extent to which one's consciousness is freed from the clutches of *kama manas,* desire, time and sensation. When the ray of the *Jivatman* is emancipated from the bondage of change, it can experience the universal pulsation of its omnipresent source. Thus it is possible to create a certain 'negative capability', in the Keatsian sense, a capacity for awareness of the unmanifest side of Nature. The greater this capacity, the more one can correct the natural tendency within incarnation of being caught up in the results and rancours of yesterday, today or tomorrow.

Authentic continuity of consciousness consists of unbroken self-conscious experience of the universality of the life-process, enjoying and relishing its unity amidst all the diversity. It is the ability to trace the Ariadne's thread of the One Life in all the seven kingdoms of nature amidst all the multitudinous forms, whilst at the same time reverencing it at its very root in a realm that is beyond manifestation, beyond the realm of form, exempt from change, undivided by subject and object. The purpose of all study of the sacred and secret science is to gain this freedom for the imagination and this depth for meditation, so that one may become better able to see to the core, and better able to discard that which obscures the Monadic spark. In practice, this means elevating, through daily discipline, one's ethical nature to the same level as one's metaphysical imagination.

One must reach a point where one's only desire or wish is on behalf of the whole, and where one's celebration of all human beings in one's own silent meditation is so real and so joyous that the boundaries of selfhood are shattered. Too often, the two wings of metaphysics and ethics are unbalanced, and spiritual aspirants find that they cannot convert metaphysics into magic. They lack the strength of mind and heart to void their sense of egoity and enclose all humanity within the vast continuity of universal self. Hence, the exercise of the metaphysical imagination must be strengthened daily through meditation, in the midst of the therapeutic practice of self-study and the cheerful performance of dharma. When ethics and metaphysics retain a durable continuity, and flow with a graceful balance, they can be synthesized, to awaken Buddhi-manasic wisdom and the soul-memory of the *sutratman*. Drawing upon that wisdom and sacrificing all strivings at its universal fire, one can make the requisite changes in consciousness, in the substance of the subtle vestures, and in one's magnetic field, so as to become effortless in the continual self-conscious enactment of the AUM.

The Gupta Vidya II, The Golden Thread

NOETIC SELF-DETERMINATION

If the general law of the conservation of energy leads modern science to the conclusion that psychic activity only represents a special form of motion, this same law, guiding the Occultists, leads them also to the same conviction — and to something else besides, which psycho-physiology leaves entirely out of all consideration. If the latter has discovered only in this century that psychic (we say even spiritual) action is subject to the same general and immutable laws of motion as any other phenomenon manifested in the objective realm of Kosmos, and that in both the organic and the inorganic (?) worlds every manifestation, whether conscious or unconscious, represents but the result of a collectivity of causes, then in Occult philosophy this represents merely the ABC of its science. . . .

But Occultism says more than this. While making of motion on the material plane and of the conservation of energy two fundamental laws, or rather two aspects of the same omnipresent law — Swara — it denies point blank that these have anything to do with the free will of man which belongs to quite a different plane.

H.P. Blavatsky

Gupta Vidya, the philosophy of perfectibility, is based upon the divine dialectic, which proceeds through progressive universalization, profound synthesis and playful integration. These primary principles are inseparably rooted in the cosmogonic archetypes and patterns of universal unity and causation. They are in sharp contrast to the expedient and evasive methodology of much contemporary thought which all too often proceeds on the basis of Aristotelian classification, statistical analysis and a sterile suspicion of intuitive insight. Whatever the karmic factors in the ancient feud between these divergent streams of thought, it is poignantly evident that their polar contrast becomes insuperable when it comes to understanding human nature. Gupta Vidya views the human situation in the light of the central conception of an immortal individuality capable of infinite perfectibility in its use of opaque and transitory vestures. The greater the degree of understanding attained of Man and Nature, the greater the effective realization of spiritual freedom and self-mastery.

In the methodology of modern thought, the more sharply its conceptions are formulated, the more inexorably it is driven to a harsh dilemma: it must either secure the comprehension of Nature at the cost of a deterministic conception of Man, or it must surrender the notions of order and causality in favour of statistical indeterminacy and randomness in Nature, thereby voiding all human action of meaning. Gupta Vidya not only dispels this dilemma, but it also explains the propensity to fall prey to it, through the arcane conception of two fundamental modes of mental activity. These were set forth by H.P. Blavatsky as "psychic" and "noetic" action. They refer to much more than 'action' in any ordinary sense, and really represent two distinct, though related, modes of self-conscious existence. They provide the prism through which the perceptive philosopher can view the complex and enigmatic relationship between human freedom and universal causality. All creative change and all dynamic activity in the universe are understood, in the perennial philosophy of Gupta Vidya, as spontaneous expressions of one abstract, pre-cosmic source symbolized as the Great Breath. In its highest ranges this is Spirit, and beneath that, it encompasses every mode of motion down to and including action on the physical plane.

> Motion as the GREAT BREATH (vide "*Secret Doctrine*", vol. i, sub voce) — ergo 'sound' at the same time — is the substratum of Kosmic-Motion. It is beginningless and endless, the one eternal life, the basis and genesis of the subjective and the objective universe; for LIFE (or Be-ness) is the *fons et origo* of existence or being. But molecular motion is the lowest and most material of its finite manifestations.
>
> H.P. Blavatsky
"Psychic and Noetic Action"

Several important consequences follow from this single origin of both subjective and objective reality. For example, the strict unity and universal causality implied by the conception of absolute abstract Motion entail the basic principle transmitted from ancient knowledge into modern science as the law of the conservation of energy. In a world of finite manifestations, such as that of molecular motion, this law has immense importance. The conception of entropy is an allied principle equally crucial in understanding the particularized motions and relationships between objects having specific kinds of energy in the world as we know it. Yet this does not really reveal much about the deeper sense in which there is collection and concentration of energy, from the highest *laya* state down through the physical plane of manifestation. There is a sense in which enormous energy is held waiting to be released from higher to lower planes. Potential energy, related to the higher aspects of the ceaseless motion of the One Life, transcends all empirical conceptions based upon observable phenomena.

This virtually inconceivable scale of modes of subtle manifestation of the Great Breath has immediate and evident implications in regard to cosmogony. But it is also highly significant when applied to the subjective side of conscious existence. Whilst the laws of physical motion and energy are natural modes of manifestation of that divine Breath, no merely objective description of them can do justice to the *subjective* side of purely physical events, much less to deeper layers of human consciousness and noumenal reality. Every plane or octave of manifest existence has both its subjective and objective side, even as every plane has its own dual aspect of activity that may variously be seen as more gross or more subtle, more concrete or more abstract. This vertical dimension of existence is often spoken of as the distinction between the subjective and the objective, though this is quite a different sense of these terms from the lateral distinction applied to any particular plane. The tendency to confuse or conflate these two senses of the subjective-objective distinction is in direct proportion to the grossness or concreteness of an individual's state of consciousness. Insofar as an individual's range of consciousness is limited to constellations of objects, persons and events, it will not be capable of comprehending the notions of metaphysical subjectivity or objectivity, or of metaphysical depth.

This is crucial when considering the seemingly abrupt transition from medieval to modern thought accompanying the movement away from a vastly inflated, but exceedingly particularized, conception of the subjective realm towards an almost obsessive concern with physical objectivity. As the capricious happenings and hearsay of the 'age of miracles' were gradually replaced by a rigid conception of external and mechanical order, it increasingly came to be understood that the inner life of man must also conform to universal laws. In what was a marked advance upon earlier notions of both physics and psychology, there emerged, in the nineteenth century, the explosive recognition that everything in the psychological realm is also subject to causality. This was powerfully put forward as part of a grandiose ethical scheme by George Godwin, the philosophical anarchist. Late in the nineteenth century several social scientists argued that if causality is to be applied to all phenomenal events and processes, it must also apply in some way to the world of what may be called psychic action. It must, in short, be applicable to all the states of mind experienced by human beings in bodies with brains.

It thus becomes vitally important to draw a clear-cut distinction between the mind and the brain, taking account of the subjective and objective aspects of both. In general, contemporary science has been either unwilling or unable to do this. Without this essential distinction, however, it is impossible to generate any firm basis for the notions of autonomy, self-determination, individuality, free thinking and potent ideation. Arcane philosophy begins at that precise point where an abyss has been discovered between the mind and brain. It is indeed a glaring gap, for though causality applies to both, it is difficult to discern clearly what the relationship could be between them, let alone to find exact correlates between the two parts of the distinction in terms of specific centres and elements.

Without the assured ability to distinguish decisively between them, the temptation is great to deny free will altogether and succumb to a reductionistic and mechanistic view of human nature. This the occultist and theurgist must deny, in theory and in practice.

> The actual fact of man's psychic (we say *manasic* or noetic) *individuality* is a sufficient warrant against the assumption; for in the case of this conclusion being correct, or being indeed . . . the *collective hallucination of the whole mankind throughout the ages,* there would be an end also to psychic individuality. Now by 'psychic' individuality we mean that self-determining power which enables man to override circumstances.
>
> Ibid.

All human beings have some experience not only of a persisting sense of individuality, but also of an ineradicable sense of being able to separate themselves from an observable objective field. They have a deep sense of being able to affect it consciously, and indeed even to control it. To dismiss so vital and universal an experience would be to betray a narrow, pseudo-philosophical prejudice towards mechanistic determinism. Not even all animals have precisely the same stimuli or reactions. Certainly, human beings in very similar environments respond quite differently to external stimuli. One cannot deny, then, that a human being can make a vital difference to his environment through his calm appraisal of it, or even through simply comparing or sharply contrasting it with something else. Either through the fugitive sense of memory or through the fervent thrill of anticipation, based upon a relaxed sense of identity projected into the past and the future, or even through heightened perceptions of the unsuspected relations between one's own circumstances and those of other beings, individuals make decisive choices among newly discovered alternatives. So long as they can ask probing questions about the degree to which they can possibly alter their mental outlook, they can truly determine for themselves, through these subtle changes of attitudes, their untapped ability to alter these circumstances.

In general, such attitudes may be rather passive or defiantly resistant to circumstances. But they may also include an intelligent acceptance of circumstances rooted in a capacity for conscious cooperation with necessity. One may completely transform one's environment through rearranging elements in it, through constructive dialogue with other agents and, above all, through an inner life of daily meditation and effortless self-transcendence. Thus free will can function, and so unfold a unitary consciousness coolly capable of deft self-determination. Having understood all this, the main challenge is to come to a clear comprehension of the self-determining power in man and, more specifically, to understand the delicate operation of the diverse faculties of the mind in the compelling context of universal causality. In this regard, the shrewd argument of George T. Ladd concerning mental faculties is crucial. Having contended that the phenomena of human consciousness must require a subject in the form of a real being, manifested immediately to itself in the phenomena of consciousness, he proceeded to consider how that real being perceives its relationship to the activity of consciousness.

> To it the mental phenomena are to be attributed as showing what it *is* by what it *does*. The so-called mental 'faculties' are only the *modes of the behaviour* in consciousness of this real being. We actually find, by the only method available, that this real being called Mind believes in certain perpetually recurring modes: therefore, we attribute to it certain faculties. . . . Mental faculties are not entities that have an existence of themselves. . . . They are the modes of the behaviour in consciousness of the mind.
>
> Ibid.

In other words, Ladd denied that one can comprehend the real being, or unit consciousness, exclusively through those recurring modes that are associated with certain 'faculties'. Just as one would find the idea of a unit being, in this metaphysical monadology, incompatible with crude physical behaviourism, it is also incompatible with psycho-physical and psychological behaviourism. Put another way, the inherent power of Manasic 'I-am-I' consciousness transcends all patterns such as those which inhere in the volatile *skandhas*. The human being can consciously transcend all behaviour patterns. He can readily transform anything through tapping his inherent powers of volition and ideation. Ladd then concluded:

> The subject of all the states of consciousness is a real unit-being, called Mind; which is of non-material nature, and acts and develops according to laws of its own, but is specially correlated with certain material molecules and masses forming the substance of the Brain.
>
> Ibid.

Full understanding of these laws, mastery over action and the capacity to coordinate the mind and brain can come only from a strong intention to attain these ends, together with a purgation of one's entire field. One cannot work with incompatible mixtures, which are inevitably explosive. One cannot infuse the potency of the noetic mind into the polluted psyche. One must purge and purify the psyche before it can absorb the higher current of transformation which is alchemical and fundamentally noetic.

The question then becomes how, in practice, one can readily recognize the subtle difference between an illusory sense of freedom and a real and valid sense of self-determination. Insofar as people are misled by everyday language and by fleeting sense-perceptions, and insofar as they have an associationist picture of mixed memories and indelible images, rendering them essentially passive in relation to mental and emotional states, they may totally fail to see that all these familiar states fall under laws of causality. They may also be unable to make significant noetic connections. Based upon luminous perceptions of noetic connections, one must learn to see their causal chains and calmly project possible consequences of persisting patterns tomorrow, next year and in the future. One must then take full responsibility for the future consequences of participation in connected patterns. The moment one recognizes and perceives significant connections, one will see that at different times one could have made a distinct difference by the way in which one reacted, by the degree of sensitivity one showed, and by the degree of self-criticism one applied to these states. The moment a human being begins to ask 'why', he demands meaning from experience and rejects uncritical acceptance or mere passivity towards anything in life, including the recognizable sequence in which mental phenomena manifest.

Through this noetic capacity to question the association and the succession of events, one can decisively alter patterns. One can thus move from an initial level of passivity to a degree of free will whilst, in the act of seeing connections and making correlations, raising questions and altering patterns. Given the Buddhist doctrine of *skandhas*, or the Hindu doctrine of *samskaras*, each personality collects, over a lifetime, persisting associated tendencies. These persisting tendencies of thought and character are reinforced by appropriate emotions, desires and habits. Hence, the mere making of sporadic alterations in the inherited pattern of tendencies will be a poor example of free will, since over a longer period of time the pattern itself is conditioned by certain basic assumptions.

To take a simple example, as long as the will to live is strong and persistent, there is a sense in which free will is illusory. One lacks the fundamental capacity to make significant changes in one's *skandhas* or personality. This is an expression of *prarabdha* karma, the karma with which one has begun life. It is already reflected in one's particular body, one's mind, one's emotions, character and personality — and, indeed, in one's established relationship to a specific heredity and environment. This is part of the karma one cannot alter easily from within. Though these ideas go far beyond anything that is conceived in ordinary behaviouristic psychology, it is vital that the complex notion of free will be raised to a higher level, making greater demands and requiring more fundamental changes in one's way of life and outlook. It is precisely at this point that the distinction between psychic and noetic action becomes crucial. One must understand the locus in consciousness of the incipient power of free will, and then distinguish this from the fundamental source of will which lies entirely outside the sphere of the personality and the field of *prarabdha karma, skandhas* and *samskaras*. Speaking of Ladd's conception of mind as the real unit being that is the subject of all states of consciousness, H.P. Blavatsky commented:

> This 'Mind' is *manas*, or rather its lower reflection, which whenever it disconnects itself, for the time being, with *kama*, becomes the guide of the highest mental faculties, and is the organ of the free will in physical man.
>
> Ibid.

Whereas *Manas* itself is noetic, and signifies what could be called the spiritual individuality, there is also that which may be called the psychic individuality — this same *Manas* in association with *kama*, or desire. This projected ray of *Manas* itself has a capacity, though intermittent, for a kind of free will. Consider a human being who is completely caught up in chaotic desires and who is extremely uncritical in relation to his experiences, his tastes, his likes — in short, to his self-image. Even that kind of person will have moments of disengagement from emotion and a relative freedom from desire. In such moments of limited objectivity the person may see what is otherwise invisible. He may see alternatives, recognize degrees, glimpse similarities and differences from other human beings in similar situations; gradually, he may sense the potential for self-determination. Even lower *Manas*, when it is disconnected from *kama*, can exercise free will, giving guidance to the mental faculties that make up the personality. This limited application of free will, however, is obviously quite different from full self-determination. The projected ray of *Manas* is the basis of the psychic nature and potentially the organ of free will in physical man. *Manas* itself is the basis of the higher self-conscious will, which has no special organ, but is capable, independent of the brain and personality, of functioning on its own. This noetic individuality is distinct from the projected ray of lower *Manas*, which is its organ, and distinct too from the physical brain and body, which are the organs of the psychic lower *Manas*. This source of spiritual will is characterized in the *Bhagavad Gita* as the *kshetrajna*, higher *Manas*, the silent Spectator, which is the voluntary sacrificial victim of all the mistakes and misperceptions of its projected ray.

The contrast between the silent Spectator and the despotic lower *Manas* explains the difference between the psychic and the noetic. Wherever there is an assertion of the egotistic will, there is an exaggeration of the astral shadow and an intensification of *kama manas*. When the projected ray of *Manas* becomes hard and cold, it tends to become parasitic upon others, taking without returning, claiming without thanking, continuously scheming without scruples. Ultimately, this not only produces a powerful *kamarupa*, but also puts one on the path towards becoming an apprentice *dugpa* or black magician. The *dugpa* or sorcerer works through coercive imposition of combative will. It accommodates nothing compassionate or sacrificial, no hint or suggestion of the supreme state of calm. This suggests a practical test in one's self-study. If one is becoming more wilful, one is becoming more and more caught up in lower psychic action. One's astral body is becoming inflamed, fattened and polluted, and one is losing one's flickering connection with the divine and silent Spectator. This is a poor way of living and ageing, a pathetic condition. If, on the other hand, one is becoming humbler and more responsive to others, more non-violent, less assertive and more open to entering into the relative reality of other beings, loosening and letting go the sense of separateness, one is becoming a true apprentice upon the path of renunciation, the path of benevolent magic. The altruistic use of noetic wisdom, true theurgy, is the teaching of Gupta Vidya.

The silent Spectator is capable of thinking and ideating on its own. It is capable of disengaging altogether from lower *Manas*, just as lower *Manas* can disengage from *kama*. This skilful process of disengagement is similar to what Plato conveys through Socrates in

Phaedo and also in the *Apology*. It is a process of consciously dying, which the philosopher practises every moment, every day. By dying unto this world, one can increasingly disengage from the will to live, the *tanha* of the astral and physical body. It is possible by conscious spiritual exercises for the individual progressively to free higher *Manas* from its lower Manasic limitations, projections, excuses, evasions and habits. It can come into its own, realizing in its higher states what Patanjali calls the state of a Spectator without a spectacle. This requires repeated entry into the Void. Even to those who have not deeply meditated upon it, the idea of supreme Voidness *(shunyata)* is challenging; it appeals to an intrinsic sense of sovereign spiritual freedom that exists in every human soul as a Manasic being. As a thinking, self-conscious agent and spectator, every individual is, in principle, capable of appreciating and understanding, at some preliminary level, the possibility of universalizing self-consciousness. But actually to expand consciousness and gain emancipation from all fetters requires a life of deep and regular meditation.

This majestic movement in consciousness towards metaphysical subjectivity is directly connected with the capacity to contact in consciousness the noetic and noumenal realm behind the proscenium of objective physical existence. It is evident, for example, that the solar system is a complex causal realm involving planetary rotation around the sun according to definite laws. From the standpoint of Gupta Vidya, everything is sevenfold.

This is as true of planets and constellations as of human beings. The solar system also involves seven planes, and each of its planets has seven globes. The physical sun is, then, the centre of revolutionary motion by the planets on the physical plane. This regulated activity is no different from anything else seen on the phenomenal plane in the manifested world. It is a representation in physical space of invisible principles. All such physical entities have correlates on the invisible plane, both subjective and objective.

Starting with the fundamental principle of universal unity and radical identity of all motion and activity in the Great Breath, there are close connections between the metaphysical aspects of all beings. Hence, there are metaphysical correlations between the subtle principles in human nature and the subtle principles of the sun and planets. Thus, there are invisible aspects of the moon which correspond to the lower principles in man, the psychic nature of the human being. There are also higher principles which correspond to *Atma-Buddhi* and to the noetic capacity of higher *Manas*. Depending upon whether a human being is mired in psychic consciousness or rises to the noetic realm, he or she will have more or less self-conscious affinities with these different aspects of the solar system. When they look to the sky at night, their responses will differ not only on the physical plane but also on these invisible planes. One person may simply be impressed by the brightness of Venus in relation to the moon, being entranced by the physical beauty of the phenomenon. Another person might be interested to think in terms of the recondite activities and functions known even to contemporary astronomy. Still another, who is deeply rooted in the philosophy of Gupta Vidya, and a practitioner of regular meditation, would see something quite different in the heavens.

It is a common observation that different people see different things and derive different meanings from the same phenomena. Different people embody different degrees and balances of psychic perception and noetic apprehension of psycho-physical phenomena. To be able to see noetically one must begin by focussing upon the Spiritual Sun. This means that one must embark upon a programme of meditation and mental discipline directed to making conscious and consistent a secure sense of immortality. True immortality belongs to the *Atma-Buddhi-Manas*, the noetic individuality, and must be made real as an active principle of selection in reference to the lower principles. A person who does this will be able, like the Vedic *hotri*, to draw upon the highest aspects of the lunar hierarchies around the full moon and also the sublime energies and hidden potencies of the Spiritual Sun.

To perceive and connect the noetic in oneself with the noetic in the cosmos requires a synthetic and serene understanding. Such understanding is the crystalline reflection of the ineffable light of *Buddhi* into the focusing field of higher *Manas*. *Buddhi*, seen from its own subjective side, is inseparable from the motion of the Great Breath, whilst its objective side is the radiant light of higher understanding. Noetic understanding is, therefore, rooted in universal unity. Its modes are markedly different from the analytical method of the lower reason, which tends to break up wholes into parts, losing all sight of integrity and meaning. No matter what the object of one's understanding, the fundamental distinction between psychic and noetic implies a subtle and vital difference between the set of properties that belongs to an assemblage of parts and the set of properties that belongs only to the whole, which is greater than the sum of its parts.

If one is going to use an analytic method, one must begin by recognizing that there are different levels of analysis requiring different categories and concepts. Merely by breaking up a phenomenon, one may not necessarily understand it. The *yogin*, according to Patanjali, does the opposite. He meditates upon each object of concentration as a whole, becomes one with it, apprehending the *Atma-Buddhi* of that phenomenon through his own *Atma-Buddhi*. He draws meanings and produces effects that would never be accessible to the analytic methods of lower *Manas*. Others, for example, may decompose sound into its component elements of vibration, yet fail to hear in them any harmony or special melody; they may talk glibly about motion and vibration, yet be deaf to the harmony produced through vibrations. A musically tone-deaf physicist may know quite a lot about the theory of sound and yet may lack the experience or ability to enjoy the experience of masters of music. Conversely, those who are masters of music, and who may know something about the analytic theory of sound, may know nothing about what the *yogin* knows who has gone beyond all audible sounds to the metaphysical meaning of vibrations.

Thus there are levels upon levels of harmony within the cosmos spanning the great octave of Spirit-Matter. Gupta Vidya, which is always concerned with vibration and harmony, provides the only secure basis for acquiring the freedom to move from plane to plane of subjective and objective existence. The arcane standpoint is integrative, and always sees the One in the many. It develops that intuitive faculty which detects what is in common to a class of objects, and at the same time, in the light of that commonality, it enjoys what is unique to each object. It is this powerful faculty of mind that the theurgist perfects. Through it, he quickly moves away from the phenomenal and even from manifest notions of harmony. And through noetic understanding he can experience the inaudible harmony and intangible resonances that exist in all manifestation. A person attentive to the great tone throughout Nature will readily appreciate the music of the spheres. Such a person can hear the sound produced by breath, not only in animals and human beings, but also in stars and planets. Such a hierophant becomes a Walker of the Skies, a Master of Compassion, in whom the power of the Great Breath has become liberated. All ordered Nature resonates and responds to the Word and Voice of such a hierophant, who lives and breathes in That which breathes beyond the cosmos, breathless.

The Gupta Vidya II, The Golden Thread

CONTINUITY AND CHOICE

Suffering arises out of exaggerated involvement in a world of colour, forms and objects, maintained by a false sense of personal identity. As long as people persist in this pseudo-continuum of existence, they necessarily forfeit the exercise of their inner creative capacities and cannot fully seize the opportunities of self-conscious evolution. Human beings produce a false sense of self out of a series of intense particularizations of will, thought and feeling, all of which become the tokens of selfhood. As a result, in the very process of fragmenting oneself into a diversity of desires and conflicting and colliding aims, or of limiting oneself by conceptions which must be concretized in some narrow programme in space and time, suffering is built into one's life. All exaggerations of the void and illusory ego, all failures to recognize the overarching One, all attempts to live as if one were the centre of the world and without any self-conscious awareness of the beyond, mean that one can only gain happiness, pleasure or fulfilment at a cost. An obscuring shadow follows all pleasure — a compulsive feedback, a necessary negation, an unavoidable depression. When people do not detach themselves and negate excessive involvement in advance of every thought, the negation must come from outside, and after a point people lose their hold over the central thread of unifying or synthesizing awareness.

Suffering is the obscuration of the light of universal understanding. As long as we live in terms of narrow conceptions of ourselves, shrunken conceptions of space and of time, and with an exaggerated intensity that will necessarily be followed by an external negation, suffering is built into our life. It is coeval with that ignorance of the real which makes what we call human life possible. Human life is a passing shadow-play in which human beings identify with roles and, like candles, are eventually snuffed out. It is a play with a brief intensity focused upon a paltry role and based upon identifications with name and form. One who experiences great suffering, or who reflects deeply upon the relationships at the very root of this process, may come to see that the world and oneself are not apart.

The world is at least partly of one's own making but it is also made by the limiting conceptions of other human beings. They have become involved in the creation of a world in which limitation is a necessary part, and they too have forgotten what they innately knew. All human beings begin life by sounding the OM. They all have a cool awareness of the ineffable when they are little children, before they begin to lisp and to speak. In the youth of their sense-organs they experience wonder in relation to the whole of life. In the process of growing up, however, they take on the illusions of others — of parents, elders, teachers, and a variety of people around them — and then they become forgetful of what they already knew. We may reawaken awareness only by self-conscious self-renewal. Awareness is like a colourless universal light for which there are as many focusing media as there are metaphysical points in abstract space. Each human being is a ray of that light. To the extent to which that ray projects out into a world of differentiated light and shade, and limitations of form and colour, it is tinctured by the colouring that comes to it from a mental environment. Philosophically, the mental environment is far more important than the external physical environment.

When one sees this process archetypally, one recognizes that there is no separation between oneself and the world except in language, reactive gestures, and in certain uncriticized assumptions. Most importantly, there is no separation of oneself from other human beings as centres of consciousness. The notions of 'mine' and 'thine', attached to pleasure and pain, to joy and suffering, are arbitrary and false. Is that which gives one great joy exclusively one's own? And, on what grounds do we assume that the suffering of human beings in numerous states of acute self-limitation is purely theirs? Does each one have his own exclusive property rights in collective human suffering and thereby have nothing to do with us? Suffering is intrinsic to the universal stream of conditioned existence. Most living is a kind of pseudo-participation in what seem to be events, but which are merely arbitrary constructions of space-time, and are largely non-events. When a human being comes to see that involvement of a single universal consciousness in a single homogeneous material medium, the very notion of the individual 'I' has dissolved.

We are all aware when we go to the dentist and submit ourselves to something that seems physically painful, through our very awareness of what is happening and our deliberate attempt to think away from our identified involvement with the part of the physical body which is suffering, we can control our sensations to some extent rather than being wholly controlled by them. If this insight could be extended, we might see that the stream of universal consciousness is like an ever-flowing river — in which all conceptions of 'I' and 'you' and 'this' and 'that' are mere superimpositions — and then we could begin to stand consciously at some remove from the process of life. Suppose a person came to listen to a discourse of the Buddha with petty expectations, because somebody said it would be quite good, or worth hearing, or fairly interesting. Someone else might have come with a deeper idea because he or she was awake as a soul and had the thought that it is a tremendous privilege to be in the magnanimous presence of a Mahatma, and hence he or she might be lit up. If one is truly lit up, one's wakefulness makes the greatest difference to the whole of one's life. It could be gathered up self-consciously at the moment of death. But even a person who comes with so profound a thought into a collective orbit where there are many souls in states of only relative wakefulness and caught up in residual illusions, may forget the original moment.

The suffering of human life is a jolt which the whole gives the part, the individual ray, to re-awaken in it a memory and awareness of the original moment. Here we can see the significance of certain meditations undertaken by Bhikshus. In Buddhist philosophy there are references to meditations on the moment of birth. Yet how are we to meditate on it when it is an event that has no sense of reality for us? It is simply a certain date on the calendar. The mystery of individuality lies in the privilege and the possibility of making one's own connections within what otherwise would be a vast, fragmented chaos of events. One could make these connections simply by habit, in terms of one's first thoughts, or in terms of the reactions of the world and the opinions of others. Or one could make them self-consciously from the standpoint of the whole. This, of course, is very difficult to experience immediately, but every human being can begin to grow in this direction.

A fearless and dispassionate examination of the past shows that a lot of what once seemed extremely important was utterly insignificant and a lot of what looked impossible to go through was relatively easy. One could take stock of one's awareness independent of external events and focus it upon intense periods in the past which seemed to be especially painful, meaningless, or terrifying, but which one came through. Then one can ask whether, just as one now feels a kind of remoteness from past events, so too at the very moment of birth, did one feel a kind of remoteness from future events? Was one really involved, or only involved in one part of oneself? Then one can shift to the moment of death and raise the difficult question whether one can see oneself dying. Can one actually see a certain moment where there is an abandonment of a corpse which, through the natural processes of life, must decay and disintegrate and, while seeing this, still hold to an immense awareness of the whole? A person who is able to imagine what it would have been like to stand at a distance from the foetus that became the baby boy or girl can also imagine being at a distance from the corpse which is being discarded. He or she can also see that there is a thread that links these moments, and that the succession is no more arbitrary than the pattern of a necklace when seen from the standpoint of the whole.

The One Life comes into a world of differentiation through prismatically differentiated rays. We can sense in the gentle quality of dawn light something that does not participate in the opalescent colours of the day, something removed from what we call heat and light, cold and shade — a quality of virginal light that is a reminder of states of matter appropriate to states of consciousness which are created and held as potential by beings in general. Then we can begin to see that the whole point of human suffering in its collective meaning is to overcome pain and the false sense of separation. This is the point in consciousness where human beings as individuals could maintain a noetic and complete wakefulness — *turiya*, a profound awareness from a standpoint which transcends the greatest magnitudes of spacetime. It goes beyond solar systems and intimates that the depths of space represent in the very core of apparently nothing, a subtle creative gestation of matter. If one can see the whole world in terms of its plastic potency, as radiant material for a single universal spiritual sun, then one gains the dignity and the divinity of being a self-conscious individuating instrument of the universal Logos.

This is the sacred teaching of all Initiates. It is the teaching of Jesus in the *Gospel According to John*, the teaching of Buddha in the *Heart Sutra*, and the teaching of Krishna in the *Bhagavad Gita* and in the *Shrimad Bhagavatam*. These beings, fully awake, see that all human life, including human suffering, is a projection of a false involvement in a false sense of self. They bear witness to the reality of universal consciousness, not as something potential but as that which can be used as plastic material for new forms of spiritual creation. Creative imagination is not an abstract immaterial force, but the most rarefied and subtle form of material energy that exists. It can be tapped by concentration. By repeated and regular attempts at concentration upon this conception of the One, negating the false sense of the self, one builds and gives coherence to one's subtler vehicles, shaping what is now chaotic matter and forming a temple, a worthy vesture for a self-conscious being aware of the divinity of all beings and capable of maintaining that awareness through waking, dreaming and deep sleep. Having entered into the void, having entered into the light beyond these states of consciousness, the awakened soul remains in it by choice, while giving the impetus to other human beings to make the same attempt. Suffering and ignorance are collective; enlightenment and spiritual creativity are universal. This is the great hope of the timeless teaching concerning true continuity of consciousness.

Within the limits of time, however, which is an illusion produced by the succession of states of consciousness, there is only a before and an after, and no full scope for creativity. Consider, for example, a moment of love. Suppose you suddenly come into contact with someone of whom you could say, like the poet Yeats, "I loved the pilgrim-soul in you." There is a magical, intense flow between two pairs of eyes, and in one instant, a taste of eternity. If two individuals later tried to understand this in terms of what was there the day before and what was there the day after, they would have simply slipped onto another plane. If two people who have such a golden moment of co-awareness later on forget it or identify it with passing and contemporary illusions, then of course they might see it simply as a date in a calendar to be remembered by ceremonial tokens. That is not the same as re-enactment, because the essential quality of that moment was the absence of before and after, or any noticeable succession of states of consciousness. It was not as if they met calculatingly with anticipations and fears, and it was not as though soon after they thought of it as a memory of an event. They simply experienced in a moment of fusion of consciousness a freedom from the false division of eternal duration into a past, a present and a future. It was as if they stood not in one city, not in one street, not in one place, but in eternal space. This is an experience which by its very nature is so profound and beautiful that many people desperately look for it. This may be where the critical mistake is made. In the very attempt to look for it, one might overlook opportunities and arenas where it is more likely to happen. The very notion of seeking it, or wanting it, of maneuvering it, is stifling.

Our experience of time involves craving and memory. Time is bound up with fragmented consciousness in a universe of change and a constantly moving world of process. At best, it is a deceptive device of convenience for gaining a sense of control in eternal duration, to serve purposes arising from the standpoint of the narrow needs of some particularized self in relation to other particularized selves, where it is useful to talk in terms of a before and an after. Consider a good physician who has seen you at different times and to whom you are more than a file. When receiving an examination, it is as if you are both friends looking together at a common medium which is the physical body you inhabit and which has certain cycles and a history. Two minds looking together at the same body can suddenly see connections between before and after. Patterns emerge and a serial view of time has practical convenience.

We have, however, another view of time which allows us to discover other types of patterns and connections. If all patterns and connections had to be discovered exclusively by individual human beings, then the human predicament would be even more grave than it now seems. Because many patterns are already given, it is a case of looking for them with a deep detachment, so that one does not cut up and fragment the process. Suddenly one may see that there is a certain moment here and another point, tendency or characteristic there with which it connects. E.M. Forster employed this idea in his novels and expressed it as a mantram — "Let us connect." To him, in pre-1914 England, the whole difference between human beings moving from the sheltered world of 1914 into the increasingly stormy and socially disordered world of Europe after the First World War, was in the extent to which they could survive the collapse of inherited identities and self-consciously create their own connections. Either human beings forge their own connections or connections will be made for them, but then they will sound arbitrary or malignant, suggesting that some dark, hostile Fate as in Thomas Hardy's novels, is causing everything. When human beings can self-consciously make these connections, they begin to live with an increasing sense of freedom from time. Time may be seen in terms of eternal duration, which is prior to it, and hence there are golden moments. Time may also be seen in terms of mere convenience, according to a calendar, to help facilitate a limited involvement between human beings, in limited roles and contexts, to take place in a reliable manner. This mode of time may even be made to approximate some broader concept of distributive justice. Time must be seen as an illusion, must be seen for what it is, if a person is to gain the real continuity of consciousness connected with true creativity.

Today there are various fascinating studies of creativity, which cite examples such as Kekule's dream that was critical in biology. Kekule dreamt one night of a serpent eating its tail and when he woke up, he got a flashing insight into the circular rather than linear nature of certain processes of growth which are fundamental in molecular biology. The more one looks at such cases, the more one comes to see that truly creative beings cannot be programmed. Even in a society fearfully hostile to creativity, creative minds can still use available resources compassionately. Typically, creativity is difficult to attain because there is too much desire to have it programmed and delivered according to a schedule set by personal consciousness. This comes out in capitalist society in its most extreme form when people feel that there must be a kind of pre-established, controlled, and mechanistic way in which one could have creativity by numbers. By emphasizing substitutability and measurability, by regarding human beings as labour-units who are convertible terms, one can evolve an aggregated view of output and product which is truly dead for the creative artist. A great potter has no sense of excitement in looking at a pot. It is already dead. What was alive was the process of visualization and the process of taking that mental image, while the potter's wheel was moving, and seeing the shape emerging. The magical moment of emergence is real. Human beings in general have a parasitic attachment to the products of creativity but the vital process of creativity eludes them because it defies ordinary modes of division of time.

Here, then, is the most critical point, both in relation to continuity of consciousness and in relation to the Demiurge. The Demiurge in the old myths and in many a rustic Hindu painting, is like Vishnu asleep, from whose navel a lotus emerges which is the universe. Mahavishnu is floating upon the great blue waters of space. Around the serpent on which this Great Being rests there is a circle within which a whitish milky curdling is taking place. Intense activity surrounds the periphery of the great wheel of eternity, on which is resting in a state of supreme, pure inactivity, the divine Demiurge, itself only an aspect of the Logos. The great Rig Vedic hymn states, "The One breathed breathless." It was alone and there was no second. Alone it breathed breathless. There is a transcending sense of boundless space, in relation to which all the notions of space that we have — of an expanding universe, of a closed universe, of solar systems, and galaxies — all of these are like maps and diagrams relating points that are already conceptually separated out and which have boundaries, but are merely partial representations or surface appearances upon the depths of a space which has no boundaries or contours, and which is never delineated in diagrams.

If continuity of consciousness is to be seen not as something individual but rather universal, embedded in the very process of the manifestation of the One in and through the many, then it is necessary to think away from conceptions of time that are arbitrary and to a view of space which is boundless. Metaphysically, the reason why the Demiurge can both be involved in space fashioning many systems, and also witness all of these like bubbles upon a surface, is because space is not empty. After three hundred years of thought and experiment, modern science is catching up with ancient wisdom and is beginning to see that there is no such thing as empty space, that the content of space is not dependent on other categories of measurement or upon other standpoints of perception. What looks like pitch-black darkness could in fact be enormously full from another and more profound understanding. In one of the great passages in the early part of *The Secret Doctrine*, the commentary upon the *Stanzas of Dzyan* says that what to the Initiate is full is very different from what appears full to the ordinary man. The more human beings self-consciously expand awareness, the more they can free their deeply felt conceptions of the world, of reality, and of themselves from the notions of part and limit, from future anticipations and a present cut up into separate particular events, and the more they can bring a conscious sense of reality to their own mental awareness of space as a void — what the Buddha called *sunyata*, Emptiness — and the more they can replace the ordinary conception of form by the Platonic, which is not bound up with anything fixed.

Archetypal forms are like flashes of light. We may represent them by external coatings or by geometrical figures, but that is to imply that they are fixed, whereas in fact they are in a ceaseless, fluid interconnection. A constant transformation is taking place in the Divine Mind from one into another appearance of a geometrical form. There is a profound statement of this conception, which has great application to the individual who wishes to meditate upon it and use it in daily life: "The world is a living arithmetic in its development and a realized geometry in its repose." Every human being is involved in that arithmetic, and therefore growth is possible for the individual. Further, beyond and above that which changes, grows and develops, each is also consubstantial with the One that breathes breathless. Therefore, for the deeper Self, the whole universe is a realized geometry in repose.

If one went to sleep with a self-conscious awareness, using such profound images to extend the conception of the very reality of the world that one will enter into when going to sleep, and if on waking up one could greet the world in terms of these great divine images, then the whole world would become a vast playground for creativity and the freely created expression of a dancing intelligence that is involved in everything. One can suddenly find immense joy, a kind of eros or love, surging within. Then of course one would not identify love with a deficiency need. Creativity has nothing to do with a sense of incompletion, except in the sense in which the whole of manifestation is necessarily incomplete. It has to do with a sense of something tremendous welling up from within. There is a necessarily unprogrammed, unpredictable nature to the creative artist in every man. A human being could look towards every context and situation, and self-consciously greet the world as a creative being, but to do this requires the courage to break with one's sniggering, supercilious, paranoid self. One must wake up and be unafraid of the divine inheritance that belongs to everyman. This, however, can never be done collectively. Individuals can only do this by choosing to strike out on their own. We have an excellent definition given in the very first essay of H.P. Blavatsky on "What is Theosophy?": 'The true Theosophist is one who independently strikes out and godward finds a path.' All create their own paths back to the original source, based upon original inspirations, unique and priceless opportunities out of each one's particular stock of experience of making reason come alive as the embodiment of beneficent forces, the eternal verities, the quintessential truths of all history.

Even though such decisions cannot be made collectively, none the less the whole of humanity is now coming closer to what is called the moment of choice, the time where consciousness must either move forward or vacate vestures because it cannot maintain the patterns of the past. This follows directly from the principle that the whole universe is continuously implicated in involution and evolution. In a universe of ceaseless motion there is a breathing in and a breathing out: one universal homogeneous spirit breaks into rays just as at dawn rays emerge out of the light. They get involved in what become in time separate forms of differentiated matter. Having become involved, they must eventually reach a point where matter has descended to the level of maximum differentiation. Then spirit is withdrawn from its involvement in the most heterogeneous matter back into its original source. This is what is symbolized in the serpent eating its tail. It led to Hegel's metaphysical theory of evolution, because it makes of every man's journey an integral part, while at the same time only a partial and to some extent apparently separate expression of one collective universal process. How can we move from this scheme to the concepts of choosing and a moment of choice, which are bound up with the notion of individual responsibility?

We may, as some have done, compare the earlier systems of philosophy to the developing states of consciousness of a child. After birth every baby resides in a state of awareness that is so bound up with the mother that it has no sense of being separate. There follows a second stage when an awareness of particularity, detail and multiplicity emerge together with a sense of being not separate but simply someone who is resting, so to speak, in the bosom of the mother, of the whole, of space. Then comes a third stage when the little child becomes enormously fascinated with its conception of itself, a kind of solipsistic or even narcissistic stage where it becomes very interested in its own feelings. It gives a kind of definition and clarity to its own desires, taking hold of itself in terms of its own wants and needs. A point surely does come, without tracing the whole process in detail, where a person begins to experience something of the joy and the thrill of having to make a decision, of taking a stand, of having to choose.

By analogy and correspondence, what seems thrilling at the time of puberty — being able to choose — may be applied on the plane of the mind to being able to choose an idea, a system of ideas, or a philosophical system. This is not merely selecting a series of particularizations, but choosing a whole way of thinking out and giving shape, direction and authentic continuity to one's mental development. All of this has become difficult to understand because of the operation of an evolutionary paradox: the necessary homogenization of the psyche is accompanied by the increasing necessity for responsible choice free of psychic influence. This may be the historical destiny of America — to foster a hazardous jelling of people from all parts of the world, producing a huge, homogenized, psychic amorphism. Everything is kept in a fluidic state so that as wise beings enter into it, they will, in taking on this plastic material and using the enormous power released by mixing and mingling, give that energy an ennobling sense of direction. This means a moment of choice is emerging for a whole race or a nation.

Many people are aware of this in America today. There was a time when glamour was attached to being decadent, but much of that nonsense has been swept away. Today the pre-packaged tins of glamour have become so boringly or pathologically familiar that there is no novelty any more attached to them. It is as if human consciousness has drained the last drop of false involvement in all of these soulless dregs of matter that are being spewed forth. This is happening because there is a complex convergence of forces and Karma is working very fast in giving people their precise allocations. There is a tremendous opportunity also for those who can work with the Promethean solar forces of the future, which at this time are extremely subtle, imperceptible yet causally crucial.

We are at a new point in history where persons cannot, as in older days, merely go by labels. Individuals have become much more sophisticated and a significant increase in self-consciousness, in regard to the eclecticism of the human mind, has emerged. The moment of choice takes a variety of forms, but in the end all the choices come back to one basic choice: living in terms of a false conception of psychic identity caught passively in a series of events happening to oneself, or living self-consciously with awareness as a noetic being. Put in a starkly simple way, one is either going to be a psychic being and behave more childishly as one grows older, or one is going to be noetic and actually grow up. To behave noetically is to reawaken something of the pristine, beautiful awareness of a baby but while one is grown up. One may be in one's forties or fifties and still have self-consciously something of the thrill found in a baby's face looking out on the world with eyes of complete truth, accepting the wonder of life.

This must be deliberately and individually chosen. The insidious legacy of vicarious atonement makes people think that this can happen to them without their having to do anything, simply by being on the side of the correct doctrine or on the side of God. Buddha came to destroy the false idea that simply by making one dramatic and tearful choice, all the rest will automatically happen. No doubt there is much wisdom in what Jesus said: "Seek ye first the kingdom of God and all else will be added unto you," but to seek the kingdom of God is to seize the critical moment of choice. "Whom choose ye this day, God or Mammon?" This formulation by itself is too narrow because its interpretations limit the magnitude of the choice to the sphere of the false self. In the presence of the light one either has to live in and for the light or one has to live like a vampire in fear of the light. Human beings have to become self-conscious, creative beings who can continuously release creativity, the light of understanding, and true sympathy, and who can thereby gain contentment and joy in a more collective sense of human welfare and a more universal sense of progress. Otherwise, they must lapse back into their habits and then, lacking responsibility, they cannot help plunging into a pattern which is one of vampirization or mere mechanical, automaton-like living.

There is a stern logic to this choice because it is not taken at any one point of time alone. Once we grasp the choice in its full sense, it is one that is taking place at every moment in time. Hence Buddha said that no moment of carelessness in relation to continuity of consciousness is possible. Eternal vigilance is the price, not only of political liberty, but even more of spiritual freedom. This is because eventually human beings who understand the logic of this choice and have made a critical choice, accept the consequences, connecting in turn to other choices, thereby creating a cumulative cycle. They also connect that cycle of ascent to various tokens of memory, objects in their lives, friends, or their contact with the Lodge where they rekindle regularly their spiritual impulses. Eventually they reach a point where they can understand the inexplicable joy, as well as the burden, of choosing a thought. Functionally, the definition of an enlightened being, of an Initiate, is a being who chooses every thought. Things do not happen to Initiates; thoughts do not come to them. They choose them. To be able to get to the ultimate capacity not only to choose every thought but to make it a living reality by mastering the power of *Kriyashakti*, totally purified creative imagination, is an exalted ideal truly inspiring and relevant to every human being. By renewing one's sense of the reality of this ideal, one can reach a point where one can give up altogether the false notion of personal or individual spiritual progress. It is replaced by a beautiful awareness that whatever happens is a kind of resignation to the universal flow of light working through one self-consciously. It is like swimming on the ocean. We appreciate that the collective pull of the ocean is divine harmony, in terms of which one cannot lose.

If good karma is that which is pleasing to the real man, to the Ishwara, the divine within, then good karma is universal harmony. None can lose if they really are unafraid of anything coming to them in terms of universal divine harmony. Fear arises only for those who would somehow like everything programmed and arranged for them, so that if things go wrong, they can blame it on the people who arranged it, and if things go right, they could forget to say thanks and take the credit. Fortunately, this small-minded view of the world cannot be supported any longer. We have reached a point where it is really the same for all. It is a matter of choosing consciously the divine harmony and saying that whatever eventually comes is not merely what I deserve but what I desire. We must come to that point in life where we are ready for everything and anything, and see the whole of life as being on the side of that in us which alone is capable of surviving. Then we shall be happy to let go that which cannot be supported by a living person who is willing self-consciously to die. At the same time we shall be assured, in a cool, relaxed and totally conscious way, of the universal currents of divine harmony within us. Then we could say that we are human beings who have chosen rightly and fundamentally. This is not once-and-for-all. We shall have to reinforce and renew it many times a day, not in the old sense of ritual but simply by becoming aware of our thinking processes. One day it could have meaning for us to say that we actually choose our thoughts and life-atoms, that we have not one reaction which is not submitted by us to the process of deliberation. Then many more shall be worthy of the most sacred of all titles in collective evolution, of being what Emerson called Man Thinking, a Manasaputra, a trustee of the sacred fire of individual and universal self-consciousness, with "the priceless boon of learning truth, the right perception of existing things, the knowledge of the non-existent."

The Gupta Vidya II, The Golden Thread

SELF-TRANSFORMATION

> *'The worlds, to the profane,' says a Commentary, 'are built up of the known Elements. To the conception of an Arhat, these Elements are themselves collectively a divine Life; distributively, on the plane of manifestations, the numberless and countless crores of lives. Fire alone is ONE, on the plane of the One Reality: on that of manifested, hence illusive, being, its particles are fiery lives which live and have their being at the expense of every other life that they consume. Therefore they are named the "DEVOURERS." ' . . . 'Every visible thing in this Universe was built by such LIVES, from conscious and divine primordial man down to the unconscious agents that construct matter'. . . . 'From the ONE LIFE formless and Uncreate, proceeds the Universe of lives. First was manifested from the Deep (Chaos) cold luminous fire (gaseous light?) which formed the curds in Space.'*
>
> The Secret Doctrine, i 249-50

Matter distributed in space manifests a series of dimensions or characteristics correlated with the different Rounds of cosmic and human evolution on earth. Just as shared perceptions of extension, colour, motion, taste and smell have developed through the persistent use of five familiar sense-organs, so too emerging humanity will experience through the sixth sense of normal clairvoyance the corresponding characteristic of matter which has been called permeability. The three so-called dimensions of length, breadth and thickness are merely the triple aspects of extension, marked out by measurements made through customary devices. To restrict the common conception of Space, as Locke did, to what is simply a single characteristic of Matter is severely to limit perception, to confine and condition it by a perspective that is not even fully three-dimensional. In order to free everyday consciousness from this narrow focus, one must sense a new dimension of depth, which is related to suffering rather than to length, breadth and thickness. Depth, which is sometimes termed height, in mystical parlance, is crucial to a person who is truly skilled in regular meditations, withdrawing the wayward mind to a still centre while visualizing an ever-extending circumference around that motionless point. Through conscientious practice this regenerative activity of consciousness can purify, elevate and intensify one's interior life. Lateral expansion can fuse with depth of concentration to generate the vibrant awareness of the vault of the luminous sphere of mystic meditation. A profounder sense of non-being can enrich the quality and range of all astral perceptions in the course of time. One becomes a modest master of one's own orchestra.

In general, a person largely sees what one expects to see, owing to an enormous routinization in sensory responses. This has been fully confirmed in contemporary experiments. Any person who perceives an unfamiliar object is apt to experience a proportionally greater variation in the retinal image than when watching a familiar object as it is removed and receding into the distance. The human organism is always adapting, through its sense-organs, all pre-existing sensations and memories of stimuli, to what is recurrent and what is unfamiliar and unexpected. Hence, physical pain and mental suffering often come through the compassion of maya, which induces fleeting shocks to the sensory apparatus lest out of a false sense of familiarity, the mechanical observer takes too much for granted, thus making the creative faculties atrophy and the brain-centres sluggish. When suddenly one is confronted with what is strangely unfamiliar, one is compelled to think and contemplate. The immortal Triad overbrooding every human being is aware, like a Pythagorean spectator, that its reflected ray is continually tempted to abdicate its responsibility — as a thinker and chooser. It becomes like a mindless robot mired in automatic responses. The more these compulsive reactions are moralized in terms of good habits and the spurious semblance of virtue, the more subtle and insidious they become, enmeshing noetic consciousness, substituting passivity for plasticity, and destroying flexibility in discriminative response to the flux of events. When restless beings encounter individuals with a very different pace of life, or who live in greater closeness to the good earth, they are forced to recognize a richer way of life, a greater awareness of depth.

In modern society, there is a constant risk of awareness being reduced to a mechanical series of automatic responses which preclude true thinking and inhibit self-examination. When reflex responses in chaotic cerebration are reinforced through familiar clusters of tawdry images and shallow emotions, perverse thoughts invade one's sphere. This is a pervasive problem in our time of accelerated change and decisive sifting. Consider a person who attempts to become attentive while reading a text but who is not used to it and whose consciousness is shackled to the wandering mind, weak sensory responses and a general lack of attention and order in daily life. Such hapless persons cannot really read exactly what is in the text and cannot focus on it, let alone see around it and probe into profound suggestions buried within and between the lines of the text. To be able to shake the system out of this false familiarity, breeding a banal contempt for the supposedly stable world outside, the greatest teacher is suffering.

In the Aquarian Age in which many see the life-process as the continually enacted and essentially hidden interplay of harmony and disharmony, suffering always comes as a benevolent teacher of wisdom. Pain serves as a shock to one's sense of identity, illusory self-image and acquired or ancestral habits. It challenges one's pride and perversity. It compels one to pause for thought and radically reappraise the meaning of life, obligations, and potentials in oneself and others. When suffering comes, it plumbs below the surface of the psyche, touching depths of untrammeled consciousness. Noumenal and noetic awareness enters into everyday experience, and is saluted by remarkable constellations of poets, singers and seers. Incidents of life once taken for granted suddenly look very different, because one's sensibility has been sharpened. Were this not so, there would be little meaning to the mere succession of events and the mere recurrence of mechanical responses to the sensory stream of consciousness.

There is constant learning, and there is the ever-present possibility of deepening the cognitive basis of awareness, the operative level of self-actualization. This is part of the evolutionary and unending process of etherealization and refinement of life in the cycle of rapid descent and painful ascent. This is an exceedingly slow and subtle process — there is nothing automatic about it — but it is ubiquitous. Such a process of refinement must involve first of all an altered mode of awareness, which for most human beings means the conscious adoption of a radically different perspective on human life and cosmic evolution. But it must also transform the range and reach of one's sense-perceptions, through a better and finer use of the sensory powers of touch, taste, smell, sight and hearing. Further, this process of etherealization and refinement must proceed through a harmonious commingling of centres in the brain-mind and spiritual heart, through inward surrender to the Sovereign Self and the silent invocation of the Light of the Logos.

One may imagine the immortal Triad as overbrooding the head, though incompletely incarnated because its reflected intelligence must consciously ascend towards the level of proper harmonization. This could be expressed in terms of metaphysical truths about consciousness which operates under laws of expansion and contraction, implying continuous creation, preservation and regeneration through destruction. These archetypal modes have been traditionally symbolized in the Hindu pantheon by Nara-Nari, Agni, Varuna and Surya, and also by Brahmā, Vishnu and Shiva. This sacred teaching about cosmic and human consciousness could also be conveyed from the standpoint of matter. The essential axiom of Gupta Vidya is the affirmation that spirit and matter are really two facets of one and the same Substance-Principle. Objectivity and subjectivity are wholly relative to centres of perception, to degrees of differentiation, and to the coadunition and consubstantiality of objects with subjects upon overlapping planes of substance. Put entirely in terms of matter, this would imply that a person whose consciousness is deepened would experience a richer awareness of the invisible aspects and mathematical points of visible matter. There would be a heightened sensitivity to the gamut of invisible relations between life-atoms, corresponding to subtle colours and rarefied sounds.

One would also be replacing an angular view by a rounded view: the greater the depth, the greater the roundedness. The price people pay for the settled three-dimensionality of their conception of the world of phenomena is that the brain-mind becomes captive to angular views. If people are not truly self-conscious, they become extremely obtuse or are hopelessly caught within narrow angles and restricted orbits of perception. Whereas a person who can intensify the depth of perception and feeling, through private pain and unspoken suffering merged in effortless awareness of the vast suffering of all humanity, gains greater depth as a human being. This is continuously enriched by meditative experience of the Silence that surrounds the mystery of *Sat* and *Asat*, Being and Non-Being. The more this becomes a way of life, the more it is possible to have a profoundly balanced view of the world and a well-rounded conception of selfhood, alchemizing and elevating personal awareness and individual sensibility to the height and breadth of universal self-consciousness and the depths of boundless space, eternal motion and endless duration.

This process of self-transformation may be illustrated by an initially shadowy circle, a very narrow segment of which seems to be lit up. There is a seemingly central focus, but it is only central to that visible segment, whilst the centre of the whole circle, most of which is obscured, remains hidden. This is analogous to the relationship between the personal ego and the individual Self. A human being with a narrow sense of identity is living only segmentally, existing only at one sensory level with reference to an unduly restricted horizon of human experience. Such a person is not properly centering, not really trying to get as full and rounded a view of himself and the world as possible. Out of this roundedness he could begin to sense a sphere of light surrounding himself in which he lives, moves and has his being. This will loosen a great deal of the fixity of categories of thought and emotional responses which, if seen clairvoyantly, reveal a sad mutilated shadow of the true Self of a human being. Herein lies the rationale for recovery through meditation of that pristine and rounded conception of the Self which is more in harmony with the music of the spheres and the Golden Egg of Brahmā in the ocean of SPACE. This transformation is indeed the psychological equivalent to the Copernican revolution, in which the sun of the *Atman* is central to the solar system. For the *Atman* to become the centre of a luminous sphere of selfhood would require a firm displacement of the false centering of consciousness, through *kama manas*, within a distorting segment of separative identity which is trapped in a fragmented view of space, time and secondary causation. The dwarfing of one's true selfhood is the crucifixion of Christos, the obscuration of the light, the plenitude, the potential and the richness within every human being on earth.

To convey this as a criterion of human stature, the greater the depth of one's inwardness, the broader, the vaster, the wider the range of one's sympathies, and the more one is able to appreciate a wider variety of experiences, situations, contexts and human beings. The more secure one's depth of consciousness, the more one is able to exercise the synthesizing gift of the Monad, capable of seeing in terms of any of the specific sub-colours, and also able to penetrate to the very centre of the white light, seeing beyond it, and benevolently using the entire range of the spectrum. What is true of colours applies equally to sounds, and ultimately to consciousness itself. This is the sacred prerogative of a human being. It is because human beings fall, owing to shared and inherited limitations, but also owing to self-created limitations, they forfeit or forget altogether this sovereign prerogative and fail to mend themselves through meditation and self-study. Hence, the healing and restorative property of sleep which Shakespeare so suggestively describes as Nature's second feast, man's great restorer. The average human being deprived of the benefit of *sushupti* or sleep would simply not survive for long. Sleep and death are Nature's modes of restoration of balance. In order to take full advantage of sleep, the seeker must initially experience the pain of forcing the mind to return to a point on which it is placed, to a chosen idea, bringing the heart back to the deepest, purest and most pristine feeling of devotion, warmth and love. If one did this again and again, then certainly one would not only become more deep in response to life but one would also become more of a spiritual benefactor to the human race, drawing freely from the infinite resources of Divine Thought and the Light of the Logos, Brahma Vach.

> Just as milliards of bright sparks dance on the waters of an ocean above which one and the same moon is shining, so our evanescent personalities — the illusive envelopes of the immortal MONAD-EGO — twinkle and dance on the waves of Maya. They last and appear, as the thousands of sparks produced by the moon-beams, only so long as the Queen of the Night radiates her lustre on the running waters of life: the period of a Manvantara; and then they disappear, the beams — symbols of our eternal Spiritual Egos — alone surviving, re-merged in, and being, as they were before, one with the Mother-Source.
>
> *The Secret Doctrine*, i 237

The Monad-Ego is the three-tongued flame, the *Atma-Buddhi-Manas* which overbroods throughout the *manvantara* myriads upon myriads of personalities, instruments and vehicles through which the great work of evolution proceeds. This is made possible by the fact that the three-tongued flame of the four wicks is connected with the myriads of sparks. Although in each life these sparks seemingly become entangled through the four derivative principles into a shallow sense of separative identity as a personal man or woman in that life, this is really an illusion. All the elements in all the personal lives throughout the *manvantara* represent the diffused intelligence which is here ascribed to a single source — the Queen of the Night

— radiating her lustre on the running waters of life. Between the hidden source of the flames throughout evolution — the Central Spiritual Sun — and the manifest source of all the myriad sparks involved in the evanescent phenomena witnessed by personal consciousness in incarnated existence, there would be a causal relationship. One is like a necessary reflection of the other. This is true cosmically. It is also true of every single human being. The astral form is like a lunar reflection of a solar light-energy that belongs to the *Atma-Buddhi-Manas* which is like the sun overbrooding every single human temple. The profoundly mysterious relation between the two is intimated by the symbol of the thread of Fohat. A very fine thread connects the solar activity of the higher principles and the lunar activity involving the reflected and parasitic intelligence of personal consciousness.

Everything can be seen, as in the Platonic scheme, as a reflection of what is higher on a more homogeneous plane. The relative reality of every single entity and event in life is a shadowy reality that presupposes something more primordial and more homogeneous. In this way, all life would trace back to the one single field of homogeneous ideation, homogeneous substance. If this is what makes the universe a cosmos — a single system — then the solemn task of the human being is to integrate life consciously and cheerfully; to do this, one must first negate the false sense of identity that belongs on the lunar plane. One must perceive in depth all the elements of being that contribute to the seeming continuity of consciousness in and through the astral form, and then reach further inwards through deep meditation to the sacred source of all consciousness and life. This alchemical work is represented in many myths as the separation of what is food for the soul from what is not, before and during after-death states. This sifting takes place through all Nature and is the deliberate undertaking of those who are pledged to self-regeneration in the service of humanity. "'Great Sifter' is the name of the 'Heart Doctrine', O Disciple."

The subtlety of this alchemical art arises from the fact that the pseudo-identity of the lunar plane involves not only the flux of fleeting emotional states but also a bewildering array of ghostly mental constructions. At a fundamental level of conceptualization, we have the tangled roots of the Ashwatha tree of samsaric illusion. This endemic tendency to hypostatize the emanations of cosmic mind was ably diagnosed by Professor Bain.

> The giving reality to abstractions is the error of Realism. Space and Time are frequently viewed as separated from all the concrete experiences of the mind, instead of being generalizations of these in certain aspects.
>
> *The Secret Doctrine,* i 251

Here Bain is referring to a long-standing tendency to reification, the cardinal error of classical realism which eventually produced a welter of conflicting interpretations of what were designated as 'universals'. These universals were abstract entities and were wholly sundered from the wealth of particulars in the world of phenomena. This generated insuperable theoretical difficulties. When the universals are applied to Space and Time, independent of all concrete experiences of the mind, they give rise to the false impression that the archetypes are remote from and unconnected with the activity of *kama manas* in the everyday world of subjects and objects. Strictly, one should recognize that at any point of time, relative to the succession of states of consciousness, there is simultaneously a non-linear clustering of conceptual frameworks that presuppose a spatio-temporal field. Bain is stating at a simple level what is crucial to the macrocosmic process at its pregenetic level. Space and Time are suffused and conceptually bound up with cosmic and human consciousness. We cannot truly separate anything from conscious life.

Every single point in space is animated by intelligence and the indwelling light of living awareness. There is nothing inanimate, nothing inert, nothing dead in the entire universe of matter and motion in Space and Time. In seeking through a series of philosophical negations to blank out all psychological concretions, and then embark upon mystic meditation in the Divine Dark, the great Night, one will view it not as an inane void but rather as intense absolute light which is also absolute darkness. All limited and limiting concepts of the contraries are derived from everyday experience of heterogeneity, in terms of which therefore, when one enters into the realm of the homogeneous, one becomes hypnotized by the contrast between the homogeneous and the heterogeneous. There is, however, a further stage of enlightenment wherein one begins to enjoy so strong, continuous and intense an awareness of the homogeneous that one cognizes the homogeneous in the heterogeneous, sees infinity in a grain of sand, eternity in an hour, the large in the small. This is the hidden message of the *Bhagavad Gita*: The cosmos is in the atom and the whole of the cosmos is like an atom. Commenting upon the mysterious fohatic thread connecting all of life, H.P. Blavatsky states:

> This relates to the greatest problem of philosophy — the physical and substantial nature of life, the independent nature of which is denied by modern science because that science is unable to comprehend it. The reincarnationists and believers in Karma alone dimly perceive that the whole secret of Life is in the unbroken series of its manifestations: whether in, or apart from, the physical body. Because if —
>
> Life, like a dome of many coloured glass, Stains the white radiance of Eternity —
>
> yet it is itself part and parcel of that Eternity; for life alone can understand life.
>
> *The Secret Doctrine*, i 238

When one is willing to gain a dynamic perception of the macrocosmic depth within microcosmic life, then one may develop a radically new mode of apprehending the world. In connection with restoring this vital continuity between all the aspects and phases of life, one must take up the difficult but important exercise of treating each day as an incarnation. It is hardly easy to grasp what this means at first. To understand truly, one can initially take four broad divisions, thus seeing a day in terms of the archetypal *process* of childhood, adolescence, adulthood and old age. One can make further and finer distinctions, once one has gained insight into the fourfold division of human life, thus transcending lumpy categories which ineffectually mediate between the atomic and the cosmic. One can gain a more mobile sense of reality, capable of reaching to the infinitesimal in consciousness, capable of rising to the transfinite. As this process becomes continuous, it inevitably affects all one's centres of perception, altering the flows of energy within the nervous system. This is why meditation must at some point give rise to a whole new set of sensory responses to the world and prepare one also for that level of cosmic consciousness where one becomes vividly conscious of the magical power of concentrated thought. When idea, image and intent are all fused in a noetic, dynamic energy which ignites the spiritual will, one gains precision and control, and can ultimately become a self-conscious agent in the transmutation of matter, the alchemical transformation of the vestures through the *tapas* and *yajna* of self-regeneration. Through calm reflection, one can begin to give a sense of reality to what are otherwise like metaphorical or vapidly abstract instances of universal consciousness, far removed from the prison-house of personal consciousness. But when one begins to enter into the activity of *Lila* itself, one can gain great strength, steadiness and spiritual sustenance, drawing apart from all forms, and gathering oneself into the mysterious interior intelligent centre of one's original spiritual consciousness.

> It is a MYSTERY, truly but only to him who is prepared to reject the existence of intellectual and conscious spiritual Beings in the Universe, limiting full Consciousness to man alone, and that only as a 'function of the Brain'. Many are those among the Spiritual Entities, who have incarnated bodily in man, since the

beginning of his appearance, and who, for all that, still exist as independently as they did before, in the infinitudes of Space.

The Secret Doctrine, i 233

One must relocate oneself within the depths of this vast general perspective of a host of Dhyani Buddhas and Bodhisattvas, exalted beings of different degrees of consciousness ranging from the most universal consciousness that even transcends the solar system to very high consciousness in this solar world and in lunar bodies. This boundless and beatific panorama is presented in many different ways in all the great mystical texts, and given *par excellence* in the universal vision of the eleventh chapter of the *Bhagavad Gita.* Through it, one may begin to see that the world as ordinarily known is but a surface revealing only pale reflections in an immense shadow-play. One can begin to apprehend the initially discomforting, but ultimately revolutionary, thought that what is going on in oneself is not even guessed by one's lower mind. Many of the problems of human beings arise because the inefficient, insecure and fear-ridden lower mind — lamed in childhood and competitive hot-houses — claims to reveal all, although it is only a small part of the whole. In truth, most of what is really going on inside a human being occurs during deep sleep, or scattered moments of awareness in waking life, which do not register at all in *kama manas.* They cannot be recorded, still less reported. Hence, the paradox known to many mystics arises — what is called life is a form of death from the standpoint of the immortal soul.

As Krishna says in the *Gita,* to the spiritually wise what men call day is the night of ignorance. It is a mere shadow-play of elemental interaction imperfectly edited by a lower mind which is naturally a helpless prisoner of its own particular perceptions, expectations and memories. This "tale told by an idiot" is independent of the true life of the immortal soul, which is well characterized as silent (since the immortal soul cannot find in the languages that belong to the heterogeneous realm any vocabulary for its own spiritual knowledge and cognition). It can, however, be reflected in the proper use of the sacred power of speech and the mystical potency of sound. The invisible entity may be bodily present on earth without abandoning its status and functions in supersensuous regions. If the overbrooding Spirit were not connected, like a daimon or indwelling tutelary genius, with personal consciousness, there would be no possibility of awareness and of learning for the soul with all its misfirings and mistakes. Even then, that learning itself is partial because what is truly happening within the real Self, the invisible entity and the immortal daimon, cannot really be summoned by the uninitiated without bringing the instruments in line with the spiritual will of the *Atma-Buddhi-Manas*.

What happens involuntarily and naturally in deep sleep must be done consciously in waking life through philosophical negation, deep meditation, calm reflection and Pythagorean self-examination. If done daily, in time it will be possible to bring closer the astral vesture and the true divine Self that otherwise is only partially involved or only inadequately incarnated. Taking this as a general truth about humanity, it connects with the complex doctrines of Rounds, Globes and Races and the eventual development that will take place in the Rounds far in the future. There will be much fuller incarnation possible, because of the radical change that would have taken place in the plasticity and resilience of the material vestures. Matter will be so markedly different that it can readily reflect Spirit with a pristine purity which is virtually independent of the entire stream of monadic and material evolution. To move self-consciously in this direction of depth perception is the willing contribution of the true pilgrim who enters the Path and takes vows for lives, vows that involve the ceaseless process of self-transformation for the sake of universal enlightenment. True disciples will consecrate each day to Hermes-Budha, to the *Manasaputras*, the descending luminous beings that make human self-consciousness possible. All Lanoos will strengthen the centre of silence within themselves until it can be used for the calm release of a new current of energy, a new line of life's meditation, which fuses thought, will and feeling in daily life for the sake of the larger whole. Wise men and women will take full advantage of this teaching to bring forth the greatest strength and sacrifice that can be released in their own lives for the sake of Universal Good, the Agathon on earth as in Heaven *(Akasha)*, the *summum bonum* which flows from *Saguna Brahman* but is gestated within the bosom of *Nirguna Brahman*, boundless Space in eternal Duration.

The Gupta Vidya II, The Golden Thread

APPENDIX I

SELECTED PASSAGES FROM GOD, NATURE AND MAN ~ VOLUME I OF *THE GUPTA VIDYA*

THE EVOLUTIONARY TIDE
ON EARTH

The source and destiny of the soul's inward life fundamentally involve the entire scope of evolution. Coeval with the manifestation of the seven worlds of the cosmic plenum is the reemergence of beings who assume once more the evolutionary pilgrimage after an immense period of rest. The emanation of matter and spirit into the objective plane of existence is but half the cycle. Its return brings all beings and forms to the bosom of absolute darkness. The period of manifestation covering trillions of years is called a *manvantara* and the corresponding period of rest, called *pralaya*, lasts for an equal duration. They are the Days and Nights of Brahmā, which were reckoned with meticulous precision by the ancient Aryans. The whole span of the *manvantara* is governed by the law of periodicity which regulates rates of activity on all planes of being. This is sometimes spoken of as 'the Great Breath' which preserves the cosmos. The essence of life is motion, growth and expansion of awareness in every atom. Each atom is at its core a monad, an expression of the highest self *(Atman)* and its vesture is the spiritual soul *(Buddhi)*. Prior to the monad's emergence in the human family, it undergoes aeons of experience in the lower kingdoms of nature, developing by natural impulse (metempsychosis) until the latent thinking faculty of *Manas* is awakened by the sacrificial efforts of beings who have risen far above the human state in *manvantaras* past. They kindle the spark of self-consciousness, making the unconscious monad a true man *(Manushya)*, capable of thought, reflection and deliberate action. The soul embarks upon a long cycle of incarnations in human form to prepare itself for entry into still greater planes of existence.

The evolutionary tide on earth is regulated by the unerring hand of cyclic law. Man passes through a series of Rounds and Races which allows him to assimilate the knowledge of every plane of existence, from the most ethereal to the most material. Man's planetary evolution describes a spiral passing from spirit into matter and returning to spirit again with a wholly self-conscious mastery of the process. Each Round is a major evolutionary period lasting many millions of years. Each Race in turn witnesses the rise and fall of continents, civilizations and nations. An earlier Race than our own, the Lemurian, lived in an idyllic Golden Age, an epoch ruled by natural religion, universal fraternity, and spontaneous devotion to spiritual teachers. Many of the myths regarding an era of childlike purity and unsullied trust in humanity's early flowering preserve the flavour of this period. As man evolved more material vestures, *kama* or passion tainted his power of thought and inflamed his irrational tendencies. The nightmare tales of Atlantean sorcerers are the heavy heirloom of contemporary humanity. The destruction of Atlantis ushered in the Aryan race of our own epoch. The Indian sages who inaugurated this period are among the torchbearers for the humanity of our time. Intuitive mystics recognize the sacred role of ancient India as mother and preserver of the spiritual heritage of present humanity. The classical Indian scriptures resonate with the authentic voice of the Verbum, uncorrupted by time and human ignorance.

Pertinent to historical insight is the doctrine of the *yugas*, the cycle of four epochs through which every Race passes, the Golden, Silver, Bronze and Iron Ages. The *yugas* indicate a broad sweep of karmic activity at any point in the life of an individual or collection of individuals. The entire globe may not be undergoing the same age simultaneously nor may any one individual be necessarily in the same epoch as his social milieu. According to Hindu calculations, *Kali Yuga* began over 5,090 years ago and will last altogether for a total of 432,000 years. This dark age is characterized by widespread confusion of roles, inversion of ethical values and enormous suffering owing to spiritual blindness. Many have celebrated the myth of the Golden Age as extolling the plenitude of man's creative potential. The doctrine of the *yugas* is not deterministic. It merely suggests the relative levels of consciousness which most human beings tend to hold in common. Thus a Golden Age vibration can be inserted into an Iron Age to ameliorate the collective predicament of mankind. The Golden Age surrounded human beings as a primordial state of divine consciousness, but their own pride and ignorance precluded its recovery. In the wonder of childhood, in archaic myths, in the sporadic illuminations of great artists and in mystical visions, one may discern shimmering glimpses of the Golden Age of universal *eros,* the rightful original estate of humanity.

The progress of humanity in harmony with cyclic law is facilitated by a mature grasp of karma and rebirth. These twin doctrines of responsibility and hope unravel many of the riddles of life and Nature. They show that every person's life and character are the outcome of previous lives and thought patterns, that each one is his or her own judge and executioner, and that all rise or fall strictly by their own merits and misdeeds. Nothing is left to chance or accident in life but everything is under the governance of a universal law of ethical causation. Man is essentially a thinker, and all thoughts initiate causes that generate suffering or bliss. The immortal Triad endures the mistakes and follies of the turbulent quaternary until such time as it can assume its rightful stature and act freely in consonance with cosmic order and natural law. As man is constantly projecting a series of thoughts and images, individual responsibility is irrevocable. Each person is the centre of any disturbance of universal harmony and the ripples of effects must return to him. Thus the law of karma or justice signifies moral interdependence and human solidarity.

Karma must not be seen as a providential means of divine retribution but rather as a universal current touching those who bear the burden of its effects. This has been called the law of spiritual gravitation. The entire scope of man's affairs – his environment, friends, family, employment and the like – are all dictated by the needs of the soul. Karma works on the soul's behalf to provide those opportunities for knowledge and experience which would aid its progress. This concept could be expanded so as to encompass all connections with other human beings of even the most casual kind, seeing them as karmically ordained not for one's own progress but for the sake of those who struggle with the dire limitations of ignorance, poverty or despair. A deeply moving account of this trial is given in *The Hero in Man*, wherein, while walking among the wretched outcasts of Dublin, the author, George William Russell ('A.E.'), rejoices in the conviction that the benevolence he feels for each benighted soul will forge a spiritual bond through which he may help them in the future. Karma means a summons to the path of action and duty. As one cannot separate one's own karma from that of one's fellow-men, one may determine to devote one's life to the remission of the karmic burden of others.

At death the true Self or immortal Triad casts off the physical and astral bodies and is released from the thraldom of passions and desires. Its natural tropism to gravitate upwards allows it to enter the rarefied plane of consciousness where its thoughts are carried to culmination, clothed in a finer body suited to that sublime existence. This state, *devachan*, is a period of rest and assimilation between lives and the basis of the popular mythology of heaven. On the other hand, the lower quaternary languishes after death in *kamaloka*, the origin of theological dogmas concerning hell and purgatory. There it dissolves by degrees back into its primary elements at a rate determined by the cohesion given them by the narcissistic personality during life on earth. Inflamed passions and poisonous thoughts sustained for long periods of time endow this entity with a vivid, vicarious and ghoulish existence. This plane of consciousness, termed 'the Astral Light' by Eliphas Lévi, is intimately connected with the lives and thoughts of most of mankind. It is the vast slag-heap of Nature into which all selfish and evil thoughts are poured and then rebound back to pollute and contaminate human life on earth. This plane of carnalized thought tends to perpetuate the horrors of the Iron Age and condemn humanity to a state of spiritual darkness.

The crucial difference between individuals lies in whether they are enslaved by the Astral Light (the region of psyche) or whether they are capable of rising above it to a calm awareness of the wisdom and compassion latent in their higher nature, the realm of nous. Beyond the region of psychic action lies the pristine sphere of noetic awareness called *Akasha*, from which empyrean individuals could derive the inspiration needed to go forth and inaugurate a Golden Age by laying down the foundations of a regenerated civilization. Sages, past and present, saluted as Men of the Word *(Brahma Vach)*, have accomplished the arduous transformation of their own natures, overcoming every vice and limitation and perfecting themselves in noetic ideation and sacrificial action. Mahatmas or Hierophants and Bodhisattvas renounce everything for the sake of suffering humanity. Solitary mystics on the ancient Bodhisattva path of service salute them as gurus, guides and preceptors and acknowledge their invisible presence as the *Guruparampara*, the sacred lineage behind their own modest labours for mankind. These wise beings are the noble trustees of the *Philosophia Perennis* and the compassionate teachers of the whole human family. The mystical pilgrimage of mankind is an authentic reflection of their ageless wisdom.

The Gupta Vidya I, "The Gupta Vidya", 10-12

TRANSCENDING AHANKARA

According to the *Stanzas of Dzyan*, both the causes of the misery of existence and the seven paths to the bliss of *moksha* have a reality which is relative to a period of manifestation. In *pralaya* they are not. Speaking of the twelve *nidanas*, or causes of being – the concatenated chain of antecedent causes and successive effects through which karma and reincarnation operate – and referring also to maya – the element of illusion which enters into all finite things as a function of the limited powers of cognition with which any observer apprehends the appearances of the one hidden noumenon – H.P. Blavatsky explains *tanha* as follows:

> 'The Causes of Existence' mean not only the physical causes known to science, but the metaphysical causes, the chief of which is the desire to exist, an outcome of Nidana and Maya. This desire for a sentient life shows itself in everything, from an atom to a sun, and is a reflection of the Divine Thought propelled into objective existence, into a law that the Universe should exist. According to esoteric teaching, the real cause of that supposed desire, and of all existence, remains forever hidden, and its first emanations are the most complete abstractions mind can conceive. These abstractions must of necessity be postulated as the cause of the material Universe which presents itself to the senses and intellect; and they underlie the secondary and subordinate powers of Nature, which, anthropomorphized, have been worshipped as God and gods by the common herd of every age.
>
> Ibid., i 44

Given the extreme persistence of *tanha*, it is a long and difficult evolutionary process to elevate consciousness beyond the realm of maya. Even human beings who have successfully generated a sense of selfhood independent of the body have attachments to the mind, through concepts, expectations and images. Even if they have gone beyond the *samskaras* and have begun to inhabit a realm of higher

Manasic ideation, they have still, out of their love of meditation or their desire to help the human race, an inherence in form. It is so difficult to transcend *ahankara* altogether, collapsing it to a zero, that there is clearly something about this illusion which is due to the Vishnu function in the universe itself. To cooperate with this, and to plumb its pure depths, one must learn to coordinate it self-consciously with the Brahmā function of expansion. From the standpoint of Buddhist metaphysics, an obsessive concern to extinguish the sense of 'I' entirely only amounts to a form of craving for nonexistence, a form of holding on to life. The same desire can exist both in a negative and a positive form. The desire to commit suicide, for example, exists in proportion to the desire to continue living.

Polarity of desire does not make the slightest difference to the intensity of craving and the intensity of conceptualization through form. This may be understood cosmically in terms of the duality of the Logos in manifestation as it incessantly acts through negative and positive, active and passive, forces. The positive force continually expands and sheds while the negative force continually gathers and fecundates. The active force falls into the veil of cosmic matter towards which it is continually attracted. This process, essential to cosmic manifestation, is the basis of limitation of consciousness in relation to manifested and differentiated matter. It is the basis, in some of the Puranic texts, for the depiction of *ahankara* as universal self-consciousness, coordinate with *Mahat* or universal mind. In these systems, however, there is a fundamental distinction between the lower forms of *ahankara*, related to an identification with a name and a form, or even individuated mind extending throughout a *manvantara*, and the highest form of *ahankara* associated with the cosmos.

Thus, owing to the universal tendency towards a mayavic inherence of consciousness in form, every human being attempting to contact the stream of pure unmodified consciousness is bound to discover certain barriers that are extremely difficult to cross, and which cannot be wholly dissolved while the capacity for incarnation still exists. Hence the rejection in Mahayana Buddhism of the desire for liberation and the necessity of cooperating with the universal sacrificial processes of the cosmos – *Adhiyajna* – in the pursuit of the Bodhisattvic ideal. With meditation one can participate through indefinite expansion in the consciousness of all beings. One can potentially be present in the consciousness of every atom, every ant, every grain of dust and every star. For most, these will merely be words, remote indeed from immediate experience. But one can nevertheless try to recognize theoretically, and beyond ordinary language, that there is an infinite possibility of expansion of the sphere of being and consciousness. In this expansion, however, it would be an error to suppose that one is doing the work oneself. In fact, one is merely becoming a vesture, a focusing instrument, of that which is intrinsic to the universe itself. Brahmā is everywhere. The creative Logos is ceaselessly breathing in and breathing out. Through this expansive force forms come into being, disappear and are replaced by new forms. Considered in its ultimate and absolute origin, this is the basis of the expansion into manifestation of what the *Stanzas of Dzyan* call "the One Form of Existence". The deliberate invocation of this expansive force is a corrective to the contracting tendency of consciousness which consolidates *ahankara* at lower levels.

Owing to *ahankara* at the level of physical name and form, human beings are, typically, terrified of death. They must instead learn to expand their consciousness and consider the myriad human beings that they once knew, or did not know, who must have been their ancestors. Where are they? Can one imagine a consciousness after the moment of death? Can one imagine a consciousness that is capable of including innumerable human beings who have disappeared as bodies and forms? One might imagine entering a gallery of ancestral photographs and understanding that none of the human beings represented there still resemble the images that portray them because their forms have all been buried or burnt. Yet if one concentrates on the pinpoints of light in their eyes, one can come to see these as a kind of collective veil upon the eternal sentient rays of light that are their true natures. "Dust thou art and unto dust shalt thou return" was not spoken of that light. It was spoken of the body, not the soul.

The Gupta Vidya I, "Consciousness and Existence", 40-41

THAT LIGHT WHICH LIVES IN ALL

If human beings start to use the *Gayatri* daily whilst their motives are yet sullied, they are in awesome danger. They risk summoning forces that will be too strong to resist or to regulate, and they will need the ever-present protection of the Rishis and Mahatmas, who are likened in Upanishadic metaphor to the ribs of an umbrella sheltering all beneath. Every human being holds the handle of this umbrella, but its ribs belong to all Humanity, for they represent the highest hierarchies of enlightened human beings who are conscious instruments of the Cosmic Will. They are the supreme divine agents of the One Law, the One Life and the One Light, and through their boundless compassion they can protect and provide opportunities to human beings, who suffer from glaring gaps between their moral stature and their mental aspiration, between their spiritual strength and their emotional stamina, between their longing for union and their communion with the One. The compassion of perfected human beings gives strength to the weak. And it gives hope to those who are sometimes awed or made afraid by the enormity of their undertaking.

Yet, whilst this allegorical umbrella provides a measure of assured protection to the fallible aspirant, enlightened beings cannot vicariously substitute for the self-conscious effort each individual must make for himself or herself to maintain the mysterious thread of life's meditation as a constant vibration. There must, however, be honesty and moral courage in recognizing the avoidable gaps in one's practice, and a clarity in discerning tendencies that make one vulnerable to delusion through likes and dislikes, delusive affections and false dependencies. One must become vigilant against the simian tricks that memory plays, and against the perverse tendency to misuse the power of thought to produce rationales which only consolidate the discontinuities in oneself. All of these persist as concessions to that part of oneself which is drowsy, lazy, cowardly and terrified of the Light; that part which is terrified of standing up confidently and moving apart from the inert mass of most beings. Before one can become a true man or woman of meditation, and so a true servant of Humanity, one must first become, in a Pauline sense, separated out of the astral and psychic plane – a being without external signs of slavish connections with human beings. One must go through the Isolation of the immortal soul, a painful period of withdrawal from lesser supports. Only then can one attain the height of what is possible, reaching the pristine source that is above the head, and that, once touched, eventually sets aflame the thousands of latent centres that are in the head, the legendary Tree of Light, Life and Cosmic Electricity in Man.

Long before this turning-point is reached, one must render reliable the steady effort to meditate. Thus it is said that if one cannot initially meditate upon the most abstract themes, one should begin by meditating upon meditation itself. Meditate upon the great Masters of Meditation, enjoying the very thought of the Buddhas of Contemplation, self-luminous beings who are masters of compassion and ceaselessly radiate currents of beneficence. In the very enjoyment of meditating upon the galaxy of Dhyanis and the host of Mahatmas, one will elevate oneself, expanding one's horizon, one's sense of kinship and one's conception of the human family. One will be thrilled that the human family can include such a vast array of self-resplendent beings, and one will begin to see this world anew.

Then, when one earnestly meditates and finds multiple obstructions arising, one will be able to see them for what they are and honestly trace them to their origins in forgetfulness, indolence and cowardice. At the same time, one will understand that the very ability one has gained to stand apart from these shadows is itself rooted in a recognition of that which is all-knowing, unforgetful, ever-awake, courageous, free, untrammelled and universally self-conscious. Even though one's deeper Self must be repeatedly invoked, one will still find a certain joy arising in oneself, a certain natural desire flowing out of deep love for that universal Self. This is the true source of all other loves and the only thing that can ultimately give meaning to all one's other altruistic urges. It is the wellspring of one's empathy for all life, for all the kingdoms of Nature, for what is in every stone and plant and tree. It is that in oneself which can resonate to the rising sun, can respond to the setting sun, and can echo back to the invisible Midnight Sun. All these are but veiled expressions of a deeper universal current of energy which is compassionate, which is sacrificial, and which is consciously emanated by the Masters of Light and Love, Compassion and Wisdom.

When one begins to develop a natural joy, hunger, longing and love for this mystic meditation, one will find that it acts as an eliminator. Many of one's lesser longings will simply fall away, and one's vanity, delusion and ego-projection will be revealed and emptied out. Yet, what was good and true at the core of them will never be lost, for that is an outflow of the fount of universal love which belongs to the *Paramatman*, the universal Self. If this meditation is real, it should arouse and deepen one's capacity to be one-pointed – single-minded and single-hearted – able to concentrate upon the appointed task at hand and able to consecrate it for the good of all. Letting go of all results, reducing one's participation in fantasy, anticipation and regret, one will become more fully engaged, more fully active and wide awake. With this, a great deal of what before looked to be oneself will become exteriorized, come out and fall away. It will all show itself for what it is – a mask, a veil. And layer by layer, veil upon veil of false selfhood will fall away until nothing remains but the one ineffable Light. It is beginningless and endless. It is the Light that is hidden in the Divine Darkness, behind all worlds, beings and manifestations. It is the One Light behind every spark of aspiration and every spark of truth, beauty and goodness in each and every being in existence. It is the Light of which Jesus spoke when he said, "If thine eye be single, thy body shall be full of Light", and it is the Light spoken of by Krishna as the lighting up in oneself of the Supreme Saviour, who then becomes visible. Let each fearless pilgrim soul meditate upon that Light which lives in all as the Highest Self. Let each devotee concentrate upon it in adoration, surrendering and subordinating all to that one fiery Self. And let each heroic seeker after undying truth will to work for its eternal habitation in every human heart.

The Gupta Vidya I, "Dateless and Deathless", 109-111

OVERCOMING ALIENATION
FROM THE SELF OF ALL

Their consciousness confined through identification with grosser forms, human beings have become alienated from their highest possibilities. They may have achieved a sense of continuity and identity on a lower plane, but at the expense of a close connection with their deeper and larger selfhood. This risk is inherent in the very process of developing and specializing a concentrated egoity or sense of 'I' in relation to a name and a body, particular conditions and memories, desires and expectations. All of this involves exercising the principle of 'I-ness', *ahankara*, in ways that generate a sense of reality, but also bind down egoity in the realm of differentiated manifestation. As a result, there is an acute frustration for that pure essence which is the angel in man. This is the *Atma-Buddhi* overbrooding *Manas*.

Through identification with *kama*, the sensorium and the *linga sharira* or astral form, *Manas* has become beclouded. Therefore, *Atma-Buddhi*, though it is inseparable from pure thought and ideation, pure *Manas* and egoity, overbroods incarnated *Manas* but only at a distance. There is a persistent alienation from active Manasic self-consciousness owing to its involvement through matter and desire with the world of differentiation. There is an agonizing separation of *Manas* from its true estate where it is one with *Atma-Buddhi*. To be one with *Atma-Buddhi* also means to be one with *Mahat*, the cosmic mind and universal consciousness. Put in another way, the alienation of the individual from the universal is repeated within the individual in a body. This becomes a protracted alienation between the Atma-Buddhic Monad in its pure state and the embodied consciousness, whereby *Manas* has been deflected and captured by *kama*. The meta-psychological process is reflected in the embodied consciousness as the illusion of separate objects and subjects.

All of this makes poignant the idea of spirit plunging deeper and deeper into material existence and then redeeming it. This does not happen automatically. Once human beings are plunged, through their claustrophobic egoity, into the world of sensation and matter, they are painfully alienated from their true selves. Unless they recognize that fact and do something to mitigate and counter their overactive tendency towards kamamanasic thought, they cannot free themselves. Unless they deliberately take steps to withdraw from identification with name and form *(namarupa)* through meditation, through abstraction and silence, through calmness and negating the illusions of the world and the false self, they will be unable to cooperate with the redemptive function of spirit. What is true of cosmic evolution on universal terms is also true of humanity at the individual and collective level. Mankind is involved in a metaphysical Fall and a potential redemption at the individual level.

Every human being must discover his true identity by asking, "Who am I?" He must initially recognize the falsity and absurdity of identifying with any mask or persona. Yet this is precisely the tendency of exteriorized language and lower manasic cerebration. All of this must be thought through and negated. He must seek to realize in daily experience the meditative state which Patanjali calls the condition of the Spectator without a spectacle. To realize this state is to experience pure 'I-am-I' consciousness without any reference to being a subject separate from other subjects or any identification with an object in a field of differentiated objects.

Owing to the long history of each human being in incarnation, the attainment of this high degree of abstraction requires a great deal of systematic work upon the vestures. To develop the capacity to give a sense of reality to pure being, apart from all desire and memory, without expectation or attachment to the temporal processes of past, present and future, requires a purification and transmutation of the life-atoms constituting the astral and physical vestures. This alchemical process of self-purification and transmutation must itself be a deliberate and self-conscious embodiment of the principles of double evolution.

The Gupta Vidya I, "Consciousness and Form", 118-120

ACCESSING UNIVERSAL MEMORY

To understand the operation of karma and memory across lifetimes, it will help to consider situations where there is a loss of memory within a single lifetime, and the nature of the opportunities afforded by the recovery of memory. For example:

> There are cases on record of long months and years of insanity, of long days of fever when almost everything done or said, was done and said unconsciously. Yet when the patients recovered they remembered occasionally their words and deeds and very fully. *Unconscious* cerebration is a phenomenon on this plane and may hold good so far as the personal mind is concerned.
>
> Ibid.

Such an abrupt break in personal memory can be prompted by fever, the influence of drugs, psychic spells, madness, infatuation, terror and fear. Similar though less serious lesions in memory occur through impulsive talk, automatic action or daydreaming, through intensity of emotion or confusion of thought. All of these processes involve the spiritual nerve-currents of the subtlest vesture, which affect in turn the intellectual nerve-currents of the mind-vesture, and, ultimately, the astral nerves and the physiological form. All of the vestures resonate and respond to each other ceaselessly, whether one notices it or not. Thus, in comparison with the self-consciousness of an Adept, human beings are behaving thoughtlessly, unself-consciously or semiconsciously most of the time. When they suddenly recall what they have been doing after a spell of oblivion, they are often terrified of confronting themselves or any honest human being.

Perhaps, however, one will not be afraid and wish to run away when confronted with the implications of one's past actions. In proportion to one's commitment to the pursuit of integrity before the traumatic episode, one will be relieved to remember what one actually did. Though shamed and shocked to discover one's actions, one can refine moral sensitivity through a chastening experience. Instead of fleeing from memory, one will gladly receive the help needed to prevent recurrences in the future. Like Immanuel Kant, who said that he was grateful to be awakened from the nonage of his dogmatic slumbers, individuals seeking participation in the humanity of the future will make every effort to overcome the unconscious cerebration of the personal mind. This unconscious cerebration – so boring, so inconvenient and so pervasive – is entirely at odds with the quickening of the Race-mind that is taking place in the present cycle. Beings will either become automata or more wide awake, morally and spiritually. The only effective contribution individuals can make to the future is through bringing ethical awareness to the centre of one's consciousness, making it the basis of every act and every attitude. If one fails to do this, one's awareness will become frenetic and manic, and certainly not honourable. Self-respect is only possible through the acquisition of moral self-consciousness, for that is the only basis of the fearlessness required to face alternatives. Only when this is possible can one look at one's accounts and have the courage to change the line of action and thus to rectify them.

Yet if all of this is only applied to the personal mind and to personal memory and consciousness, it will only yield an ego-centered sense of ethics and moral awareness. In becoming concerned with one's motives and moral life, one should not just become more preoccupied with oneself. Meta-psychologically, holding oneself up as a victim of the world is little different from holding oneself up as entirely responsible for the whole world. If one forgets that other people are moral agents, and sees them only as puppets upon the stage of one's moral life, one becomes outwardly permissive, yet inwardly self-righteous. In a position of responsibility, yesterday's libertine becomes today's tyrant. Whilst powerless, the crypto-power maniac is content to play the role of the victim, acting out martyrdom whilst wallowing in judgementalism.

But it is rapidly becoming impossible to live unless one truly loves other human beings and lives for them. Unless one can learn to live for children, one cannot live for the future. Nor is this merely a matter of words or exhilarated emotions. It is a function of one's capacity to hold a transcendental vibration in one's consciousness, thereby giving life to what is real and turning away from what is dying with no fear, but with calm compassion. Only thus can the subjective matrix of personal self-reference be dissolved from above below.

Collective humanity is presently undergoing a crisis that is both painful and fortunate. During this psychological Vietnamization of the world, there is no escape. There are corpses, shells, wounded and deformed beings everywhere in the astral light. They may seem to be other people, but they all affect elements in oneself which are distorted and deformed. This is not actually new; a noble seer like H.P. Blavatsky spoke in the nineteenth century of modern civilization being a necropolis. The Rishi sees astral forms and auras not in some psychic way but calmly and consistently, everywhere and all the time. Without the slightest disturbance to his or her state of consciousness, everything is known and nothing is hidden. Naturally, the eyes of a seer are eyes of deep wisdom and immense compassion for humanity. And when the seer speaks, it is from a universal standpoint.

> Behold the Hosts of Souls. Watch how they hover o'er the stormy sea of human life, and how, exhausted, bleeding, broken-winged, they drop one after other on the swelling waves. Tossed by the fierce winds, chased by the gale, they drift into the eddies and disappear within the first great vortex.
>
> *The Voice of the Silence*

This vision of the spiritual travail of humanity, caught in the darkness of loneliness and despair, of spiritual failure and desperation, is overwhelming. It cannot be either understood or assimilated by personal consciousness, but requires a universal vision of karma and human experience. Authentic impersonality in consciousness must be restored, whether through contemplation of the vastitude of starry Nature, through adoration of heroic figures and scenes in distant epochs or through meditation upon universal ideas. To connect oneself to the fathomless resources of the akashic light, one will need a conception of the karmic recording process which goes beyond any analogy to the individual brain or a computer. Instead, one must conceive of every atom in every blade of grass as intimately and eternally involved with every other sentient atom throughout the whole cosmos. This is difficult to conceive of because of the immense thoughtlessness, callousness and insensitivity of much human interaction. Caught up in their self-conceptions, individuals imagine that they are isolated in consciousness from each other, or if they take interaction seriously, they tend to blame each other for the disturbances they experience. To counter this narrow view, one might re-read some of the great plays of Shakespeare: in the great duet between the frightened apprentice Macbeth and the more accomplished black magician, Lady Macbeth, who nonetheless goes mad in terror at the end, we see the agitation of nature consonant with human beings. Not only is there a resonant response to every human emotion on the sounding-board of Nature, but one may even, if perceptive, discern in these responses of Nature the archetypal processes that envelop the human individual in birth and in death.

Kama loka and *devachan* are objective resonances of human consciousness; as permanent possibilities in nature they are present everywhere and always. If, with all their implications regarding soul-memory and the cycle of reincarnation, they are not perceived continuously, it is because human beings are so isolated in their personal awareness and bodily identification that they are blind to the causal matrices they are continually elaborating. Without overcoming this obscuration of consciousness it is not possible to consult the book of memory and the book of judgement at the dawn and twilight of incarnation in a constructive manner. During life, individual karma and memory must be inserted into the vast living fabric of visible and invisible Nature, which is conscious and responsive at every point, having nothing to do with any mechanistic conceptions of the recording of information.

> Personal memory is a fiction of the physiologist. There are cells in our brain that receive and convey sensations and impressions but this once done, their mission is accomplished. These cells of the supposed "organ of memory" are the *receivers* and *conveyors* of all the pictures and impressions of the past, not their *retainers*. Under various conditions and stimuli, they can receive instantaneously the reflection of these astral images back again, and this is called *memory, recollection, remembrance*; but they do not preserve them.... But the Universal Memory preserves every motion, the slightest wave and feeling that ripples the waves of differentiated nature, of man or of the Universe.
>
> *Lucifer*, October 1891

Once one understands that in universal memory everything is not only recorded but felt, one can no longer hold to a separative concept of ethics. Instead, one will turn to the perspective of the poets, the seers, the Great Compassionaters who have always taught that every thought affects every plant and every star. Whilst caught up in a separative conception of ethics, one may hold oneself responsible for hurting another person, but not necessarily every leaf and plant on earth. Yet, when human beings generate maleficent vibrations, every element in Nature is wounded. Innumerable ripples reach out throughout all differentiated Nature, and they are all preserved in the universal memory, not merely as information about individual lives, but as part of the constitutive basis for living beings in general. When this observation is coupled with a consideration of the problem of unconscious cerebration, at the level of the personal mind, the entire nature of the quest for continuity of consciousness is transformed. Instead of simply insisting to oneself that one should be more responsible or more effective, that one should learn from past failures so as to acquire virtue in an egocentric sense, such personal conceptions are supplanted by a sensitivity to universal responsibility, universal causation and the operation of karmic law within the framework of universal unity.

The Gupta Vidya I, "Resonance and Vibration", 215-218

THE UNIVERSAL MEMORY
OF MANKIND

... not all human beings live in the same dimension of space-time. They may be grouped according to divergent states of consciousness; hence there could be within a single family, within a community, certainly within a nation, people representing differences of consciousness so vast that they constitute a virtual sub-species of humanity. In the most propitious cases these beings, having achieved a certain level of personal invulnerability, would always be universalizing and elevating themselves. But others, despite the best will in the world, have consolidated or inherited extremely tenacious tendencies that push them constantly towards the shadow-play of the physical senses. They are, therefore, blinded to the joyous possibilities of what would otherwise be the natural upward arc of the metaphysical imagination. Human beings of all sorts may be characterized in terms of these marked divergences in consciousness which invariably reflect the closeness or looseness of the relation between the immortal triad and the mutable quaternary, between spiritual will and material ossification. *What might be called a human being's basic level of self-consciousness is directly proportional to that Monad's evolution as an independent centre of primordial formless intelligence.* In any particular case, the degree of this noetic individuation is a direct function of how that ray of self-consciousness has, over a period of eighteen million years, used life-atoms and the vestures, either universalizing itself or failing to do so. This is the secret history of every human soul.

Looked at in the aggregate, all immortal souls presently experiencing the complexities of this earth chain in the Fourth Round are themselves the inheritors of an evolution that goes back to prior Rounds and earlier periods of evolution. In the first three Rounds, before reaching the stage of nascent self-consciousness, every Monad would have acquired a wealth of spiritual experiences in ethereal vestures, all of which is part of the universal memory of mankind. Each unfolding Round of evolution is like a day of Brahmā, composed of one revolution of the wheel of the planetary chain or one circling of the Monadic Hosts around the seven globes. In the Fourth Round, human evolution reaches the high-point of physical development, crowning its work with the development of the perfect physical vesture. This point of maximum involution of spirit into matter represents the fullest development of physical consciousness. After attaining this threshold, evolution begins its return movement towards spirit. In this vast perspective of human evolution, humanity has already passed that point of intense involvement in differentiation at the atomic and molecular level. This is evident in the subtlety and refinement of the human cellular structure, nervous system and specialized organs. There is an immeasurable gap between, for example, the human hand and an animal's paw. Each human being carries in his hands and other organs instruments that are the product of an extraordinary specialization of natural intelligence. But this privilege – having a hand with a firm thumb, five fingers and all its mounds corresponding to the different planets – is too little considered and too often taken for granted.

Even those fortunate enough to have had access to the arcane teachings regarding Rounds and globes, the correspondences and analogies between Nature and Man, have neglected this meditation. Though supposedly liberated from both theistic and materialistic conceptions of evolution, they have succumbed to superficial views of spirituality. Few, if any, have thought to connect the ten virtues with the twice-five fingers of the two hands. However many have reflected upon the phrase "constitutionally incapable of deviating from the right path", few have tried to understand irreversibility even on the physical plane, to recognize that it might apply to leading a little child by the hand across precipitous terrain. There is no point in being *more or less* reliable when guiding a child along the edge of an abyss; one needs nothing less than absolute irreversible stability. Gandhi understood this well and tirelessly attempted to impress it upon his followers. Even disregarding so extreme a case, one can remind oneself that such a firm stability is the indispensable basis of industrial civilization. People must be prompt and reliable in going about their work. No matter how much they may be driven by lesser or distracting motives, they either turn up at work at a certain time or accept, and expect, the inevitable consequences. This works all the way through Nature and society, so much so that it is taken to be common sense. The difficulty, then, is for people to bring to bear this stringent sense of reliability upon the inner life, with its whirling thoughts, chaotic feelings and everyday moral choices.

The fundamental problem is to generate a sufficient sense of reality for the inner pilgrimage when it is freely chosen and when it is neither baited by external rewards nor buffeted by internal fears. Not all human beings are the same in this regard. Some need the stimulus of fear more than others. This is due to the aggregate character of all the impressions they have made upon the life-atoms in their vestures during their incarnations over the past eighteen million years. At any given time, through one's predominant state of consciousness, one establishes a link with elementals, which on different planes belong by affinity to quite different classes. They themselves function in groups and are connected with the five visible and two invisible elements of Nature. They are also therefore connected, by analogy, with other globes of the earth chain, and are consubstantial with matter, either in a rarefied form corresponding to the first three Rounds or in an extremely dense state connected with the point of maximum differentiation in the Fourth Round.

Viewed in a larger time scale than is ordinarily accessible to human beings, the entire process of Nature is circular; every Round on the descending scale is but a more concrete repetition of the one preceding it. Similarly, every globe within a Round on the descending arc is a materialized copy of a more ethereal sphere which preceded it in the successive descents of consciousness through the three higher planes of the earth chain. On the fourth globe in the Fourth Round, humanity has completed the involutionary arc of this process and is now engaged in the difficult push upwards and inwards towards the source of all life-energy. The immense suffering of present humanity comes from the lapses of irresponsible beings who lost touch with the great evolutionary thrust. Regardless of the exact nature of these collective failures of prior civilizations, and regardless of the particular burdens that these failures have placed on present humanity, it is now necessary for all human beings to learn to move upwards self-consciously in the ascending arc.

In practice, this means that human beings must acquire greater control over their conscious energies, a much greater capacity to withdraw from external stimuli and deformed images. This internal refinement of consciousness is the method of evolution itself, which acts to spiritualize and etherealize the complex nature of all beings, bringing them successively on to the levels of the globes in the descending arc of evolution. Thus, on the ascending arc the fifth globe corresponds to the third globe of the descending arc, the sixth to the second and the seventh to the first. A corresponding relationship exists between the Rounds themselves. This upward process is essentially the sublimation of matter and its impressibility by intelligence, which is the constructive function of thinking beings in the creative use of matter. The general sum-total of impulse given by thought to matter includes the laser-sharp contributions of legions of Adepts as well as the more haphazard effusions of millions of laggard souls. Without being an Adept, it is impossible to assess the awesome nature of this sum-total. Most human beings are, by definition, active at a middle level of consciousness and therefore are unable to understand the enormous range of alchemy that arises in human experience. They touch only a minute segment of meaningful experience in any given lifetime. Whilst the humanity of a particular Race and Round will act under a general limiting curve of consciousness, present humanity falls far short in optimizing its opportunities under the curves that apply to it, and this is largely through compulsive identification with lower classes of elementals negatively impressed in the past.

The Gupta Vidya I, "Purity and Pollution", 241-243

MAKING MORE ROOM FOR OTHERS

At the head of the host of virgin ascetics called the Kumaras stands Maha Shiva, the Mahayogin, the supreme exemplar of effortless asceticism and the highest creative meditation.

> Siva-Rudra is the Destroyer, as Vishnu is the preserver; and both are the regenerators of spiritual as well as of physical nature. To live as a plant, the *seed* must die. To live as a conscious entity in the Eternity, the passions and senses of man must first DIE before his body does. 'To live is to die and to die is to live,' has been too little understood in the West. Siva, the *destroyer*, is the *creator* and the Saviour of Spiritual man, as he is the good gardener of nature. He weeds out the plants, human and cosmic, and kills the passions of the physical, to call to life the perceptions of the spiritual, man.
>
> Ibid., 459

Shiva is the destroyer of passions and of the physical senses, which are constant impediments to the development of higher spiritual perceptions and to the growth of the inner spiritual man. The more desperately a human being tries to stave off ageing, the more rapidly Shiva will destroy that being. Shiva wants every human being to grow older and to die, so that by suffering he may learn that there is no other true dharma for a human being than to overcome illusion. Nature shows this all the time. If a plant is to grow, the seed must die, and if there is to be fruit for the harvest and for succeeding years, the plant must die. To live as a conscious entity in eternity, one must kill out *tanha,* the powerful force impelling beings into involuntary reincarnation. If no self-conscious effort is made during life to overcome this force, then even the small element of choice that one might have had at the moment of death is weakened. Nothing is sadder than to see the old encouraged to cling to life and to fear death. This corrupting tendency is derived from the decadent period of fallen Egyptian civilization. Whether disguised as pseudo-science or pseudo-medicine or pseudo-religion, it is nothing more than a piteous selfishness bound up with the delusion of carnal immortality.

To live as a conscious human being is to make more room for others, and this is what the present cycle is intended to teach. Every human being must come to live in the recognition that other and finer human beings will follow him. This lesson is particularly acute in the so-called modern civilization of the West, with its false and illusive conceptions of history and progress. Every time the lesson of gratitude to ancestors and benefactors has been taught over the last centuries, it has been forgotten. It is not enough to give ritual thanks one day each year. One must learn ceaseless gratitude to ancestors and a continuous sense of obligation to descendants. This does not involve transferring one's anxieties onto children. They should rather be greeted as souls and shown by example how joyous true discipline can be. Otherwise, by the age of thirteen, children will become mother superiors, witches, pontificators, constantly engaged in passing judgements. This is awful enough amongst those who have never had the advantage of association with Gupta Vidya; those who know something of its pristine philosophy and persist in gossip and image-crippling are on the way to becoming grey magicians and worse. Jesus said it all two thousand years ago, but millions of people since then, twisting and abusing his name, failed to take in the central lesson.

To live is to die, to make more room for others. One must age gracefully, must start letting go by the age of twenty-eight, if one wants to learn how to do so at the moment of death. One must learn to cooperate with Shiva, the destroyer, who is also the creator and saviour of spiritual man, the good gardener of Nature. Through this cooperation will come a sifting of the unnecessary, a cleansing of thought, a rhythm of breathing. It will become easier to focus the mind. The more one develops a strong sense of external duty, the more one can cultivate a living awareness of the internal necessities of the soul. Long before one is prepared to engage in direct occult training, with its magical wisdom and spiritual creativity, one must learn to act economically, lightly and precisely, in a manner that refines one's spiritual nature and diffuses benevolence.

By becoming a devotee of Shiva the soul has a better chance to connect with the mind, to use the mind as a creative instrument, and to govern the body as a faithful vehicle. One will know that the soul is at work through the heart when one's capacity for loving others grows to such an extent that one has no thought of oneself. There will be a gradual diminution of the passions and an increase in the perceptions of the spiritual man. Contemporary fascination with Tantra is merely a way of evading the issue of celibacy. Those caught up in it will not develop the Third Eye; they will instead be incinerated, for there is no fooling around in the realm of spiritual fire. Go slow, but do not compensate. Shiva teaches the anchorite to be totally honest, he is the friend of that in oneself which is cheerfully modest but morally courageous.

The Gupta Vidya I, "Spiritual Progenitors", 302-304

PROMETHEUS, CHRIST, ARE IN EVERY HEART

A.E.'s mysticism emphasizes understanding through love, and he embroiders mystical naturalism with suggestions of the rich void beyond and throughout nature. He emphasizes man's identity with all nature because he sees the soul in nature and in humanity. "The great heart of the earth is full of laughter", one of his characters says, "do not put yourselves apart from its joy, for its soul is your soul and its joy is your true being." As the veil of visible nature is dissolved before the mystic's sight, time itself is seen as an illusion from a metaphysical standpoint. Consciousness is expanded or constricted by its apprehension of time. The mystic senses a vibration prior to visible nature, though insofar as it is expressible, it too has a beginning and an end. Mystical experience is timeless though located in time, and the mystic is hard pressed to describe the crossings between the unmanifest and the manifest. Speaking of the hour of twilight as a metaphor for that time when "the Mystic shall be at home", A.E. calls it "the hour for memory".

> Wherever it is spent, whether in the dusky room or walking home through the blue evening, all things grow strangely softened and united; the magic of the old world reappears. The commonplace streets take on something of the grandeur and solemnity of starlit avenues of Egyptian temples; the public squares in the mingled glow and gloom grow beautiful as the Indian grove where Sakuntala wandered with her maidens; the children chase each other through the dusky shrubberies, as they flee past they look at us with long remembered glances: lulled by the silence, we forget a little while the hard edges of the material and remember that we are *spirits*.

When the horizon set by one's awareness of time is foreshortened, memory is reduced to recent particulars redolent with echoes of childhood remembrance. As that horizon is expanded through a sense of eternity, recollection arises with a profound awareness of mythic time, and the soul gazes within the archaic history of humanity. Soul-memory exhibits natural affinities to strange dreams, insignificant in detail yet suggesting a cosmic drama in which each creature plays an appropriate role. Soul-memory also portrays to waking consciousness what would otherwise be witnessed only in *sushupti* or Devachan. If most individuals see nature as a static created world comprising myriad separate entities, the mystic beholds *natura naturans,* a dynamic process constantly unleashing creative energies.

The mystical experience is grounded in the commonality of human life.

> For this in truth it seems to me to mean: all knowledge is a revelation of the self to the self, and our deepest comprehension of the seemingly apart divine is also our furthest inroad to self-knowledge; Prometheus, Christ, are in every heart; the story of one is the story of all; the Titan and the Crucified are humanity.
>
> *The Hero in Man*

Precisely because Christ is incarnate in all humanity, every human being has golden moments and mystical glimpses, yet because Prometheus is bound for ever within us, such moments and glimpses are obliterated in waking life through indulgence, egotism, obsession with results and the concern for salvation. And if these barriers to deeper unity are bypassed without genuine self-transcendence, they become still stronger obstacles: passivity, aggression, fantasy and malignant interference in the lives of others. To thread passing moments into a continuous current in life, one must hold firmly to a selfless line of thought and motivation.

The Gupta Vidya I, "The Hero in Man", 306-307

ASSISTING THE DIVINE EVOLUTION OF IDEAS

. . . all the Dhyanis, all the *devas* and the higher potencies, are entitled to the grateful reverence of humanity, and man ought to be ever striving to help the divine evolution of ideas by becoming to the best of his ability a co-worker with Nature in the cyclic task of augmenting self-consciousness.

Philosophically, this work is consonant with the intrinsic logic of manifestation. Patanjali, the great teacher of yoga, declared that the entire universe exists for the sake of the human soul. It is part of the programme of evolution, cosmic and human, that there should be universal enlightenment. Hence, the point and force of taking a vow lies in an individual's becoming fully aware of the inmost purpose of evolution and the privilege of being incarnated. An individual who does this becomes a living link on earth with wise beings who constitute a mighty Fraternity, who are ideating at a level that is sufficiently homogeneous to reach all humanity on the subtlest plane in deep sleep and in deep meditation. But for beings below that level, even to attempt to do this is to help to make possible the percolation into the consciousness of human beings of that universal current which is the impulse of life itself from the standpoint of the immortal soul. If enough people do this, in due course language and thought will change, and, at some point, the modes of human interaction must also change. Human beings must be able to create patterns of life relevant to those future races that will enact at a high level of deliberation and control what was felt intuitively by the earliest races, especially the Third Root Race.

To take a vow is to assist in the divine evolution of ideas. It is to recognize that there is a great deal in oneself which – by atavism, abuse and misuse, the karma of other lives and the karma attached to whole classes of life-atoms over long periods of time – does not want to cooperate intelligently. To overcome these obstructions requires proper attention, the potent power of thought, the spiritual force of the will and the universal energy of feeling. These have become appropriated and dissipated, concretized and wasted, and also, on occasion, badly abused. It is to offset deliberately this downward tendency of the lunar nature that one self-consciously reorients one's attitude of mind, state of being and sphere of magnetic influence around the supernal light of the solar ray which is *Atma-Buddhi*. Thus a vow is made holy. And hence, the ever-unknowable and incognizable *Karana* alone has its shrine and altar on the holy and ever-untrodden ground of the heart. In spiritually developed cultures sacred truths simply could not be uttered indiscriminately by anyone.

Speakers, not speech, bring words to life. For a number of complex reasons connected with the larger purpose of evolution, as against the long-standing exploitation through corrupt and ignorant priestcraft alienated from the true source of wisdom, there is in Kali Yuga the necessary process of widespread access to authentic spiritual teachings. This can give rise to the illusion that one need simply utter certain words to enter into the current of potent ideation. In reality, if one is unfamiliar with the arcane properties of light and sound that are inextricably connected with great ideas, one may actually release a strong force which works as an agent of disintegration, disruption, delusion, decay and death. So one must spend much time in silence, making a repeated and sincere regular effort to enter this state of communion – "invisible, intangible, unmentioned, save through 'the still small voice' of our spiritual consciousness". Only so can one activate the voice of conscience, which in time becomes the voice of spiritual consciousness. At a further stage this becomes the voice of the daimon and at its highest level it is the *chitkala*, the voice which is infallibly and constantly available to the individual. Before one can reach that stage, one must silence other voices. One must draw within; one must "give Nature time to speak". It is a veritable tragedy that when people assemble, they fear silence and ceaselessly transmit to one another mundane, meaningless detail. This needlessly reduces the length of life and restricts the power of the spiritual will. The most crucial training involves deliberate speech and creative silence, that true reverential silence in which all the faculties are at once alert and relaxed, free from any rush to manifest. This is the decisive difference between the sacred and the profane, the holy and the polluted.

One must first learn to listen to that still, small voice of one's spiritual consciousness and the integral teaching of the Gupta Vidya directed towards *Buddhi*, the voice of spiritual intuition in every human being. Because that voice is not initially available, a person may begin by calmly reading and reading again, aloud but also silently, some of the great passages in spiritual texts. This can begin to arouse *Buddhi*. The ordinary mind is in a rush; but *Buddhi* is calm, gentle and assured, like a living spring that flows from the ground. Many people cannot begin this, however, because of a false lower Manasic identification of vitality and wakefulness with manifestation. When they do not manifest, they become drowsy and fall asleep. Unable to keep spiritually awake and Manasically active, they become mediumistic and are taken over by every kind of lower astral force in the elemental universe. They fall prey to a corruption of the faculties because the lunar mind becomes mixed and mingled with anything lurking in the astral light. Many people are imprisoned in a false dichotomy between a loud but weak manifesting tendency and an equally feeble mediumistic tendency.

The aim of true meditation, of developing the mind but also, in time, unfolding the intuition, is to rise above this dichotomy to a relaxed yet heightened awareness that flows in a continuous and steady stream. To be able to do this one has to loosen the hold exercised by the illusion – through ignorance, association of ideas and habits of speech – that there is some entity called the personality. In fact, there is only a vast collection of tendencies. All attempts on the personal plane to gain continuity are only shadowy reflections, a kind of imitative activity that draws fitfully from the true light of awareness of the immortal soul, but which has no chance to manifest continuously because of the overactive personal consciousness. One must see through this illusion at the core to dissociate from it. One must learn through asceticism in speech how one tends to use the personal pronoun, the 'I'; one must see that most of what one views as oneself is merely a set of tendencies, and that by identifying with them one has created a false 'I'. After a point, this aggregate becomes so ossified that one cannot show reverence, be grateful, be calm, or meditate, and hence one cannot withdraw into the inmost sanctuary. One cannot get away from pessimism – a sure sign of corruption of truly human consciousness, which is always marked in its pure form by an inward optimism that is the Buddhic light of awareness of the inner joy of life, behind the veil of manifestation.

The Gupta Vidya I, "Levels of Manifestation", 366-368

THE FLAME OF THE *KARANA*

The dispelling of the illusion of separateness needs both a preliminary toughness and, ultimately, a readiness to plunge into the stream. *The Voice of the Silence* says, "The pilgrim who would cool his weary limbs in running waters, yet dares not plunge for terror of the stream, risks to succumb from heat." One has to try to withdraw into oneself for the purpose of communion and quiet contemplation, for the purpose of surrender, as many mystics have put it, but also for the purpose of a pure consecration of all energies to this invisible, intangible, unmentioned ground of the altar upon which will shine the flame of the *Karana*. To honour the soul, making one's spirit the sole mediator between oneself and the Universal Spirit, one's good actions the only priests, and one's sinful intentions the only sacrificial victims to the Presence, means having no doubts about the undertaking. Doubts must be thrown into the sacrificial fire of surrender and contemplation. All worries and hesitations are like vermin. They are the encrusted mental deposits made by lower thoughts and emotions that consolidate greedy, hungry, bitter and sour elementals, all of which must be thrown into the fire. In this light one can understand the therapeutic teaching and wise instruction of Jesus, which has to do with authentic initiation, and not with hypocritical public prayer or the mumbo-jumbo of exclusive claims.

> 'When thou prayest thou shalt not be as the hypocrites are . . . but enter into *thine inner chamber and having shut thy door, pray to thy Father which is in secret.*' (Matt. vi) Our Father is *within us*, 'in Secret', our 7th principle, in the 'inner chamber' of our Soul perception. 'The Kingdom of Heaven' and of God '*is within us*' says Jesus, not *outside*.
>
> The Secret Doctrine, i 280

There is a direct analogy between the light that shines in the "inner chamber" and the subtle creative light of the first twilight at the dawn of the *Maha-Manvantara*. This Initial Existence is a *conscious spiritual quality* which, in the manifested solar world, resembles the film of divine breath to the gaze of the entranced seer. A reflection of the Absolute, it is designated the One Life, and is a film for creative or formative purposes. Manifesting in seven states, each with seven subdivisions, it is the basis of the six *shaktis*, the highest powers available to the initiated seer, which exist in germ in every single human being. These six *shaktis* are in their unity represented by the Light of the Logos, *Daiviprakriti*, the noumenal light of the dawn of manifestation, also called Vach, Kwan Yin, Sarasvati, Isis and, in some alchemical texts, the Virgin of the World. This Initial Existence has an intimate correspondence with the twin twilights that enclose each terrestrial day. In both the potent hour of readiness before the dawn and the hour of memory at dusk, human beings can withdraw from the external physical plane of manifestation and approach their true spiritual state of being. The universal and cosmic resonances of these timeless moments remind the soul of forgotten truths that pertain to the largest cycles and are a permanent presence in the innermost chambers of the soul. Ancient wisdom has always taught the use of certain periods of time through which, by analogy and correspondence, one can come more easily into the subtle luminous vestures, into the *karana sharira,* and, ultimately, into the *anandamaya kosha*.

The hidden light-energy and noumenal matter of the highest principles persist throughout an evolutionary period as the true raiment of the immortal soul that comes through a vast course of collective monadic life and over eighteen million years of self-consciousness and human existence. It is easier to experience this light through meditation upon the whole host of perfected beings during certain times because these beings have entered the creative light of which Jesus spoke. To understand this philosophically, it is important to think through the metaphysical distinction between the brute energy inherent in matter and the intelligence which guides and directs that energy.

> ... what is called 'unconscious Nature' is in reality an aggregate of forces manipulated by semi-intelligent beings (Elementals) guided by High Planetary Spirits, (Dhyan Chohans), whose collective aggregate forms the manifested *verbum* of the unmanifested LOGOS, and constitutes at one and the same time the MIND of the Universe and its immutable LAW.
>
> Three distinct representations of the Universe in its three distinct aspects are impressed upon our thought by the esoteric philosophy: the PRE-EXISTING (evolved from) the EVER-EXISTING; and the PHENOMENAL – the world of illusion, the reflection, and shadow thereof.
>
> *The Secret Doctrine*, i 277-278

The Ever-Existing is the eternal divine ground of all being. The Pre-Existing is the most subtle, primary, luminous emanation which is totally unmanifest from the point of view of what is called the world, but which is the most potent manifestation. A human being truly concerned to acquire Demiurgic control over the power of thought will deliberate and hold back expression, not in frustration but in order to dwell upon each thought and let it settle. The unmanifest reality of an idea becomes evident only when one can hold an idea for the benefit of others and see that this power of retention truly helps. It will help others far more if silent than if verbalized without having been assimilated through contemplation. Many people sincerely and mistakenly think that by making a slogan out of this they can do it; genuinely to curb the desire to manifest is to have a profound sense of reality in the unmanifest. To live in the causal realm, and in the *karana sharira*, one must see the ideas behind words, and also behind one's own mind. Profound ideas take shape when dwelt upon in the silence and solitude of the immovable mind, far from the noisy speech of the manifesting movable mind. That which is supernally true spontaneously subsists in silence.

The Gupta Vidya I, "Levels of Manifestation", 368-370

APPENDIX II

SELECTED PASSAGES FROM THE GOLDEN THREAD ~ VOLUME II OF *THE GUPTA VIDYA*

DEVOTION AND DUTY

During the primeval dawn of human evolution, the whole of humanity was suffused with a spontaneous devotion to Gurus and Preceptors, to the golden chain of transmission of the Guruparampara, a galaxy of known and unknown teachers. Simultaneously, all found no pain but a pure pleasure in the performance of the daily duties of life, revealing an intimate connection between devotion and duty. The conception of such a humanity differs totally from our own. It is like a Golden Age far removed from our time, because for many centuries we have engendered, with extraordinary violence and pertinacity, the falsehood of a separate identity for each human being, supposedly gestated at birth and terminated at death. People tend not to think about death and live as if they have a kind of invulnerability. But they blunder through without any knowledge of who they are, and find themselves oppressed by a sense of inward confusion, which only allows them to speak and think in terms of comparison and contrast. They are driven by their dwarfed conceptions of success and failure and are trapped in differentiated consciousness based on unending comparison and contrast. At the same time, this consciousness assumes an apparent stability not intrinsic to it, but involving a shutting out of the archetypal moments of birth and death. In time, this means forgetfulness, an indifference to the primary facts that apply to all humanity — that there is a great continuity to the human pilgrimage, that death is followed by rebirth, that this is true not only for particular souls but also that there is a continuous passage from generation to generation.

The whole process is so vast that the moment we try to limit it, in terms of crude conceptions of duty or obligation, we also feel that any personal devotion we show is gratuitous. Captivated by personal differentiated consciousness, we live under the sway of the specious idea that the universe is for one's own private benefit and that each one is favouring the world, favouring other human beings, by an egocentric stance, by supererogatory acts, and that if one is devoted one has set up some kind of claim upon the object of devotion. All of this thinking is distorted, inverted, and perverted, bound up with the descent of consciousness into matter. At a certain point of material density and fragmentation of consciousness, the pale reflection of the unmanifest light of the Immortal Triad assumes a false centrality. This would be like a shift from the self-luminous centre of a circle to a lit-up region which only seems luminous by contrast with the shadow around. The latter is the spurious ego, the limited personal consciousness. Given this condition, every human being can, at one level, understand that there is something very beautiful and elevating, something extremely authentic, in poetic accounts of a Golden Age of primordial humanity, when human beings moved naturally and related to each other beautifully. They were spontaneously held together by an effortless sense of moral and spiritual solidarity with the whole of nature, with those before and those yet to come, and above all, with their great Teachers. Though we can resonate with such an Age, we also know that if we have to ask questions about it, we already presuppose that it is estranged from us.

What good, then, can come of talking about devotion for a person who has become totally convinced that he has no capacity for any feeling, any devotion for anyone else? Who is that person? A cerebral machine, chatting away, insecure, confused yet making judgments? Is that the whole of that person? But if he has assumed this is all he or anyone else is, how can talking about devotion make a difference? Suppose such a person were told that there are great beings like Krishna and the Buddha, hosts of hierophants who are seated in meditation and constantly engaged in ideation upon universal good, who have so vast a perspective of endless time, boundless space and ceaseless motion, that they can see the rises and falls of civilizations and epochs in perspective. Suppose he were told that they can see the antics of human beings in much smaller spans of time and space with unwavering compassion, and also that they can see the root illusion. These beings are involved in universal welfare and uplifting the whole of humanity. Any human being who can vibrate in mind, heart and self to the tune of the great universal impulse of these mighty beings, may serve as a focal point through whom some mitigation of human misery and some elevation of consciousness is possible.

The Gupta Vidya II, "The Inmost Sanctuary", 89-90

THE *ANAHATA* VIBRATION

Buddhi Yoga requires a fixity and steadfastness in intuitive intelligent determination which is superior to *Karma Yoga,* the yoga of works, as a means of gaining enlightenment. It involves an eye capable of recognizing essentials, which, once awakened, will give a decisiveness without wavering or wandering. Through this resolute intellect, one's actions may become shadowless — *nischaya*. Even though one may be obscured, as a member of the human family participating in the world's pain, ignorance and turbulence, nonetheless one inwardly preserves the dignity of the power of choice. It is, therefore, possible to touch within oneself that level of absolute resolve which ensures that something essential will never be abandoned, or diluted or doubted, never weakened by careless speech nor lost in the chaos of compulsive acts, but always protected from discursive and dissecting Manasic reasoning. Every human being enjoys such moments of assurance. Otherwise it would not be possible to survive. Even fools and knaves have a few moments of *sushupti* at night inspiring them to awaken in the morning to greet another day. Were it not for this abiding sense of assurance about one's minimum dignity within the core of one's being, one could not go on.

This sense of one's distinct place in the total scheme of things is what Spinoza called the *conatus,* the urge or will to sustain rational and spiritual self-preservation. This is not merely an intellectual notion, but a biological fact. When a person begins to approach death, the *anahata* vibration in the spiritual heart ceases to sound in the *linga sharira*. The Sage or Seer can recognize this cessation of sound and a subtle alteration in the rate of breathing several months before the time of physical death. Throughout this period, the human being is engaged in a protracted review of the whole of his or her life, a review which is too often chaotic and confused, a jumble of recent memories and childhood events. Only at the time of separation from the physical body is the soul enabled to view in an orderly and rapid manner the entire film of an entire life. In the final preparation for this there is an ebbing of the connection between the sound vibration in the spiritual heart and the *karana sharira* and the vibration in the *linga sharira,* and therefore also in the *sthula sharira.* Once this ebbing begins, the person has begun to withdraw or die.

The sense of resolve and human dignity is so weak in human beings today that vast numbers, in the phrase of T.S. Eliot, are only "living and partly living". They have become so disgusted with the world, so confused about the events of our times and the precipitous decline of humane values throughout the globe, that they are hardly incarnated. They are mostly asleep or sleepwalking, drowsy or passive, or they mechanically go about their duties. They maintain none of that minimal wakefulness that is found in many a humble villager who, through desperation and poverty, maintains intact the light in the eyes, the light of *Manas* and human self-awareness. Paradoxically, one can sometimes sense the ray and radiance of pure consciousness in the most desperate and despised of human beings, whilst others have, alas, been educated beyond their capacity to make use of their knowledge. Between the head and the heart there is a terrible chasm, or even a battle. Many tend to be lost and therefore they live and partly live. It is as if the will to live, the *conatus,* has weakened; nothing remains but an automatism of habit and the power of cohesion in the *skandhas.* This is the pitiable condition referred to by Lord Krishna when he speaks of those who are wedded to the fruits of action. The plight of those who have conditioned themselves only to act for the sake of results is an indictment of modern education in Kali Yuga. The Iron Age arms too many people to live only in terms of what is perceptible, measurable and tangible. Having reduced all to the terms of a utilitarian consciousness, they come to view their fellow human beings in a crude Lockean fashion: "Every human being is a threat to you, unless you can join interests with him." If a person is neither a threat nor an accomplice in some selfish interest, he is a stranger. Today vast numbers of human beings live in cities of strangers. They live alone amidst humanity, unloved, with no sense of warmth. Such is the tragic condition of 'modern man'.

The Gupta Vidya II, "Buddhi Yoga and Svadharma", 104-105

RENUNCIATION AND SELF-REGENERATION

Shiva is the supreme principle of potent ideation and constructive imagination, bridging the unconditioned and the conditioned, the unlimited and the limited, the boundless and what is bounded in the realm of time. Shiva represents a noumenal intelligence ceaselessly at work in the life process through all the elemental, mineral, vegetable and animal kingdoms of Nature. Shiva is also accessible to each and every human being, not only the highest and the holiest, but also the most sinful and depraved whenever they have a flash of true repentance. The mundane realm, of course, is that wherein most human beings encounter a host of difficulties, because they cannot connect disparate elements of fleeting experience or else are victims of false connections that bombard them from outside. Human beings must resolve to stand on their own. They need to wake up to the fact that each is alone in this world, that in the end each is the custodian of his or her own hopes and promises, and that each is the only agent able to make a radical change in his or her own kingdom. This is not a task that can be transferred to any other agent.

A person who comes to understand this is ready to contemplate Shiva as a *yogin*, as the archetypal Man of Renunciation, as the paradigm of the pilgrim soul who has been through every possible experience of every possible human being. But Shiva can also be seen constantly at work destroying the froth of complacent illusion through disintegration. Shiva represents the universal frustration of all the foolish and faulty plans of deluded souls. In other words, Shiva epitomizes the insight that most of human history is based upon a terrible expenditure of emotion, an attempt to force upon this world schemes which must inevitably be frustrated because they are based upon the lie of separateness and cannot be supported by the cosmos. Beyond the lower realms of Nature and beyond the human realm, Shiva is the living metaphysical link between the unmanifest and the manifest Logos.

Since most problems arise in the middle or human realm, wherein individuals must learn to take a stand, Shiva is initially most relevant as the archetype of every seeker on earth. There is a specific point at which individuals are ready to take stock of the sum total of their experiences and to cut through the compulsive succession of dreamy, illusionary experiences. For the individual at this crossroad, Shiva becomes the paradigm of the perfect human being who is fully self-conscious. Within all the traumas and tragedies of human beings there lies latent the seed of self-awareness which enables an individual — whether in a future life, or at the moment of death, or many years later in this life — to cut through the froth. Shiva represents the pristine seed of a new beginning rooted in the Truth that makes one fearless. This signifies a new kind of courage — to see all the phases of life together and to cut through the process of *samsara*.

Unfortunately, too many human beings are ready to renounce only after they have been burnt out by their previous refusals to renounce and by the enormous burden of their exaggerated and ever-growing attachments. There is, therefore, a certain sadness in the eyes of a person who starts the climb towards the mountains, often at an advanced age, in the hope that at least his few remaining years may not be wasted in delusion. When one renounces separateness, one's life opens itself up to all human lives, to the enormity and vast Himalayan scope of the human pilgrimage, encompassing not only friends and relatives, but all human beings — strangers in the city, strangers in the streets, millions upon millions of persons who live and toil in extreme conditions of deprivation and desolation. Everywhere human beings are caught up without meaning in a life that is extremely hard economically or enormously wasteful in its focus upon providing for the passing fancies and endless consumption of other human beings. Everywhere there is the pain of emptiness, of fatigue, excess and self-indulgence. But there is also the pain of actual deprivation and the pain of loneliness.

The challenge of Shiva today is to learn to relate to all these beings.

What has always been true has now come much more to a head. Many human beings are living lives of utter waste, yet the very impulse that gives one the courage to go back to sleep after a trying day can become something more. It can become the courage to renounce the whole concept of the self bound up with memories and frustrations. It can quicken a sense of a larger self, a sense of involvement in the self of all humanity, and a concern for the wider horizon of human consciousness transcending the visible, the partial and the transitory.

In that fearless willingness to renounce, such a person has not only the actual inspiration of Shiva as an ideal or object — whether as a *linga,* or a statue, or as the author of certain texts, or as the supreme god Maheshvara who presides over and transcends the process of creation — but also as an actual hierophantic *yogin.* In Gupta Vidya, Shiva is Dakshinamurti, the Initiator of Initiates, responsible for the Mysteries in the Third, Fourth and Fifth Root-Races. Shiva was involved in all the triumphs and travails of the human race going back to Atlantean times, and Shiva will also be involved in all the heroic struggles of human beings for millions of years into the future, until the emergence of the Sixth Race. It is as if all the knowledge of all human souls in their desperate gropings towards the Mysteries is engraved within his sphinx-like face. He is the silent witness to their terrible failures. At the same time, he also bears shining witness to the vital hint of hope that all may one day begin anew and make a fresher, cleaner, better start.

Shiva, then, has a universal meaning, whether one has explicitly heard or thought much about him or not. No human being who experiences suffering and deep disappointment, no one who is frightened by what lies ahead when death draws near or who deeply reflects upon the suffering of humanity can help but see that something new is needed to understand the human predicament. Something is needed which involves going within, and it comes from silence rather than speech, from brooding rather than verbalizing. It involves thinking deeply and with total honesty about oneself, acknowledging every tendency of prevarication, doubt, procrastination, contradiction, ambivalence, ill will, envy, jealousy, hatred, pride and vulnerability. The willingness to enter into the dungeon within the psyche in which these demons exist, and the strength to come out of it courageously, vindicate Shiva. Shiva represents the assured capacity to reduce delusions to ashes. The fire of spiritual perception and objective honesty, the light of pure *Manas*, can burn out psychic dross which is powerful only because of a misplaced allegiance to a false persona. This is a long and painful process of purification. It takes years and lives to complete. If it is a true beginning, however, it will have the benediction of all those who have made similar beginnings and who have attained to some level of success on the side of that which is strong in the human race.

What characterizes wise beings, Initiates, Teachers and Mahatmas is the unconditional faith they can place in every single human being, against all odds, despite the past and whatever the record. This is not faith in something merely potential, but faith in that which is omnipresent, sacred and indestructible. It is like a cry to the divine and an affirmation of willingness to persist, to be tested, to sift and select ever more clearly and wisely. Such a faith implies increasing silence, with less propensity to manifest in the coming years, so that one begins to take on the burden of living with more deliberation and more dignity. This resolve and the very desire to make it, as well as the willingness to persist in it, draw upon that which Shiva represents. Rather than being a negative view of human despair, it is a fearless recognition of the myriads of forgotten instances of extraordinary redemption. Something Christ-like and Buddha-like has happened again and again among millions of human beings, and yet it has been accompanied by a colossal sense of waste, suffering and frustration caused by false consolidation of the ego. All this involves vast magnitudes. To talk of Shiva is thus to get beyond a narrow focus upon one's own horizon and to take one's own place within the larger whole. This is not something vague. It requires hard work, the effort of thinking through the problem and beginning to look at all beings in a different way.

While many of the obstacles that emerge are the familiar ones, they appear in different forms. One of them provides a clue to the subtle connection between love and asceticism. Shiva represents that strength which results from voluntary self-control carried to its highest point, where it becomes effortless and full of joy. As the paradigm of *yogins,* Shiva is often depicted as besmeared with ashes, carrying a necklace of skulls. This signifies a clarity of vision in which there is no truck with human fantasy, desire or ambition. It represents a courageous recognition of the underground in which most human beings live. This terrible Hades exists owing to the ugliness of human presumption. While there is so much of this everywhere and everyone can see it in themselves, nonetheless, something else that transcends understanding is involved in this perception. A kind of veiling has taken place. One could not see all this ugliness if one were not more than the sum total of all that is repellent, if there were not a seed of Platonic divine discontent moving one constantly towards an ineffable beauty. Shiva stands outside time. He carries in his right hand the drum, which represents the cyclic beat of time, but he himself is beyond time. Even the iconography and mythology of Shiva are amongst the oldest that exist. They precede all known religions and go back at least five to seven thousand years, to ancient coins and seals. They are part of the prehistoric folk memory of mankind. Shiva always has to do with the truth of the human condition, the truth of human failure, the truth of human persistence, and especially the truth of the possibility of human redemption which can only come with freedom from illusion.

The Gupta Vidya II, "Shiva and Self-Regeneration", 112-114

THE SELF-NEGATION
OF SHANKARACHARYA

History represents in recent centuries a harsh but also a necessary negation of the absurdities, errors and illusions of the past. When that happens with so many minds, when so many wills are blunted, hearts hurt and human beings lamed and crippled, suddenly we know that springtime is near. The Golden Age is next door. Suddenly we realize what we always might have known — that there are children in this world, that other people exist, that while ten men are gloomy there are another hundred who are happy. Those who are engrossed in being happy do not go around certifying their happiness to the gloomy. The gloomy want certainty, but there is no certitude to be attained anywhere in the realm of differentiation. This is a philosophical truth which everyone knew as a little child. The intuitive negation of childhood, a beautiful sharing with no 'mine' and 'thine,' was followed by cruel adolescent affirmations which are intensely ugly especially to others and sometimes to oneself. Then came the prolonged adolescence of those who are petrified that they might actually have to assume minimal responsibilities. But when men will not negate, Nature negates. Nature's power of negation is vaster than the collective power of negation of history, and both seem more awesome and decisive than the capacity of an individual to negate. Against this, however, we have the tremendous affirmation through the supreme negation of Sri Shankaracharya.

The individual who knows that at the root is the persisting illusion of separateness, is vaster than the universe, and can dissolve it instantly by breaking down at will the baseless, insubstantial fabric of his imagination. Anyone who can do that has begun to wake up. There are people who will not wake up voluntarily because they repeatedly fell asleep during eighteen million years and are now frightened to settle accounts. They are themselves negated by suffering which comes as healing compassion, and are negated by others in the course of intolerable inhuman encounter. Self-negation is shown by the timeless religion of responsibility and the hidden science of divine wisdom. The invisible sun in every man as the *Atman*, the spectator, ever radiates endless energy for the sake of all. According to this teaching, darkness is prior to what we call light; glamour or unwisdom is beginningless. It is what the ancients called Chaos, Gaia, or *Mahamaya*. There is a chaos prior to any cosmos. There are many myriads of systems, galaxies and galactic clusters in the vast spaces of the heavens, but if there were no primordial chaos one would be forever trapped within the same universe. Before Adam was Chaos, the primordial matter, in which is hidden the light that is the soundless sound. In the beginning was the Word. Primordial chaos is necessary for the universe, but whether we think it necessary or not, we have no choice. We are caught. We can get out, because we have in us the light that was hidden in the darkness, which lighteth up every man who comes into the world.

The Crest Jewel of Wisdom speaks only to those who are prepared to negate the world of appearances:

> Gaining at length human life, hard to win, and manhood, and an understanding of the revealed teachings, he who strives not for liberation in the Divine Self, deluded in heart, self-destroying, slays himself through grasping at the unreal. Who, then, is the very self of folly but he who, deluded, follows selfish purposes, after he had gained a human body and manhood hard to win? Even though they recite the scriptures, and sacrifice to the gods, and fulfil all works, and worship the divinities — without awakening to the unity of the Divine Self, liberation is not attained even in a hundred aeons.

From the standpoint of the Sage, the innumerable ways in which human beings are enmeshed in the *Mahamaya* are not very interesting. The Sage can recognize anyone who is fully awake behind a semi-sleepy projection. Those who really want to emerge from behind the false personal mask will receive what they deserve in mathematically exact proportion. This is a truth about consciousness on all planes. One must deserve to go beyond all the external forms and modes and, through the eternal soul-memory now awakened of the soundless sound behind the great vibrations of the universe, to light up in the lower mind a self-conscious reflection of the invisible sun that overbroods the egg.

Albert Einstein said there are no hitching posts in the universe. There are no boundaries except arbitrary and conventional ones assigned by human beings who happen to think that they occupy a fixed point of space and time, when in fact space is curved and time is relative. They do not understand the inner meaning of spatial coordinates and of clock time. Although there are no hitching posts, there are innumerable hooking points. When people really begin to enjoy the thought that at any point of space-time they could break out of the boundedness of the universe, they can experience through self-knowledge what they have forgotten. The ancients taught that God is a circle with its centre everywhere and circumference nowhere. Human beings can find in the inmost depths of abstract meditation an active centre of intense, motionless, joyous consciousness. Abiding in universal welfare and doing nothing, as beings of light they enjoy pure unmoving spiritual will in, through and independently of, all material vestures. Even if we somewhat understand all of this, it is still very difficult to light the lamp of discernment. The moment we think, "Let me do this," "May I be that," we only create karma and imprison ourselves. But the moment we say, "Let me begin," and also recognize that there is a chaos we cannot explain and that there are no hitching posts, then we begin like true pilgrims to walk along the Path. It leads to invisible summits lost in glorious Nirvanic light which may be glimpsed from foothills and mountains arduously climbed in cheerful enjoyment, although one is aware of the many pitfalls on the way. The only hooking points are found within. They form the seven-knotted bamboo staff of the ascetic. If you were a Montagnard you would cherish the serene strength of the individual and know what the Communards forget, that communities are doomed to fail from the start when men are afraid to be alone. At the same time, if a human being in distress came for help, the Montagnard will take care of him and then return to solitude.

The soul is ensnared through the power of misidentification in the chaos of primordial matter. If we enjoy narcissistically the illusions of the ever-changing reflective soul, then we forget the light of divine discernment, the Sleeping Beauty in the castle. She can only be awakened by Prince Charming, the androgynous *Manas*, the power of noetic thought, ideation and imagination. Real thinking has a self-sustaining quality determined by the grasp, the vision, the scope and the strength of the universal ideas that provide mental nourishment. When one truly begins to walk the inner Path, one does not need any reference point in external space and time, and can see the moment of birth as if it were this morning's dawn and can see the moment of death as if it were this evening's twilight. Thousands of previous lives seem like twinkling stars in the sky.

The real Gurus who truly know teach just by being themselves. They are self-existing, self-manifesting embodiments of the wisdom of compassion, crowned with the Crest Jewel of pure insight. Their very existence is testimony. Shankara spoke to disciples who were already free from the delusion of the *personal* 'I' but who were stuck in the illusion of the *individual* 'I.' His teaching is not about the hereafter, not about the now and then, not about the always and everywhere, but about That. The supreme affirmation is TAT TVAM ASI — 'That Thou Art'. That is the oldest teaching which Shankara explained by reference to reason, to experience, to states of consciousness, to vestures of matter in the fivefold classification, and also by references to madmen, *yogins* and free men. Universal self-awareness is the potential privilege and birthright of every human being, but no one can attain to it except by fulfilling the qualifications, embodying the conditions that approximate the posture and the position of a true learner.

The Crest Jewel could be in your hands. Use it, Shankara says, because by use you make it sufficiently your own to recognize that the greatest lies are 'I' and 'thou.' All amounts to an 'it' and 'it' equals THAT. THAT equals zero. Your sphere becomes luminous when you wholly adopt the standpoint of the Logos in the cosmos, God in man, and then enjoy the universe through every pair of eyes. Heal yourself, and others through yourself, by luminous thoughts and adamantine compassion.

The Gupta Vidya II, "The Crest Jewel", 132-134

ALL LEARNING IS RECOLLECTION

The vital essence of the Pythagorean teaching was to encourage the emergence of whole men and women. They cannot be manufactured, but must truly create themselves. Great Teachers assist in the self-production of whole human beings by making a holistic teaching come alive. Pythagoras was an originator of true science, religion and philosophy in the Near Eastern cycle which he initiated. The teaching of Pythagoras was also that of Buddha and later on of Shankara. Two thousand five hundred years ago Buddha taught his disciples first to become *shravakas,* listeners. When they had spent a sufficient time in listening and learning, as in the earlier Hindu tradition with its emphasis upon *brahmacharya,* a period of probation, then they could become *sramanas,* men of action. We find this also in the Pythagorean tradition, where neophytes are *acousticoi,* those who listen. This has reference not to something mechanical or rigid and therefore false, but to a balanced training in the art of perfecting through wisdom the conservation of energy. The purification of thought, the calming and harmonizing of feelings, was undertaken for the sake of the appropriate manifestation of the Inner Self through proper speech and fitting conduct.

Pythagoras taught a threefold division of humankind and a threefold division of desire. All men may be compared to people who attend a festival. There are those who are motivated by the love of gain and who go to buy and sell. There are those motivated by the love of honour and they go to compete with and emulate each other in attaining standards of excellence. Then there are those who are concerned with neither gain nor glory because they have either worn out these toys or thought through these illusions, or they are born with a natural indifference to them. Such are wholly concerned with the love of wisdom. Lovers of wisdom may be compared to those who at festivals are like spectators, not participating but at the same time not making external judgements, not buying and selling, not comparing and contrasting, but merely learning what is common to all men, learning something about the noble art of living. They do not do what is unnecessary. They try to find out what is intimated behind the forms in the vaster human drama in which all the world is a stage and men and women merely players. The play is the thing. Quiet attention is the beginning of the way to wisdom in the Pythagorean tradition.

Reincarnation, the philosophy of palingenesis, is also fundamental. Every human being has been involved as a spectator in a variety of spectacles, has played a multiple diversity of roles. In this perspective, all learning is recollection, and much of what is seen is the restoration of Soul-memory. What people think is new is mostly a recollection from where and whence they know naught, but which nonetheless acts as a divine prompting within them and sometimes saves them, in times of trouble and of trial, from making mistakes which would propel them further back than when they made them before, because by now they should have learnt something. The School which Pythagoras founded was one in which every kind of learning could be pursued, not for the purpose of integrating the isms and the sects of the time, but rather for coming down, from above below, so as to be able to see the synthesizing principles, in *theoria* and *praxis*, contemplation and conduct.

After the passing of Pythagoras, the pupils of his School separated out. Schisms ensued between the so-called scientific people, who spent their time making claims, arguing and attacking each other, and those who initially espoused simple enthusiasms and were mocked by the others. The latter were left solely with their disarming trust, faith and devotion, which helped to continue the transmission of the tradition. All of this was known in advance by that wise Promethean called Pythagoras. He wanted separation and self-selection to take place not only among the many who were influenced, but equally among the few who were experiencing the rigours of training, those who had the moral fibre to endure the extremely difficult ascent to wisdom. The claim that the path is easy is the facile excuse of those who do not truly intend to make the ascent, because they have failed many times before and are inwardly so terrified of failure before they start that they would rather not risk even the first test.

There is much protection in the time-tested moral codes of every true community of seekers. This is suggested in the proverbs and the folklore of all societies. Pythagoras taught that there must be an inward quiescence of the soul, a stilling of the mind in which the true receptivity of the heart can enable real learning to take place. A person concentrating while learning carpentry, or while training for athletics, is quiet. Individuals who concentrate while preparing and studying for anything are quiet. Could any less be required of a person who would study and persevere while seeking the divine science of the dialectic, as Hierocles called the Pythagorean teaching? The art of free ascent of the soul towards the upper realms, indicated in the concluding words of the *Golden Verses*, is portrayed as the unveiling of latent perceptions of realities that are hidden. Anyone who is in earnest must give Nature time to speak. It is only upon the serene surface of the unruffled mind that the visions gathered from the invisible may find true and proper representation.

The Gupta Vidya II, "Pythagoras and His School", 138-140

THE GLORIOUS VESTURE OF IMMORTALITY

There are different ways by which we could see in ourselves the embryo of that boundless love and compassion which is the fruit of self-knowledge at its height, where a man becomes self-consciously a universal embodiment of the Logos, having no sense of identity except in the very act of mirroring universal light.

There must be a tremendous integrity to a teaching and discipline which says that every step counts, that every failure can be used, and that the ashes of your failures will be useful in regrafting and rejuvenating what is like a frail tree that has to be replanted again and again. But the tree one is planting is the tree of immortality. One is trying to bring down into the lesser vehicles of the more differentiated planes of matter the glorious vesture of immortality, which showed more clearly when one was a baby, which one saluted in the first cry of birth, and of which one becomes somewhat aware at the moment of death.

There is a hint at the moments of birth and death, something like an intimation of the hidden glory of man, but during life one is not so awake. This becomes a problem of memory and forgetfulness. The chain of decline is started. It was classically stated in the second chapter of the *Gita*: "He who attendeth to the inclinations of the senses, in them hath a concern; from this concern is created passion, from passion anger, from anger is produced delusion, from delusion a loss of the memory, from the loss of memory loss of discrimination, and from loss of discrimination loss of all!" Every man is fragmenting himself, spending himself, limiting himself, finitizing himself, localizing himself, to such a degree, with such an intensity and irregularity, and such a frenetic, feverish restlessness, that he is consuming himself. Physiologically, we know that we cannot beat the clock time processes of the changes in the physical body. Therefore we cannot expect to find the elixir of immortality on the physical plane. But we all know that by attending to the very process of growth and change, and by awareness of what happens to us in sickness, that we do have some control and can make a difference by our very attitude and acceptance of the process. If you are very ill, by worrying about it you are going to make yourself worse, but there are people who are really quite ill, who by acceptance have gained something of the aroma of well-being.

These are everyday facts having analogues and roots in a causal realm of ideation and creative imagination which gives shape and form to the subtle vehicle, through which a transmission could take place of the immortal, indestructible and inexhaustible light of the Logos which is in every man and came into the world with every child. It is the radiance of Shekinah, the *nur* of Allah, the light of *St. John*. It is a light that looks like darkness and is not to be mistaken for those things that have a glamour on the sensory plane. To bring it down or make it transmit through the causal realm and become a living *tejas* or light-energy issuing forth from the fingers and all the windows and apertures of the human body is, of course, asking for a great deal. But what one is asking is meaningful, and we have got to try to understand.

The Gupta Vidya II, "Meditation and Self-Study", 309-310

THE INMOST SANCTUARY

Restoration of the right relationship between the Master in the inmost sanctuary and the incarnated consciousness is gained only through a sacrificial process of self-purification. Obscuring and polluting tendencies nurtured in the mind through its misuse over many lives must be removed by a self-chosen and self-administered therapy. Like the Pandava brothers exiled from their kingdom through their own folly, or like the master held prisoner in his own house by those who should be his servants in the parable of Jesus, the pristine divine ray of the Logos in man is trapped and stripped of its sovereign place in human life unless consciously sought by the aspirant. This invocation of wisdom through the supplication of the mind to the spirit was seen by the ancient Greeks as the cultivation of *sophrosyne* — the subordination of the inferior element to the superior. It is shown in *The Voice of the Silence* as the *shila* virtue — the attunement of thought, will and feeling to the pulsation of divine harmony, *Alaya-Akasha*. The mind stands as the critical link between the divine and the animal nature. The recovery and right use of the privilege of human existence depend upon the subordination of the elements of the lower *rupa* existence to the spiritual ideation of *Arupa Manas*.

The sacrificial posture and selfless motive required for this self-purification can be readily grasped through a telling analogy. There is not a modern metropolis which does not maintain the equipment needed to neutralize the effluvia of human waste and thereby reduce the danger of infection to its population. Similarly, a large number of devices are available, both to cities and to individuals, for the purpose of removing sediments and impurities from drinking water, through distillation, filtration and osmosis, to make it available in a purer and fresher form. With the human mind the same principles of public health and civic responsibility would require that each individual and every society strive to purify the muddy stream of human passions which pollute those coming into contact with it.

Every human being has received the crystalline waters of life in a pure and unsullied condition, and therefore everyone has the karmic responsibility for every failure to return these waters to the ocean of life in a pristine condition. Insofar as this responsibility has been neglected by individuals, under karma in successive lives they are self-condemned to immersion in the waters they themselves have poisoned. Under the laws of karma affecting the processes of reincarnation and the transmigration of life-atoms, individuals owe it to their neighbours and their descendants, as well as to themselves, to purify their mental emanations.

In practice, this implies a continuous cleansing of one's thoughts, one's words and one's actions; these in turn fundamentally depend upon the purification of the will. Unfortunately, purification of the will, which is vital to the spiritual regeneration of humanity, is itself seriously misunderstood as a consequence of the process of pollution of consciousness and magnetism. Mired in the morbid obscuration of higher consciousness, too many people suppose that a bolstering of the lower will is a means to survival. Nothing could be farther from the truth. The higher spiritual will does not itself need to be strengthened, but it may be released through the removal of obscurations and hindrances. So long as the will is activated by the individual only on behalf of passions and the illusion of the persona, that will is not worth having. Hence, many people have discovered that the will cannot be released on behalf of lesser purposes. This predicament is conspicuous in those diseased societies which place an inordinate emphasis upon the personal will. Will itself is a pure colourless principle which cannot be dissociated from the energy of the *Atman* released through breathing. Thus when human beings breathe benevolently, blessing others with every breath, they can release the beneficent will-energy of the *Atman*. As soon as the will is released on behalf of the personal ego, however, against other human beings, it is blunted. This inevitable paralysis of the antagonistic lower will is indeed a beneficent and therapeutic aspect of karma.

Viewed from a collective standpoint, many human beings can be seen as having been weakened because they have absorbed life-atoms from others who have misused spiritual knowledge and the potency of the higher will. Throughout the world perhaps one in ten persons has insistently used the will against other human beings in this or previous lives. This may have been for the sake of bolstering the insecure identity of the *persona* or, worse, through the misuse of spiritual knowledge connected with false meditation, indulgence in drugs and mediumistic practices. Since 1966 contemporary society has witnessed the emergence of a number of centres of pseudo-spiritual activity; now it is witnessing the inevitable psychological breakdown of many who were responsible for this moral pollution. The waves of spiritual influence initiated by the descent of Krishna offer golden opportunities to all souls, including those inverted natures self-blocked from inward growth by their own failures on the Path in previous lives. Amongst these there were some too cowardly to make a new beginning, who sought instead to compensate for their own weakness and delusion by cashing in on the currents of the 1975 Cycle. Having forfeited timely opportunities offered through compassion, they are self-destroyed when Krishna takes a firm stand on behalf of the entire human family because they are unable to generate a genuine concern for others. Never having generated an interest in the welfare of the vast majority of mankind, they are self-condemned. Sadly, they cast a long shadow over a much larger class of weaker souls who are affected by them, no doubt through their own delusions and vulnerabilities.

Persons are sometimes drawn into dangerous orbits of misused knowledge through loose talk about such sacred subjects as *kundalini, kriyashakti* and the activation of the higher spiritual centres in man. Ordinary people who enjoy a normal measure of spiritual health wisely avoid those places where they are likely to hear profane chatter. Through a natural sense of spiritual good taste they simply shun those places where self-deluded con men congregate to make a living off the gullible. Today, because the moral and spiritual requirements for participation in the humanity of the future have become more evident to many people, the market for such deceptive opportunism has begun to diminish. The America of P.T. Barnum, who said that a sucker is born every moment, has been replaced to a large extent by the America of Abraham Lincoln, where, as is well known, one cannot fool all the people all the time. Although many souls have to travel a great distance along the path of self-integration, they have learnt enough not to be duped by pseudo-spiritual blandishments. Just as they have learnt not to believe everything conveyed by the mass media and not to leap at every free offer or supermarket discount, they have also learnt to pass up invitations for instant development of *kundalini* and every facile promise of spiritual development that dispenses with the judicious control of the emotions and passions.

Even in the difficult area of sexuality the idea of strength through celibacy (e.g. Gabrielle Brown, *The New Celibacy*, 1980) has gained some currency amongst many people, young and old, who find the burden of ego-games and unequal experimentation intolerable. There is nothing wrong with the sacred act of communion and procreation, and as the ancient Jews believed, God is pleased when a man and a woman come together in true unison. Nor need this issue be obscured by pseudo-arguments concerning the Malthusian spectre of over-population. As the economist E.F. Schumacher pointed out, even if the entire population of the globe were concentrated in America, this would result in a population density no greater than that of Great Britain, a nation long noted for the spaciousness and greenery of its countryside. North America itself, over its ancient and almost entirely unwritten history, has supported many varied civilizations, some of which displayed a much greater spiritual maturity than is evidenced in its recent history. Broadly, one cannot understand the physical facts of life on earth, much less the spiritual facts of life, through a language of conflicting claims and counter-claims, rationalizations and compensatory illusions, or pseudo-sophisticated statistical arguments based upon a selfish and shallow view of the nature of the human psyche.

The purification and release of the will must be comprehended in terms of human individuality, and therefore must be considered in the light of the mystery of every human soul. Since this mystery encompasses an entire series of reincarnations extending over eighteen million years, it can only begin to be appreciated through careful consideration of the motley evidence offered by one's participation in varied states of consciousness in the present life. Any individual concerned to recover the spontaneity and benevolence of the spiritual will must be willing to examine courageously the manner and extent to which he or she has become the servant not of the divine Ego, but rather of the lower astral form and its attendant *incubi* and *succubi*.

> For this 'Astral' — the shadowy 'double' (in the animal as in man) is not the companion of the *divine* Ego but of the *earthly body*. It is the link between the personal SELF, the lower consciousness of *Manas* and the Body, and is the vehicle of *transitory, not of immortal life*. Like the shadow projected by man, it follows his movements and impulses slavishly and mechanically, and leans therefore to matter without ever ascending to Spirit.
>
> H.P. Blavatsky
> "Occultism Versus the Occult Arts"

Plato explains, in a myth in the *Timaeus*, that when the Demiurge was fashioning the form of man, he endowed the human body with a stomach. This was done, according to the myth, out of compassion because otherwise man, unlike the animal, would be in danger of eating continually. Not only would this be disastrous for human health, but it would needlessly preoccupy consciousness with the intake and elimination of physical food. If human consciousness is to mature fully, it cannot be preoccupied with the *persona*, with the stomach and the libido, with physical space, time and motion. Consciousness must be freed to contemplate eternal motion, boundless space and infinite duration. This liberation from the bonds of the *persona* cannot be accomplished all at once but must be attempted again and again, through persistent efforts over a lifetime of meditation.

The radical reorientation of consciousness, away from the *persona* and towards the Divine, requires ceaseless striving and unremitting patience. Such continuity cannot be sustained over a lifetime unless it can be sustained for a year or even a week. In this arena, where clean beginnings and steadiness of application are crucial, one may gain great help from the example of the good gardener, who comes again and again to tend seedlings and plants, and yet allows nature time to work its magic. In fact, people who actually do some planting can gain considerable benefit through the restoration of their contact with the earth and by gaining an organic sense of growth. They can learn that all life is sacred, including the human body, and that every form of life can and should be treated with due respect. To recover this lost sense of the inviolable integrity of nature, however, one must be able to insert oneself into the whole, gaining intimations of what it is like to be a single blade of grass in a field or a single tree in a vast forest. As a modest experiment one might go to a nursery and purchase a seed, a pot and some soil. If one asks properly, the clerk will give whatever instructions are necessary and then one can take these materials home, carefully and with respect. Then after planting the seed in the soil with humility and love, treating it not as a symbol but as life, one can set the pot firmly upright in a place prepared for it. Each day one can give to the growing plant what it requires by way of water and nourishment, but it is important to do this with an assurance and confidence that comes with humility before nature. Forgetting oneself and without anxiety, one can observe the process of organic growth. In doing this properly, one will also be sowing in oneself the seeds of a new confidence rooted not in fear, not in deceit, but rather in fearlessness and truth, the source of authentic humility.

The Gupta Vidya II, "The Inmost Sanctuary", 357-360

ABANDONING THE *ANTASKARANA*

It is only through the Guru that the chela has the golden opportunity of lighting up 'the Nachiketas flame' of discernment and daring. Once lit, it must be sedulously guarded and tended by the chela, and eventually fanned into the fire of wisdom-sacrifice *(jnana yajna)* which gives light to all and takes from none. Established on this hoary Path, a stage will definitely come when all indifference to earthly reward will be natural and easy. In the *Katha Upanishad* Nachiketas simply could not see the point of the glittering gifts Yama, the god of death, offered him: riches, kingship, kingdoms and earthly happiness. All these had no meaning for Nachiketas because he knew too well the deceptive trappings of a life he had long since outgrown. He sought only the secret of immortality, and was unreservedly willing to honour the privilege of receiving the secret and retaining it with constant gratitude. Every skill and faculty is needed while climbing the steep mountain precipices of the secret Path. It must never be forgotten that all the needed resources are within oneself, and they will all have to be summoned and utilized, on this razor-edged Path. Having heard about the Path and having grasped that one cannot evade this recognition, however partial or fleeting, one must see the profound sense in which the Path is difficult to tread.

The powerful metaphors — indeed the entire parable — of the *Katha Upanishad* have manifold layers and levels of meaning, all pointing to the secret spiritual heart. In *The Voice of the Silence* the Paramita Path is connected with *antaskarana*, the inward bridge between the impersonal and personal selves. The time will come when the seeker must choose between the two, for either must prevail. One cannot both be upon the Path and also maintain the absurd but prevalent misconception that there is a personal entity inside oneself, a 'ghost in the machine', to whom things are happening and who is holding the reins in life's journey. This is the root illusion in the eyes of enlightened seers; no such entity really exists; there is only a bundle of propensities and reflexes, images and fantasies. The concatenation of elemental entities comprising the shadowy self are engaged in their own activity, propelled by the *gunas* expounded in the closing chapters of the *Bhagavad Gita*. The evanescent and everchanging personality may cling to the illusory misconception that it is acting freely, but it is no more than a congeries of numerous life-atoms pursuing their own predetermined proclivities. The celebrated metaphor of the chariot, also deployed in Plato's *Phaedrus*, is given a vast extension in the *Katha Upanishad* as it is applicable to cosmic as well as to human activity. The *Katha Upanishad* may be seen not only as a philosophical dialogue, but also as an alchemical text, replete with deeply evocative, enigmatic and magical mantrams.

At some point one must mentally let go of the route by which one has come, what Gautama Buddha called the Raft and *The Voice of the Silence* terms the *antaskarana* bridge. This letting go is depicted in the image of the complete sacrifice *(mahasmashana)* of the 'assemblage of sins' and the *namarupa* (name and form) to the impersonal, immortal Self upon the altar of the secret heart. For a *Manasa* to be engaged in embodied existence means that an impersonal cosmos has made an immense sacrifice. This is symbolized physically by the sacrifice of the father giving of his life-essence, and mentally by the magnanimous sacrifice of a great being giving freely of his spiritual essence so that evolution may go on. It is also evident in the noble sacrifice of the mother who, over a period of painful gestation, gives everything to the astral body *(linga sharira)* of the soul coming into the world, just as the maternal matrix of *Akasha* nourishes the embryo of the globe. The impersonal has sacrificed for the sake of manifestation on the personal plane. This must be deliberately reversed through an intense awareness of what one owes to one's father, mother, and all one's teachers, especially to one's spiritual parents and preceptors. The conscious reversal involves taking everything one has, with all one's powers and limitations, and readily sacrificing it for the sake of the self-conscious re-emergence on the plane of manifestation of the inward god, the inner sovereign, who otherwise would remain the silent Self. One must allow that Self within, who is no different from the Self of all, to assume divine kingship within the human estate.

No one can tap the highest resources without becoming secure enough to want nothing for the puny, shadowy self. Moved solely by desires that elevate the whole of humanity and the entirety of creation, and established in that proper mental posture, one can abandon the *antaskarana* bridge, because one can re-create it at will. Seeing one's personal self as no different from other personal selves, one can do the bidding of the divine through the instrumentality of anything in Nature, including, therefore, the use of one's *persona*, in which one has renounced absolutely all proprietary interest. Becoming aware of the life-atoms in one's vesture, one realizes that there is no such thing as the 'personal self' save in a metaphorical sense. Life-atoms are constantly streaming in and out as part of the ceaseless spiritual transmutation of matter on seven planes and the awesome law of sacrifice within the seven kingdoms of Nature. The true *hotri* or hierophant is an initiated alchemist able to send forth beneficent emanations through a mighty current of concentrated thought, mystic meditation, noetic vision and unconditional compassion, consciously quickening the upward movement of all the available life-atoms. To such a sage or magus, the *antaskarana* Path does not have its former significance, except as a drawbridge to be extended at will in the service of universal welfare.

The Gupta Vidya II, "The Nachiketas Flame", 376-378

ENDLESS REGENERATION

. . . infinity is actually mirrored in the infinitesimal. One can get a sense of depth, not merely by expansion or by elevation of consciousness, but also by intense concentration upon what is near at hand. Hence in yogic practices such as those given in the *Bhagavad Gita,* emphasis is given to concentration upon the point between the eyes as a starting point for meditation. In the thirteenth chapter, Shri Krishna points out that Deity, which seems so far away, is also closer than anything else. This sense of the closeness of Deity is something one can experience in human life when one is privileged to be present either at the birth of a baby or at the deathbed of a human soul who is leaving the body. At such moments and at other times in life — at solemn ceremonies, joyous festivals, and sometimes in fleeting moments in human relationships — one can experience a depth of feeling, of self-transcendence and self-forgetfulness, of pure joy and serenity, which is healing, calming and soothing to the soul. The influence of these intimations of immanent immortality is so real that in such moments one can feel the touch of the divine.

All of this is expressed in the great metaphor of Kalahansa, sometimes translated as 'the Swan in and out of time'. Kalahansa is black, representing Divine Darkness, the plenum of all potentiality. Imagine a mighty cosmic bird with black wings which correspond to infinity and eternity. Although at rest, that same bird emanates or emerges as a white bird in space and time. Kalahansa in eternity is behind Kalahansa in time. This powerful metaphor represents the descent of Dhyanis from Divine Darkness — from what seems to be motionless absolute stillness — into the world of Becoming, where there is rhythmic motion amidst burgeoning life, growth, decay and death, but also endless regeneration. Kalahansa stands for all the endless cycles *(Kalachakra)*: the cycles of the seasons, the cycles of the year, the cycles represented by the revolutions of the planets, but also the cycles of day and night and the cycles that human beings experience — in sleeping and waking, in living and dying, in birth and death and rebirth.

In all the vast cycles of time and manifestation, there is a representation of a certain rhythm which itself is a reflection of the inbreathing and the outbreathing of the Great Bird. Even when still and motionless, it is breathing in and breathing out. This means that there is an analogue to physical breathing in mental breathing, in the breathing of the organs and centres of the subtle vestures, and even a kind of spiritual breathing. There is also a diastolic and systolic movement in the spiritual heart that is only dimly reflected in the diastole and systole of the physical heart, beautiful and wondrous as it is. Therefore, in the very act of being alive there is a gratitude for life itself. There is in life itself an ultimate form of worship, piety and prayer, of celebration and reverence for the divine. This is the basis of all folk cultures, as well as all the festive gatherings of human beings over thousands upon thousands of years, where the birth or death of one being is greeted as relevant to all. There is a recognition, but also a transcendence, an insertion and immersion, of what is deeply significant and sacred in the lives of individuals into the great stream of collective life, and ultimately into the unending stream of the universal pilgrimage of humanity.

The Gupta Vidya II, "Kalahansa and Kalachakra", 401

APPENDIX III

SELECTED PASSAGES FROM THE PILGRIMAGE OF HUMANITY ~ VOLUME III OF *THE GUPTA VIDYA*

REINCARNATION AND SPIRITUAL REBIRTH

Just as the global rebirth of humanity mirrors the archetypal birth of humanity in the Third Root Race, so too the authentic spiritual renewal of every human being reflects and resonates with the wider cycle of the race. Prior to physical birth each monad has had the meta-psychological experience of being catapulted into what the Orphics called the tomb of the soul, but also that which the Ionians regarded as the temple of the human body. And whilst every baby enters the world voicing the AUM, each with a unique accent and intonation, it is given to very few to end their lives with the sacred Sound. This is the difference which human life makes, with its saga of fantasy and forgetfulness. What one sensed in one's pristine innocence at the moment of birth and which is witnessed through the enigmatic sounding of the Word becomes wholly obscured by the time of death unless one has deliberately and self-consciously sought out the path leading to spiritual rebirth. Through the complex processes of karmic precipitation and conscious and unconscious exercise of the powers of choice, each human being differentiates from others, self-selecting his or her own destiny. To minimize the dangers to the soul and to maximize the continuity of spiritual self-consciousness between the commencement and close of incarnation, one must learn to look back and forwards over the entire span of a lifetime, breaking it up into successive septenary cycles and their sub-phases. All cycles participate in birth, in adolescence, in slow and painful maturation, in the shedding of illusions, and in a sort of death or disintegration leading to new beginnings. In some portions of the globe the wheel revolves so rapidly that most human beings have been through many lives within one lifetime, and though this poignant fact is little understood by other persons, even those who experience it acutely do not think through its implications.

One cannot really comprehend such primal verities without silent contemplation. As Krishna hinted in the *Uttara Gita*, every time one opens one's mouth, the astral shadow is lengthened. In the demanding discipline of preparation for spiritual rebirth, there are very few who could hope to match or even approach the example of the Kanchipuram Shankaracharya, who perfected his *svadharma* over the past half century, provided sagely counsel to myriad devotees, and then retreated under a vow of silence. There is evidently a Himalayan difference between mighty Men of Meditation and the motley host of deluded mortals called fools by Puck in *A Midsummer Night's Dream*. Nevertheless, the folly of mortals is largely a protected illusion. If a human being knew from the age of seven everything that was going to happen in his or her life from that moment to the time of death, life would be intolerably difficult. Similarly, if one knew exactly what tortures one had committed or connived at in the time of the Inquisition or elsewhere in the history of the world – and there is no portion of the globe which has not witnessed terrible misdeeds – it would be very hard to avoid being overwhelmed by such knowledge. Every human being has at times, like Pilate, opted out of responsibilities upon the unrecorded scenes of history. Whilst all, like Ivan in Dostoevsky's *The Brothers Karamazov*, would like to think of themselves as holding to the principle that it is never justifiable to harm even a single child, each person bears the heavy burden of karmic debts, every one of which will have to be repaid in full before the irreversible attainment of conscious immortality is feasible.

To begin to raise such questions about oneself is to realize that they cannot be answered in the utilitarian calculus of the age of commerce, which is the only crude morality of the market-place. Many people simply refuse to be priced, bought and sold or even appraised, in terms of market values or competitive criteria, especially in a time of spurious inflation. One has indeed to find out what is one's own true value. One must gain an inward recognition of the elusive truth of the axiom, "To thine own self be true . . . and thou canst not then be false to any man." Looking at the whole of one's life in terms of what one feels is the truest thing about oneself, one must search out the deepest, most abiding hope that one holds, apart from all fantasy myths. For most human beings, this hope is much the same. It is the hope to conclude one's life without being a nuisance or hindrance to others. It is the wish to finish one's life without harming other human beings, but making some small contribution to the sum-total of good, so that at the moment of death one may look back over life and feel that one has lived the best one knew how.

Broadly, too many human beings torture themselves with an appalling amount of useless guilt, owing to their utter lack of knowledge of the mathematics of the soul. Just as it is useless and unconstructive to become guilty or evasive about one's checkbook balance, because the figures do not lie and the facts cannot be denied, it is equally fruitless and destructive to become immersed in guilt-fantasies with regard to one's whole life. Even a little knowledge of the relevance of simple mathematics to the realm of meta-psychology can save one from recurring though needless despair. Every attempt to blot out awareness of responsibility for karma through giving way to emotional reactions obscures the impersonal continuity of one's real existence and is an insult to the divine origin of one's self-consciousness.

> In each of us that golden thread of continuous life – periodically broken into active and passive cycles of sensuous existence on Earth, and super-sensuous in Devachan – *is* from the beginning of our appearance upon this earth. It is the *Sutratma*, the luminous thread of immortal *impersonal* monadship, on which our earthly lives or evanescent *Egos* are strung as so many beads – according to the beautiful expression of Vedantic philosophy. . . Without this principle – the emanation of the very essence of the pure divine principle *Mahat* (Intelligence), which radiates direct from the *Divine mind* – we would be surely no better than animals.
>
> *The Secret Doctrine*, ii 513

In order to insert one's own efforts to recover this Mahatic awareness into the regeneration of humanity by the Mahatmas and the Avatar, one must learn to work first with the cycles of the seasons of nature. The period of fourteen days beginning with the winter solstice and culminating on the fourth of January, which is sacred to Hermes-Budha, may be used as a period of *tapas* for the sake of generating calm and sacrificial resolves. The precious time between January and March may be spent in quiet inward gestation of the seeds of the coming year. Care needs to be taken if one is to avoid excess and idle excitement at the time of the vernal equinox and deceptive dreams about the carefree, indolent summer. From March until June there is an inevitable and necessary descent into manifestation, but if the summer solstice is to find one prepared for the season of flourishing, one must not give way to the extravagances of anticipation and memory. If one observes this solstice with one's resolves intact, then one is in a good position to maintain inward continuity, free from wastefulness and fatigue, until the onset of autumn. Then arriving at the autumnal equinox, not having accumulated a series of debts and liabilities owing to lost opportunities and forgotten resolves, one will be able to maintain the critical detachment needed to participate in the season of withdrawal and regeneration, culminating in the return of the winter solstice.

By setting oneself realistic goals and working with the rhythms of nature, it is possible over a period of seven years to nurture within oneself the seedlings of the virtues – "the nurslings of immortality" – needed to become a true servant of the Servants of Humanity. Owing to the dual nature assumed by *Mahat* when it manifests and falls into matter as self-consciousness, it is necessary to correct for the terrestrial attractions of the moon of the mind if one would recover the illumination of the solar power of understanding. As Longfellow said, one may hit the mark by aiming a little bit above the mark because every arrow feels the earth's gravity. One must allow for the sagging or declination of the curve, but whilst one allows for it, one must not hesitate to resolve with inner strength and cool confidence.

Spiritual rebirth initially means being born again with new eyes and with the ability to see each successive year and cycle as truly new. This noetic perspective can be gained only by linking each year or cycle with its predecessors, not in detail but in essence. And infallibly, if one is able to live consciously and self-consciously throughout the cycles and seasons of life, one will be able to use the thread of continuity at the moment of death. *Sutratma-Buddhi* thus becomes *Manas-Sutratman,* and both arise through the fiery, Fohatic energy of the *Mahat-Atman.*

Those who are serious about engaging in spiritual self-regeneration in the service of others could begin with the simplest assumption: death is inevitable but the moment of death is uncertain. This is in no wise a morbid or gloomy assumption, for death always comes as a deliverer and a friend to the immortal soul. If one can remotely resonate to the words of Krishna and feel in the invisible heart the ceaseless vibration of one's essential immortality, then one will understand that being born is like putting on clothes and dying is like taking them off. At this point in human evolution it is too late to indulge in body identification along with its consequent denial of the ubiquity of death and suffering for mortal vestures. It is a mark of spiritual maturity to recognize that human life involves risk and pain. Were it otherwise, it could hold no promise. Even if one is not yet prepared for the Himalayan heights of spiritual mountain climbing, nonetheless, one may begin to discern and hearken to the light of daring that burns in the heart. Whatever one's mode of self-measurement, that measure should be in favour of what is strong, what is true, what is noble and what is beautiful in oneself. All the Avatars concur in the strength of affirmation that the spirit is willing, even though the flesh is weak. Unlike the preachers of discouragement who emphasize the element of weakness in the flesh, the true prophets of the divine destiny of mankind place the stress upon the willingness of the spirit.

The Gupta Vidya III, "The Rebirth Of Humanity", 21-24

INTENSIFY YOUR IDEAL THOUGHTS

Owing to the relentless pressure of the age, it is more and more necessary to abjure separative thinking and join the larger perspective of the majority of mankind. The intensity of the struggle happily compels individuals to choose. Those who pretend to remain indifferent to the prospects of the future only doom themselves to the "arid wastes of matter . . . to vegetate there through a long series of lives, content henceforth with feverish hallucinations instead of spiritual perceptions, with passions instead of love, with the rind instead of the fruit." Unless they scorn selfish assumptions, they will come to resemble the squirrel on its ceaselessly revolving wheel, whirling round and round chewing the nut of nihilism. But once spiritual starvation and material satiety move them to forget self, they will recognize the necessity of an intellectual and moral reform. The privilege of beginning this fundamental reform within oneself, and working for its fulfilment on behalf of other human beings, is extended by the Brotherhood of Bodhisattvas to every true friend of the human race.

> This reform cannot be accomplished except through Theosophy and, let us say it, Occultism, or the wisdom of the East. Many are the paths leading to it, but Wisdom is forever one. Artists foresee it, those who suffer dream of it, the pure in spirit know it. Those who work for others cannot remain blind before its reality even though they do not always know it by name. It is only the light-headed and empty-minded, the selfish and vain drones deafened by the sound of their own buzzing, who can ignore this high ideal.
>
> H.P. Blavatsky
La Revue Theosophique, March 1889

Whilst many have dreamt of ideal wisdom, some actually know it. They know it in their bones and in their blood; they have tested and tasted it; they have found that it works, and made it the basis of their thought and their lives. In the best cases, they have made it the basis of their unlimited devotion to the interests of others, and in the unselfishness of their service they have become invulnerable and indifferent towards the world and its evanescent opinions.

This is a very high state indeed. But in contemplating it, one should not fall prey to self-recrimination and recurring doubt. To do so would only reaffirm the contagious materialism that one wishes to leave behind. It does not matter at what level a human being approaches Divine Wisdom. Even if one can embody only one percent of the ideal, one must hold fast to the conviction that what is real in oneself and can be realized in practice is the only element that truly counts. This alone must be taken as the focus of one's concentration. Whilst it is always possible at any given time to say that one can only do so much, and no more, it is also always possible to enjoy and contemplate the ideal in meditation. The ideal can, and must, be separated from the limitations of incarnated existence. Thus, two different types of development emerge. First of all, one is intensifying through devotion to the ideal the architectonics of one's thought with regard to the ideal. This will be elaborated in *devachan* after death in the celestial condition of dreams of goodwill and creativity which can cut grooves in the *karana sharira*, the causal body, and affect lives to come. At the same time, one may recognize in other aspects of the vestures, particularly in the *linga sharira* or astral form, that one is unfortunately enslaved by many habits.

Under the karmic curve of the present life, one cannot enormously increase one's power of concentration however much one tries, because one lacks the strength to resist negative forces. Therefore, whilst maximizing development within the present lifetime, individuals must also recognize how little they can do and consequently how modest and honest they must be in the day to day walk of life. By understanding this dual process affecting both the present life and future lives, one can awaken a balanced courage and a spirit of unconditionality in one's commitment to an ideal.

> To take the first step on this ideal path requires a perfectly pure motive; no frivolous thought must be allowed to divert our

eyes from the goal; no hesitation, no doubt must fetter our feet. Yet, there are men and women perfectly capable of all this, and whose only desire is to live under the aegis of their Divine Nature. Let these, at least, have the courage to live this life and not to hide it from the sight of others! No one's opinion could ever be above the rulings of our own conscience, so, let that conscience, arrived at its highest development, be our guide in all our common daily tasks. As to our inner life, let us concentrate all our attention on our chosen Ideal, and let us ever look *beyond* without ever casting a glance at the mud at our feet.

Ibid.

It may be natural enough and even nutritionally sound for children to eat a little dirt, but it is unnatural and unhealthy for adults to savour the mentally negative or psychically muddy. They must rather train themselves always to look beyond, towards the stars and towards the future. By gazing towards the radiant though distant summit of enlightenment, they can keep their heads above the waters of chaos. By learning to float, by learning to tread water, they can begin to swim, and even to deal with the shifting tides of the psychic nature. Under karma, these forces work differently for different people. Some can concentrate on that which is universal and impersonal for long periods of time; others find that they cannot do so for more than a few minutes at a time. Again, the length of meaningful meditation is less important than the authenticity of the attempt. The more one can calmly accept the limits of one's abilities, the more those limits will expand. Here as everywhere the greater one's application the greater one's results. And like many physical habits, these mental exercises must be established at an early age. What is easy for the young is not so easy for the old. If one acquires healthy mental habits whilst young one should be grateful for the auspicious karma. If one does not recognize the need for a mental reform until later in life, again, one should be grateful for the recognition itself, as for the counsel required to carry out the reform. One must desire reform, and having embarked upon it, persevere with courage. One must become a true friend of oneself and strive without guilt, enjoying progress, without falling into the anxious traps that began with 'original sin'. Like Job, one must learn that one's burden is neither greater nor less than one can bear, and thus become receptive to every form of good.

The Gupta Vidya III, "The Aquarian Tide", 28-30

THE IMPERISHABLE SOUL-MEMORY

In the ancient and archetypal view of noetic magic, there is a summoning from latency to active potency of arcane knowledge that was originally impressed in the imperishable soul-memory of all humanity. Going all the way back to the middle of the Third Root Race, when self-consciousness had been attained, human beings were in astral vestures that were capable of effortless and benevolent use of the spiritual senses. Human beings, therefore, through their intuitive knowledge of the correlations of sound, colour and number, were able to communicate effortlessly. In that Golden Age, shrouded in the myths and mists of antiquity, they showed spontaneous reverence to Magus-Teachers, Hierophant-Adepts moving openly among human beings, teaching in fabled "concord groves" all over the earth. Seated under banyan trees (varieties of *ficus religiosa*), they bestowed divine wisdom upon those who were ready to learn. In that idyllic time the vast human inheritance of spiritual wisdom and scientific magic was assimilated into the *karana sharira*, the permanent vesture of the monad. It is in that inmost vesture, which is the container of all soul-memories, that the original wisdom and theurgy of humanity lie latent to this day.

It is suggestive and significant that contemporary physicists, like Roger Jones, have come to see that a great deal of what is known in particle physics and quantum mechanics points to a necessary transcendence of conventional space and time. This is strikingly reminiscent of the recondite concept of the *karana sharira*. A few intuitive scientists find the idea of such a causal field or morphogenetic matrix intensely meaningful because it intimates modes of action that are independent of many of the restrictions that hold in ordinary space and time. Because it allows for what would appear from a physical standpoint to be simultaneous transmission, it suggests the operation of laws very different from those applicable to the objective-seeming world of disparate material entities. Hence, it may have application or relevance to some of the energy fields and the "broken symmetry" that pertain to fundamental particles. Considered in relation to noetic consciousness and benevolent magic, the significance of the *karana sharira* is that it is the ground of the latent knowledge called to active potency by Hermes.

Hermes is the paradigm of the oldest sacred tradition, going back a million years ago to India *(Bharata Dwipa)*. There, among the Initiates, the basis was laid in all the Mystery Schools for the manasic development of the seminal civilizations of the Fifth Race. When the most creative minds of the Aquarian Age gain a sufficient knowledge of Sanskrit, they will come to see that all latter-day sciences are but pale and poor fragments compared with the systematic ontology and epistemology of *Brahma Vidya, Theosophia* or *Dzyan*. With reference to astronomy, to physics, physiology and to chemistry, to the mathematical and geometrical sciences, even to mechanics, transmission devices and aerial transport, the lost knowledge of the ancients was overwhelming. Some of this knowledge, still accessible through scattered texts, is being slowly recovered today by remarkable young scholars like David Pingree, who has dedicated his life to the translation of available Sanskrit texts in astronomy. This is only one small field within a vast body of information, but by the end of the century many such texts should be accessible to those who can effectively use them.

The foreshortened view of the emergence and growth of civilization which has characterized the last two hundred years is rooted in a habit of mind extending back over a period of some two thousand years, but nonetheless a minor incident in human evolution. Historians tend to focus upon the material aspects of civilization and cultures, to become obsessed with power and violence; yet since a nation's spiritual decline accompanies its material ascent, such a truncated approach can only distort the truth and mislead the unwary. Any attempt to account for this messianic history of recent millennia must begin fundamentally with a recognition that many human souls were badly scarred in decadent Atlantis, and, having lost the Third Eye, were left merely with an external sense of power connected to a crude conception of energy which still mesmerizes them through awe of tangible bigness and gross strength.

This is reminiscent of Plato's memorable reference to the contest between the Gods and the Giants. Whilst such events go back far beyond even the declining period of Egyptian dynasties, it does not, after all, characterize the entire million-year history of the Fifth Root Race. Certainly, such a shrunken perspective does little or no justice to the more than eighteen million years of human existence on this globe, or to the immeasurable reservoir of soul-memories garnered in the earliest golden ages. Every major culture reflects, to some degree, these finest and persistent intuitions in human beings. That is what gives many people a kind of reverence, however confused, before the Native Americans and other so-called 'primitive' peoples. Even if many of these cultures have lost their spiritual knowledge, and so have fallen to the mercy of inferior races, these same Monads may yet recover and re-enact their wisdom in future civilizations.

This process has recurred again and again. It was played out before the days of Magna Graecia in events that were encapsulated by Herodotus in his brief work, *Euterpe*. Therein he acknowledged the debt of gratitude that the Greeks owed to the grand Egyptian civilization which preceded it. This is even more explicit in Plato, who made Socrates speak of Solon, and the great Egyptian teachers of Sais, next to whom the Greeks were as little children. Yet whilst the reverence of Herodotus for predecessors was genuine, and expressed with almost religious awe, he also wrote that more familiar kind of historical narrative through which he is known as the "Father of History". In an often overlooked passage, he commended the Persians for their exemplary bravery and sense of truth, which, he said, were lacking among the Greeks. The courage to tell the truth and stand by it, the sense of the sacredness of a man's word of honour – these, he thought, were virtues that the Greeks could learn from the ancient Persians.

At the same time, however, Herodotus, in dealing with the Persian legal system, began to generate some of the snobbery that long prevailed among Athenians when they contemplated their *polis* and its democratic institutions. Through dramatized contrasts with the corrupt despotism of Persian institutions, Herodotus managed to compress, and devalue, the scope and successive phases of Persian civilization. In virtually every subsequent account of the supposed history of ancient civilizations, this same compression is found compounded. It arises because of decadence and the disappearance from active human memory of the greatest epochs of antiquity. This has led to the extraordinary and confusing conclusion that all the collective knowledge of the human race can somehow be made readily available to the common man. Some even insist that the less one knows, the more one has a right to demand all and sundry information.

This puny standpoint is seriously threatened by the fact that the seminal periods of human evolution are hidden and secret, and yet span millions of years which are inaccessible except through initiation. The profoundest truths were never written about in popular chronicles. They were available only in glyphs and symbols, in monuments, in secret libraries in central Asia and elsewhere. They were not for the eyes of curious crowds. In any event, even ordinary people in more mature cultures have a natural reticence about spiritual wisdom. Just as, in old age, those beset by a sense of failure, a fear of death and a feeling of audience deprivation seek refuge in reminiscence, so too cultures grow infatuated with telling their inflated history only after they have begun to decay. They become compulsively autobiographical, repeatedly retelling their life story. The truly creative, mindful of the enormous potency of mathematical and spiritual knowledge, are careful to protect that knowledge. They will make it available to those who can use it constructively; but they will keep it away from those who may abuse it, delude others and harm themselves.

The Gupta Vidya III, "Aquarian Civilization", 34-36

REINCARNATION AND CYCLIC EVOLUTION

In order to tap the vast potential of soul-wisdom in any single epoch of human evolution, it is vital to retain a reverential standpoint towards the known and the unknown, as well as towards That which is inherently Unknowable. At all times human beings seem to be surrounded by clusters of familiar objects and inexplicable events. Yet, with a minimal degree of introspection, individuals may discern that their mundane experience is largely conditioned by habitual states of consciousness. If they remain sensitive to the ebb and flow of the tides of earthly existence, yet aware of the strange illusion of temporal succession, they may ardently seek to reach beyond conventional norms of logic and morality so as to establish a firm foundation for cognition and conduct. Within the limits of every epoch, individuals foster an ideal image of themselves and formulate diverse strategies for the attainment of goals in different sectors of human life. Depending upon the clarity and care with which the ideal of excellence is pursued, it can exercise a civilizing influence upon individuals, cultures and societies. Whilst much of human striving and motivation may be comprehended within the scope of dominant civilizations and their goals, a more fundamental perspective is needed to understand the rise and fall of long-lived cultures.

The intuitive seeker of Gupta Vidya turns to the cryptic teaching of cyclic evolution, suspended between the impenetrable mystery of *Parabrahm* and the pivotal laws of karma and reincarnation. Affirming the immeasurable ontological abundance of TAT in the infinitudes of space and the triple hypostases of the *Atman* as the universal basis of harmonious manifestation, Gupta Vidya portrays cyclic evolution as encompassing incremental degrees of self-knowledge and self-regeneration, and at the same time affording illimitable refinement in the noetic apprehension of cosmic order and justice. In practice this means that the elements of mystery and discipline – wisdom and method, symbolized by the Tibetan bell and *dorje* – are correlative components of human growth and experience. No single testament of wisdom can embrace the exhaustless potential of TAT. And yet, not even a glimmering of spiritual insight is without value in the pursuit of universal good. Each successive phase of manifest existence, whether of individual Monads or of the entire human race, is new and unprecedented in a Heraclitean sense. Yet, every unfolding moment epitomizes the vast sum-total of the past, is replete with the rich potential of the future, and evanescently bubbles upon the infinite ocean of eternity.

When probing the meaning and significance of the Aquarian Age or any of the major and minor cycles of human evolution, it is helpful to retain a sense of mystery as well as an undaunted resolve to sift essential insights gleaned through an alert Manasic intelligence, whilst shedding vested illusions. The potential mystery pervading the present epoch is archetypally represented by *soma*, and the formative forces of the emerging cosmopolis may be glimpsed through contemplating the zodiacal transition from the Piscean to the Aquarian Age. *Soma* is the arcane symbol of initiation. The zodiacal ages indicate the alchemical transmutation of the meta-psychological elements underlying formative change. If initiation is to be understood as individuation through the universalization of consciousness, it must also be retained intact with increasing continuity of consciousness through the etherealization and specialization of the vestures needed for effective incarnation.

The alchemical significance of these interrelated processes was suggested by H.P. Blavatsky in her gnostic interpretation of the cosmogonic myths of Chaldea, Egypt, Greece and, above all, India. Each points to the physico-chemical principle of primordial creation:

> The first revelation of the Supreme Cause in its triple manifestation of spirit, force, and matter; the divine *correlation*, at its starting-point of evolution, allegorized as the marriage of *fire* and water, products of electrifying spirit, union of the male

active principle with the female passive element, which become the parents of their tellurian child, cosmic matter, the *prima materia*, whose spirit is ether, the ASTRAL LIGHT!

Isis Unveiled I, 156

Shiva, as Dakshinamurti, the Hierophant of Hierophants, descends from the empyrean in a pillar of fire, and remains aloof and invulnerable like the world-mountain Meru, an allegorical representation of primal cosmogony.

Within the mysterious recesses of the mountain – the matrix of the universe – the gods (powers) prepare the atomic germs of organic life, and at the same time the life-drink, which, when tasted, awakens in man-matter the man *spirit*. The *soma*, the sacrificial drink of the Hindus, is that sacred beverage. For, at the creation of the *prima materia,* while the grossest portions of it were used for the physical embryo-world, the more divine essence of it pervaded the universe, invisibly permeating and enclosing within its ethereal waves the newly-born infant, developing and stimulating it to activity as it slowly evolved out of the eternal chaos.

Isis Unveiled I, 156

Like the swans who separate milk from water, seekers of Gupta Vidya must learn to distil the divine *Akashic* essence out of the matrix of organic elements. The process of distillation takes place within the alembic of noetic consciousness and the secret sanctuary in the temple of the human form, not in any terrestrial location.

A genuine understanding of the awakening of the "man spirit" could begin with a calm consideration of the extraordinary commencement of human activity on this globe over eighteen million years ago. At the time of the initial lighting up of Manasic self-consciousness, there was an awakening of the potent fires of self-knowledge in all human beings. This sacred heritage has enabled the immortal soul to maintain intact its sutratmic thread throughout myriads of lives upon earth. It is the continuity of this spiritual thread that enables individuals to learn and recollect in any lifetime. None of the facile theories of behavioural conditioning or social imitation can account for the elusive mystery inherent in the infant's learning of a language. Still less can they satisfactorily explain xenoglossy. Many little children spontaneously speak ancient and forgotten tongues, including those which are not even found in exhaustive glossaries of modern languages.

Dr. Ian Stevenson, in his fascinating study of xenoglossy, has investigated a number of such cases, including that of a child in New York who spoke a language which simply could not be readily identified, but which, on detailed investigation, was found to be a long unspoken tongue from Central Asia. Similarly, in other studies concerning what often seem to be the nonsensical sounds of babies, it has been shown that what looked like nonsense had a definite meaning. Not only are there significant patterns in the sounds made by infants all over the world, but there are also recurrent features in a wide variety of children's games, which often seem simple, but are often more complex than adult sports. The significance of all such evidence for a universal grammar independent of cultures is sharpened by consideration of the work of Noam Chomsky in philosophic linguistics. Chomsky has effectively shown that there is no sound evidence to suggest that in learning the alphabet children are actually being conditioned from the outside. Rather, it seems as if there is a kind of innate response to sounds on the part of infants. The learning of language essentially provides a telling example of how children bring back memories from other lives. More broadly, all knowledge is recollection in a Socratic sense. In alchemical terms, the signature of language is found in the Soul, and the sigils are learnt in childhood.

The relationship between sutratmic continuity and present learning is likely to remain obscure unless one is ready to probe deeply into the simplest things of life. For example, whilst it may seem easy to learn to walk, anyone who has ever made the effort to teach a cat or dog to walk on two legs would soon discover that it is exceedingly difficult. Circus trainers are able to get four-legged animals to walk like two-legged human beings for short lengths of time. With proper stimuli they can produce predictable responses. But these patterned responses are quite different from the intrinsic Manasic ability of children to hold their heads and spines erect and to be able to function as self-moving beings. The Socratic conception of the *psuche* as a self-moving agent, together with the Platonic idea of *nous* as the matter-moving mind, points to the initiatory potential inherent within every human being. Whenever an individual makes a new beginning, initiating a considered line of activity during a day, a week, a month or a year, such a commencement could signify the start of a new phase of learning. Whether one takes as the starting-point of such an endeavour one's birthday or any other cyclic reference-point in life, one is recognizing the permanent possibility for all individuals of making fresh ventures into the unknown. Ordinarily, human beings are protected by not knowing too much about their previous lives or knowing too much even about the immediate future of this one. Since individuals learn to live in ignorance of the unknown, and at the same time venture on the basis of what they do know, clearly there is an indestructible element in every immortal soul which enables a human being again and again to make a fresh start. This permanent element is not simply the *Atma-Buddhi* or Divine Monad, but also the distilled and assimilated wisdom of past lives gathered in the *sutratman*, the repository of the fragrant aroma of past learning.

If every human being brings this precious inheritance of prior efforts towards individuation into the present life, and if all have passed through several initiations in distant lives, what relevance does this have to the onset of the Aquarian Age? Commencing on June 19, 1902, and having completed its first degree, the Aquarian Age has already brought about an unprecedented heightening of self-consciousness, and it holds a tremendous potential for the future. Something of the fundamental significance of the Aquarian Age can be glimpsed by recollecting that the year 1902 was not unconnected with the increasing concern to fly in the air. In the nineteenth century, on the other hand, the ocean was the common term of reference for many people in regard to travel, exploration and geopolitics. If people in the last century took many of their analogies and metaphors from the nautical world, this was because they had such an impressive collection of imposing sailing ships and modern steamships. In Greenwich and in Plymouth, from Cathay to Cape Horn, the romance and excitement of the pioneering exploration of the world's oceans fired the imagination of adults and children alike. Beginning in the sixteenth century, the rapid expansion of sea trade lay at the basis of the commercial and cultural growth of European civilization. By the close of the Victorian Age, the idea of a maritime civilization had become crystallized in the minds of such writers as Mahan and Fisher and consolidated the image of a globe governed by sea power. The construction of large ocean liners capable of sailing thousands of miles at considerable rates of speed provided ordinary people with basic metaphors concerning the conduct of life. The exacting skills needed in navigation received an attention reminiscent of older conceptions in literature and myth, viewing man as the captain of his soul. Yet now, in the twentieth century, with the vast elaboration upon what the Wright Brothers began, there is a fundamentally new outlook that has emerged with reference to the atmosphere surrounding the earth.

Even early in the century, artists and visionaries were stimulated by grand, if sometimes fanciful, conceptions of what the implications of flight could mean to human beings in general. By the time of the First World War, shrewd politicians like Winston Churchill perceived with almost prophetic clarity the significant change in the balance of power brought about by the airplane and the appalling dangers that this new capacity could unleash. For most people, despite pioneering efforts by individuals and businesses, it was not until after the Second World War that they were able on a large scale to travel by air. Then suddenly they experienced what otherwise could only have been done by climbing mountains – they gained some sense of what it is like at different elevations. In the past few decades this upward ascent has passed beyond the proximate atmosphere of the earth, reaching into the empyrean of space. Tapping the theoretical insights of a few and drawing upon the cooperative labours of specialized teams of scientists and engineers, a small coterie of intrepid individuals has travelled into space and brought back beautiful images of the earth as a shining gem suspended in the void. Spacecraft with intricate instruments have ventured towards Mercury, Venus, Mars, Jupiter and Saturn, linked to earth only by the finest etheric threads of electrical impulse, and returning copious information regarding long-recognized globes in our solar system.

Broadly, the Aquarian Age is typified by the concept of vertical ascent, whereas during the nineteenth century and before, the idea of horizontal movement was far more prevalent. This is not to minimize the importance of the great circumnavigations of the globe conducted in the maritime era, nor to discount the considerable knowledge gained by daring explorers and naturalists in regard to diverse forms of life. At their best, the nineteenth century naturalists discovered valuable principles of continuity in living form and developed significant intuitions into the geometry of dynamic growth. But now, in the twentieth century, principally because of air travel, people are much more conscious of the enormous relevance of factors such as altitude and atmosphere in relation to the elevation of consciousness. Through the beneficent invention of pressurized cabins, vast numbers of people have had the opportunity to observe that the earth does not seem the same when seen from an airplane as it does when seen on the plains.

All of this merely suggests that there has been a vital change taking place in human consciousness progressively over the last eighty years. From a merely empirical standpoint the entry of human beings into the airy regions is conclusive of nothing. From the standpoint of the Gupta Vidya, however, these outward changes are emblematic of the shift in the fundamental perspective of human experience. The nature and significance of this change cannot be comprehended through conventional and pseudo-rationalistic schemes of popular astrology. Caught up in erratic frameworks and outdated calculations, most astrologers are no more aware of the true meaning of the Aquarian Age than the average person. Few, if any, have deeply reflected upon the precession of the equinoxes, or upon the essential differences between the Taurean, Piscean and Aquarian Ages. Nonetheless, an increasingly large number of individuals have begun to sense a new awakening of human consciousness. Whether they interpret this from a purely personal standpoint, or connect it to some form of secular or sectarian millennial thinking, they can discern that a fundamental change is taking place in the global atmosphere of human life. Some who are sensitive see this in terms of a subtle beauty and alteration in the atmosphere of the earth itself, whilst those who are more perceptive detect a similar change in the atmosphere that surrounds each human being. In general, there is a growing recognition and widespread acknowledgement of a fresh opportunity for human souls at the present time of metamorphosis. Such glimmerings provide an array of opportunities which bring with them fresh avenues for awakening and growth.

Philosophically, all awakening is self-awakening. Self-consciousness represents an extraordinary privilege as well as a burden. It is a privilege because it brings with it the ability to choose, and through choices to comprehend connections between causes and consequences. It is a burden because it also brings with it the obligation to act in harmony with one's most fundamental perceptions. It is not possible to prove oneself worthy of the privilege of self-awakening through fulfillment of obligations and commitments without strengthening a practical sense of self-transcendence through contemplation and meditation. Whilst the Aquarian Age has already seen a surfeit of schemes for meditation which appeal to the suggestibility and gullibility of people who think that they can get something for nothing, the authentic and therapeutic teaching with regard to the true nature of contemplation is now available to more human beings than ever before. In their essentials, meditation and contemplation are neither episodic nor dependent upon any technique. Rather, they require the unremitting watchfulness of the mind and heart for the sake of restoration of purity of consciousness.

It is only through purity of thought, word and deed that the inexpressible yearning of the inner man for the infinite can find the fulfillment of its aspiration. It is only through the perfected continuity of the will, incessantly striving towards the highest ideal of divine manhood, that spiritual awakening through meditation can take place. There can be no increment of individuation or continuity of consciousness through any form of passivity. To give focus to aspiration, as *The Voice of the Silence* teaches, the mind needs breadth and depth and points to draw it towards the Diamond Soul. For example, one could take the Four Golden Links – Universal Unity and Causation, Human Solidarity, Karma and Reincarnation – as axiomatic starting-points for meditation. Beginning with an intellectual comprehension of these universal axioms, and deriving deductive inferences regarding particulars, a preliminary grasp of the true aim of meditation must be gained. Then, having worked out some tentative conception of the scheme of causes and effects to be comprehended, it is possible to pass inductively and intuitively from a contemplation of the known phenomena of the world of effects to the as yet unknown causes in the noumenal and unmanifest realm. Thus constructing and using a Jacob's Ladder of ideation, an individual can insert himself or herself into the evolutionary programme and explore the opportunities that it offers to the entire globe. It is the prospect and promise of this inward ascent in consciousness that so many people dimly feel, and which makes them sense the privilege of being alive at a critical moment in human evolution.

The Gupta Vidya III, "The Aquarian Elixir", 69-74

THE STREAM OF INCARNATION

If the highest *jnanis* are also the purest *bhaktas,* responding in magical sympathy to the cosmic will of Krishna, entering the stream of incarnation or abiding in the regions of invisible space only for the sake of service, can souls on earth who aspire to learn take any other standard? In the present period of human transformation, the opportunities for growth are great although the law of retrogression claims its toll amongst the weak. It may help to recall Longfellow's reminder that "Dust thou art, to dust returnest, was not spoken of the soul." One need not be like a dumb driven creature; but through unassuming heroism one may live a real life of earnest striving after the good. In a time of profanation one must refine the potent energy of thought through the living idea of the sacred, and though one might have humour and humanity, this need never be at the expense of another human being. One should recognize that *ahimsa* sweetens the breath, that non-violence dignifies the human being and straightens the spine, and that prostration adds inches to one's stature and health to one's frame. Integrity resides in the ability to recognize the difference between what one knows and what one does not know, coupled with a commitment to make good use of the divine gift of the power of learning right until the moment of death, so that one may arrive at the farther shore of earthly life with a sense of having contributed to that which was vaster and more profound than anything that could be contained in the compass of one lifetime.

To recover one's own inheritance as a Manasic being, and to resonate to the Avataric vibration which reverberates throughout the invisible world, one must raise one's horizons of thought. One must renounce the confined chronologies and parsimonious ontologies of Western thought. Almost by definition, a Westerner is an individual who believes in only one life. Yet there are many both in America and throughout the world who take rebirth for granted, integrating it into their way of life. Whilst there is a risk that one may speak in terms of many lives but act in terms of one life (which is cheating), once the mind and heart are firmly fixed upon the idea of karma, there is a spontaneous recovery of the capacity to learn and to show reverence and kinship to other human souls. Like the majority of mankind and the ancient inhabitants of the New World, the early Americans, including the Founding Fathers, believed in reincarnation. What, then, is the point of cowardice? Reincarnation is not merely a fashionable topic of conversation for actors and prostitutes sharing autobiographies, nor is it only designed for behind-the-scenes discussions. It should be brought out into the open, as the great sages have always done. If one has doubts, one must ask oneself if there is any reason to affirm another alternative. If so, then freely adopt the philosophy of the behaviourists and nihilists who openly expect to end their existence at death. As Jesus taught, either blow hot or blow cold, for the lukewarm are spewed forth.

If you choose the language of karma and the logic of reincarnation, universal unity and causation, and human solidarity, then you must also accept that theory is only as good as its practice. On this clarified and purified basis it becomes possible to make some small difference by one's life to the lives of others through showing true reverence and humility and an authentic agnosticism because of the ineffability of the One, the universality of the Law of Karma, the intricacy and exactitude of philosophical astrology, and the mysterious mathematics of sum-totals pertaining to the series of reincarnations. Thus one may learn to take an accurate account of the heavy toll exacted by the blockage of the Divine Light in the interior principles. A strenuous effort is required to learn the ABC's of occultism, and it would be folly to expect to discover the origins of consciousness through the self-restricted evidence of only one of its states. The ontological depths of *Prajna* can only be approached after there is a thorough mastery of the psychological and moral planes of human existence. Through firm detachment and unwavering attention, one must make oneself invulnerable to the siren calls of the past and cloying fantasies about the future, for the *narjol* is not safe until after having crossed beyond the regions of illusion, in which, as the *Anugita* teaches:

> ... fancies are the gadflies and mosquitoes, in which grief and joy are cold and heat, in which delusion is the blinding darkness, avarice, the beasts of prey and reptiles, and desire and anger are the obstructors.
>
> *The Secret Doctrine* II, 637

Above all, if one would seek freedom from the forests of delusion, from the enslavement of *Manas* to the senses, one must turn to the one and only source which can give protection and refuge, the *Kshetragna* within the sun. This is not to be understood in terms of any of the foolish salvation myths built up by failed disciples, but rather because of the logic and the law of the reflection of supernal light. Try to see the world not from below above but from above below. Try to see the world through the eyes of all those *yogins*, Mahatmas, who live both in the Himalayan crests of consciousness and in the lowliest heart of every sincere and aspiring human being. They can pass through any metal or substance named by man, and be simultaneously in many places. Established in the transcendental freedom of *Mahat,* they travel at will throughout the planes of the globe, though this has nothing to do with pseudo-occult notions of astral travel. They are Masters; their life-atoms are so pure that they can never hurt a single being. Supremely benevolent, men of truth who never know what it is to foster a lie, they are perfected in the practice of *Karma Yoga,* using many guises, playing jokes, veiling themselves constantly and thereby always guarding and protecting each and every human being without exception. They are what they are before they ever take illusory birth in the races of man, and they do not become anything different. Taking on illusory bodies of form from time to time for the instruction of mankind, Avatars create before mortal eyes a re-enactment of the path towards supreme enlightenment, but it is only a foolish fancy that supposes, for example, that Christ was not Christ, that Buddha was not Buddha, aeons before taking birth in a mortal frame. It was only for the sake of instruction that Jesus the Chrestos became Christos seemingly in three years, or that Gautama the Prince became the Enlightened Buddha through his travail in the forest on behalf of mankind.

Buddha taught that the entire world is like a lake of lotuses, each representing beings in different stages of *maya*. He explained that his life was not for the sake of those few who had already approached the Light of the Spiritual Sun, nor for those so deeply plunged in the mud of *maya* and *moha* that they could make no significant progress in their present incarnation, but rather for those in the middle, struggling to come out, those who need the assurance and the confidence that they too can move further up through the swirling currents of earth life and reach the surface of the waters and open to the sun. All such births of spiritual Teachers of Mankind are conscious incarnations of beings who knew millions of years ago who they were, and who, in enacting their self-knowledge that spells out as self-conquest, assume a compassionate veil.

The Gupta Vidya III, "The Healing of Souls", 83-85

CHOOSING LOVE OF THE LIGHT

If one's thinking is noetic, based upon that which is larger and more universal, and if, in this light, one considers calmly the lower and that which is lesser, one will be an optimistic person, glad that there are billions of human beings in the world, happy that children are being born, and above all, eager to greet the future. If, on the other hand, one is amongst those unfortunate people who have made pernicious alliances with the dark side of the moon, coming under its shadow through preoccupation with one's own shadow, one is *in extremis*. For such, no matter how many years of physical life may remain, it is, in fact, too late. At the moment of death, they will find that they have wasted their lives. Through meditation upon the shadow, through fascination with excreta, they have become afraid of the light. No one else has done this to them. They have excluded themselves from the school of human evolution and are unable to move onward with the awesome pilgrimage of humanity.

There are many such people in the world today, and, owing to their own selfishness, they are experiencing an extreme form of psychological terror. They, along with their inordinate selfishness, must and will disappear. Like *rakshasa* ghouls of the graveyard, they will make a great deal of noise before they are finished, but disappear they will because it is too late in Manasic evolution for abnormal selfishness. All human beings are, of course, concerned with survival and self-preservation to some degree, but there is a world of difference between this furtive selfishness and frenetic ego sickness. Ego sickness is abnormal selfishness; it has already created by the power of thought the very avenging demons which will destroy it. These *incubi* and *succubi* pursue the abnormally selfish in sleep and in waking life, all the time, until these dark monsters — created out of greed, out of fear of being wrong and making a fresh start, out of fear of the facts of spiritual life, out of exploitation of the patience and kindness, the generosity and magnanimity of others — surround their creator and close in for the kill.

This is no mere figure of speech, though it was graphically illustrated by Aldous Huxley in *The Devils of Loudun*. It is not merely a possibility, but a grave fact in the metaphysical realms of human existence beyond the veil of physical life. It is rooted in the capacity of manasic thought-energy to disturb and impress the atoms of the astral light. Drawing from the science of optics, accessible in a crude form to her readers in the nineteenth century, H.P. Blavatsky explains:

> . . . the rays of thought have the same potentiality for producing forms in the astral atmosphere as the sunrays have with regard to a lens. Every thought so evolved with energy from the brain, creates *nolens volens* a shape.
>
> H.P. Blavatsky

One may have the illusion of free will, but this production of astral forms through the power of thought proceeds involuntarily. In the case of an ordinary human being, both this form and the process of its formation are entirely unconscious. One simply does not know what one has done. By contrast, however, in the case of an Adept, who chooses each thought with a beneficent and well-directed motive, the mental emanation can be sent forth with enough of his will and intelligence to accomplish his purpose. The Adept needs no visible media, no complex computer or elaborate postal service. He can instantly transmit a thought over millions of miles. Thus, all Adepts are in immediate and effortless communication with each other, and Adepts in the Army of the Voice are able to take orders from their Chief, who transmits the will of the Logos instantly to agents all over the globe, who thereby know what exactly they have to do.

Whilst this instant alertness to the Light of the Logos and the Voice of Vach will not be earned by humanity as a whole until future Rounds, the moment has come for men and women everywhere to choose between love of the Light and morbid slavery to shadows. The logic of Manasic evolution implies a division between forms fostered by astral attachment and vestures evolved through altruistic meditation. Each alternation of day and night, each cycle of birth, death and reincarnation, each pulse-beat and each breath taken is a living moment of choice, a link in the endless chain of potential spiritual growth. With every mental exhalation, one emanates into the common atmosphere either fresh blessings for all or the foul snares of one's future bondage. As the Monad's karma accumulates over the aeons, it does so amidst the vastly larger totals affecting the entire race, which are continuously adjusted by the Lipikas under the impersonal guidance of the laws of invisible Nature. It is the unwavering will of the Logos that every sentient atom of life shall realize its ultimate unity with the One Life, and become thereby an active centre of beneficent light energy, consecrated to the law of sacrifice – the law of its own being.

Manasic humanity today is at a moment like the dawn of Venus, filled with the promise of a future wherein societies and civilizations founded upon the sacrificial love of wisdom will flourish. Every dawn dispels the shadows of the night; they are wise in their time who learn to love the light they cannot yet see in its fullness, whose harbinger they can recognize in the bright messenger of the dawn. In a few brief hours on the clock of human evolution, the Sun of Truth will arise for all who are courageous enough to turn towards the East, and mankind will rediscover itself. Having chosen the noetic light of *Buddhi* within, it will find itself in the company and service of the Servants of the Logos, and engaged in the compassionate travail of the true City of Man.

The Gupta Vidya III, "The Vigil Night of Humanity", 93-94

STRENGTHENING SUTRATMAN

In a universe of justice the voluntary discipline of sacrifice presupposes the power of choice of every single human being. *Manas* spells moral responsibility, and it connotes freedom of choice as well as the fearless acceptance of the full consequences of past choices. A Manasic being welcomes everything that comes under merciful karma as a necessary consequence of choices in other lives, self-determination at the moment of birth, and the continuous stream of self-definition originating at the causal level of ideation. The truly Manasic being would never condescend to assign any portion of his character or circumstance entirely to an outside agency or source – whether heredity, environment, the collective Karma of society or humanity. All such alibis, excuses and evasions would be morally unworthy of a Manasic being. One might coolly consider these mitigating factors when one wishes to understand the unknown karma of other beings, especially as one cannot arrogate to oneself the vicarious burden of responsibility which other persons must assume voluntarily. It is with selfless humility and spontaneous reverence before the mystery of every Ego that the Bodhisattva seeks broader explanations for the sake of a compassionate understanding, a non-moralistic or constructive appraisal of the spiritual predicament of human souls. If one thinks seriously about the metaphysical basis of sacrifice, the ethics of responsibility would logically follow, including the moral codes of discipleship. Also, one would see with the clarity of compassion that what is customarily called living is largely a series of pathetic contortions based upon a sad legacy of fears inherited from past lives of irresponsibility and evasion.

Persisting in such a course of self-destruction can only lead at some point to a total rupture of the connection with the Divine, unless there is a courageous if traumatic confrontation with these downward tendencies. For humanity as a whole, there eventually must come such a crucial moment of choice in the Fifth Round, but for individuals who have entered the Path, it can come much earlier than for the majority of mankind. When the twin gifts of *Manas* – moral responsibility and noetic choice – are strengthened through use by a burgeoning Buddhic awareness of cosmic sacrifice, then, as the *Stanzas* teach:

> The thread between the *silent watcher* and his *shadow* (man) becomes stronger – with every reincarnation.

This is what should happen in every human life, and if it does not, there is something seriously wrong. In every incarnation the *sutratman* should become stronger between the Silent Watcher – the overbrooding Dhyani or Divine Prototype at the upper rung of the ladder of being – and the lunar shadow at the lower rung. Gupta Vidya teaches that the two highest classes of Dhyanis – the Watchers connected with the seventh principle and the Architects connected with the sixth principle – furnished the various races of humanity with divine Kings and Instructors:

> It is the latter who taught humanity their arts and sciences, and the former who revealed to the incarnated Monads that had just shaken off their vehicles of the lower Kingdoms – and who had, therefore, lost every recollection of their divine origin – the great spiritual truths of the transcendental worlds.
>
> *The Secret Doctrine* I, 267

If, despite this sacred lineage and divine descent which lends to man the sacrificial light of self-consciousness, he nonetheless desecrates the gift of creative imagination through moral turpitude, then there is a tragic loosening or sundering of the vital connection with the immortal Monad. Turpitude means taking pride in what is vile and base and pleasure in what is shameful; it is bravado in the service of Satan. Such terrible misuse of the will and the potency of thought imperils the life-giving connection between the higher Triad and the lower quaternary, and gravely increases the risk of running loose and "astray into the lunar path".

There is enormous moral danger in any pseudo-scientific categories of thought or pseudo-religious forms of worship that encourage disguised irresponsibility in the name of pseudo-freedom or pseudo-determinism or pseudo-salvation. Once one goes astray into the lunar path, all manner of unholy alliances are made between the astral form and nefarious swarms of tortured elementals, soulless elementaries and evil sorcerers, as also massive legions of malignant, gangrenous and leprous thoughtforms going back to Atlantean times. One becomes the helpless prey of whole classes of images intimately associated with the appalling abuse of spiritual knowledge, creative potency and mental energies. This inevitably attracts a host of soul-ailments and diseases, and those who succumb to them face formidable obstructions to finding a human form or congenial conditions in which one can foster spiritual intuitions. Even if, at one level, one wants to aspire heavenward, the entire system seems to conspire against the promise of progress owing to spinal blockages, mental deposits and astral deformities.

To purge oneself of spiritual pollution and to heal the moral scars it leaves in the lunar vesture, one must meditate deeply and continuously, with an intensely devout wish to restore and strengthen the fragile connection with the immortal spirit of *Atma-Buddhi*. One must immerse oneself in the Buddhic current of the healing waters of wisdom, the elixir of *Hermes*, the indestructible spark of divine conscience, which is consubstantial with the fiery essence of the Dhyanis (the Angirasa descended from Agni). This is like bathing in the luminous stream of Divine Wisdom, the only Jordan whose waters can baptize in the name of the Father in Heaven, the *Mahaguru* on earth, the God in man. The therapeutic restoration of the right relationship between the reflected ray and its divine parent cannot come by ritual chanting and monotonous mutterings, by what is mistaken for prayer, worship or meditation.

Rectification must proceed from intense thought, conscious strengthening of the strongest altruistic feelings in oneself, and by an unconditional vow and irreversible determination. This would be enormously helped by invoking and activating the higher faculties which have their analogues with lower *manas* and with *prana*. The manifest energy of *prana* must reflect something of the continuity and self-luminous, self-created spiritual energy of the invisible *Atman*. The polarity of *kama* must be purified through devotion and directed by that inward tropism and vertical movement towards the Divine Triad which could confer the benediction of gratitude and reverence towards the *Ishtaguru* and the Brotherhood of Bodhisattvas. Lower *manas* must be brought into firm alignment with higher *Manas*, especially through the use of silence and conscious control of speech. If there are daily duties to perform, one should take a universal ideal, a potent *mantram*, dwell upon these and then look upon obligations as sacred, with a joyous recognition of responsibility and choice.

The Gupta Vidya III, "The Path of Renunciation", 118-120

CREATING A FORWARD IMPULSE

Control of thought and speech is an essential ingredient of soul etiquette and spiritual discrimination. It represents good taste at the highest level, where one may enrich a spontaneous longing for Brahma Vach, the *Agathon*, the Ineffable Good. Out of repeated meditation one must gain such a strong, lively and self-perpetuating sense of the Ineffable Good at the core of the Divine Darkness behind the shimmering veils of the universe, that one is securely anchored in that state of spiritual awareness. And therefore, as Plato suggested in the Allegory of the Cave, when seemingly descending into the world of heterogeneity, one is able to use wisely one's eyes and ears and above all, one's tongue, so that one is acutely conscious of every available opportunity to give a forward impulse to human evolution. Where one encounters anything meretricious on the lower planes, it will roll off like water off a duck's back. It simply will not inhere because of the intense activation and vigilant preservation of one's noetic awareness. The importance of this mental discipline will soon become evident to those who are courageous enough to become steadfast in its practice, not for their protection, but for the sake of universal enlightenment. Not only can they begin to discharge their debt to the sacred Teaching by converting it into what they could use, but they could actively contribute to the creation of the magnetic field in which spiritual instruction could be integrated into new modes of secular monasticism.

It is the responsibility of those who have received the Teaching to test themselves by experiments and exercises, by resolutions and by vows, for the sake of other human beings who have not been so privileged, and therefore cannot understand how they are constantly harming themselves by the sounds emitted through their tongues and vocal chords. They have created recurrent karma even through a single violent outburst. Given the mathematics of the process, it takes a long time to create a strong field of refined vibrations. Destruction takes very little time, and through violence masses of life-atoms have stamped on them some memory of revenge. As W.Q. Judge explains in "The Persian Student's Doctrine", at some point they will return and take their toll for the abuse given to them. Many people are self-alienated because they have misused too many life-atoms for too long and therefore fear that something like nemesis is coming to them. This supposedly malign fate is nothing other than what they themselves have summoned, but unless they grasp the logic of karma and reincarnation, there is little they can do to mitigate their own misery.

If one has been so fortunate as to encounter these teachings, then instead of vainly brooding over what one might have done ten lives ago, one should right now release the strongest vibration of which one is capable. One will be doing so in a magnetic field in which there are unknown but tougher beings than oneself who are also doing it in their own consciousness. One will have the benefit of that collective current as well as the inestimable benediction of Initiates. If one attempts this earnestly, one will begin to feel worthy of inhabiting the human form, with its far-ranging faculties of perception and action, which myriads of ancestors and their spiritual instructors have produced and perfected over aeons. The golden opportunity is open to all to correct the persisting mistakes of the past and to insert the strongest current into the immediate future, and that means one has to get to the root-cause which is the immovable mind. Just as one can sense the depths of the ocean or the idea of bare space, one can make the mind immovable and inconceivably strong. One may associate it with an inward posture and meditate upon its potential fixity, analogous to the snowy pillars of Amarnath. As Robert Crosbie suggests, one should meditate upon the idea of steadiness itself. One might think of familiar examples of what is fixed, from the pole-star to the unthanked lamp that lights a city street for stragglers in the night. Above all, if one would learn steadfastness in maintaining the highest spiritual vibration, one must meditate upon the Bodhisattvas and Mahatmas, and Shiva, the patron and paradigm of true ascetics.

The initiation of any sacred sound-vibration, when based upon exact spiritual knowledge, can set the keynote of an entire epoch. In that Avataric tradition, when Krishna struck a keynote, as with Buddha, Shankara and Pythagoras, the highest karma of a cycle was determined. This has a bearing upon the classes of souls drawn into incarnation as well as the pressures that vacate souls unable to keep pace with the current, and also upon all the invisible forces and energies that have been rearranged and affected. At all times there are people who may be contemporaneous with the sounding of such a keynote, but apart from a vague sense that something is going on, they may not be able to participate in it because, as Buddha said in the *Dhammapada,* the ladle of a soup bowl, even though it serves the most delicious soup over the lifetime of that bowl, will never become the taste of the soup. Mere physical proximity makes no difference to consciousness. Spiritual teachers think and speak in terms of millennia and of millions of beings, and in many a Buddhist text it is said that the Buddha taught all three worlds. In these worlds there are those who, by self-conscious awareness of what is seminal, can receive the reverberation of the keynote and become capable of benefiting by its translation into uses that may be exemplary and helpful to other beings. There would be no survival for the human race over eighteen million years but for the continuous compassion of the Brotherhood of Bodhisattvas.

The Gupta Vidya III, "The Verbum", 191-192

A TRUE SENSE OF SELF-EXISTENCE

The fundamental distinction between liberation and renunciation implies that true love is proportional to spiritual wakefulness. The capacity to love all life-atoms depends upon one's understanding of their various orders and functions within the World Soul. Through appropriate arrangement and discipline, they must be given a chance to become apprenticed in discipleship, even at the level of unself-consciousness and incipient consciousness. No mere facility with intellectual constructions or recourse to ritual techniques is going to sustain the tremendous power of attention needed for this learning. This capacity of the soul for wakefulness is dependent upon previous lives of meditation, renunciation and service. Thus, in the metapsychological perspective of Gupta Vidya, there is no basis for understanding soul powers and the development of magical possibilities, whether in their beneficent or maleficent uses, apart from an understanding of karma and reincarnation.

Every human being has brought into the world some distinctive experience of the immortal soul and its theurgic powers, some indelible marks of past proficiency and past deficiency. Spiritual growth cannot, therefore, be explained by the principle of desire operating in the present. Filtered through the distorting prism of *kama manas*, the ideal principle of aspiration becomes a concretized impression of temporal and temporary desires. Such illusory impressions are merely projections out of *tanha*, the root desire to exist and subsist in a form or body in a world that is limited in space and time. There can be no true wakefulness, no release of the spiritual will, and no moral and mental growth based upon such an obscured and distorted sense of self-existence.

> The real person or thing does not consist solely of what is seen at any particular moment, but is composed of the sum of all its various and changing conditions from its appearance in the material form to its disappearance from the earth. It is these

'sum-totals' that exist from eternity in the 'future', and pass by degrees through matter, to exist for eternity in the 'past'.

Ibid., 37

    The deeper conception of time which is needed to understand these karmic sum-totals can only arise from an extraordinary detachment. Burdened by individual and collective karma on the one hand, confronted by the necessity of supreme detachment on the other, many find it difficult to retain a vital enthusiasm for the world. They must realize that even the most magnanimous souls cannot give themselves fully to every living being without voiding every element of meretricious attraction to the shadowy self. Detachment from the personal self is necessary for those who wish to view the world without bondage to attachments and illusions. The inner ray of *Alaya* cannot be freed for the exhilaration of universal compassion until it is disengaged in consciousness from its own reflection localized in time and space upon the waves of differentiated matter. This disengagement, equivalent to awakening true continuity of consciousness, proceeds through an undivided process of unfoldment that may be represented by an orderly series of law-governed phases. If these stages are not clearly understood, the nature of detachment may be distorted and its motives debased. Each stage accompanies a growing transcendence of the illusion of time and comprehension of Karma. At the same time, each stage represents a growing awakening to essential degrees of *Alaya* or noetic intelligence. Souls progress from the restraint of the lower self or personality by the divine Self or individuality to the restraint of the Self divine by the Eternal, in which even the latent consciousness of desire and *tanha* is torn out. Thus the soul is merged in self-consciousness with the eternal essence of *Alaya*.

    The first problem of withdrawal of consciousness from form may be understood best through the relationship between karmic attachment and memory. So long as karmic attachment operates through personal memories, individuals will experience pleasant and unpleasant reactions. As Shri Shankaracharya taught, "So long as we experience pleasure and pain, karma is still working through us." The more violent these emotional reactions, the stronger is the dead weight of karma. In extreme cases, a terrible and intensely traumatic experience in previous lives, coupled perhaps with a short or non-existent devachan, may bring about a tremendous burden on consciousness in the present incarnation. Attracted, under karma, to parents and companions bound by likes and dislikes, one may likewise experience emotional extremism. But, whatever its cause, volatility is invariably symptomatic of a high degree of karmic bondage. Its victims must learn painfully over a lifetime to void a false sense of reality or romance, of security or expectation. The seeming burdens of karma are in direct proportion to the delusions that must be voided.

An Initiate, seeing the aura of a human being mired in delusion, knows that at the moment of that being's death one question remains: Has his understanding of the ABCs of life improved since his birth? If so, the individual can begin to discharge the debt of karma. Thus, if he is fortunate, the individual will gravitate to environments where there is little attention to likes and dislikes and where the options for the personality are fewer. Through successive incarnations, Karma compassionately reduces opportunities for protracted delusion until the individual is compelled to learn essential lessons. In terms of the self-conscious pursuit of moral and metaphysical ideals, Karma operates with the same dispassion, progressively narrowing the margins for error. Individuals vary in their degrees of wakefulness in proportion to their kamic attachment. They burden consciousness with fragmented memories, which must be distinguished from soul reminiscence, a reflection of universal memory beyond parochial and ephemeral likes and dislikes. As an individual learns to overcome the blurring of attention induced by personal memory, he will receive greater aid through moral allegiance to chosen ideals. Plato and Gandhi wisely recognized that most people in the Age of Zeus, Kali Yuga, are burdened by hostile memories and desperately in need of hospitable ideals.

Transmitting ideals to children and pupils through example and through precept is both beneficent and constructive. Their capacity for credible ideals increases with practice, and, as attention is focussed upon the possibilities of the future, it continues to develop. Naturally, ideals recede as they are approached, but they are nonetheless essential; they provide directions, if not destinations, and propel the individual ever forwards. As long as there are ideals, pointing to the imaginative possibilities of the foreseeable future, one can appreciate the salutary lessons of karma without becoming overburdened by collective memories of failure. Ultimately, all potent and transcendental ideals have their origins in Divine Thought, and their realization cannot be restricted to the solitary pilgrimage of any individual soul. As presented in the portraits of perfect enlightenment in various scriptures, they represent the source and apex of universal spiritual unfoldment. The true mystery of ideals is bound up with that of Avatars and Manus, the exalted incarnations and prototypes guiding and overbrooding manifestation, but rooted in the unmanifest Divine Thought and the Host of Anupadaka.

The Gupta Vidya III, "Spiritual Wakefulness", 216-218

VOLUNTARY REINCARNATION

Thus the entire message of Gautama Buddha constitutes a wonderful unity, universal in scope, applicable to all human beings, and powerfully re-stated by different Teachers in different ways. Buddha gave to one and all the prospect of validating and pursuing a single-minded spiritual quest for meaning, enlightenment and redemption. He taught, not escape into some celestial retreat, but the gaining of *nirvana* in *samsara*, progressive enlightenment in the company of one's fellows and voluntary reincarnation for the sake of sharing the hard-won fruits of self-knowledge and inner peace with suffering humanity. His own exemplary life was the beautiful and lustrous realization of three paramount principles – the principle of regeneration, the principle of renunciation and the principal of reverence. We must regenerate ourselves as he did, we must gain more and more wisdom and compassion and then renounce the fruits of our spiritual strivings; thus, by a series of steps, each greater than the last, we come to the final step, the supreme renunciation of individual bliss which he superbly demonstrated in his own life. Above all, we must take refuge in the Tathagata light of Buddha and in the Order of Disciples he came to re-establish upon the earth. We must show reverence to the Buddhas and to all beings, for without reverence nothing worthwhile is possible in human life.

The Gupta Vidya III, "The Message of Buddha", 228

BETWEEN DEATH AND REBIRTH

Asanprajnata samadhi arises out of meditation on a seed though it is itself seedless. Here supreme detachment frees one from even the subtlest cognition and one enters *nirbija samadhi,* meditation without a seed, which is self-sustaining because free of any supporting focalization on an object. From the standpoint of the succession of objects of thought – the type of consciousness all human beings experience in a chaotic or fragmentary way and a few encounter even in meditation on a seed – *nirbija samadhi* is non-existence or emptiness, for it is absolutely quiescent consciousness. Nonetheless, it is not the highest consciousness attainable, for it is the retreat of mind to a neutral *(laya)* centre from which it can begin to operate on a wholly different plane of being. This elevated form of pure consciousness is similar to a state experienced in a disembodied condition between death and rebirth, when consciousness is free of the involvement with vestures needed for manifestation in differentiated matter. Just as an individual becomes unconscious when falling into deep dreamless sleep, because consciousness fails to remain alert except in conditions of differentiation, so too consciousness in a body becomes unconscious and forgetful of its intrinsic nature on higher planes. *Samadhi* aims to restore that essential awareness self-consciously, making the alert meditator capable of altering planes of consciousness without any loss of awareness.

The Gupta Vidya III, "Samadhi Pada", 273

APPENDIX IV

THE AFTER-DEATH STATES

DIALOGUE ON THE MYSTERIES OF THE AFTER LIFE

On The Constitution Of The Inner Man

M. Of course it is most difficult, and, as you say, "puzzling" to understand correctly and distinguish between the various *aspects*, called by us the "principles" of the real EGO. It is the more so as there exists a notable difference in the numbering of those principles by various Eastern schools, though at the bottom there is the same identical substratum of teaching in all of them.

X. Are you thinking of the Vedantins. They divide our seven "principles" into five only, I believe?

M. They do; but though I would not presume to dispute the point with a learned Vedantin, I may yet state as my private opinion that they have an obvious reason for it. With them it is only that compound spiritual aggregate which consists of various mental aspects that is called *Man* at all, the physical body being in their view something beneath contempt, and merely an *illusion*. Nor is the Vedanta the only philosophy to reckon in this manner. Lao-Tze in his *Tao-te-King*, mentions only five principles, because he, like the Vedantins, omits to include two principles, namely, the spirit (Atma) and the physical body, the latter of which, moreover, he calls "the cadaver." Then there is the *Taraka Raja Yoga* School. Its teaching recognizes only three "principles" in fact; but then, in reality, their *Sthulopadhi,* or the physical body in its *jagrata* or waking conscious state, their *Sukshmopadhi,* the same body in *svapna* or the dreaming state, and their *Karanopadhi* or "causal body," or that which passes from one incarnation to another, are all dual in their aspects, and thus make six. Add to this Atma, the impersonal divine principle or the immortal element in Man, undistinguished from the Universal Spirit, and you have the same seven, again, as in the esoteric division.[15]

X. Then it seems almost the same as the division made by mystic Christians: body, soul and spirit?

M. Just the same. We could easily make of the body the vehicle of the "vital Double"; of the latter the vehicle of Life or *Prana;* of *Kamarupa* or (animal) soul, the vehicle of the *higher* and the *lower* mind, and make of this six principles, crowning the whole with the one immortal spirit. In Occultism, every qualificative change in the state of our consciousness goes to man a new aspect, and if it prevails and becomes part of the living and acting EGO, it must be (and is) given a special name, to distinguish the man in that particular state from the man he is when he places himself in another state.

X. It is just that which is so difficult to understand.

M. It seems to me very easy, on the contrary, once that you have seized the main idea, *i.e.,* that man acts on this, or another plane of consciousness, in strict accordance with his mental and spiritual condition. But such is the materialism of the age that the more we explain, the less people seem capable of understanding what we say. Divide the terrestrial being called man into three chief aspects, if you like; but, unless you make of him a pure animal, you cannot do less. Take his objective *body;* the feeling principle in him – which is only a little higher than the *instinctual* element in the animal – or the vital elementary soul; and that which places him so immeasurably beyond and higher than the animal – *i.e.,* his *reasoning* soul or "spirit." Well, if we take these three groups or representative entities, and subdivide them, according to the occult teaching, what do we get?

First of all Spirit (in the sense of the Absolute, and therefore indivisible ALL) or Atma. As this can neither be located nor conditioned in philosophy, being simply that which IS, in Eternity, and as the ALL cannot be absent from even the tiniest geometrical or mathematical point of the universe of matter or substance, it ought

---

[15] See "*The Secret Doctrine*" for a clearer explanation.

not to be called, in truth, a "human" principle at all. Rather, and at best, it is that point in metaphysical Space which the human Monad and its vehicle man, occupy for the period of every life. Now that point is as imaginary as man himself, and in reality is an illusion, a *maya*; but then for ourselves as for other personal Egos, we are a reality during that fit of illusion called life, and we have to take ourselves into account – in our own fancy at any rate if no one else does. To make it more conceivable to the human intellect, when first attempting the study of Occultism, and to solve the ABC of the mystery of man, Occultism calls it the *seventh* principle, the synthesis of the six, and gives it for vehicle the *Spiritual* Soul, *Buddhi*. Now the latter conceals a mystery, which is never given to anyone with the exception of irrevocably pledged *chelas,* those at any rate, who can be safely trusted. Of course there would be less confusion, could it only be told; but, as this is directly concerned with the power of projecting one's double consciously and at will, and as this gift like the "ring of Gyges" might prove very fatal to men at large and to the possessor of that faculty in particular, it is carefully guarded. Alone the adepts, who have been tried and can never be found wanting, have the key of the mystery fully divulged to them . . . Let us avoid side issues, however, and hold to the "principles".

This divine soul or *Buddhi*, then, is the Vehicle of the Spirit. In conjunction, these two are one, impersonal, and without any attributes (on this plane, of course), and make two spiritual "principles." If we pass on to the *Human* Soul (*Manas*, the *mens*) everyone will agree that the intelligence of man is *dual* to say the least: *e.g.,* the high-minded man can hardly become low-minded; the very intellectual and spiritual-minded man is separated by an abyss from the obtuse, dull and material, if not animal-minded man. Why then should not these men be represented by two "principles" or two aspects rather? Every man has these two principles in him, one more active than the other, and in rare cases, one of these is entirely stunted in its growth; so to say paralysed by the strength and predominance of the other *aspect,* during the life of man. These, then, are what we call the two principles or aspects of *Manas*, the higher and the lower; the former, the higher *Manas*, or the thinking, conscious EGO gravitating toward the Spiritual Soul (*Buddhi*); and the latter, or its instinctual principle attracted to *Kama*, the seat of animal desires and passions in man. Thus, we have *four* "principles" justified; the last three being (1) the "Double" which we have agreed to call Protean, or Plastic Soul; the vehicle of (2) the life *principle;* and (3) the physical body. Of course no Physiologist or Biologist will accept these principles, nor can he make head or tail of them. And this is why, perhaps, none of them understand to this day either the functions of the spleen, the physical vehicle of the Protean Double, or those of a certain organ on the right side of man, the seat of the above mentioned desires, nor yet does he know anything of the pineal gland, which he describes as a horny gland with a little sand in it, and which is the very key to the highest and divinest consciousness in man – his omniscient, spiritual and all-embracing mind. This seemingly useless appendage is the pendulum which, once the clockwork of the *inner* man is wound up, carries the spiritual vision of the EGO to the highest planes of perception, where the horizon open before it becomes almost infinite. . . .

X. But the scientific materialists assert that after the death of man nothing remains; that the human body simply disintegrates into its component elements, and that what we call soul is merely a temporary self-consciousness produced as a by-product of organic action, which will evaporate like steam. Is not theirs a strange state of mind?

M. Not strange at all, that I see. If they say that self-consciousness ceases with the body, then in *their* case they simply utter an unconscious prophecy. For once that they are firmly convinced of what they assert, no conscious after-life is possible for them.

X. But if human self-consciousness survives death as a rule, why should there be exceptions?

M. In the fundamental laws of the spiritual world which are

immutable, no exception is possible. But there are rules for those who see, and rules for those who prefer to remain blind.

X. Quite so, I understand. It is an aberration of a blind man, who denies the existence of the sun because he does not see it. But after death his spiritual eyes will certainly compel him to see?

M. They will not compel him, nor will he see anything. Having persistently denied an after-life during this life, he will be unable to sense it. His spiritual senses having been stunted, they cannot develop after death, and he will remain blind. By insisting that he *must* see it, you evidently mean one thing and I another. You speak of the spirit from the Spirit, or the flame from the Flame – of Atma in short – and you confuse it with the human soul – *Manas*. . . . You do not understand me, let me try to make it clear. The whole gist of your question is to know whether, in the case of a downright materialist, the complete loss of self-consciousness and self-perception after death is possible? Isn't it so? I say: It is possible. Because, believing firmly in our Esoteric Doctrine, which refers to the *post-mortem* period, or the interval between two lives or births as merely a transitory state, I say: – Whether that interval between two acts of the illusionary drama of life lasts one year or a million, that *post-mortem* state may, without any breach of the fundamental law, prove to be just the same state as that of a man who is in a dead swoon.

X. But since you have just said that the fundamental laws of the after-death state admit of no exceptions, how can this be?

M. Nor do I say now that they admit of exceptions. But the spiritual law of continuity applies only to things which are truly real. To one who has read and understood *Mundakya Upanishad* and *Vedanta-Sara* all this becomes very clear. I will say more: it is sufficient to understand what we mean by *Buddhi* and the duality of *Manas* to have a very clear perception why the materialist may not have a self-conscious survival after death: because *Manas*, in its lower aspect, is the seat of the terrestrial mind, and, therefore, can give only that perception of the Universe which is based on the evidence of that mind, and not on our spiritual vision. It is said in our Esoteric school that between *Buddhi* and *Manas,* or *Iswara* and *Pragna,*[16] there is in reality no more difference than *between a forest and its trees, a lake and its waters,* just as *Mundakya* teaches. One or hundreds of trees dead from loss of vitality, or uprooted, are yet incapable of preventing the forest from being still a forest. The destruction or *post-mortem* death of one personality dropped out of the long series, will not cause the smallest change in the Spiritual divine *Ego,* and it will ever remain the same EGO. Only, instead of experiencing *Devachan* it will have to immediately reincarnate.

X. But as I understand it, Ego-*Buddhi* represents in this simile the forest and the personal minds the trees. And if *Buddhi* is immortal, how can that which is similar to it, *i.e., Manas-Taijasi,*[17] lose entirely its consciousness till the day of its new incarnation? I cannot understand it.

M. You cannot, because you will mix up an abstract representation of the whole with its casual changes of form; and because you confuse *Manas-Taijasi,* the *Buddhi*-lit human soul, with the latter, animalized. Remember that if it can be said of *Buddhi* that it is unconditionally immortal, the same cannot be said of *Manas,* still less of *taijasi,* which is an attribute. No *post-mortem* consciousness or *Manas-Taijasi,* can exist apart from *Buddhi,* the divine soul, because the first (*Manas*) is, in its lower aspect, a qualificative attribute of the terrestrial personality, and the second (*taijasi*) is identical with the first, and that it is the same *Manas* only with the light of *Buddhi*

---

[16] *Iswara* is the collective consciousness of the manifested deity, Brahmâ, *i.e.,* the collective consciousness of the Host of Dhyan Chohans; and *Pragna* is their individual wisdom.

[17] *Taijasi* means the radiant in consequence of the union with *Buddhi* of *Manas,* the human, illuminated by the radiance of the divine soul. Therefore *Manas-Taijasi* may be described as radiant mind; the *human* reason lit by the light of the spirit; and *Buddhi-Manas* is the representation of the divine *plus* the human intellect and self-consciousness.

reflected on it. In its turn, *Buddhi* would remain only an impersonal spirit without this element which it borrows from the human soul, which conditions and makes of it, in this illusive Universe, *as it were something separate* from the universal soul for the whole period of the cycle of incarnation. Say rather that *Buddhi-Manas* can neither die nor lose its compound self-consciousness in Eternity, nor the recollection of its previous incarnations in which the two – *i.e.*, the spiritual and the human soul, had been closely linked together. But it is not so in the case of a materialist, whose human soul not only receives nothing from the divine soul, but even refuses to recognize its existence. You can hardly apply this axiom to the attributes and qualifications of the human soul, for it would be like saying that because your divine soul is immortal, therefore the bloom on your cheek must also be immortal; whereas this bloom, like *taijasi,* or spiritual radiance, is simply a transitory phenomenon.

X. Do I understand you to say that we must not mix in our minds the noumenon with the phenomenon, the cause with its effect?

M. I do say so, and repeat that, limited to *Manas* or the human soul alone, the radiance of Taijasi itself becomes a mere question of time; because both immortality and consciousness after death become for the terrestrial personality of man simply conditioned attributes, as they depend entirely on conditions and beliefs created by the human soul itself during the life of its body. Karma acts incessantly; we reap *in our after*-life only the fruit of that which we have ourselves sown, or rather created, in our terrestrial existence.

X. But if my Ego can, after the destruction of my body, become plunged in a state of entire unconsciousness, then where can be the punishment for the sins of my past life?

M. Our philosophy teaches that Karmic punishment reaches the Ego only in the next incarnation. After death it receives only the reward for the unmerited sufferings endured during its just past existence.[18] The whole punishment after death, even for the materialist, consists therefore in the absence of any reward and the utter loss of the consciousness of one's bliss and rest. Karma – is the child of the terrestrial Ego, the fruit of the actions of the tree which is the objective personality visible to all, as much as the fruit of all the thoughts and even motives of the spiritual "I"; but Karma is also the tender mother, who heals the wounds inflicted by her during the preceding life, before she will begin to torture this Ego by inflicting upon him new ones. If it may be said that there is not a mental or physical suffering in the life of a mortal, which is not the fruit and consequence of some sin in this, or a preceding existence, on the other hand, since he does not preserve the slightest recollection of it in his actual life, and feels himself not deserving of such punishment, but believes sincerely he suffers for no guilt of his own, this alone is quite sufficient to entitle the human soul to the fullest consolation, rest and bliss in his *post-mortem* existence. Death comes to our spiritual selves ever as a deliverer and friend. For the materialist, who, notwithstanding his materialism, was not a bad man, the interval between the two lives will be like the unbroken and placid sleep of a child; either entirely dreamless, or with pictures of which he will have no definite perception. For the believer it will be a dream as vivid as life and full of realistic bliss and visions. As for the bad

---

[18] Some Theosophists have taken exception to this phrase, but the words are those of the Masters, and the meaning attached to the word "unmerited" is that given above. In the T.P.S. pamphlet No. 6, a phrase, criticised subsequently in *Lucifer* was used, which was intended to convey the same idea. In form however it was awkward and open to the criticism directed against it; but the essential idea was that men often suffer from the effects of the actions done by others, effects which thus do not strictly belong to their own Karma, but to that of other people – and for these sufferings they of course deserve compensation. If it is true to say that nothing that happens to us can be anything else than Karma – or the direct or indirect effect of a cause – it would be a great error to think that every evil or good which befalls us is due *only to our* personal Karma. (*Vide* further on.)

and cruel man, whether materialist or otherwise, he will be immediately reborn and suffer his hell on earth. To enter *Avitchi* is an exceptional and rare occurrence.

X. As far as I remember, the periodical incarnations of *Sutratma* [19] are likened in some Upanishad to the life of a mortal which oscillates periodically between sleep and waking. This does not seem to me very clear, and I will tell you why. For the man who awakes, another day commences, but that man is the same in soul and body as he was the day before; whereas at every new incarnation a full change takes place not only in his external envelope, sex and personality, but even in his mental and psychic capacities. Thus the simile does not seem to me quite correct. The man who arises from sleep remembers quite clearly what he has done yesterday, the day before, and even months and years ago. But none of us has the slightest recollection of a preceding life or any fact or event concerning it. . . . I may forget in the morning what I have dreamed during the night, still I know that I have slept and have the certainty that I lived during sleep; but what recollection have I of my past incarnation? How do you reconcile this?

M. Yet some people do recollect their past incarnations. This is what the Arhats call *Samma-Sambuddha* – or the knowledge of the whole series of one's past incarnations.

X. But we ordinary mortals who have not reached *Samma-Sambuddha*, how can we be expected to realize this simile?

M. By studying it and trying to understand more correctly the

---

[19] Our immortal and reincarnating principle in conjunction with the *Manas*ic recollections of the preceding lives is called *Sutratma*, which means literally the Thread-Soul; because like the pearls on a thread so is the long series of human lives strung together on that one thread. *Manas* must become *taijasi*, the radiant, before it can hang on the *Sutratma* as a pearl on its thread, and so have full and absolute perception of itself in the Eternity. As said before, too close association with the terrestrial mind of the human soul alone causes this radiance to be entirely lost.

characteristics of the three states of sleep. Sleep is a general and immutable law for man as for beast, but there are different kinds of sleep and still more different dreams and visions.

X. Just so. But this takes us from our subject. Let us return to the materialist who, while not denying dreams, which he could hardly do, yet denies immortality in general and the survival of his own individuality especially.

M. And the materialist is right for once, at least; since for one who has no inner perception and faith, there is no immortality possible. In order to live in the world to come a conscious life, one has to believe first of all in that life during one's terrestrial existence. On these two aphorisms of the Secret Science all the philosophy about the *post-mortem* consciousness and the immortality of the soul is built. The Ego receives always according to its deserts. After the dissolution of the body, there commences for it either a period of full clear consciousness, a state of chaotic dreams, or an utterly dreamless sleep indistinguishable from annihilation; and these are the three states of consciousness. Our physiologists find the cause of dreams and visions in an unconscious preparation for them during the waking hours; why cannot the same be admitted for the *post-mortem* dreams? I repeat it, *death is sleep*. After death begins, before the spiritual eyes of the soul, a performance according to a programme learnt and very often composed unconsciously by ourselves; the practical carrying out of *correct* beliefs or of illusions which have been created by ourselves. A Methodist, will be Methodist, a Mussulman, a Mussulman, of course, just for a time -in a perfect fool's paradise of each man's creation and making These are the *post-mortem* fruits of the tree of life. Naturally, our belief or unbelief in the fact of conscious immortality is unable to influence the unconditioned reality of the fact itself, once that it exists; but the belief or unbelief in that immortality, as the continuation or annihilation of separate entities, cannot fail to give colour to that fact in its application to each of these entities. Now do you begin to understand it?

X. I think I do. The materialist, disbelieving in everything that cannot be proven to him by his five senses or by scientific reasoning, and rejecting every spiritual manifestation, accepts life as the only conscious existence. Therefore, according to their beliefs so will it be unto them. They will lose their personal Ego, and will plunge into a dreamless sleep until a new awakening. Is it so?

M. Almost so. Remember the universal esoteric teaching of the two kinds of conscious existence: the terrestrial and the spiritual. The latter must be considered real from the very fact that it is the region of the eternal, changeless, immortal cause of all; whereas the incarnating Ego dresses itself up in new garments entirely different from those of its previous incarnations, and in which all except its spiritual prototype is doomed to a change so radical as to leave no trace behind.

X. Stop! . . . Can the consciousness of my terrestrial *Egos* perish not only for a time, like the consciousness of the materialist, but in any case so entirely as to leave no trace behind?

M. According to the teaching, it must so perish and in its fulness, all except that principle which, having united itself with the Monad, has thereby become a purely spiritual and indestructible essence, one with it in the Eternity. But in the case of an out and out materialist, in whose personal "I" no *Buddhi* has ever reflected itself, how can the latter carry away into the infinitudes one particle of that terrestrial personality? Your spiritual "I" is immortal; but from your present Self it can carry away into after life but that which has become worthy of immortality, namely, the aroma alone of the flower that has been mown by death.

X. Well, and the flower, the terrestrial "I"?

M. The flower, as all past and future flowers which blossomed and died, and will blossom again on the mother bough, the *Sutratma*, all children of one root of *Buddhi*, will return to dust. Your present "I," as you yourself know, is not the body now sitting before me, nor yet is it what I would call *Manas-Sutratma* – but *Sutratma-Buddhi*.

X. But this does not explain to me at all, why you call life after death immortal, infinite, and real, and the terrestrial life a simple phantom or illusion; since even that *post-mortem* life has limits, however much wider they may be than those of terrestrial life.

M. No doubt. The spiritual Ego of man moves in Eternity like a pendulum between the hours of life and death. But if these hours marking the periods of terrestrial and spiritual life are limited in their duration, and if the very number of such stages in Eternity between sleep and awakening, illusion and reality, has its beginning and its end, on the other hand the spiritual "Pilgrim" is eternal. Therefore are the hours of his *post-mortem* life – when, disembodied he stands face to face with truth and not the mirages of his transitory earthly existences during the period of that pilgrimage which we call "the cycle of rebirths" – the only reality in our conception. Such intervals, their limitation notwithstanding, do not prevent the Ego, while ever perfecting itself, to be following undeviatingly, though gradually and slowly, the path to its last transformation, when that Ego having reached its goal becomes the divine ALL. These intervals and stages help towards this final result instead of hindering it; and without such limited intervals the divine Ego could never reach its ultimate goal. This Ego is the actor, and its numerous and various incarnations the parts it plays. Shall you call these parts with their costumes the individuality of the actor himself? Like that actor, the Ego is forced to play during the Cycle of Necessity up to the very threshold of *Para-nirvana,* many parts such as may be unpleasant to it. But as the bee collects its honey from every flower, leaving the rest as food for the earthly worms, so does our spiritual individuality, whether we call it Sutratma or Ego. It collects from every terrestrial personality into which Karma forces it to incarnate, the nectar alone of the spiritual qualities and self-consciousness, and uniting all these into one whole it emerges from its chrysalis as the glorified Dhyan Chohan. So much the worse for those terrestrial personalities from which it could collect nothing. Such personalities cannot assuredly outlive consciously their terrestrial existence.

X. Thus then it seems, that for the terrestrial personality, immortality is still conditional. Is then immortality itself *not* unconditional?

M. Not at all. But it cannot touch the *non-existent*. For all that which exists as SAT, ever aspiring to SAT, immortality and Eternity are absolute. Matter is the opposite pole of spirit and yet the two are one. The essence of all this, *i.e.*, Spirit, Force and Matter, or the three in one, is as endless as it is beginningless; but the form acquired by this triple unity during its incarnations, the externality, is certainly only the illusion of our personal conceptions. Therefore do we call the after-life alone a reality, while relegating the terrestrial life, its terrestrial personality included, to the phantom realm of illusion.

X. But why in such a case not call sleep the reality, and waking the illusion, instead of the reverse?

M. Because we use an expression made to facilitate the grasping of the subject, and from the standpoint of terrestrial conceptions it is a very correct one.

X. Nevertheless, I cannot understand. If the life to come is based on justice and the merited retribution for all our terrestrial suffering, how, in the case of materialists many of whom are ideally honest and charitable men, should there remain of their personality nothing but the refuse of a faded flower!

M. No one ever said such a thing. No materialist, if a good man, however unbelieving, can die forever in the fulness of his spiritual individuality. What was said is, that the consciousness of one life can disappear either fully or partially; in the case of a thorough materialist, no vestige of that personality which disbelieved remains in the series of lives.

X. But is this not annihilation to the Ego?

M. Certainly not. One can sleep a dead sleep during a long railway journey, miss one or several stations without the slightest recollection or consciousness of it, awake at another station and continue the journey recollecting other halting places, till the end of that journey, when the goal is reached. Three kinds of sleep were mentioned to you: the dreamless, the chaotic, and the one so real, that to the sleeping man his dreams become full realities. If you believe in the latter why can't you believe in the former? According to what one has believed in and expected after death, such is the state one will have. He who expected no life to come will have an absolute blank amounting to annihilation in the interval between the two rebirths. This is just the carrying out of the programme we spoke of, and which is created by the materialist himself. But there are various kinds of materialists, as you say. A selfish wicked Egoist, one who never shed a tear for anyone but himself, thus adding entire indifference to the whole world to his unbelief, must drop at the threshold of death his personality forever. This personality having no tendrils of sympathy for the world around, and hence nothing to hook on to the string of the Sutratma, every connection between the two is broken with last breath. There being no Devachan for such a materialists, the Sutratma will re-incarnate almost immediately. But those materialists who erred in nothing but their disbelief, will oversleep but one station. Moreover, the time will come when the ex-material perceive himself in the Eternity and perhaps repent that he lost even one day, or station, from the life eternal.

X. Still would it not be more correct to say that death is birth new Life or a return once more to the threshold of eternity?

M. You may if you like. Only remember that births differ, and that there are births of "still-born" beings, which are *failures.* More-over with your fixed Western ideas about material life, the words "living" and "being" are quite inapplicable to the pure subjective *post-mortem* existence. It is just because of such ideas – a few philosophers who are not read by the many and who themselves are too confused to present a distinct picture of it – that all your conceptions of life and death have finally become so narrow. On the one hand, they have led to crass materialism, and on the other, to the still more material conception of the other life which ritualists have formulated in their Summer-land. There the souls of men eat, drink and marry, and live in a Paradise quite as sensual as that of Mohammed, but even less philosophical. Nor are average conceptions of the uneducated Christians any better, but are still more material, if possible. What between truncated Angels, brass trumpets, golden harps, streets in paradisiacal cities with jewels, and hell-fires, it seems like a scene at a Christmas pantomime. It is because of these narrow conceptions that you such difficulty in understanding. And, it is also just because the life of the disembodied soul, while possessing all the vividness of reality, as in certain dreams, is devoid of every grossly objective form of terrestrial life, that the Eastern philosophers have compared it with visions during sleep.

H.P. Blavatsky
Lucifer, January, 1889
https://www.theosophytrust.org/398-dialogue-on-the-mysteries-of-the-after-life

ON THE VARIOUS POST MORTEM STATES

The Physical and the Spiritual Man

Enquirer. I am glad to hear you believe in the immortality of the Soul.

Theosophist. Not of "the Soul," but of the divine Spirit; or rather in the immortality of the re-incarnating Ego.

Enquirer. What is the difference?

Theosophist. A very great one in our philosophy, but this is too abstruse and difficult a question to touch lightly upon. We shall have to analyse them separately, and then in conjunction. We may begin with Spirit.

We say that the Spirit (the "Father in secret" of Jesus), or *Atman*, is no individual property of any man, but is the Divine essence which has no body, no form, which is imponderable, invisible and indivisible, that which does not *exist* and yet *is*, as the Buddhists say of Nirvana. It only overshadows the mortal; that which enters into him and pervades the whole body being only its omnipresent rays, or light, radiated through *Buddhi*, its vehicle and direct emanation. This is the secret meaning of the assertions of almost all the ancient philosophers, when they said that "the *rational* part of man's soul"[1] never entered wholly into the man, but only overshadowed him more or less through the *irrational* spiritual Soul or *Buddhi*.[2]

Enquirer. I laboured under the impression that the "Animal Soul" alone was irrational, not the Divine.

---

[1] In its generic sense, the word "rational" meaning something emanating from the Eternal Wisdom

[2] *Irrational* in the sense that as a *pure* emanation of the Universal mind it can have no individual reason of its own on this plane of matter, but like the Moon, who borrows her light from the Sun and her life from the Earth, so *Buddhi*, receiving its light of Wisdom from Atma, gets its rational qualities from *Manas*. *Per se*, as something homogeneous, it is devoid of attributes.

Theosophist. You have to learn the difference between that which is negatively, or *passively* "irrational," because undifferentiated, and that which is irrational because too *active* and positive. Man is a correlation of spiritual powers, as well as a correlation of chemical and physical forces, brought into function by what we call "principles."

Enquirer. I have read a good deal upon the subject, and it seems to me that the notions of the older philosophers differed a great deal from those of the mediaeval Kabalists, though they do agree in some particulars.

Theosophist. The most substantial difference between them and us is this. While we believe with the Neo-Platonists and the Eastern teachings that the spirit (Atma) never descends hypostatically into the living man, but only showers more or less its radiance on the *inner* man (the psychic and spiritual compound of the *astral*) principles, the Kabalists maintain that the human Spirit, detaching itself from the ocean of light and Universal Spirit, enters man's Soul, where it remains throughout life imprisoned in the astral capsule. All Christian Kabalists still maintain the same, as they are unable to break quite loose from their anthropomorphic and Biblical doctrines.

Enquirer. And what do you say?

Theosophist. We say that we only allow the presence of the radiation of Spirit (or Atma) in the astral capsule, and so far only as that spiritual radiancy is concerned. We say that man and Soul have to conquer their immortality by ascending towards the unity with which, if successful, they will be finally linked and into which they are finally, so to speak, absorbed. The individualization of man after death depends on the spirit, not on his soul and body. Although the word "personality," in the sense in which it is usually understood, is an absurdity if applied literally to our immortal essence, still the latter is, as our individual Ego, a distinct entity, immortal and eternal, *per se. It is only in the case of black magicians or of criminals beyond redemption, criminals who have been such during a long series of lives* – that the shining thread, which links the spirit to the *personal* soul from the moment of the birth of the child, is violently snapped, and the disembodied entity becomes divorced from the personal soul, the latter being annihilated without leaving the smallest impression of itself on the former. If that union between the lower, or personal Manas, and the individual reincarnating Ego, has not been effected during life, then the former is left to share the fate of the lower animals, to gradually dissolve into ether, and have its personality annihilated. But even then the Ego remains a distinct being. It (the spiritual Ego) only loses one Devachanic state – after that special, and in that case indeed useless, life – as that idealized *Personality*, and is reincarnated, after enjoying for a short time its freedom as a planetary spirit almost immediately.

Enquirer. It is stated in *Isis Unveiled* that such planetary Spirits or Angels, "the gods of the Pagans or the Archangels of the Christians," will never be men on our planet.

Theosophist. Quite right. Not "*such*," but *some* classes of higher Planetary Spirits. They will never be men on this planet, because they are liberated Spirits from a previous, earlier world, and as such they cannot re-become men on this one. Yet all these will live again in the next and far higher Mahamanvantara, after this "great Age," and "Brahma *pralaya*," (a little period of 16 figures or so) is over. For you must have heard, of course, that Eastern philosophy teaches us that mankind consists of such "Spirits" imprisoned in human bodies? The difference between animals and men is this: the former are ensouled by the "principles" *potentially*, the latter *actually*. [3] Do you understand now the difference?

Enquirer. Yes; but this specialisation has been in all ages the stumbling-block of metaphysicians.

Theosophist. It was. The whole esotericism of the Buddhistic philosophy is based on this mysterious teaching, understood by so

---

[3] *Vide* "Secret Doctrine," Vol. II., stanzas.

few persons, and so totally misrepresented by many of the most learned modern scholars. Even metaphysicians are too inclined to confound the effect with the cause. An Ego who has won his immortal life as spirit will remain the same inner self throughout all his rebirths on earth; but this does not imply necessarily that he must either remain the Mr. Smith or Mr. Brown he was on earth, or lose his individuality. Therefore, the astral soul and the terrestrial body of man may, in the dark hereafter, be absorbed into the cosmical ocean of sublimated elements, and cease to feel his last *personal* Ego (if it did not deserve to soar higher), and the *divine* Ego still remain the same unchanged entity, though this terrestrial experience of his emanation may be totally obliterated at the instant of separation from the unworthy vehicle.

Enquirer. If the "Spirit," or the divine portion of the soul, is pre-existent as a distinct being from all eternity, as Origen, Synesius, and other semi-Christians and semi-Platonic philosophers taught, and if it is the same, and nothing more than the metaphysically-objective soul, how can it be otherwise than eternal? And what matters it in such a case, whether man leads a pure life or an animal, if, do what he may, he can never lose his individuality?

Theosophist. This doctrine, as you have stated it, is just as pernicious in its consequences as that of vicarious atonement. Had the latter dogma, in company with the false idea that we are all immortal, been demonstrated to the world in its true light, humanity would have been bettered by its propagation.

Let me repeat to you again. Pythagoras, Plato, Timæus of Locris, and the old Alexandrian School, derived the *Soul* of man (or his higher "principles" and attributes) from the Universal World Soul, the latter being, according to their teachings, *Æther* (Pater-Zeus). Therefore, neither of these "principles" can be *unalloyed* essence of the Pythagorean *Monas*, or our *Atma-Buddhi*, because the *Anima Mundi* is but the effect, the subjective emanation or rather radiation of the former. Both the *human* Spirit (or the individuality), the re-incarnating Spiritual Ego, and Buddhi, the Spiritual soul, are pre-existent. But, while the former exists as a distinct entity, an individualization, the soul exists as pre-existing breath, an unscient portion of an intelligent whole. Both were originally formed from the Eternal Ocean of light; but as the Fire-Philosophers, the mediaeval Theosophists, expressed it, there is a visible as well as invisible spirit in fire. They made a difference between the *anima bruta* and the *anima divina*. Empedocles firmly believed all men and animals to possess two souls; and in Aristotle we find that he calls one the reasoning soul, *nous*, and the other, the animal soul, *psuche*. According to these philosophers, the reasoning soul comes from *within* the universal soul, and the other from *without*.

Enquirer. Would you call the Soul, *i. e.*, the human thinking Soul, or what you call the Ego – matter?

Theosophist. Not matter, but *substance* assuredly; nor would the word "matter," if prefixed with the adjective, *primordial*, be a word to avoid. That matter, we say, is co-eternal with Spirit, and is not our visible, tangible, and divisible matter, but its extreme sublimation. Pure Spirit is but one remove from the *no*-Spirit, or the absolute *all*. Unless you admit that man was evolved out of this primordial Spirit-matter, and represents a regular progressive scale of "principles" from *meta*-Spirit down to the grossest matter, how can we ever come to regard the *inner* man as immortal, and at the same time as a spiritual Entity and a mortal man?

Enquirer. Then why should you not believe in God as such an Entity?

Theosophist. Because that which is infinite and unconditioned can have no form, and cannot be a being, not in any Eastern philosophy worthy of the name, at any rate. An "entity" is immortal, but is so only in its ultimate essence, not in its individual form. When at the last point of its cycle, it is absorbed into its primordial nature; and it becomes spirit, when it loses its name of Entity.

Its immortality as a form is limited only to its life-cycle or the *Mahamanvantara*; after which it is one and identical with the

Universal Spirit, and no longer a separate Entity. As to the *personal Soul* – by which we mean the spark of consciousness that preserves in the Spiritual Ego the idea of the personal "I" of the last incarnation – this lasts, as a separate distinct recollection, only throughout the Devachanic period; after which time it is added to the series of other innumerable incarnations of the Ego, like the remembrance in our memory of one of a series of days, at the end of a year. Will you bind the infinitude you claim for your God to finite conditions? That alone which is indissolubly cemented by *Atma* (*i.e.*, Buddhi-Manas) is immortal. The soul of man (*i.e.*, of the personality) *per se* is neither immortal, eternal nor divine. Says the *Zohar* (vol. iii., p.616), "the soul, when sent to this earth, puts on an earthly garment, to preserve herself here, so she receives above a shining garment, in order to be able to look without injury into the mirror, whose light proceeds from the Lord of Light." Moreover, the *Zohar* teaches that the soul cannot reach the abode of bliss, unless she has received the "holy kiss," or the reunion of the soul *with the substance from which she emanated* – spirit. All souls are dual, and, while the latter is a feminine principle, the spirit is masculine. While imprisoned in body, man is a trinity, unless his pollution is such as to have caused his divorce from the spirit. "Woe to the soul which prefers to her divine husband (spirit) the earthly wedlock with her terrestrial body," records a text of the *Book of the Keys*, a Hermetic work. Woe indeed, for nothing will remain of that personality to be recorded on the imperishable tablets of the Ego's memory.

Enquirer. How can that which, if not breathed by God into man, yet is on your own confession of an identical substance with the divine, fail to be immortal?

Theosophist. Every atom and speck of matter, not of substance only, is *imperishable* in its essence, but not in its *individual consciousness*. Immortality is but one's unbroken consciousness; and the *personal* consciousness can hardly last longer than the personality itself, can it? And such consciousness, as I already told you, survives only throughout Devachan, after which it is reabsorbed, first, in the *individual*, and then in the *universal* consciousness. Better enquire of your theologians how it is that they have so sorely jumbled up the Jewish Scriptures. Read the Bible, if you would have a good proof that the writers of the *Pentateuch*, and *Genesis* especially, never regarded *nephesh*, that which God breathes into Adam (*Gen.* ch. ii.), as the *immortal* soul. Here are some instances: – "And God created . . . . every *nephesh* (life) that moveth" (*Gen.* i. 21), meaning animals; and (*Gen.* ii. 7) it is said: "And man became a *nephesh*" (living soul), which shows that the word *nephesh* was indifferently applied to *immortal* man and to *mortal* beast. "And surely your blood of your *nepheshim* (lives) will I require; at the hand of every beast will I require it, and at the hand of man" (*Gen.* ix. 5), "Escape for *nephesh*" (escape for thy *life*, it is translated), (*Gen.* xix. 17). "Let us not kill him," reads the English version (*Gen.* xxxvii. 21.) "Let us not kill his *nephesh*," is the Hebrew text. "*Nephesh* for *nephesh*," says Leviticus (xvii. 8). "He that killeth any man shall surely be put to death," literally "He that smiteth the *nephesh* of a man" (*Lev.* xxiv. 17); and from verse 18 and following it reads: "And he that killeth a beast (*nephesh*) shall make it good. . . . Beast for beast," whereas the original text has it "nephesh for nephesh." How could man *kill* that which is immortal? And this explains also why the Sadducees denied the immortality of the soul, as it also affords another proof that very probably the Mosaic Jews – the uninitiated at any rate – never believed in the soul's survival at all.

On Eternal Reward and Punishment, and on Nirvana

Enquirer. It is hardly necessary, I suppose, to ask you whether you believe in the Christian dogmas of Paradise and Hell, or in future rewards and punishments as taught by the Orthodox churches?

Theosophist. As described in your catechisms, we reject them absolutely; least of all would we accept their eternity. But we believe firmly in what we call the *Law of Retribution*, and in the absolute justice and wisdom guiding this Law, or Karma. Hence we positively refuse to accept the cruel and unphilosophical belief in eternal reward or eternal punishment. We say with Horace:

> "Let rules be fixed that may our rage contain,
> And punish faults with a proportion'd pain;
> But do not flay him who deserves alone
> A whipping for the fault that he has done."

This is a rule for all men, and a just one. Have we to believe that God, of whom you make the embodiment of wisdom, love and mercy, is less entitled to these attributes than mortal man?

Enquirer. Have you any other reasons for rejecting this dogma?

Theosophist. Our chief reason for it lies in the fact of re-incarnation. As already stated, we reject the idea of a new soul created for every newly-born babe. We believe that every human being is the bearer, or *Vehicle*, of an *Ego* coeval with every other Ego; because all *Egos* are *of the same essence* and belong to the primeval emanation from one universal infinite *Ego*. Plato calls the latter the *logos* (or the second manifested God); and we, the manifested divine principle, which is one with the universal mind or soul, not the anthropomorphic, extra-cosmic and *personal* God in which so many Theists believe. Pray do not confuse.

Enquirer. But where is the difficulty, once you accept a manifested principle, in believing that the soul of every new mortal is *created* by that Principle, as all the Souls before it have been so created?

Theosophist. Because that which is *impersonal* can hardly create, plan and think, at its own sweet will and pleasure. Being a universal *Law*, immutable in its periodical manifestations, those of radiating and manifesting its own essence at the beginning of every new cycle of life, IT is not supposed to create men, only to repent a few years later of having created them. If we have to believe in a divine principle at all, it must be in one which is as absolute harmony, logic, and justice, as it is absolute love, wisdom, and impartiality; and a God who would *create* every soul for the space of *one brief span of life*, regardless of the fact whether it has to animate the body of a wealthy, happy man, or that of a poor suffering wretch, hapless from birth to death though he has done nothing to deserve his cruel fate – would be rather a senseless *fiend* than a God. (*Vide infra*, "On the Punishment of the Ego".) Why, even the Jewish philosophers, believers in the Mosaic Bible (esoterically, of course), have never entertained such an idea; and, moreover, they believed in re-incarnation, as we do.

Enquirer. Can you give me some instances as a proof of this?

Theosophist. Most decidedly I can. Philo Judaeus says (in "*De Somniis*," p. 455): "The air is full of them (of souls); those which are nearest the earth, descending to be tied to mortal bodies, παλινδρομοῦσι αὖθις, *return to other bodies, being desirous to live in them.*" In the *Zohar*, the soul is made to plead her freedom before God: "Lord of the Universe! I am happy in this world, and do not wish to go into another world, where I shall be a handmaid, and be exposed to all kinds of pollutions."[4] The doctrine of fatal necessity, the everlasting immutable law, is asserted in the answer of the Deity: "Against thy will thou becomest an embryo, and against thy will thou art born."[5] Light would be incomprehensible without darkness to make it manifest by contrast; good would be no longer good without evil to show the priceless nature of the boon; and so personal virtue could claim no merit, unless it had passed through the furnace of temptation. Nothing is eternal and unchangeable, save the concealed Deity. Nothing that is finite – whether because it had a beginning, or must have an end – can remain stationary. It must either progress or recede; and a soul which thirsts after a reunion with its spirit, which alone confers upon it immortality, must purify itself through cyclic transmigrations onward toward the only land of bliss and eternal rest, called in the *Zohar*, "The Palace of Love"; in the Hindu religion, "Moksha"; among the Gnostics, "The Pleroma of Eternal Light"; and by the Buddhists, "Nirvana". And all these states are temporary, not eternal.

---

[4] "*Zohar*," Vol. 11., p. 96.
[5] "*Mishna*," "*Aboth*," Vol. IV, p. 29.

Enquirer. Yet there is no re-incarnation spoken of in all this.

Theosophist. A soul which pleads to be allowed to remain where she is, *must be pre-existent*, and not have been created for the occasion. In the *Zohar* (vol. iii., p. 61), however, there is a still better proof. Speaking of the re-incarnating *Egos* (the *rational* souls), those whose last personality has to fade out *entirely*, it is said: "All souls which have alienated themselves in heaven from the Holy One – blessed be His Name – have thrown themselves into an abyss at their very existence, and have anticipated the time when they are to descend once more on earth." "The Holy One" means here, esoterically, the Atman, or *Atma-Buddhi*.

Enquirer. Moreover, it is very strange to find *Nirvana* spoken of as something synonymous with the Kingdom of Heaven, or the Paradise, since according to every Orientalist of note Nirvana is a synonym of annihilation!

Theosophist. Taken literally, with regard to the personality and differentiated matter, not otherwise. These ideas on re-incarnation and the trinity of man were held by many of the early Christian Fathers. It is the jumble made by the translators of the New Testament and ancient philosophical treatises between soul and spirit, that has occasioned the many misunderstandings. It is also one of the many reasons why Buddha, Plotinus, and so many other Initiates are now accused of having longed for the total extinction of their souls – "absorption unto the Deity," or "reunion with the universal soul," meaning, according to modern ideas, annihilation. The personal soul must, of course, be disintegrated into its particles, before it is able to link its purer essence forever with the immortal spirit. But the translators of both the *Acts* and the *Epistles*, who laid the foundation of the *Kingdom of Heaven*, and the modern commentators on the Buddhist *Sutra of the Foundation of the Kingdom of Righteousness*, have muddled the sense of the great apostle of Christianity as of the great reformer of India. The former have smothered the word ψυχικος, so that no reader imagines it to have any relation with *soul;* and with this confusion of *soul* and *spirit* together, *Bible* readers get only a perverted sense of anything on the subject. On the other hand, the interpreters of Buddha have failed to understand the meaning and object of the Buddhist four degrees of Dhyana. Ask the Pythagoreans, "Can that spirit, which gives life and motion and partakes of the nature of light, be reduced to nonentity?" "Can even that sensitive spirit in brutes which exercises memory, one of the rational faculties, die and become nothing?" observe the Occultists. In Buddhistic philosophy *annihilation* means only a dispersion of matter, in whatever form or *semblance* of form it may be, for everything that has form is temporary, and is, therefore, really an illusion. For in eternity the longest periods of time are as a wink of the eye. So with form. Before we have time to realize that we have seen it, it is gone like an instantaneous flash of lightning, and passed for ever. When the Spiritual *entity* breaks loose forever from every particle of matter, substance, or form, and re-becomes a Spiritual breath: then only does it enter upon the eternal and unchangeable *Nirvana*, lasting as long as the cycle of life has lasted – an eternity, truly. And then that Breath, existing *in Spirit*, is *nothing* because it is *all;* as a form, a semblance, a shape, it is completely annihilated; as absolute Spirit it still *is*, for it has become *Be-ness* itself. The very word used, "absorbed in the universal essence," when spoken of the "Soul" as Spirit, means "*union with.*" It can never mean annihilation, as that would mean eternal separation.

Enquirer. Do you not lay yourself open to the accusation of preaching annihilation by the language you yourself use? You have just spoken of the Soul of man returning to its primordial elements.

Theosophist. But you forget that I have given you the differences between the various meanings of the word "Soul," and shown the loose way in which the term "Spirit" has been hitherto translated. We speak of an *animal*, a *human*, and a *spiritual*, Soul, and distinguish between them. Plato, for instance, calls "rational SOUL" that which we call *Buddhi*, adding to it the adjective of "spiritual," however; but that which we call the reincarnating Ego, *Manas*, he calls *Spirit*, *Nous*, etc., whereas we apply the term *Spirit*, when standing alone and without any qualification, to Atma alone. Pythagoras repeats our archaic doctrine when stating that the *Ego* (*Nous*) is eternal with Deity; that the soul only passed through various stages to arrive at divine excellence; while *thumos* returned to the earth, and even the *phren*, the lower *Manas*, was eliminated. Again, Plato defines *Soul* (Buddhi) as "the motion that is able to move itself." "Soul," he adds (*Laws* X.), "is the most ancient of all things, and the commencement of motion," thus calling *Atma-Buddhi* "Soul," and *Manas* "Spirit," which we do not.

> "Soul was generated prior to body, and body is posterior and secondary, as being according to nature, ruled over by the ruling soul." "The soul which administers all things that are moved in every way, administers likewise the heavens."

> "Soul then leads everything in heaven, and on earth, and in the sea, by its movements – the names of which are, to will, to consider, to take care of, to consult, to form opinions true and false, to be in a state of joy, sorrow, confidence, fear, hate, love, together with all such primary movements as are allied to these. ... Being a goddess herself, she ever takes as an ally *Nous*, a god, and disciplines all things correctly and happily; but when with *Annoia* – not *nous* – it works out everything the contrary."

In this language, as in the Buddhist texts, the negative is treated as essential existence. *Annihilation* comes under a similar exegesis. The positive state is essential being, but no manifestation as such. When the spirit, in Buddhistic parlance, enters *Nirvana*, it loses objective existence, but retains subjective being. To objective minds this is becoming absolute "nothing"; to subjective, NO-THING, nothing to be displayed to sense. Thus, their Nirvana means the certitude of individual immortality *in Spirit*, not in Soul, which, though "the most ancient of all things," is still – along with all the other *Gods* – a finite emanation, in *forms* and individuality, if not in substance.

Enquirer. I do not quite seize the idea yet, and would be thankful to have you explain this to me by some illustrations.

Theosophist. No doubt it is very difficult to understand, especially to one brought up in the regular orthodox ideas of the Christian Church. Moreover, I must tell you one thing; and this is that unless you have studied thoroughly well the separate functions assigned to all the human "principles" and the state of all these *after death*, you will hardly realize our Eastern philosophy.

On the Various "Principles" in Man

Enquirer. I have heard a good deal about this constitution of the "inner man" as you call it, but could never make "head or tail on't" as Gabalis expresses it.

Theosophist. Of course, it is most difficult, and, as you say, "puzzling" to understand correctly and distinguish between the various *aspects*, called by us the "principles" of the real EGO. It is the more so as there exists a notable difference in the numbering of those principles by various Eastern schools, though at the bottom there is the same identical substratum of teaching.

Enquirer. Do you mean the Vedantins, as an instance? Don't they divide your seven "principles" into five only?

Theosophist. They do; but though I would not presume to dispute the point with a learned Vedantin, I may yet state as my private opinion that they have an obvious reason for it. With them it is only that compound spiritual aggregate which consists of various mental aspects that is called *Man* at all, the physical body being in their view something beneath contempt, and merely an *illusion*. Nor is the Vedanta the only philosophy to reckon in this manner. Lao-Tze, in his *Tao-te-King*, mentions only five principles, because he, like the Vedantins, omits to include two principles, namely, the spirit (Atma) and the physical body, the latter of which, moreover, he calls "the cadaver." Then there is the *Taraka Raja Yoga* School. Its teaching recognises only three "principles" in fact; but then, in reality, their *Sthulopadi*, or the physical body, in its waking conscious state, their *Sukshmopadhi*, the same body in *Svapna*, or the dreaming state, and their *Karanopadhi* or "causal body," or that which passes from one incarnation to another, are all dual in their aspects, and thus make six. Add to this Atma, the impersonal divine principle or the immortal element in Man, undistinguished from the Universal Spirit, and you have the same seven again.[6] They are welcome to hold to their division; we hold to ours.

Enquirer. Then it seems almost the same as the division made by the mystic Christians: body, soul and spirit?

Theosophist. Just the same. We could easily make of the body the vehicle of the "vital Double"; of the latter the vehicle of Life or *Prana;* of *Kamarupa,* or (animal) soul, the vehicle of the *higher* and the *lower* mind, and make of this six principles, crowning the whole with the one immortal spirit. In Occultism every qualificative change in the state of our consciousness gives to man a new aspect, and if it prevails and becomes part of the living and acting Ego, it must be (and is) given a special name, to distinguish the man in that particular state from the man he is when he places himself in another state.

Enquirer. It is just that which it is so difficult to understand.

Theosophist. It seems to me very easy, on the contrary, once that you have seized the main idea, *i.e.,* that man acts on this or another plane of consciousness, in strict accordance with his mental and spiritual condition. But such is the materialism of the age that the more we explain the less people seem capable of understanding what we say. Divide the terrestrial being called man into three chief aspects, if you like, and unless you make of him a pure animal you cannot do less. Take his objective *body;* the thinking principle in him – which is only a little higher than the *instinctual* element in the animal – or the vital conscious soul; and that which places him so immeasurably beyond and higher than the animal – *i.e.,* his *reasoning* soul or "spirit." Well, if we take these three groups or representative entities, and subdivide them, according to the occult teaching, what do we get?

---

[6] See "*The Secret Doctrine*" for a clearer explanation: Vol. I, p. 157.

First of all, Spirit (in the sense of the Absolute, and therefore, indivisible ALL), or Atma. As this can neither be located nor limited in philosophy, being simply that which is in Eternity, and which cannot be absent from even the tiniest geometrical or mathematical point of the universe of matter or substance, it ought not to be called, in truth, a "human" principle at all. Rather, and at best, it is in Metaphysics, that point in space which the human Monad and its vehicle man occupy for the period of every life. Now that point is as imaginary as man himself, and in reality is an illusion, a *maya;* but then for ourselves, as for other personal Egos, we are a reality during that fit of illusion called life, and we have to take ourselves into account, in our own fancy at any rate, if no one else does. To make it more conceivable to the human intellect, when first attempting the study of Occultism, and to solve the A B C of the mystery of man, Occultism calls this *seventh* principle the synthesis of the sixth, and gives it for vehicle the *Spiritual* Soul, *Buddhi.* Now the latter conceals a mystery, which is never given to any one, with the exception of irrevocably pledged *chelas,* or those, at any rate, who can be safely trusted. Of course, there would be less confusion, could it only be told; but, as this is directly concerned with the power of projecting one's double consciously and at will, and as this gift, like the "ring of Gyges," would prove very fatal to man at large and to the possessor of that faculty in particular, it is carefully guarded. But let us proceed with the "principles." This divine soul, or Buddhi, then, is the vehicle of the Spirit. In conjunction, these two are one, impersonal and without any attributes (on this plane, of course), and make two spiritual "principles." If we pass on to the *Human* Soul, *Manas* or *mens,* everyone will agree that the intelligence of man is *dual* to say the least: *e.g.,* the high-minded man can hardly become low-minded; the very intellectual and spiritual-minded man is separated by an abyss from the obtuse, dull, and material, if not animal-minded man.

Enquirer. But why should not man be represented by two "principles" or two aspects, rather?

Theosophist. Every man has these two principles in him, one more active than the other, and in rare cases, one of these is entirely stunted in its growth, so to say, or paralysed by the strength and predominance of the other *aspect*, in whatever direction. These, then, are what we call the two principles or aspects of *Manas*, the higher and the lower; the former, the higher Manas, or the thinking, conscious EGO gravitating toward the spiritual Soul (Buddhi); and the latter, or its instinctual principle, attracted to *Kama*, the seat of animal desires and passions in man.

Thus, we have *four* "principles" justified; the last three being (1) the "Double," which we have agreed to call Protean, or Plastic Soul; the vehicle of (2) the life *principle;* and (3) the physical body. Of course no physiologist or biologist will accept these principles, nor can he make head or tail of them. And this is why, perhaps, none of them understand to this day either the functions of the spleen, the physical vehicle of the Protean Double, or those of a certain organ on the right side of man, the seat of the above-mentioned desires, nor yet does he know anything of the pineal gland, which he describes as a horny gland with a little sand in it, which gland is in truth the very seat of the highest and divinest consciousness in man, his omniscient, spiritual and all-embracing mind. And this shows to you still more plainly that we have neither invented these seven principles, nor are they new in the world of philosophy, as we can easily prove.

Enquirer. But what is it that reincarnates, in your belief?

Theosophist. The Spiritual thinking Ego, the permanent principle in man, or that which is the seat of *Manas*. It is not Atma, or even Atma-Buddhi, regarded as the dual *Monad*, which is the *individual*, or *divine* man, but Manas; for Atman is the Universal ALL, and becomes the HIGHER-SELF of man only in conjunction with *Buddhi*, its vehicle, which links IT to the individuality (or divine man). For it is the Buddhi-Manas which is called the *Causal body*, (the United 5th and 6th Principles) and which is *Consciousness*, that connects it with every personality it inhabits on earth. Therefore, Soul being a generic term, there are in men three *aspects* of Soul – the terrestrial, or animal; the Human Soul; and the Spiritual Soul; these, strictly speaking, are one Soul in its three aspects. Now of the first aspect, nothing remains after death; of the second (*nous* or Manas) only its divine essence *if left unsoiled* survives, while the third in addition to being immortal becomes *consciously* divine, by the assimilation of the higher Manas. But to make it clear, we have to say a few words first of all about Reincarnation.

Enquirer. You will do well, as it is against this doctrine that your enemies fight the most ferociously.

Theosophist. You mean the Spiritualists? I know; and many are the absurd objections laboriously spun by them over the pages of *Light*. So obtuse and malicious are some of them, that they will stop at nothing. One of them found recently a contradiction, which he gravely discusses in a letter to that journal, in two statements picked out of Mr. Sinnett's lectures. He discovers that grave contradiction in these two sentences: "Premature returns to earth-life in the cases when they occur may be due to Karmic complication . . ."; and "there is no *accident* in the supreme act of divine justice guiding evolution." So profound a thinker would surely see a contradiction of the law of gravitation if a man stretched out his hand to stop a falling stone from crushing the head of a child!

Why Do We Not Remember Our Past Lives?

Enquirer. You have given me a bird's eye view of the seven principles; now how do they account for our complete loss of any recollection of having lived before?

Theosophist. Very easily. Since those "principles" which we call physical, and none of which is denied by science, though it calls them by other names,[7] are disintegrated after death with their constituent elements, *memory* along with its brain, this vanished memory of a

---

[7] Namely, the body, life, passional and animal instincts, and the astral eidolon of every man (whether perceived in thought or our mind's eye, or objectively and separate from the physical body), which principles we call *Sthula sarira, Prana, Kama rupa,* and *Linga sarira (vide supra).*

vanished personality, can neither remember nor record anything in the subsequent reincarnation of the EGO. Reincarnation means that this Ego will be furnished with a *new* body, a *new* brain, and a *new* memory. Therefore it would be as absurd to expect this *memory* to remember that which it has never recorded as it would be idle to examine under a microscope a shirt never worn by a murderer, and seek on it for the stains of blood which are to be found only on the clothes he wore. It is not the clean shirt that we have to question, but the clothes worn during the perpetration of the crime; and if these are burnt and destroyed, how can you get at them?

Enquirer. Aye! how can you get at the certainty that the crime was ever committed at all, or that the "man in the clean shirt" ever lived before?

Theosophist. Not by physical processes, most assuredly; nor by relying on the testimony of that which exists no longer. But there is such a thing as circumstantial evidence, since our wise laws accept it, more, perhaps, even than they should. To get convinced of the fact of re-incarnation and past lives, one must put oneself in *rapport* with one's real permanent Ego, not one's evanescent memory.

Enquirer. But how can people believe in that which they *do not know*, nor have ever seen, far less put themselves in *rapport* with it?

Theosophist. If people, and the most learned, will believe in the Gravity, Ether, Force, and what not of Science, abstractions "and working hypotheses," which they have neither seen, touched, smelt, heard, nor tasted – why should not other people believe, on the same principle, in one's permanent Ego, a far more logical and important "working hypothesis" than any other?

Enquirer. What is, finally, this mysterious eternal principle? Can you explain its nature so as to make it comprehensible to all?

Theosophist. The EGO which re-incarnates, the *individual* and immortal – not personal – "I", the vehicle, in short, of the Atma-Buddhic MONAD, that which is rewarded in Devachan and punished on earth, and that, finally, to which the reflection only of the *Skandhas*, or attributes, of every incarnation attaches itself. [8]

Enquirer. What do you mean by *Skandhas*?

Theosophist. Just what I said: "attributes," among which is *memory*, all of which perish like a flower, leaving behind them only a feeble perfume. Here is another paragraph from H. S. Olcott's "*Buddhist Catechism*"[9] which bears directly upon the subject. It deals with the question as follows: "The aged man remembers the incidents of his youth, despite his being physically and mentally changed. Why, then, is not the recollection of past lives brought over by us from our last birth into the present birth? Because memory is included within the Skandhas, and the Skandhas having changed with the new existence, a memory, the record of that particular existence, develops. Yet the record or reflection of all the past lives must survive, for when Prince Siddhartha became Buddha, the full sequence of His previous births were seen by Him. . . . and anyone who attains to the state of *Jhana* can thus retrospectively trace the line of his lives." This proves to you that while the undying qualities of the personality – such as love, goodness, charity, etc. – attach themselves to the immortal Ego, photographing on it, so to speak, a permanent image of the divine aspect of the man who was, his material Skandhas (those which generate the most marked Karmic effects) are as evanescent as a flash of lightning, and cannot impress the new brain of the new personality; yet their failing to do so impairs in no way the identity of the re-incarnating Ego.

---

[8] There are five *Skandhas* or attributes in the Buddhist teachings: "Rupa (form or body), material qualities; *Vedana*, sensation; *Sanna*, abstract ideas; *Samkhara*, tendencies of mind; *Vinnana*, mental powers. Of these we are formed; by them we are conscious of existence; and through them communicate with the world about us."

[9] By H. S. Olcott, President and Founder of the Theosophical Society. The accuracy of the teaching is sanctioned by the Rev. H. Sumangala, High Priest of the Sripada and Galle, and Principal of the *Widyodaya Parivena* (College) at Colombo, as being in agreement with the Canon of the Southern Buddhist Church.

Enquirer. Do you mean to infer that that which survives is only the Soul-memory, as you call it, that Soul or Ego being one and the same, while nothing of the personality remains?

Theosophist. Not quite; something of each personality, unless the latter was an *absolute* materialist with not even a chink in his nature for a spiritual ray to pass through, must survive, as it leaves its eternal impress on the incarnating permanent Self or Spiritual Ego.[10] (See On *post mortem* and *post natal* Consciousness.) The personality with its Skandhas is ever changing with every new birth. It is, as said before, only the part played by the actor (the true Ego) for one night. This is why we preserve no memory on the physical plane of our past lives, though the *real* "Ego" has lived them over and knows them all.

Enquirer. Then how does it happen that the real or Spiritual man does not impress his new personal "I" with this knowledge?

Theosophist. How is it that the servant-girls in a poor farm-house could speak Hebrew and play the violin in their trance or somnambulic state, and knew neither when in their normal condition? Because, as every genuine psychologist of the old, not your modern, school, will tell you, the Spiritual Ego can act only when the personal Ego is paralysed. The Spiritual "I" in man is omniscient and has every knowledge innate in it; while the personal self is the creature of its environment and the slave of the physical memory. Could the former manifest itself uninterruptedly, and without impediment, there would be no longer men on earth, but we should all be gods.

Enquirer. Still there ought to be exceptions, and some ought to remember.

Theosophist. And so there are. But who believes in their report? Such sensitives are generally regarded as hallucinated hysteriacs, as

---

[10] Or the *Spiritual*, in contradistinction to the personal *Self*. The student must not confuse this Spiritual Ego with the "HIGHER SELF" which is *Atma*, the God within us, and inseparable from the Universal Spirit.

crack-brained enthusiasts, or humbugs, by modern materialism. Let them read, however, works on this subject, pre-eminently *"Reincarnation, a Study of Forgotten Truth"* by E. D. Walker, F. T. S., and see in it the mass of proofs which the able author brings to bear on this vexed question. One speaks to people of soul, and some ask "What is Soul?" "Have you ever proved its existence?" Of course it is useless to argue with those who are materialists. But even to them I would put the question: "Can you remember what you were or did when a baby? Have you preserved the smallest recollection of your life, thoughts, or deeds, or that you lived at all during the first eighteen months or two years of your existence? Then why not deny that you have ever lived as a babe, on the same principle?" When to all this we add that the reincarnating Ego, or *individuality*, retains during the Devachanic period merely the essence of the experience of its past earth-life or personality, the whole physical experience involving into a state of *in potentia*, or being, so to speak, translated into spiritual formulae; when we remember further that the term between two rebirths is said to extend from ten to fifteen centuries, during which time the physical consciousness is totally and absolutely inactive, having no organs to act through, and therefore *no existence*, the reason for the absence of all remembrance in the purely physical memory is apparent.

Enquirer. You just said that the SPIRITUAL EGO was omniscient. Where, then, is that vaunted omniscience during his Devachanic life, as you call it?

Theosophist. During that time it is latent and potential, because, first of all, the Spiritual Ego (the compound of Buddhi-Manas) is *not* the HIGHER SELF, which being one with the Universal Soul or Mind is alone omniscient; and, secondly, because Devachan is the idealized continuation of the terrestrial life just left behind, a period of retributive adjustment and a reward for unmerited wrongs and sufferings undergone in that special life. It is omniscient only *potentially* in Devachan, and *de facto* exclusively in Nirvana, when the Ego is merged in the Universal Mind-Soul. Yet it rebecomes *quasi* omniscient during those hours on earth when certain abnormal conditions and physiological changes in the body make the *Ego* free from the trammels of matter. Thus the examples cited above of somnambulists, a poor servant speaking Hebrew, and another playing the violin, give you an illustration of the case in point. This does not mean that the explanations of these two facts offered us by medical science have no truth in them, for one girl had, years before, heard her master, a clergyman, read Hebrew works aloud, and the other had heard an artist playing a violin at their farm. But neither could have done so as perfectly as they did had they not been ensouled by THAT which, owing to the sameness of its nature with the Universal Mind, is omniscient. Here the higher principle acted on the Skandhas and moved them; in the other, the personality being paralysed, the individuality manifested itself. Pray do not confuse the two.

On Individuality and Personality

Enquirer. But what is the difference between the two? I confess that I am still in the dark. Indeed it is just that difference, then, that you cannot impress too much on our minds.[11]

---

[11] Even in his *Buddhist Catechism*, Col. Olcott, forced to it by the logic of Esoteric philosophy, found himself obliged to correct the mistakes of previous Orientalists who made no such distinction, and gives the reader his reasons for it. Thus he says: "The successive appearances upon the earth, or 'descents into generation,' of the *tanhaically* coherent parts (Skandhas) of a certain being, are a succession of personalities. In each birth the PERSONALITY differs from that of a previous or next succeeding birth. Karma, the DEUS EX MACHINA, masks (or shall we say reflects?) itself now in the personality of a sage, again as an artisan, and so on throughout the string of births. But though personalities ever shift, the one line of life along which they are strung, like beads, runs unbroken; it is ever that *particular line*, never any other. It is therefore individual, an individual vital undulation, which began in Nirvana, or the subjective side of nature, as the light or heat

Theosophist. I try to; but alas, it is harder with some than to make them feel a reverence for childish impossibilities, only because they are *orthodox*, and because orthodoxy is respectable. To understand the idea well, you have to first study the dual sets of "principles": the *spiritual*, or those which belong to the imperishable Ego; and the *material*, or those principles which make up the ever-changing bodies or the series of personalities of that Ego. Let us fix permanent names to these, and say that:

I. *Atma*, the *"Higher Self,"* is neither your Spirit nor mine, but like sunlight shines on all. It is the universally diffused *"divine principle,"* and is inseparable from its one and absolute *Meta*-Spirit, as the sunbeam is inseparable from sunlight.

II. *Buddhi* (the spiritual soul) is only its vehicle. Neither each separately, nor the two collectively, are of any more use to the

---

undulation through aether began at its dynamic source; is careering through the objective side of nature under the impulse of Karma and the creative direction of *Tanha* (the unsatisfied desire for existence); and leads through many cyclic changes back to Nirvana. Mr. Rhys-Davids calls that which passes from personality to personality along the individual chain 'character,' or 'doing.' Since 'character' is not a mere metaphysical abstraction, but the sum of one's mental qualities and moral propensities, would it not help to dispel what Mr. Rhys-Davids calls 'the desperate expedient of a mystery' (*Buddhism*, p. 101) if we regarded the life-undulation as individuality, and each of its series of natal manifestations as a separate personality? The perfect individual, Buddhistically speaking, is a Buddha, I should say; for Buddha is but the rare flower of humanity, without the least supernatural admixture. And as countless generations ('four *asankheyyas* and a hundred thousand cycles,' Fausboll and Rhys-Davids' *Buddhist Birth Stories*, p. 13) are required to develop a *man* into a Buddha, and *the iron will to become one* runs throughout all the successive births, what shall we call that which thus wills and perseveres? Character? One's individuality: an individuality but partly manifested in any one birth, but built up of fragments from all the births?" (*Bud. Cat., Appendix* A. 137) body of man, than sunlight and its beams are for a mass of granite buried in the earth, *unless the divine Duad is assimilated by, and reflected in,* some *consciousness.* Neither Atma nor Buddhi are ever reached by Karma, because the former is the highest aspect of Karma, *its working agent* of ITSELF in one aspect, and the other is unconscious *on this plane.* This consciousness or mind is,

III. *Manas,*[12] the derivation or product in a reflected form of *Ahamkara,* "the conception of I," or EGO-SHIP. It is, therefore, when inseparably united to the first two, called the SPIRITUAL EGO, and *Taijasi* (the radiant). This is the real Individuality, or the divine man. It is this Ego which – having originally incarnated in the *senseless* human form animated by, but unconscious (since it had no consciousness) of, the presence in itself of the dual monad – made of that human-like form *a real man.* It is that Ego, that "Causal Body," which overshadows every personality Karma forces it to incarnate into; and this Ego which is held responsible for all the sins committed through, and in, every new body or personality – the evanescent masks which hide the true Individual through the long series of rebirths.

Enquirer. But is this just? Why should this Ego receive punishment as the result of deeds which it has forgotten?

Theosophist. It has not forgotten them; it knows and remembers its misdeeds as well as you remember what you have done yesterday. Is it because the memory of that bundle of physical compounds called "body" does not recollect what its predecessor (the

---

[12] MAHAT or the "Universal Mind" is the source of Manas. The latter is Mahat, *i.e.,* mind, in man. Manas is also called *Kshetrajna,* "embodied Spirit," because it is, according to our philosophy, the *Manasa-putras,* or "Sons of the Universal Mind," who *created,* or rather produced, the *thinking* man, "manu," by incarnating in the *third Race* mankind in our Round. It is Manas, therefore, which is the real incarnating and permanent *Spiritual Ego,* the INDIVIDUALITY, and our various and numberless personalities only its external masks.

personality *that was)* did, that you imagine that the real Ego has forgotten them? As well say it is unjust that the new boots on the feet of a boy, who is flogged for stealing apples, should be punished for that which they know nothing of.

Enquirer. But are there no modes of communication between the Spiritual and human consciousness or memory?

Theosophist. Of course there are; but they have never been recognised by your scientific modern psychologists. To what do you attribute intuition, the "voice of the conscience," premonitions, vague undefined reminiscences, etc., etc., if not to such communications? Would that the majority of educated men, at least, had the fine spiritual perceptions of Coleridge, who shows how intuitional he is in some of his comments. Hear what he says with respect to the probability that "all thoughts are in themselves imperishable." "If the intelligent faculty (sudden 'revivals' of memory) should be rendered more comprehensive, it would require only a different and appropriate organization, the *body celestial* instead of the *body terrestrial,* to bring before every human soul *the collective experience of its whole past existence* (*existences,* rather)." And this *body celestial* is our Manasic EGO.

On the Reward and Punishment of the Ego

Enquirer. I have heard you say that the *Ego,* whatever the life of the person he incarnated in may have been on Earth, is never visited with *post-mortem* punishment.

Theosophist. Never, save in very exceptional and rare cases of which we will not speak here, as the nature of the "punishment" in no way approaches any of your theological conceptions of damnation.

Enquirer. But if it is punished in this life for the misdeeds committed in a previous one, then it is this Ego that ought to be rewarded also, whether here, or when disincarnated.

Theosophist. And so it is. If we do not admit of any punishment outside of this earth, it is because the only state the Spiritual Self knows of, hereafter, is that of unalloyed bliss.

Enquirer. What do you mean?

Theosophist. Simply this: crimes and sins committed on a plane of objectivity and in a world of matter, cannot receive punishment in a world of pure subjectivity. We believe in no hell or paradise as localities; in no objective hell-fires and worms that never die, nor in any Jerusalems with streets paved with sapphires and diamonds. What we believe in is a post-mortem state or mental condition, such as we are in during a vivid dream. We believe in an immutable law of absolute Love, Justice, and Mercy. And believing in it, we say: "Whatever the sin and dire results of the original Karmic transgression of the now incarnated Egos,[13] no man (or the outer material and periodical form of the Spiritual Entity) can be held, with any degree of justice, responsible for the consequences of his birth. He does not ask to be born, nor can he choose the parents that will give him life. In every respect he is a victim to his environment, the child of circumstances over which he has no control; and if each of his transgressions were impartially investigated, there would be

---

[13] It is on this transgression that the cruel and illogical dogma of the Fallen Angels has been built. It is explained in Vol. II. of *The Secret Doctrine.* All our "Egos" are thinking and rational entities (*Manasaputras*) who had lived, whether under human or other forms, in the precedent *life-cycle* (Manvantara), and whose Karma it was to incarnate in the *man* of this one. It was taught in the MYSTERIES that, having delayed to comply with this law (or having "refused to create" as Hinduism says of the *Kumaras* and Christian legend of the Archangel Michael), *i. e.*, having failed to incarnate in due time, the bodies predestined for them got defiled (*Vide* Stanzas VIII. and IX. in the "Slokas of Dzyan," Vol. II. *Secret Doctrine,* pp. 19 and 20), hence the original sin of the senseless forms and the punishment of the *Egos*. That which is meant by the rebellious angels being hurled down into Hell is simply explained by these pure Spirits or Egos being imprisoned in bodies of unclean matter, flesh.

found nine out of every ten cases when he was the one sinned against, rather than the sinner. Life is at best a heartless play, a stormy sea to cross, and a heavy burden often too difficult to bear. The greatest philosophers have tried in vain to fathom and find out its *raison d'etre*, and have all failed except those who had the key to it, namely, the Eastern sages. Life is, as Shakespeare describes it:

". . . . but a walking shadow – a poor player,
That struts and frets his hour upon the stage,
And then is heard no more. It is a tale
Told by an idiot, full of sound and fury,
Signifying nothing. . . . ."

Nothing in its separate parts, yet of the greatest importance in its collectivity or series of lives. At any rate, almost every individual life is, in its full development, a sorrow. And are we to believe that poor, helpless man, after being tossed about like a piece of rotten timber on the angry billows of life, is, if he proves too weak to resist them, to be punished by a *sempiternity* of damnation, or even a temporary punishment? Never! Whether a great or an average sinner, good or bad, guilty or innocent, once delivered of the burden of physical life, the tired and worn-out Manu ("thinking Ego") has won the right to a period of absolute rest and bliss. The same unerringly wise and just rather than merciful Law, which inflicts upon the incarnated Ego the Karmic punishment for every sin committed during the preceding life on Earth, provided for the now disembodied Entity a long lease of mental rest, *i.e.*, the entire oblivion of every sad event, aye, to the smallest painful thought, that took place in its last life as a personality, leaving in the soul-memory but the reminiscence of that which was bliss, or led to happiness. Plotinus, who said that our body was the true river of Lethe, for "souls plunged into it forget all," meant more than he said. For, as our terrestrial body is like Lethe, so is our *celestial body* in Devachan, and much more.

Enquirer. Then am I to understand that the murderer, the transgressor of law divine and human in every shape, is allowed to go unpunished?

Theosophist. Who ever said that? Our philosophy has a doctrine of punishment as stern as that of the most rigid Calvinist, only far more philosophical and consistent with absolute justice. No deed, not even a sinful thought, will go unpunished; the latter more severely even than the former, as a thought is far more potential in creating evil results than even a deed.[14] We believe in an unerring law of Retribution, called KARMA, which asserts itself in a natural concatenation of causes and their unavoidable results.

Enquirer. And how, or where, does it act?

Theosophist. Every labourer is worthy of his hire, saith Wisdom in the Gospel; every action, good or bad, is a prolific parent, saith the Wisdom of the Ages. Put the two together, and you will find the "why." After allowing the Soul, escaped from the pangs of personal life, a sufficient, aye, a hundredfold compensation, Karma, with its army of Skandhas, waits at the threshold of Devachan, whence the *Ego* re-emerges to assume a new incarnation. It is at this moment that the future destiny of the now-rested Ego trembles in the scales of just Retribution, as *it* now falls once again under the sway of active Karmic law. It is in this rebirth which is ready for *it*, a rebirth selected and prepared by this mysterious, inexorable, but in the equity and wisdom of its decrees infallible LAW, that the sins of the previous life of the Ego are punished. Only it is into no imaginary Hell, with theatrical flames and ridiculous tailed and horned devils, that the Ego is cast, but verily on to this earth, the plane and region of his sins, where he will have to atone for every bad thought and deed. As he has sown, so will he reap. Reincarnation will gather around him all those other Egos who have suffered, whether directly or indirectly, at the hands, or even through the unconscious instrumentality, of the

---

[14] "Verily, I say unto you, that whosoever looketh at a woman to lust after her, hath committed adultery with her already in his heart." (*Matthew.* v., 28.)

past *personality*. They will be thrown by Nemesis in the way of the *new* man, concealing the *old*, the eternal EGO, and...

Enquirer. But where is the equity you speak of, since these *new* "personalities" are not aware of having sinned or been sinned against?

Theosophist. Has the coat torn to shreds from the back of the man who stole it, by another man who was robbed of it and recognises his property, to be regarded as fairly dealt with? The new "personality" is no better than a fresh suit of clothes with its specific characteristics, colour, form and qualities; but the *real* man who wears it is the same culprit as of old. It is the *individuality* who suffers through his "personality." And it is this, and this alone, that can account for the terrible, still only *apparent*, injustice in the distribution of lots in life to man. When your modern philosophers will have succeeded in showing to us a good reason, why so many apparently innocent and good men are born only to suffer during a whole life-time; why so many are born poor unto starvation in the slums of great cities, abandoned by fate and men; why, while these are born in the gutter, others open their eyes to light in palaces; while a noble birth and fortune seem often given to the worst of men and only rarely to the worthy; while there are beggars whose *inner* selves are peers to the highest and noblest of men; when this, and much more, is satisfactorily explained by either your philosophers or theologians, then only, but not till then, you will have the right to reject the theory of reincarnation. The highest and grandest of poets have dimly perceived this truth of truths. Shelley believed in it, Shakespeare must have thought of it when writing on the worthlessness of Birth. Remember his words:

> "Why should my birth keep down my mounting spirit?
> Are not all creatures subject unto time?
> There's legions now of beggars on the earth,
> That their original did spring from Kings,
> And many monarchs now, whose fathers were
> The riff-raff of their age......."

Alter the word "fathers" into "egos" – and you will have the truth.

H.P. Blavatsky
The Key to Theosophy, 101-142

ON THE KAMA-LOKA AND DEVACHAN

On the Fate of the Lower "Principles"

Enquirer. You spoke of *Kama-loka*, what is it?

Theosophist. When the man dies, his lower three principles leave him forever; *i. e.* body, life, and the vehicle of the latter, the astral body or the double of the *living* man. And then, his four principles – the central or middle principle, the animal soul or *Kama-rupa*, with what it has assimilated from the lower Manas, and the higher triad find themselves in *Kama-loka*. The latter is an astral locality, the *limbus* of scholastic theology, the *Hades* of the ancients, and, strictly speaking, a *locality* only in a relative sense. It has neither a definite area nor boundary, but exists *within* subjective space; *i. e.* is beyond our sensuous perceptions. Still it exists, and it is there that the astral *eidolons* of all the beings that have lived, animals included, await their *second death*. For the animals it comes with the disintegration and the entire fading out of their *astral* particles to the last. For the human *eidolon* it begins when the Atma-Buddhi-Manasic triad is said to "separate" itself from its lower principles, or the reflection of the *ex-personality*, by falling into the Devachanic state.

Enquirer. And what happens after this?

Theosophist. Then the *Kama-rupic* phantom, remaining bereft of its informing thinking principle, the higher *Manas*, and the lower aspect of the latter, the animal intelligence, no longer receiving light from the higher mind, and no longer having a physical brain to work through, collapses.

Enquirer. In what way?

Theosophist. Well, it falls into the state of the frog when certain portions of its brain are taken out by the vivisector. It can think no more, even on the lowest animal plane. Henceforth it is no longer even the lower Manas, since this "lower" is nothing without the "higher."

Enquirer. And is it *this* nonentity which we find materializing in Seance rooms with Mediums?

Theosophist. It is this nonentity. A true nonentity, however, only as to reasoning or cogitating powers; still an *Entity*, however astral and fluidic, as shown in certain cases when, having been magnetically and unconsciously drawn toward a medium, it is revived for a time and lives in him by *proxy*, so to speak. This "spook," or the *Kama-rupa*, may be compared with the *jelly-fish*, which has an ethereal gelatinous appearance so long as it is in its own element, or water (the *medium's specific AURA*), but which, no sooner is it thrown out of it, than it dissolves in the hand or on the sand, especially in sunlight. In the medium's Aura, it lives a kind of vicarious life and reasons and speaks either through the medium's brain or those of other persons present. But this would lead us too far, and upon other people's grounds, whereon I have no desire to trespass. Let us keep to the subject of reincarnation.

Enquirer. What of the latter? How long does the incarnating *Ego* remain in the Devachanic state?

Theosophist. This, we are taught, depends on the degree of spirituality and the merit or demerit of the last incarnation. The average time is from ten to fifteen centuries, as I already told you.

Enquirer. But why could not this Ego manifest and communicate with mortals as Spiritualists will have it? What is there to prevent a mother from communicating with the children she left on earth, a husband with his wife, and so on? It is a most consoling belief, I must confess; nor do I wonder that those who believe in it are so averse to give it up.

Theosophist. Nor are they forced to, unless they happen to prefer truth to fiction, however "consoling." Uncongenial our doctrines may be to Spiritualists; yet, nothing of what we believe in and teach is half as selfish and cruel as what they preach.

Enquirer. I do not understand you. What is selfish?

Theosophist. Their doctrine of the return of Spirits, the real "personalities" as they say; and I will tell you why. If *Devachan* – call it "paradise" if you like, a "place of bliss and of supreme felicity," if it is anything – is such a place (or say *state*), logic tells us that no sorrow or even a shade of pain can be experienced therein. "God shall wipe away all the tears from the eyes" of those in paradise, we read in the book of many promises. And if the "Spirits of the dead" are enabled to return and see all that is going on earth, and especially *in their homes*, what kind of bliss can be in store for them?

Why Theosophists Do Not Believe in the Return of Pure "Spirits"

Enquirer. What do you mean? Why should this interfere with their bliss?

Theosophist. Simply this; and here is an instance. A mother dies, leaving behind her little helpless children – orphans whom she adores – perhaps a beloved husband also. We say that her "Spirit" or *Ego* – that individuality which is now all impregnated, for the entire Devachanic period, with the noblest feelings held by its late *personality*, *i.e.*, love for her children, pity for those who suffer, and so on – we say that it is now entirely separated from the "vale of tears," that its future bliss consists in that blessed ignorance of all the woes it left behind. Spiritualists say, on the contrary, that it is as vividly aware of them, *and more so than before*, for "Spirits see more than mortals in the flesh do." We say that the bliss of the *Devachanee* consists in its complete conviction that it has never left the earth, and that there is no such thing as death at all; that the *post-mortem* spiritual *consciousness* of the mother will represent to her that she lives surrounded by her children and all those whom she loved; that no gap, no link, will be missing to make her disembodied state the most perfect and absolute happiness. The Spiritualists deny this point blank. According to their doctrine, unfortunate man is not liberated even by death from the sorrows of this life. Not a drop from the life-cup of pain and suffering will miss his lips; and *nolens volens*, since he sees everything now, shall he drink it to the bitter dregs. Thus, the loving wife, who during her lifetime was ready to save her husband sorrow at the price of her heart's blood, is now doomed to see, in utter helplessness, his despair, and to register every hot tear he sheds for her loss. Worse than that, she may see the tears dry too soon, and another beloved face shine on him, the father of her children; find another woman replacing her in his affections; doomed to hear her orphans giving the holy name of "mother" to one indifferent to them, and to see those little children neglected, if not ill-treated. According to this doctrine the "gentle wafting to immortal life" becomes without any transition the way into a new path of mental suffering! And yet, the columns of the "Banner of Light," the veteran journal of the American Spiritualists, are filled with messages from the dead, the "dear departed ones," who all write to say how very *happy* they are! Is such a state of knowledge consistent with bliss? Then "bliss" stands in such a case for the greatest curse, and orthodox damnation must be a relief in comparison to it!

Enquirer. But how does your theory avoid this? How can you reconcile the theory of Soul's omniscience with its blindness to that which is taking place on earth?

Theosophist. Because such is the law of love and mercy. During every Devachanic period the Ego, omniscient as it is *per se*, clothes itself, so to say, with the *reflection* of the "personality" that was. I have just told you that the *ideal* efflorescence of all the abstract, therefore undying and eternal qualities or attributes, such as love and mercy, the love of the good, the true and the beautiful, that ever spoke in the heart of the living "personality," clung after death to the Ego, and therefore followed it to Devachan. For the time being, then, the Ego becomes the ideal reflection of the human being it was when last on earth, and *that* is not omniscient. Were it that, it would never be in the state we call Devachan at all.

Enquirer. What are your reasons for it?

Theosophist. If you want an answer on the strict lines of our philosophy, then I will say that it is because everything is *illusion* (*Maya*) outside of eternal truth, which has neither form, colour, nor limitation. He who has placed himself beyond the veil of maya – and such are the highest Adepts and Initiates – can have no Devachan. As to the ordinary mortal, his bliss in it is complete. It is an *absolute* oblivion of all that gave it pain or sorrow in the past incarnation, and even oblivion of the fact that such things as pain or sorrow exist at all. The *Devachanee* lives its intermediate cycle between two incarnations surrounded by everything it had aspired to in vain, and in the companionship of everyone it loved on earth. It has reached the fulfilment of all its soul-yearnings. And thus it lives throughout long centuries an existence of *unalloyed* happiness, which is the reward for its sufferings in earth-life. In short, it bathes in a sea of uninterrupted felicity spanned only by events of still greater felicity in degree.

Enquirer. But this is more than simple delusion, it is an existence of insane hallucinations!

Theosophist. From your standpoint it may be, not so from that of philosophy. Besides which, is not our whole terrestrial life filled with such delusions? Have you never met men and women living for years in a fool's paradise? And because you should happen to learn that the husband of a wife, whom she adores and believes herself as beloved by him, is untrue to her, would you go and break her heart and beautiful dream by rudely awakening her to the reality? I think not. I say it again, such oblivion and *hallucination* – if you call it so – are only a merciful law of nature and strict justice. At any rate, it is a far more fascinating prospect than the orthodox golden harp with a pair of wings. The assurance that "the soul that lives ascends frequently and runs familiarly through the streets of the heavenly Jerusalem, visiting the patriarchs and prophets, saluting the apostles, and admiring the army of martyrs" may seem of a more pious character to some. Nevertheless, it is a hallucination of a far more delusive character, since mothers love their children with an immortal love, we all know, while the personages mentioned in the "heavenly Jerusalem" are still of a rather doubtful nature. But I would, still, rather accept the "new Jerusalem," with its streets paved like the show windows of a jeweller's shop, than find consolation in the heartless doctrine of the Spiritualists. The idea alone that the *intellectual conscious souls* of one's father, mother, daughter or brother find their bliss in a "Summer land" – only a little more natural, but just as ridiculous as the "New Jerusalem" in its description – would be enough to make one lose every respect for one's "departed ones." To believe that a pure spirit can feel happy while doomed to witness the sins, mistakes, treachery, and, above all, the sufferings of those from whom it is severed by death and whom it loves best, without being able to help them, would be a maddening thought.

Enquirer. There is something in your argument. I confess to having never seen it in this light.

Theosophist. Just so, and one must be selfish to the core and utterly devoid of the sense of retributive justice, to have ever imagined such a thing. We are with those whom we have lost in material form, and far, far nearer to them now, than when they were alive. And it is not only in the fancy of the *Devachanee*, as some may imagine, but in reality. For pure divine love is not merely the blossom of a human heart, but has its roots in eternity. Spiritual holy love is immortal, and Karma brings sooner or later all those who loved each other with such a spiritual affection to incarnate once more in the same family group. Again we say that love beyond the grave, illusion though you may call it, has a magic and divine potency which reacts on the living. A mother's *Ego* filled with love for the imaginary children it sees near itself, living a life of happiness, as real to *it* as when on earth – that love will always be felt by the children in flesh. It will manifest in their dreams, and often in various events – in *providential* protections and escapes, for love is a strong shield, and is not limited by space or time. As with this Devachanic "mother," so with the rest of human relationships and attachments, save the purely selfish or material. Analogy will suggest to you the rest.

Enquirer. In no case, then, do you admit the possibility of the communication of the living with the *disembodied spirit*?

Theosophist. Yes, there is a case, and even two exceptions to the rule. The first exception is during the few days that follow immediately the death of a person and before the *Ego* passes into the Devachanic state. Whether any living mortal, save a few exceptional cases – (when the intensity of the desire in the dying person to return for some purpose forced the higher consciousness *to remain awake*, and therefore it was really the *individuality*, the "Spirit" that communicated) – has derived much benefit from the return of the spirit into the *objective* plane is another question. The spirit is dazed after death and falls very soon into what we call *"pre-devachanic* unconsciousness." The second exception is found in the *Nirmanakayas*.

Enquirer. What about them? And what does the name mean for you?

Theosophist. It is the name given to those who, though they have won the right to Nirvana and cyclic rest – (*not* "Devachan," as the latter is an illusion of our consciousness, a happy dream, and as those who are fit for Nirvana must have lost entirely every desire or possibility of the world's illusions) – have out of pity for mankind and those they left on earth renounced the Nirvanic state. Such an adept, or Saint, or whatever you may call him, believing it a selfish act to rest in bliss while mankind groans under the burden of misery produced by ignorance, renounces Nirvana, and determines to remain invisible *in spirit* on this earth. They have no material body, as they have left it behind; but otherwise they remain with all their principles even *in astral life* in our sphere. And such can and do communicate with a few elect ones, only surely not with *ordinary* mediums.

Enquirer. I have put you the question about *Nirmanakayas* because I read in some German and other works that it was the name given to the terrestrial appearances or bodies assumed by Buddhas in the Northern Buddhistic teachings.

Theosophist. So they are, only the Orientalists have confused this terrestrial body by understanding it to be *objective* and *physical* instead of purely astral and subjective.

Enquirer. And what good can they do on earth?

Theosophist. Not much, as regards individuals, as they have no right to interfere with Karma, and can only advise and inspire mortals for the general good. Yet they do more beneficent actions than you imagine.

Enquirer. To this Science would never subscribe, not even modern psychology. For them, no portion of intelligence can survive the physical brain. What would you answer them?

Theosophist. I would not even go to the trouble of answering, but would simply say, in the words given to "M. A. Oxon," "Intelligence *is* perpetuated after the body is dead. Though it is not a question of the brain only. . . . It is reasonable to propound the indestructibility of the human spirit from what we know" (*Spirit Identity*, p. 69).

Enquirer. But "M. A. Oxon" is a Spiritualist?

Theosophist. Quite so, and the only *true* Spiritualist I know of, though we may still disagree with him on many a minor question. Apart from this, no Spiritualist comes nearer to the occult truths than he does. Like any one of us he speaks incessantly "of the surface dangers that beset the ill-equipped, feather-headed muddler with the occult, who crosses the threshold without counting the cost."[1] Our only disagreement rests in the question of "Spirit Identity." Otherwise, I, for one, coincide almost entirely with him, and accept the three propositions he embodied in his address of July, 1884. It is this eminent Spiritualist, rather, who disagrees with us, not we with him.

Enquirer. What are these propositions?

Theosophist. "1. That there is a life coincident with, and independent of the physical life of the body."

---

[1] "Some things that I *do* know of Spiritualism and some that I do *not*."

"2. That, as a necessary corollary, this life extends beyond the life of the body" (we say it extends throughout Devachan).

"3. That there is communication between the denizens of that state of existence and those of the world in which we now live."

All depend, you see, on the minor and secondary aspects of these fundamental propositions. Everything depends on the views we take of Spirit and Soul, or *Individuality* and *Personality*. Spiritualists confuse the two "into one"; we separate them, and say that, with the exceptions above enumerated, no *Spirit* will revisit the earth, though the animal Soul may. But let us return once more to our direct subject, the Skandhas.

Enquirer. I begin to understand better now. It is the Spirit, so to say, of those Skandhas which are the most ennobling, which, attaching themselves to the incarnating Ego, survive, and are added to the stock of its angelic experiences. And it is the attributes connected with the material Skandhas, with selfish and personal motives, which, disappearing from the field of action between two incarnations, reappear at the subsequent incarnation as Karmic results to be atoned for; and therefore the Spirit will not leave Devachan. Is it so?

Theosophist. Very nearly so. If you add to this that the law of retribution, or Karma, rewarding the highest and most spiritual in Devachan, never fails to reward them again on earth by giving them a further development, and furnishing the Ego with a body fitted for it, then you will be quite correct.

A Few Words about the Skandhas

Enquirer. What becomes of the other, the lower Skandhas of the personality, after the death of the body? Are they quite destroyed?

Theosophist. They are and yet they are not – a fresh metaphysical and occult mystery for you. They are destroyed as the working stock in hand of the personality; they remain as *Karmic effects*, as germs, hanging in the atmosphere of the terrestrial plane, ready to come to life, as so many avenging fiends, to attach themselves to the new personality of the Ego when it reincarnates.

Enquirer. This really passes my comprehension, and is very difficult to understand.

Theosophist. Not once that you have assimilated all the details. For then you will see that for logic, consistency, profound philosophy, divine mercy and equity, this doctrine of Reincarnation has not its equal on earth. It is a belief in a perpetual progress for each incarnating Ego, or divine soul, in an evolution from the outward into the inward, from the material to the Spiritual, arriving at the end of each stage at absolute unity with the divine Principle. From strength to strength, from the beauty and perfection of one plane to the greater beauty and perfection of another, with accessions of new glory, of fresh knowledge and power in each cycle, such is the destiny of every Ego, which thus becomes its own Saviour in each world and incarnation.

Enquirer. But Christianity teaches the same. It also preaches progression.

Theosophist. Yes, only with the addition of something else. It tells us of the *impossibility* of attaining Salvation without the aid of a miraculous Saviour, and therefore dooms to perdition all those who will not accept the dogma. This is just the difference between Christian theology and Theosophy. The former enforces belief in the Descent of the Spiritual Ego into the *Lower Self;* the latter inculcates the necessity of endeavouring to elevate oneself to the Christos, or Buddhi state.

Enquirer. By teaching the annihilation of consciousness in case of failure, however, don't you think that it amounts to the annihilation of *Self*, in the opinion of the non-metaphysical?

Theosophist. From the standpoint of those who believe in the resurrection of the body *literally*, and insist that every bone, every artery and atom of flesh will be raised bodily on the Judgment Day – of course it does. If you still insist that it is the perishable form and finite qualities that make up *immortal* man, then we shall hardly understand each other. And if you do not understand that, by limiting the existence of every Ego to one life on earth, you make of Deity an ever-drunken Indra of the Puranic dead letter, a cruel Moloch, a god who makes an inextricable mess on Earth, and yet claims thanks for it, then the sooner we drop the conversation the better.

Enquirer. But let us return, now that the subject of the Skandhas is disposed of, to the question of the consciousness which survives death. This is the point which interests most people. Do we possess more knowledge in Devachan than we do in Earth life?

Theosophist. In one sense, we can acquire more knowledge; that is, we can develop further any faculty which we loved and strove after during life, provided it is concerned with abstract and ideal things, such as music, painting, poetry, etc., since Devachan is merely an idealized and subjective continuation of earth-life.

Enquirer. But if in Devachan the Spirit is free from matter, why should it not possess all knowledge?

Theosophist. Because, as I told you, the Ego is, so to say, wedded to the memory of its last incarnation. Thus, if you think over what I have said, and string all the facts together, you will realize that the Devachanic state is not one of omniscience, but a transcendental continuation of the personal life just terminated. It is the rest of the soul from the toils of life.

Enquirer. But the scientific materialists assert that after the death of man nothing remains; that the human body simply disintegrates into its component elements; and that what we call soul is merely a temporary self-consciousness produced as a bye-product of organic action, which will evaporate like steam. Is not theirs a strange state of mind?

Theosophist. Not strange at all, that I see. If they say that self-consciousness ceases with the body, then in their case they simply utter an unconscious prophecy, for once they are firmly convinced of what they assert, no conscious after-life is possible for them. For there *are* exceptions to every rule.

On Post Mortem and Post-Natal Consciousness [2]

Enquirer. But if human self-consciousness survives death as a rule, why should there be exceptions?

Theosophist. In the fundamental principles of the spiritual world no exception is possible. But there are rules for those who see, and rules for those who prefer to remain blind.

Enquirer. Quite so, I understand. This is but an aberration of the blind man, who denies the existence of the sun because he does not see it. But after death his spiritual eyes will certainly compel him to see. Is this what you mean?

Theosophist. He will not be compelled, nor will he see anything. Having persistently denied during life the continuance of existence after death, he will be unable to see it, because his spiritual capacity having been stunted in life, it cannot develop after death, and he will remain blind. By insisting that he *must* see it, you evidently mean one thing and I another. You speak of the spirit from the spirit, or the flame from the flame – of Atma, in short – and you confuse it with the human soul – Manas. . . . You do not understand me; let me try to make it clear. The whole gist of your question is to know whether, in the case of a downright materialist, the complete loss of self-consciousness and self-perception after death is possible? Isn't it so? I answer, It is possible. Because, believing firmly in our Esoteric Doctrine, which refers to the *post-mortem* period, or the interval between two lives or births, as merely a transitory state, I say, whether that interval between two acts of the illusionary drama of life lasts one year or a million, that *post-mortem* state may, without

---

[2] A few portions of this chapter and of the preceding were published in *Lucifer* in the shape of a "Dialogue on the Mysteries of After Life," in the January number, 1889. The article was unsigned, as if it were written by the editor, but it came from the pen of the author of the present volume.

any breach of the fundamental law, prove to be just the same state as that of a man who is in a dead faint.

Enquirer. But since you have just said that the fundamental laws of the after death state admit of no exceptions, how can this be?

Theosophist. Nor do I say that it does admit of an exception. But the spiritual law of continuity applies only to things which are truly real. To one who has read and understood *Mundakya Upanishad* and Vedanta-Sara all this becomes very clear. I will say more: it is sufficient to understand what we mean by Buddhi and the duality of Manas to gain a clear perception why the materialist may fail to have a self-conscious survival after death. Since Manas, in its lower aspect, is the seat of the terrestrial mind, it can, therefore, give only that perception of the Universe which is based on the evidence of that mind; it cannot give spiritual vision. It is said in the Eastern school, that between Buddhi and Manas (the *Ego*), or Iswara and Pragna [3] there is in reality no more difference than *between a forest and its trees, a lake and its waters*, as the *Mundakya* teaches. One or hundreds of trees dead from loss of vitality, or uprooted, are yet incapable of preventing the forest from being still a forest.

Enquirer. But, as I understand it, Buddhi represents in this simile the forest, and Manas-taijasi [4] the trees. And if Buddha is immortal, how can that which is similar to it, *i. e.*, Manas-taijasi, entirely lose its consciousness till the day of its new incarnation? I cannot understand it.

---

[3] Iswara is the collective consciousness of the manifested deity, Brahma, *i. e.*, the collective consciousness of the Host of Dhyan Chohans (*vide The Secret Doctrine*); and *Pragna* is their individual wisdom

[4] *Taijasi* means the radiant in consequence of its union with *Buddhi; i.e., Manas*, the human soul, illuminated by the radiance of the divine soul. Therefore, Manas-taijasi may be described as radiant mind; the *human* reason lit by the light of the spirit; and Buddhi-Manas is the revelation of the divine *plus* human intellect and self-consciousness.

Theosophist. You cannot, because you will mix up an abstract representation of the whole with its casual changes of form. Remember that if it can be said of Buddhi-Manas that it is unconditionally immortal, the same cannot be said of the lower Manas, still less of Taijasi, which is merely an attribute. Neither of these, neither Manas nor Taijasi, can exist apart from Buddhi, the divine soul, because the first (*Manas*) is, in its lower aspect, a qualificative attribute of the terrestrial personality, and the second (*Taijasi*) is identical with the first, because it is the same Manas only with the light of Buddhi reflected on it. In its turn, Buddhi would remain only an impersonal spirit without this element which it borrows from the human soul, which conditions and makes of it, in this illusive Universe, *as it were something separate* from the universal soul for the whole period of the cycle of incarnation. Say rather that *Buddhi-Manas* can neither die nor lose its compound self-consciousness in Eternity, nor the recollection of its previous incarnations in which the two – *i.e.*, the spiritual and the human soul – had been closely linked together. But it is not so in the case of a materialist, whose human soul not only receives nothing from the divine soul, but even refuses to recognise its existence. You can hardly apply this axiom to the attributes and qualifications of the human soul, for it would be like saying that because your divine soul is immortal, therefore the bloom on your cheek must also be immortal; whereas this bloom, like Taijasi, is simply a transitory phenomenon.

Enquirer. Do I understand you to say that we must not mix in our minds the noumenon with the phenomenon, the cause with its effect?

Theosophist. I do say so, and repeat that, limited to Manas or the human soul alone, the radiance of Taijasi itself becomes a mere question of time; because both immortality and consciousness after death become, for the terrestrial personality of man, simply conditioned attributes, as they depend entirely on conditions and beliefs created by the human soul itself during the life of its body.

Karma acts incessantly: we reap *in our after-life* only the fruit of that which we have ourselves sown in this.

Enquirer. But if my Ego can, after the destruction of my body, become plunged in a state of entire unconsciousness, then where can be the punishment for the sins of my past life?

Theosophist. Our philosophy teaches that Karmic punishment reaches the Ego only in its next incarnation. After death it receives only the reward for the unmerited sufferings endured during its past incarnation.[5] The whole punishment after death, even for the materialist, consists, therefore, in the absence of any reward, and the utter loss of the consciousness of one's bliss and rest. Karma is the child of the terrestrial Ego, the fruit of the actions of the tree which is the objective personality visible to all, as much as the fruit of all the thoughts and even motives of the spiritual "I"; but Karma is also the tender mother, who heals the wounds inflicted by her during the preceding life, before she will begin to torture this Ego by inflicting upon him new ones. If it may be said that there is not a mental or physical suffering in the life of a mortal which is not the direct fruit and consequence of some sin in a preceding existence; on the other hand, since he does not preserve the slightest recollection of it in his actual life, and feels himself not deserving of such punishment, and therefore thinks he suffers for no guilt of his own, this alone is sufficient to entitle the human soul to the fullest consolation, rest, and bliss in his *post-mortem* existence. Death comes to our spiritual

---

[5] Some Theosophists have taken exception to this phrase, but the words are those of Master, and the meaning attached to the word "unmerited" is that given above. In the T. P. S. pamphlet No. 6, a phrase, criticised subsequently in LUCIFER, was used which was intended to convey the same idea. In form, however, it was awkward and open to the criticism directed against it; but the essential idea was that men often suffer from the effects of the actions done by others, effects which thus do not strictly belong to their own Karma – and for these sufferings they of course deserve compensation.

selves ever as a deliverer and friend. For the materialist, who, notwithstanding his materialism, was not a bad man, the interval between the two lives will be like the unbroken and placid sleep of a child, either entirely dreamless, or filled with pictures of which he will have no definite perception; while for the average mortal it will be a dream as vivid as life, and full of realistic bliss and visions.

Enquirer. Then the personal man must always go on suffering *blindly* the Karmic penalties which the Ego has incurred?

Theosophist. Not quite so. At the solemn moment of death every man, even when death is sudden, sees the whole of his past life marshalled before him, in its minutest details. For one short instant the *personal* becomes one with the *individual* and all-knowing *Ego*. But this instant is enough to show to him the whole chain of causes which have been at work during his life. He sees and now understands himself as he is, unadorned by flattery or self-deception. He reads his life, remaining as a spectator looking down into the arena he is quitting; he feels and knows the justice of all the suffering that has overtaken him.

Enquirer. Does this happen to everyone?

Theosophist. Without any exception. Very good and holy men see, we are taught, not only the life they are leaving, but even several preceding lives in which were produced the causes that made them what they were in the life just closing. They recognise the law of Karma in all its majesty and justice.

Enquirer. Is there anything corresponding to this before re-birth?

Theosophist. There is. As the man at the moment of death has a retrospective insight into the life he has led, so, at the moment he is reborn on to earth, the *Ego*, awaking from the state of Devachan, has a prospective vision of the life which awaits him, and realizes all the causes that have led to it. He realizes them and sees futurity, because it is between Devachan and re-birth that the *Ego* regains his full *manasic* consciousness, and rebecomes for a short time the god he was, before, in compliance with Karmic law, he first descended into matter and incarnated in the first man of flesh. The "golden thread" sees all its "pearls" and misses not one of them.

What Is Really Meant by Annihilation

Enquirer. I have heard some Theosophists speak of a golden thread on which their lives were strung. What do they mean by this?

Theosophist. In the Hindu Sacred books, it is said that that which undergoes periodical incarnation is the *Sutratma*, which means literally the "Thread Soul." It is a synonym of the reincarnating Ego – Manas conjoined with *Buddhi* – which absorbs the Manasic recollections of all our preceding lives. It is so called, because, like the pearls on a thread, so is the long series of human lives strung together on that one thread. In some *Upanishad*, these recurrent rebirths are likened to the life of a mortal which oscillates periodically between sleep and waking.

Enquirer. This, I must say, does not seem very clear, and I will tell you why. For the man who awakes, another day commences, but that man is the same in soul and body as he was the day before; whereas at every incarnation a full change takes place not only of the external envelope, sex, and personality, but even of the mental and psychic capacities. The simile does not seem to me quite correct. The man who arises from sleep remembers quite clearly what he has done yesterday, the day before, and even months and years ago. But none of us has the slightest recollection of a preceding life or of any fact or event concerning it. . . . I may forget in the morning what I have dreamt during the night, still I know that I have slept and have the certainty that I lived during sleep; but what recollection can I have of my past incarnation until the moment of death? How do you reconcile this?

Theosophist. Some people do recollect their past incarnations during life; but these are Buddhas and Initiates. This is what the Yogis call *Samma-Sambuddha*, or the knowledge of the whole series of one's past incarnations.

Enquirer. But we ordinary mortals who have not reached *Samma-Sambuddha*, how are we to understand this simile?

Theosophist. By studying it and trying to understand more correctly the characteristics and the three kinds of sleep. Sleep is a general and immutable law for man as for beast, but there are different kinds of sleep and still more different dreams and visions.

Enquirer. But this takes us to another subject. Let us return to the materialist who, while not denying dreams, which he could hardly do, yet denies immortality in general and the survival of his own individuality.

Theosophist. And the materialist, without knowing it, is right. One who has no inner perception of, and faith in, the immortality of his soul, in that man the soul can never become *Buddhi-taijasi*, but will remain simply *Manas*, and for *Manas* alone there is no immortality possible. In order to live in the world to come a conscious life, one has to believe first of all in that life during the terrestrial existence. On these two aphorisms of the Secret Science all the philosophy about the *post-mortem* consciousness and the immortality of the soul is built. The Ego receives always according to its deserts. After the dissolution of the body, there commences for it a period of full awakened consciousness, or a state of chaotic dreams, or an utterly dreamless sleep undistinguishable from annihilation, and these are the three kinds of sleep. If our physiologists find the cause of dreams and visions in an unconscious preparation for them during the waking hours, why cannot the same be admitted for the *post-mortem* dreams? I repeat it: *death is sleep*. After death, before the spiritual eyes of the soul, begins a performance according to a programme learnt and very often unconsciously composed by ourselves: the practical carrying out of *correct* beliefs or of illusions which have been created by ourselves. The Methodist will be Methodist, the Mussulman a Mussulman, at least for some time – in a perfect fool's paradise of each man's creation and making. These are the *post-mortem* fruits of the tree of life. Naturally, our belief or unbelief in the fact of conscious immortality is unable to influence the unconditioned reality of the fact itself, once that it exists; but the belief or unbelief in that immortality as the property of independent or separate entities, cannot fail to give colour to that fact in its application to each of these entities. Now do you begin to understand it?

Enquirer. I think I do. The materialist, disbelieving in everything that cannot be proven to him by his five senses, or by scientific reasoning, based exclusively on the data furnished by these senses in spite of their inadequacy, and rejecting every spiritual manifestation, accepts life as the only conscious existence. Therefore according to their beliefs so will it be unto them. They will lose their personal Ego, and will plunge into a dreamless sleep until a new awakening. Is it so?

Theosophist. Almost so. Remember the practically universal teaching of the two kinds of conscious existence: the terrestrial and the spiritual. The latter must be considered real from the very fact that it is inhabited by the eternal, changeless and immortal Monad; whereas the incarnating Ego dresses itself up in new garments entirely different from those of its previous incarnations, and in which all except its spiritual prototype is doomed to a change so radical as to leave no trace behind.

Enquirer. How so? Can my conscious terrestrial "I" perish not only for a time, like the consciousness of the materialist, but so entirely as to leave no trace behind?

Theosophist. According to the teaching, it must so perish and in its fulness, all except the principle which, having united itself with the Monad, has thereby become a purely spiritual and indestructible essence, one with it in the Eternity. But in the case of an out-and-out materialist, in whose personal "I" no *Buddhi* has ever reflected itself, how can the latter carry away into the Eternity one particle of that terrestrial personality? Your spiritual "I" is immortal; but from your present self it can carry away into Eternity that only which has become worthy of immortality, namely, the aroma alone of the flower that has been mown by death.

Enquirer. Well, and the flower, the terrestrial "I"?

Theosophist. The flower, as all past and future flowers which have blossomed and will have to blossom on the mother bough, the *Sutratma*, all children of one root or Buddhi – will return to dust. Your present "I," as you yourself know, is not the body now sitting before me, nor yet is it what I would call Manas-Sutratma, but Sutratma-Buddhi.

Enquirer. But this does not explain to me, at all, why you call life after death immortal, infinite and real, and the terrestrial life a simple phantom or illusion; since even that *post-mortem* life has limits, however much wider they may be than those of terrestrial life.

Theosophist. No doubt. The spiritual Ego of man moves in eternity like a pendulum between the hours of birth and death. But if these hours, marking the periods of life terrestrial and life spiritual, are limited in their duration, and if the very number of such stages in Eternity between sleep and awakening, illusion and reality, has its beginning and its end, on the other hand, the spiritual pilgrim is eternal. Therefore are the hours of his *post-mortem* life, when, disembodied, he stands face to face with truth and not the mirages of his transitory earthly existences, during the period of that pilgrimage which we call "the cycle of re-births" – the only reality in our conception. Such intervals, their limitation notwithstanding, do not prevent the Ego, while ever perfecting itself, from following undeviatingly, though gradually and slowly, the path to its last transformation, when that Ego, having reached its goal, becomes a divine being. These intervals and stages help towards this final result instead of hindering it; and without such limited intervals the divine Ego could never reach its ultimate goal. I have given you once already a familiar illustration by comparing the *Ego*, or the *individuality*, to an actor, and its numerous and various incarnations to the parts it plays. Will you call these parts or their costumes the individuality of the actor himself? Like that actor, the Ego is forced to play during the cycle of necessity, up to the very threshold of *Paranirvana*, many parts such as may be unpleasant to it. But as the bee collects its honey from every flower, leaving the rest as food for the earthly worms, so does our spiritual individuality, whether we call it Sutratma or Ego. Collecting from every terrestrial personality, into which Karma forces it to incarnate, the nectar alone of the spiritual qualities and self-consciousness, it unites all these into one whole and emerges from its chrysalis as the glorified *Dhyan Chohan*. So much the worse for those terrestrial personalities from which it could collect nothing. Such personalities cannot assuredly outlive consciously their terrestrial existence.

Enquirer. Thus, then, it seems that, for the terrestrial personality, immortality is still conditional. Is, then, immortality itself *not* unconditional?

Theosophist. Not at all. But immortality cannot touch the *non-existent:* for all that which exists as SAT, or emanates from SAT, immortality and Eternity are absolute. Matter is the opposite pole of spirit, and yet the two are one. The essence of all this, *i.e.,* Spirit, Force and Matter, or the three in one, is as endless as it is beginningless; but the form acquired by this triple unity during its incarnations, its externality, is certainly only the illusion of our personal conceptions. Therefore do we call *Nirvana* and the Universal life alone a reality, while relegating the terrestrial life, its terrestrial personality included, and even its Devachanic existence, to the phantom realm of illusion.

Enquirer. But why in such a case call sleep the reality, and waking the illusion?

Theosophist. It is simply a comparison made to facilitate the grasping of the subject, and from the standpoint of terrestrial conceptions it is a very correct one.

Enquirer. And still I cannot understand, if the life to come is based on justice and the merited retribution for all our terrestrial suffering, how in the case of materialists, many of whom are really honest and charitable men, there should remain of their personality nothing but the refuse of a faded flower.

Theosophist. No one ever said such a thing. No materialist, however unbelieving, can die for ever in the fulness of his spiritual individuality. What was said is that consciousness can disappear either fully or partially in the case of a materialist, so that no conscious remains of his personality survive.

Enquirer. But surely this is annihilation?

Theosophist. Certainly not. One can sleep a dead sleep and miss several stations during a long railway journey, without the slightest recollection or consciousness, and awake at another station and continue the journey past innumerable other halting-places till the end of the journey or the goal is reached. Three kinds of sleep were mentioned to you: the dreamless, the chaotic, and the one which is so real, that to the sleeping man his dreams become full realities. If you believe in the latter why can't you believe in the former; according to the after-life a man has believed in and expected, such is the life he will have. He who expected no life to come will have an absolute blank, amounting to annihilation, in the interval between the two re-births. This is just the carrying out of the programme we spoke of, a programme created by the materialists themselves. But there are various kinds of materialists, as you say. A selfish, wicked Egoist, one who never shed a tear for anyone but himself, thus adding entire indifference to the whole world to his unbelief, must, at the threshold of death, drop his personality forever. This personality having no tendrils of sympathy for the world around and hence nothing to hook on to Sutratma, it follows that with the last breath every connection between the two is broken. There being no Devachan for such a materialist, the Sutratma will re-incarnate almost immediately. But those materialists who erred in nothing but their disbelief will oversleep but one station. And the time will come when that ex-materialist will perceive himself in the Eternity and perhaps repent that he lost even one day, one station, from the life eternal.

Enquirer. Still, would it not be more correct to say that death is birth into a new life, or a return once more into eternity?

Theosophist. You may if you like. Only remember that births differ, and that there are births of "still-born" beings, which are *failures* of nature. Moreover, with your Western fixed ideas about material life, the words "living" and "being" are quite inapplicable to the pure subjective state of *post-mortem* existence. It is just because, save in a few philosophers who are not read by the many, and who themselves are too confused to present a distinct picture of it, it is just because your Western ideas of life and death have finally become so narrow, that on the one hand they have led to crass materialism, and on the other, to the still more material conception of the other life, which the spiritualists have formulated in their Summer-land. There the souls of men eat, drink, marry, and live in a paradise quite as sensual as that of Mohammed, but even less philosophical. Nor are the average conceptions of the uneducated Christians any better, being if possible still more material. What between truncated angels, brass trumpets, golden harps, and material hell-fires, the Christian heaven seems like a fairy scene at a Christmas pantomime.

It is because of these narrow conceptions that you find such difficulty in understanding. It is just because the life of the disembodied soul, while possessing all the vividness of reality, as in certain dreams, is devoid of every grossly objective form of terrestrial life, that the Eastern philosophers have compared it with visions during sleep.

Definite Words for Definite Things

Enquirer. Don't you think it is because there are no definite and fixed terms to indicate each "Principle" in man, that such a confusion of ideas arises in our minds with respect to the respective functions of these "Principles"?

Theosophist. I have thought of it myself. The whole trouble has arisen from this: we have started our expositions of, and discussion about, the "Principles," using their Sanskrit names instead of coining immediately, for the use of Theosophists, their equivalents in English. We must try and remedy this now.

Enquirer. You will do well, as it may avoid further confusion; no two theosophical writers, it seems to me, have hitherto agreed to call the same "Principle" by the same name.

Theosophist. The confusion is more apparent than real, however. I have heard some of our Theosophists express surprise at, and criticize several essays speaking of these "principles"; but, when examined, there was no worse mistake in them than that of using the word "Soul" to cover the three principles without specifying the distinctions. The first, as positively the clearest of our Theosophical writers, Mr. A. P. Sinnett, has some comprehensive and admirably-written passages on the "Higher Self."[6] His real idea has also been misconceived by some, owing to his using the word "Soul" in a general sense. Yet here are a few passages which will show to you how clear and comprehensive is all that he writes on the subject:

"The human soul, once launched on the streams of evolution as a human individuality,[7] passes through alternate periods of physical and relatively spiritual existence. It passes from the one plane, or stratum, or condition of nature to the other under the guidance of its Karmic affinities; living in incarnations the life which its Karma has pre-ordained; modifying its progress within the limitations of circumstances, and, – developing fresh Karma by its use or abuse of opportunities, – it returns to spiritual existence (Devachan) after each physical life, – through the intervening region of Kamaloka – for rest and refreshment and for the gradual absorption into its essence, as so much cosmic progress, of the life's experience gained "on earth" or during physical existence. This view of the matter will, moreover, have suggested many collateral inferences to anyone thinking over the subject; for instance, that the transfer of consciousness from the Kamaloka to the Devachanic stage of this progression would

---

[6] *Vide* Transactions of the "*London Lodge of the Theos. Soc.*," No. 7, Oct., 1885.

[7] The "re-incarnating Ego," or "Human Soul," as he called it, the *Causal Body* with the Hindus.

necessarily be gradual[8]; that in truth, no hard-and-fast line separates the varieties of spiritual conditions, that even the spiritual and physical planes, as psychic faculties in living people show, are not so hopelessly walled off from one another as materialistic theories would suggest; that all states of nature are all around us simultaneously, and appeal to different perceptive faculties; and so on. . . . It is clear that during physical existence people who possess psychic faculties remain in connection with the planes of superphysical consciousness; and although most people may not be endowed with such faculties, we all, as the phenomena of sleep, even, and especially . . . those of somnambulism or mesmerism, show, are capable of entering into conditions of consciousness that the five physical senses have nothing to do with. We – the souls within us – are not as it were altogether adrift in the ocean of matter. We clearly retain some surviving interest or rights in the shore from which, for a time, we have floated off. The process of incarnation, therefore, is not fully described when we speak of an *alternate* existence on the physical and spiritual planes, and thus picture the soul as a complete entity slipping entirely from the one state of existence to the other. The more correct definitions of the process would probably represent incarnation as taking place on this physical plane of nature by reason of an efflux emanating from the soul. The Spiritual realm would all the while be the proper habitat of the Soul, which would never entirely quit it; *and that non-materializable portion of the Soul which abides permanently on the spiritual plane may fitly,* perhaps, be spoken of as the HIGHER SELF."

This "Higher Self" is ATMA, and of course it is "non-materializable," as Mr. Sinnett says. Even more, it can never be "objective" under any circumstances, even to the highest spiritual

---

[8] The length of this "transfer" depends, however, on the degree of spirituality in the ex-personality of the disembodied Ego. For those whose lives were very spiritual this transfer, though gradual, is very rapid. The time becomes longer with the materialistically inclined.

perception. For *Atman* or the "Higher Self" is really Brahma, the ABSOLUTE, and indistinguishable from it. In hours of *Samadhi*, the higher spiritual consciousness of the Initiate is entirely absorbed in the ONE essence, which is Atman, and therefore, being one with the whole, there can be nothing objective for it. Now some of our Theosophists have got into the habit of using the words "Self" and "Ego" as synonymous, of associating the term "Self" with only man's higher individual or even personal "Self" or *Ego*, whereas this term ought never to be applied except *to the One universal Self*. Hence the confusion. Speaking of Manas, the "causal body," we may call it – when connecting it with the Buddhic radiance – the "HIGHER EGO," never the "Higher Self." For even Buddhi, the "Spiritual Soul," is not the SELF, but the vehicle only of SELF. All the other *"Selves"* – such as the "Individual" self and "personal" self – ought never to be spoken or written of without their qualifying and characteristic adjectives.

Thus in this most excellent essay on the "Higher Self," this term is applied to the *sixth principle* or *Buddhi* (of course in conjunction with Manas, as without such union there would be no *thinking* principle or element in the spiritual soul), and has in consequence given rise to just such misunderstandings. The statement that "a child does not acquire its *sixth* principle – or become a morally responsible being capable of generating Karma – until seven years old," proves what is meant therein by the HIGHER SELF. Therefore, the able author is quite justified in explaining that after the "Higher Self" has passed into the human being and saturated the personality – in some of the finer organizations only – with its consciousness "people with psychic faculties may indeed perceive this Higher Self through their finer senses from time to time." But so are those, who limit the term "Higher Self" to the Universal Divine Principle, "justified" in misunderstanding him. For, when we read, without being prepared for this shifting of metaphysical terms,[9] that while "fully manifesting on the physical plane . . . the Higher Self still remains a conscious spiritual Ego on the corresponding plane of Nature" – we are apt to see in the "Higher Self" of this sentence, "Atma," and in the spiritual Ego, "Manas," or rather *Buddhi-Manas*, and forthwith to criticise the whole thing as incorrect.

To avoid henceforth such misapprehensions, I propose to translate literally from the Occult Eastern terms their equivalents in English, and offer these for future use:

The Higher Self is { Atma the inseparable ray of the Universal and ONE SELF. It is the God *above*, more than within, us. Happy the man who succeeds in saturating his *inner Ego* with it!

The Spiritual *divine* Ego is { the Spiritual soul or *Buddhi*, in close union with *Manas*, the mind-principle, without which it is no EGO at all, but only the Atmic *Vehicle*.

The Inner, or Higher "Ego" is { *Manas*, the "Fifth" Principle, so called, independently of Buddhi. The Mind-Principle is only the Spiritual Ego when merged *into one* with Buddhi, no materialist being supposed to have in him *such* an Ego, however great his intellectual capacities. It is the permanent *Individuality* or the "Reincarnating Ego."

---

[9] "Shifting of *Metaphysical terms*" applies here only to the shifting of their translated equivalents from the Eastern expressions; for to this day there never existed any such terms in English, every Theosophist having to coin his own terms to render his thought. It is nigh time, then, to settle on some definite nomenclature.

The Lower, or Personal "Ego" is { the physical man in conjunction with his *lower* Self, *i. e.*, animal instincts, passions, desires, etc. It is called the "false personality," and consists of the *lower Manas* combined with Kama-rupa, and operating through the Physical body and its phantom or "double."

The remaining "Principle" "*Prana*," or "Life," is, strictly speaking, the radiating force or Energy of Atma – as the Universal Life and the One Self, – Its lower or rather (in its effects) more physical, because manifesting, aspect. Prana or Life permeates the whole being of the objective Universe; and is called a "principle" only because it is an indispensable factor and the *deus ex machina* of the living man.

Enquirer. This division being so much simplified in its combinations will answer better, I believe. The other is much too metaphysical.

Theosophist. If outsiders as well as Theosophists would agree to it, it would certainly make matters much more comprehensible.

H.P. Blavatsky
The Key to Theosophy, 143-176

DIALOGUES BETWEEN THE TWO EDITORS

On Astral Bodies, Or Doppelgangers

M.C. Every country in the world believes more or less in the "double" or doppelganger. The simplest form of this is the appearance of a man's phantom, the moment after his death, or at the instant of death, to his dearest friend. Is this appearance the *mayavi rupa*?

H.P.B. It is; because produced by the thought of the dying man.

M.C. Is it unconscious?

H.P.B. It is unconscious to the extent that the dying man does not generally do it knowingly; nor is he aware that he so appears. What happens is this. If he thinks very intently at the moment of death of the person he either is very anxious to see, or loves best, he may appear to that person. The thought becomes objective; the double, or shadow of a man, being nothing but the faithful reproduction of him, like a reflection in a mirror, that which the man does, even in thought, that the double repeats. This is why the phantoms are often seen in such cases in the clothes they wear at the particular moment, and the image reproduces even the expression on the dying man's face. If the double of a man bathing were seen it would seem to be immersed in water; so when a man who has been drowned appears to his friend, the image will be seen to be dripping with water. The cause for the apparition may be also reversed; *i.e.*, the dying man may or may not be thinking at all of the particular person his image appears to, but it is that person who is sensitive. Or perhaps his sympathy or his hatred for the individual whose wraith is thus evoked is very intense physically or psychically; and in this case the apparition is created by, and depends upon, the intensity of the thought. What then happens is this. Let us call the dying man A, and him who sees the double B. The latter, owing to love, hate, or fear, has the image of A so deeply impressed on his psychic memory, that actual magnetic attraction and repulsion are established between the two, whether one knows of it and feels it, or not. When A dies, the sixth sense or psychic spiritual intelligence of the *inner man in* B becomes cognizant of the change in A, and forthwith apprises the physical senses of the man, by projecting before his eye the form of A, as it is at the instant of the great change. The same when the dying man longs to see someone; *his* thought telegraphs to his friend, consciously or unconsciously along the wire of sympathy, and becomes objective. This is what the "Spookical" Research Society would pompously, but none the less muddily, call *telepathic impact.*

M.C. This applies to the simplest form of the appearance of the double. What about cases in which the double does that which is contrary to the feeling and wish of the man?

H.P.B. This is impossible. The "Double" cannot act, unless the keynote of this action was struck in the brain of the man to whom the "Double" belongs, be that man just dead, or alive, in good or in bad health. If he paused on the thought a second, long enough to give it form, before he passed on to other mental pictures, this one second is as sufficient for the *objectivizations* of his personality on the astral waves, as for your face to impress itself on the sensitized plate of a photographic apparatus. Nothing prevents your form, then, being seized upon by the surrounding Forces – as a dry leaf fallen from a tree is taken up and carried away by the wind – being made to caricature or distort your thought.

M.C. Supposing the double expresses in actual words a thought uncongenial to the man, and expresses it – let us say to a friend far away, perhaps on another continent? I have known instances of this occurring.

H.P.B. Because it then so happens that the created image is taken up and used by a "Shell." Just as in seance-rooms when "images" of the dead – which may perhaps be lingering unconsciously in the memory or even the auras of those present – are seized upon by the Elemental or Elemental Shadows and made objective to the audience, and even caused to act at the bidding of the strongest of the many different wills in the room. In your case, moreover, there must exist a connecting link – a telegraph wire – between the two persons, a point of psychic sympathy, and on this the thought travels instantly. Of course there must be, in every case, some strong reason why that particular thought takes that direction; it must be connected in some way with the other person. Otherwise such apparitions would be of common and daily occurrence.

M.C. This seems very simple; why then does it only occur with exceptional persons?

H.P.B. Because the plastic power of the imagination is much stronger in some persons than in others. The mind is dual in its potentiality: it is physical and metaphysical. The higher part of the mind is connected with the spiritual soul or Buddhi, the lower with the animal soul, the Kama principle. There are persons who never think with the higher faculties of their mind at all; those who do so are the minority and are thus, in a way, *beyond, if* not above, the average of human kind. These will think even upon ordinary matters on that *higher* plane. The idiosyncrasy of the person determines in which "principle" of the mind the thinking is done, as also the faculties of a preceding life, and sometimes the heredity of the physical. This is why it is so very difficult for a materialist – the metaphysical portion of whose brain is almost atrophied – to raise himself, or for one who is naturally spiritually minded, to descend to the level of the matter-of-fact vulgar thought. Optimism and pessimism depend on it also in a large measure.

M.C. But the habit of thinking in the higher mind can be developed – else there would be no hope for persons who wish to alter their lives and raise themselves? And that this is possible must be true, or there would be no hope for the world.

H.P.B. Certainly it can be developed, but only with great difficulty, a firm determination, and through much self-sacrifice. But it is comparatively easy for those who are born with the gift. Why is it that one person sees poetry in a cabbage or a pig with her little ones, while another will perceive in the loftiest things only their lowest and most material aspect, will laugh at the "music of the spheres," and ridicule the most sublime conceptions and philosophies? This difference depends simply on the innate power of the mind to think on the higher or on the lower plane, with the *astral (in* the sense given to the word by St. Martin), or with the physical brain. Great intellectual powers are often no proof of, but are impediments to spiritual and right conceptions; witness most of the great men of science. We must rather pity than blame them.

H.P. Blavatsky
Lucifer, December, 1888
https://www.theosophytrust.org/399-dialogues-between-the-two-editors

WHY DO WE ALL FEAR DEATH?

Unhappily – or shall we say, happily – man in this dark cycle is denied, as a collective whole, the faculty of foresight. Whether we take into our mystic consideration the average business man, the profligate, the materialist, or the bigot, it is always the same. Compelled to confine his attention to the day's concern, the business man but imitates the provident ant by laying by a provision against the winter of old age; while the elect of fortune and Karmic illusions tries his best to emulate the grasshopper in his perpetual buzz and summer-song. The selfish care of the one and the utter recklessness of the other make both disregard and often remain entirely ignorant of any serious duty towards Human kind. As to the latter two, namely the materialist and the bigot, their duty to their neighbours and charity to all begin and end at home. Most men love but those who share their respective ways of thinking, and care nothing for the future of the races or the world; nor will they give a thought, if they can help it, to *post-mortem* life. Owing to their respective psychical temperaments each man expects death will usher him either through golden porches into a conventional heaven, or through sulphurous caverns into an asbestos hell, or else to the verge of an abyss of non-existence. And lo, how all of them – save the materialist – do fear death to be sure! May not this fear lie at the bottom of the aversion of certain people to Theosophy and Metaphysics? But no man in this century – itself whirling madly towards its gaping tomb – has the time or desire to give more than a casual thought either to the grim visitor who will not miss one of us, or to Futurity.

They are, perhaps, right as to the latter. The future lies in the present and both include the Past. With a rare occult insight Rohel made quite an *esoterically* true remark, in saying that "the future does not come from before to meet us, but comes streaming up from behind over our heads." For the Occultist and average Theosophist the Future and the Past are both included in each moment of their lives, hence in the eternal PRESENT. The Past is a torrent madly rushing by, that we face incessantly, without one second of interval; every wave of it, and every drop in it, being an event, whether great or small. Yet, no sooner have we faced it, and whether it brings joy or sorrow, whether it elevates us or knocks us off our feet, than it is carried away and disappears behind us, to be lost sooner or later in the great Sea of Oblivion. It depends on us to make every such event non-existent to ourselves by obliterating it from our memory; or else to create of our past sorrows Promethean Vultures – those "dark-winged birds, the embodied memories of the Past," which, in Sala's graphic fancy wheel and shriek over the Lethean lake." In the first case, we are real philosophers; in the second – but timid and even cowardly soldiers of the army called mankind, and commanded in the great battle of Life by "King Karma." Happy those of its warriors by whom Death is regarded as a tender and merciful mother. She rocks her sick children into sweet sleep on her cold, soft bosom but to awake them a moment after, healed of all ailing, happy, and with a tenfold reward for every bitter sigh or tear. *Post-mortem* oblivion of every evil – to the smallest – is the most blissful characteristic of the "paradise" *we* believe in. Yes: oblivion of pain and sorrow and the vivid recollection only, nay once more the living over of every happy moment of our terrestrial drama; and, if no such moment ever occurred in one's sad life, then, the glorious realization of every legitimate, well-earned, yet unsatisfied desire we ever had, as true as life itself and intensified seventy-seven times sevenfold. . . .

* * * * * * *

Christians – the Continental especially – celebrate their New Year days with special pomp. That day is the *Devachan* of children and servants, and everyone is supposed to be happy, from Kings and Queens down to the porters and kitchen-malkins. The festival is, of course, purely pagan, as with very few exceptions are all our *holy days*. The dear old pagan customs have not died out, not even in Protestant England, though here the New Year is no longer a sacred day – more's the pity. The presents, which used to be called in old

Rome *strenæ* (now, the French *étrennes*), are still mutually exchanged. People greet each other with the words: *Annum novum faustum felicemque tibi,* as of yore; the magistrates, it is true, sacrifice no longer a white swan to Jupiter, nor priests a white steer to Janus. But magistrates, priests and all devour still in commemoration of swan and steer, big fat oxen and turkeys at their Christmas and New Year's dinners. The gilt dates, the dried and gilt plums and figs have now passed from the hands of the tribunes on their way to the Capitol unto the Christmas trees for children. Yet, if the modern Caligula receives no longer piles of copper coins with the head of Janus on one side of them, it is because his own effigy replaces that of the god on every coin, and that coppers are no longer touched by royal hands. Nor has the custom of presenting one's Sovereigns with *strenæ* been abolished in England so very long. D'Israeli tells us in his *Curiosities of Literature* of 3,000 gowns found in Queen Bess's wardrobe after her death, the fruits of her New Year's tax on her faithful subjects, from Dukes down to dustmen. As the success of any affair on that day was considered a good omen for the whole year in ancient Rome, so the belief exists to this day in many a Christian country, in Russia pre-eminently so. Is it because instead of the New Year, the mistletoe and the holly are now used on Christmas day, that the symbol has become Christian? The cutting of the mistletoe off the sacred oak on New Year's day is a relic of the old Druids of pagan Britain. Christian Britain is as pagan in her ways as she ever was.

But there are more reasons than one why England is bound to include the New Year as a sacred day among Christian festivals. The 1st of January being the 8th day after Christmas, is, according to both profane and ecclesiastical histories, the festival of Christ's circumcision, as six days later is the Epiphany. And it is as undeniable and as world-known a fact as any, that long before the advent of the three Zoroastrian Magi, of Christ's circumcision, or his birth either, the 1st of January was the first day of the civil year of the Romans, and celebrated 2,000 years ago as it is now. It is hard to see the reason, since Christendom has helped itself to the Jewish

Scriptures, and along with them their curious chronology, why it should have found it unfit to adopt also the Jewish *Rosh-Hashonah* (the head of the year), instead of the pagan New Year. Once that the 1st Chapter of *Genesis* is left headed in every country with the words, "Before Christ, 4004," consistency alone should have suggested the propriety of giving preference to the Talmudic calendar over the pagan Roman. Everything seemed to invite the Church to do so. On the undeniable authority of revelation Rabbinical tradition assures us that it was on the 1st day of the month of *Tisri,* that the Lord God of Israel created the world – just 5,848 years ago. Then there's that other historical fact, namely that our father Adam was likewise created on the first anniversary of that same day of *Tisri* – a year after. All this is very important, pre-eminently suggestive, and underlines most emphatically our proverbial western ingratitude. Moreover, if we are permitted to say so, it is dangerous. For that identical first day of *Tisri* is also called "Yom Haddin," the Day of Judgment. The Jewish *El Shaddai,* the Almighty, is more active than the "Father" of the Christians. The latter will judge us only after the destruction of the Universe, on the Great Day when the Goats and the Sheep will stand, each on their allotted side, awaiting eternal bliss or damnation. But El Shaddai, we are informed by the Rabbins, sits in judgment on every anniversary of the world's creation – *i.e.* on every New Year's Day. Surrounded by His archangels, the God of Mercy has the astro-sidereal minute books opened, and the name of every man, woman and child is read to Him aloud from these Records, wherein the minutest thoughts and deeds of every human (or is it only Jewish?) being are entered. If the good deeds outnumber the wicked actions, the mortal whose name is read lives through that year. The Lord plagues for him some Christian Pharaoh or two, and hands him over to him to shear. But if the bad deeds outweigh the good – then woe to the culprit; he is forthwith condemned to suffer the penalty of death during that year, and is sent to Sheol.

This would imply that the Jews regard the gift of life as something very precious indeed. Christians are as fond of their lives as Jews, and both are generally scared out of their wits at the approach of Death. Why it should be so has never been made clear. Indeed, this seems but a poor compliment to pay the Creator, as suggesting the idea that none of the Christians care particularly to meet the Unspeakable Glory of the "Father' face to face. Dear, loving children!

A pious Roman Catholic assured us one day that it was not so, and attributed the scare to *reverential awe*. Moreover, he tried to persuade his listeners that the Holy Inquisition burnt her "heretics" out of pure Christian kindness. They were put out of the way of terrestrial mischief in this way, he said, for Mother Church knew well that Father God would take better care of the roasted victims than any mortal authority could, while they were raw and living. This may be a mistaken view of the situation, nevertheless, it was meant in all Christian charity.

We have heard a less charitable version of the real reason for burning heretics and all whom the Church was determined to get rid of; and by comparison this reason colours the Calvinistic doctrine of predestination to eternal bliss or damnation with quite a roseate hue. It is said to be stated in the secret records of the Vatican archives, that burning to the last atom of flesh, after breaking all the bones into small fragments, was done with a predetermined object. It was that of preventing the "enemy of the Church," from taking his part and share even in the last act of the drama of the world – as theologically conceived – namely in "the Resurrection of the Dead," or of all flesh, on the great Judgment Day. As cremation is to this hour opposed by the Church on the same principle – to wit, that a cremated "Sleeper" will upon awakening at the blast of the angel's trumpet, find it impossible to gather up in time his scattered limbs – the reason given for the *auto da fé* seems reasonable enough and quite likely. The sea will give up the dead which are in it, and death and hell will deliver up their dead *(Vide "Revelation"* xx. 13); but terrestrial fire is not to be credited with a like generosity, nor supposed to share in the asbestosian characteristics of the orthodox hellfire. Once the body is cremated it is as good as annihilated with regard to the last rising of the dead. If the occult reason of the inquisitorial *autos da fé* rests on fact – and personally we do not entertain the slightest doubt of it, considering the authority it was received from – then the Holy Inquisition and Popes would have very little to say against the Protestant doctrine of Predestination. The latter, as warranted in Revelation, allows some chance, at least, to the "Damned" whom hell delivers at the last hour, and who may thus yet be pardoned. While if things took place in nature as the theology of Rome decreed that they should, the poor "Heretics" would find themselves worse off than any of the "damned." Natural query: which of the two, the God of the Calvinists or the Jesuit of God, he who first invented burning, beats the other in refined and diabolical cruelty? Shall the question remain in 1890, *sub judice,* as it did in 1790?

H.P. Blavatsky
Excerpted from "1890! On The New Year's Morrow"
Lucifer, January, 1890
https://theosophytrust.org/362-1890-on-the-new-years-morrow

LIFE AND DEATH

A Conversation Between a Great Eastern Teacher, H. P. B., Colonel Olcott and an Indian Reported by H. P. Blavatsky

"Master," said Narayan to Thakur, in the midst of a very hot dispute with the poor Babu, "what is it he is saying, and can one listen to him without being disgusted? He says that nothing remains of the man after he is dead, but that the body of the man simply resolves itself into its component elements, and that what we call the soul, and he calls the temporary consciousness, separates itself, disappearing like the steam of hot water as it cools."

"Do you find this so very astonishing?" said the Master. "The Babu is a Chârvâka[1] and he tells you only that which every other Chârvâka would have told you."

"But the Chârvâkas are mistaken. There are many people who believe that the real man is not his physical covering, but dwells in the mind, in the seat of consciousness. Do you mean to say that in any case the consciousness may leave the soul after death?"

"In his case it may," answered Thakur quietly: "because he firmly believes in what he says."

Narayan cast an astonished and even frightened look at Thakur, and the Babu – who always felt some restraint in the presence of the latter – looked at us with a victorious smile.

"But how is this?" went on Narayan. "The Vedânta teaches us that the spirit of the spirit is immortal, and that the human soul does not die in Parabrahman. Are there any exceptions?"

"In the fundamental laws of the spiritual world there can be no exceptions; but there are laws for the blind and laws for those who see."

"I understand this, but in this case, as I have told him already, his

---

[1] A sect of Bengali Materialists.

full and final disappearance of consciousness is nothing but the aberration of a blind man, who, not seeing the sun, denies its existence, but all the same he will see the sun with his spiritual sight after he is dead."

"He will not see anything," said the Master. "Denying the existence of the sun now, he could not see it on the other side of the grave."

Seeing that Narayan looked rather upset, and that even we, the Colonel and myself, stared at him in the expectation of a more definite answer, Thakur went on reluctantly:

"You speak about the spirit of the spirit, that is to say about the Atmâ, confusing this spirit with the soul of the mortal, with *Manas*. No doubt the spirit is immortal, because being without beginning it is without end; but it is not the spirit that is concerned in the present conversation. It is the human, self-conscious soul. You confuse it with the former, and the Babu denies the one and the other, soul and spirit, and so you do not understand each other."

"I understand him," said Narayan.

"But you do not understand me," interrupted the Master. "I will try to speak more clearly. What you want to know is this. Whether the full loss of consciousness and self-feeling is possible after death, even in the case of a confirmed Materialist. Is that it?"

Narayan answered: "Yes; because he fully denies everything that is an undoubted truth for us, that in which we firmly believe."

"All right," said the Master. "To this I will answer positively as follows, which, mind you, does not prevent me from believing as firmly as you do in our teaching, which designates the period between two lives as only temporary. Whether it is one year or a million that this entr'acte lasts between the two acts of the illusion life, the posthumous state may be perfectly similar to the state of a man in a very deep fainting-fit, without any breaking of the fundamental rules. Therefore the Babu in his personal case is perfectly right."

"But how is this?" said Colonel Olcott; "since the rule of immortality does not admit of any exceptions, as you said."

"Of course it does not admit of any exceptions, but only in the case of things that really exist. One who like yourself has studied *Mândukya Upanishad* and *Vedânta-Sara* ought not to ask such questions," said the Master with a reproachful smile.

"But it is precisely *Mândukya Upanishad*," timidly observed Narayan, "which teaches us that between the *Buddhi* and the *Manas*, as between the *Îshvara* and *Prajnâ*, there is no more difference in reality than between a forest and its trees, between a lake and its waters."

"Perfectly right," said the Master, "because one or even a hundred trees which have lost their vital sap, or are even uprooted, cannot prevent the forest from remaining a forest."

"Yes," said Narayan, "but in this comparison, *Buddhi* is the forest, and *Manas-Taijasi* the trees, and if the former be immortal, then how is it possible for the *Manas-Taijasi*, which is the same as *Buddhi*, to lose its consciousness before a new incarnation? That is where my difficulty lies."

"You have no business to have any difficulties," said the Master, "if you take the trouble not to confuse the abstract idea of the whole with its casual change of form. Remember that if in talking about *Buddhi* we may say that it is unconditionally immortal, we cannot say the same either about *Manas*, or about *Taijasi*. Neither the former nor the latter have any existence separated from the Divine Soul, because the one is an attribute of the terrestrial personality, and the second is identically the same as the first, only with the additional reflection in it of the *Buddhi*. In its turn, *Buddhi* would be an impersonal spirit without this element, which it borrows from the human soul, and which conditions it and makes out of it something which has the appearance of being separate from the Universal Soul, during all the cycle of the man's incarnations. If you say therefore that *Buddhi-Manas* cannot die, and cannot lose consciousness either in eternity or during the temporary periods of suspension, you would be perfectly right; but to apply this axiom to the qualities of *Buddhi-Manas* is the same as if you were arguing that as the soul of Colonel Olcott is immortal the red on his cheeks is also immortal. And so it is evident you have mixed up the reality, *Sat*, with its manifestation. You have forgotten that united to the *Manas* only, the luminosity of *Taijasi* becomes a question of time, as the immortality and the posthumous consciousness of the terrestrial personality of the man become conditional qualities, depending on the conditions and beliefs created by itself during its lifetime. Karma acts unceasingly, and we reap in the next world the fruit of that which we ourselves have sown in this life."

"But if my Ego may find itself after the destruction of my body in a state of complete unconsciousness, then where is the punishment for the sins committed by me in my lifetime?" asked the Colonel, pensively stroking his beard.

"Our Philosophy teaches us," answered Thakur, "that the punishment reaches the Ego only in its next incarnation, and that immediately after our death we meet only the rewards for the sufferings of the terrestrial life, sufferings that were not deserved by us. So, as you may see, the whole of the punishment consists in the absence of reward, in the complete loss of the consciousness of happiness and rest. Karma is the child of the terrestrial Ego, the fruit of the acts of his visible personality, even of the thoughts and intentions of the spiritual I. But at the same time it is a tender mother, who heals the wounds given in the preceding life before striking this Ego and giving him new ones. In the life of a mortal there is no mishap or sorrow which is not a fruit and direct consequence of a sin committed in his preceding incarnation; but not having preserved the slightest recollection of it in his present life, and not feeling himself guilty, and therefore suffering unjustly, the man deserves consolation and full rest on the other side of the grave. For our spiritual Ego, Death is always a redeemer and a friend. It is either the peaceful sleep of a baby, or a sleep full of blissful dreams and reveries."

"As far as I remember, the periodical incarnations of *Sûtrâtmâ* [2] are compared in the *Upanishads* to the terrestrial life which is spent, term by term, in sleeping and waking. Is that so?" I asked, wishing to renew the first question of Narayan.

"Yes, it is so; that is a very good comparison."

"I do not doubt it is good," I said, "but I hardly understand it. After the awakening, the man merely begins a new day, but his soul, as well as his body, are the same as they were yesterday; whereas in every new incarnation not only his exterior, sex, and even personality, but, as it seems to me, all his moral qualities, are changed completely. And then, again, how can this comparison be called true, when people, after their awakening, remember very well not only what they were doing yesterday, but many days, months, and even years ago, whereas, in their present incarnations, they do not preserve the slightest recollection about any past life, whatever it was. Of course a man, after he is awakened, may forget what he has seen in his dreams, but still he knows that he was sleeping and that during his sleep he lived. But about our previous life we cannot say even that we lived. What do you say to this?"

"There are some people who do remember some things," enigmatically answered Thakur, without giving a straight answer to my question.

"I have some suspicions on this point," I answered, laughingly, "but it cannot be said about ordinary mortals. Then how are we, who

---

[2] In the Vedânta, *Buddhi*, in its combinations with the moral qualities, consciousness, and the notions of the personalities in which it was incarnated, is called *Sûtrâtmâ*, which literally means the "thread soul," because a whole long row of human lives is strung on this thread like the pearls of a necklace. The *Manas* must become Taijasi in order to reach and to see itself in eternity, when united to *Sûtrâtmâ*. But often, owing to sin and associations with the purely terrestrial reason, this very luminosity disappears completely.

have not reached as yet the *Samma Sambuddha*,³ to understand this comparison?"

"You can understand it when you better understand the characteristics of the three kinds of what we call sleep."

"This is not an easy task you propose to us," said the Colonel, laughingly. "The greatest of our physiologists got so entangled in this question that it became only more confused."

"It is because they have undertaken what they had no business to undertake, the answering of this question being the duty of the psychologist, of whom there are hardly any among your European scientists. A Western psychologist is only another name for a physiologist, with the difference that they work on principles still more material. I have recently read a book by Maudsley which showed me clearly that they try to cure mental diseases without believing in the existence of the soul."

"All this is very interesting," I said, "but it leads us away from the original object of our questions, which you seem reluctant to clear for us, Thakur Sahib. It looks as if you were confirming and even encouraging the theories of the Babu. Remember that he says he disbelieves the posthumous life, the life after death, and denies the possibility of any kind of consciousness exactly on the grounds of our not remembering anything of our past terrestrial life."

"I repeat again that the Babu is a Chârvâka, who only repeats what he was taught. It is not the system of the Materialists that I confirm and encourage, but the truth of the Babu's opinions in what concerns his personal state after death."

"Then do you mean to say that such people as the Babu are to be excepted from the general rule?"

"Not at all. Sleep is a general and unchangeable law for man as well as for every other terrestrial creature, but there are various

---

³ The knowledge of one's past incarnations. Only Yogis and Adepts of the Occult Sciences possess this knowledge, by the aid of the most ascetic life.

sleeps and still more various dreams."

"But it is not only the life after death and its dreams that he denies. He denies the immortal life altogether, as well as the immortality of his own spirit."

"In the first instance he acts according to the canons of modern European Science, founded on the experience of our five senses. In this he is guilty only with respect to those people who do not hold his opinions. In the second instance again he is perfectly right. Without the previous interior consciousness and the belief in the immortality of the soul, the soul cannot become *Buddhi* Taijasi. It will remain *Manas*.[4] But for the *Manas* alone there is no immortality. In order to live a conscious life in the world on the other side of the grave, the man must have acquired belief in that world, in this terrestrial life. These are the two aphorisms of the Occult Science, on which is constructed all our Philosophy in respect to the posthumous consciousness and immortality of the Soul. *Sûtrâtmâ* gets only what it deserves. After the destruction of the body there begins for the *Sûtrâtmâ* either a period of full awakening, or a chaotic sleep, or a sleep without reveries or dreams. Following your physiologists who found the causality of dreams in the unconscious preparation for them. in the waking state, why should not we acknowledge the same

---

[4] Without the full assimilation with the Divine Soul, the terrestrial soul, or *Manas*, cannot live in eternity a conscious life. It will become *Buddhi-Taijasi*, or *Buddhi-Manas*, only in case its general tendencies during its lifetime lead it towards the spiritual world. Then full of the essence and penetrated by the light of its Divine Soul, the *Manas* will disappear in *Buddhi*, will assimilate itself with *Buddhi*, still preserving a spiritual consciousness of its terrestrial personality; otherwise *Manas*, that is to say, the human mind, founded on the five physical senses, our terrestrial or our personal soul, will be plunged into a deep sleep without awakening, without dreams, without consciousness, till a new reincarnation. [In this article, *Sûtrâtmâ* is used for the principle later called the Higher *Manas*, and *Manas* for that later called the Lower *Manas*, or *Kama-Manas*. – Eds.

with respect to the posthumous dreams? I repeat what *Vedânta Sara* teaches us: Death is sleep. After death, there begins before our spiritual eyes a representation of a programme that was learned by heart by us in our lifetime, and was sometimes invented by us, the practical realization of our true beliefs, or of illusions created by ourselves. These are the posthumous fruit of the tree of life. Of course the belief or disbelief in the fact of conscious immortality cannot influence the unconditioned actuality of the fact itself once it exists. But the belief or disbelief of separate personalities cannot but condition the influence of this fact in its effect on such personalities. Now I hope you understand."

"I begin to understand. The Materialists, disbelieving everything that cannot be controlled by their five senses and their so-called scientific reason and denying every spiritual phenomenon, point to the terrestrial as the only conscious existence. Accordingly they will get only what they have deserved. They will lose their personal I; they will sleep the unconscious sleep until a new awakening. Have I understood rightly?"

"Nearly. You may add to that that the Vedântins, acknowledging two kinds of conscious existence, the terrestrial and the spiritual, point only to the latter as an undoubted actuality. As to the terrestrial life, owing to its changeability and shortness, it is nothing but an illusion of our senses. Our life in the spiritual spheres must be thought an actuality because it is there that lives our endless, never-changing immortal I, the *Sûtrâtmâ*. Whereas in every new incarnation it clothes itself in a perfectly different personality, a temporary and short-lived one, in which everything except its spiritual prototype is doomed to traceless destruction."

"But excuse me, Thakur. Is it possible that my personality, my terrestrial conscious I, is to perish tracelessly?"

"According to our teachings, not only is it to perish, but it must perish in all its fullness, except this principle in it which, united to *Buddhi*, has become purely spiritual and now forms an inseparable whole. But in the case of a hardened Materialist it may happen that neither consciously nor unconsciously has anything of its personal I ever penetrated into *Buddhi*. The latter will not take away into eternity any atom of such a terrestrial personality. Your spiritual I is immortal, but from your present personality it will carry away only that which has deserved immortality, that is to say only the aroma of the flowers mowed down by death."

"But the flower itself, the terrestrial I?"

"The flower itself, as all the past and future flowers which have blossomed and will blossom after them on the same maternal branch, *Sûtrâtmâ*, children of the same root, *Buddhi*, will become dust. Your real I is not, as you ought to know yourself, your body that now sits before me, nor your *Manas-Sûtrâtmâ*, but your *Sûtrâtmâ-Buddhi*."

"But this does not explain to me why you call our posthumous life immortal, endless, and real, and the terrestrial one a mere shadow. As far as I understand, according to your teaching, even our posthumous life has its limits, and being longer than the terrestrial life, still has its end."

"Most decidedly. The spiritual Ego of the man moves in eternity like a pendulum between the hours of life and death, but if these hours, the periods of life terrestrial and life posthumous, are limited in their continuation, and even the very number of such breaks in eternity between sleep and waking, between illusion and reality, have their beginning as well as their end, the spiritual Pilgrim himself is eternal. Therefore the hours of his posthumous life, when unveiled he stands face to face with truth and the short-lived mirages of his terrestrial existences are far from him, compose or make up, in our ideas, the only reality. Such breaks, in spite of the fact that they are finite, do double service to the *Sûtrâtmâ*, which, perfecting itself constantly, follows without vacillation, though very slowly, the road leading to its last transformation, when, reaching its aim at last, it becomes a Divine Being. They not only contribute to the reaching of this goal, but without these finite breaks *Sûtrâtmâ-Buddhi* could never reach it. *Sûtrâtmâ* is the actor, and its numerous and different incarnations are the actor's parts. I suppose you would not apply to these parts, and so much the less to their costumes, the term of personality. Like an actor the soul is bound to play, during the cycle of births up to the very threshold of *Paranirvâna*, many such parts, which often are disagreeable to it, but like a bee, collecting its honey from every flower, and leaving the rest to feed the worms of the earth, our spiritual individuality, the *Sûtrâtmâ*, collecting only the nectar of moral qualities and consciousness from every terrestrial personality in which it has to clothe itself, forced by Karma, unites at last all these qualities in one, having then become a perfect being, a Dhyân Chohan. So much the worse for such terrestrial personalities from whom it could not gather anything. Of course, such personalities cannot outlive consciously their terrestrial existence."

"Then the immortality of the terrestrial personality still remains an open question, and even the very immortality is not unconditioned?"

"Oh no, you misunderstand me," said the Master. "What I mean is that immortality does not cover the non-existing; for everything that exists in *Sat*, or has its origin in *Sat*, immortality as well as infinity, are unconditioned. *Mulaprakriti* is the reverse of *Parabrahman*, but they are both one and the same. The very essence of all this, that is to say, spirit, force and matter, have neither end nor beginning, but the shape acquired by this triple unity during its incarnations, their exterior so to speak, is nothing but a mere illusion of personal conceptions. This is why we call the posthumous life the only reality, and the terrestrial one, including the personality itself, only imaginary."

"Why in this case should we call the reality sleep, and the phantasm waking?"

"This comparison was made by me to facilitate your comprehension. From the standpoint of your terrestrial notions it is perfectly accurate."

"You say that the posthumous life is founded on a basis of perfect justice, on the merited recompense for all the terrestrial sorrows. You say that *Sûtrâtmâ* is sure to seize the smallest opportunity of using the spiritual qualities in each of its incarnations. Then how can you admit that the spiritual personality of our Babu, the personality of this boy, who is so ideally honest and noble, so perfectly kind, in spite of all his disbeliefs, will not reach immortality, and will perish like the dust of a dried flower?"

"Who, except himself," answered the Master, "ever doomed him to such a fate? I have known the Babu from the time he was a small boy, and I am perfectly sure that the harvest of the *Sûtrâtmâ* in his case will be very abundant. Though his Atheism and Materialism are far from being feigned, still he cannot die for ever in the whole fullness of his individuality."

"But, Thakur Sahib, did not you yourself confirm the rectitude of his notions as to his personal state on the other side of the grave, and do not these notions consist in his firm belief that after his death every trace of consciousness will disappear?"

"I confirmed them, and I confirm them again. When travelling in a railway train you may fall asleep and sleep all the time, while the train stops at many stations; but surely there will be a station where you will awake, and the aim of your journey will be reached in full consciousness. You say you are dissatisfied with my comparison of death to sleep, but remember, the most ordinary of mortals knows three different kinds of sleep – dreamless sleep, a sleep with vague chaotic dreams, and at last a sleep with dreams so very vivid and clear that for the time being they become a perfect reality for the sleeper. Why should not you admit that exactly the analogous case happens to the soul freed from its body? After their parting there begins for the soul, according to its deserts, and chiefly to its faith, either a perfectly conscious life, a life of semi-consciousness, or a dreamless sleep which is equal to the state of non-being. This is the realization of the programme of which I spoke, a programme previously invented and prepared by the Materialist. But there are Materialists and Materialists. A bad man, or simply a great egotist, who adds to his full disbelief a perfect indifference to his fellow beings, must unquestionably leave his personality forever at the threshold of death. He has no means of linking himself to the *Sûtrâtmâ*, and the connection between them is broken forever with his last sigh; but such Materialists as our Babu will sleep only one station. There will be a time when he will recognize himself in eternity, and will be sorry he has lost a single day of the life eternal. I see your objections – I see you are going to say that hundreds and thousands of human lives, lived through by the *Sûtrâtmâ*, correspond in our Vedântin notions to a perfect disappearance of every personality. This is my answer. Take a comparison of eternity with a single life of a man, which is composed of so many days, weeks, months, and years. If a man has preserved a good memory in his old age he may easily recall every important day or year of his past life, but even in case he has forgotten some of them, is not his personality one and the same through all his life? For the Ego every separate life is what every separate day is in the life of a man."

"Then, would it not be better to say that death is nothing but a birth for a new life, or, still better, a going back to eternity?"

"This is how it really is, and I have nothing to say against such a way of putting it. Only with our accepted views of material life the words 'live' and 'exist' are not applicable to the purely subjective condition after death; and were they employed in our Philosophy without a rigid definition of their meanings, the Vedântins would soon arrive at the ideas which are common in our times among the American Spiritualists, who preach about spirits marrying among themselves and with mortals. As amongst the true, not nominal Christians, so amongst the Vedântins – the life on the other side of the grave is the land where there are no tears, no sighs, where there is neither marrying nor giving in marriage, and where the just realize their full perfection."

H. P. Blavatsky
Lucifer, October, 1892

APPENDIX V

OTHER SOURCES

ON THE MYSTERIES OF REINCARNATION
Periodical Re-Births

Enquirer. You mean, then, that we have all lived on earth before, in many past incarnations, and shall go on so living?

Theosophist. I do. The life-cycle, or rather the cycle of conscious life, begins with the separation of the mortal animal-man into sexes, and will end with the close of the last generation of men, in the seventh round and seventh race of mankind. Considering we are only in the fourth round and fifth race, its duration is more easily imagined than expressed.

Enquirer. And we keep on incarnating in new personalities all the time?

Theosophist. Most assuredly so; because this life-cycle or period of incarnation may be best compared to human life. As each such life is composed of days of activity separated by nights of sleep or of inaction, so, in the incarnation-cycle, an active life is followed by a Devachanic rest.

Enquirer. And it is this succession of births that is generally defined as re-incarnation?

Theosophist. Just so. It is only through these births that the perpetual progress of the countless millions of Egos toward final perfection and final rest (as long as was the period of activity) can be achieved.

Enquirer. And what is it that regulates the duration, or special qualities of these incarnations?

Theosophist. Karma, the universal law of retributive justice.

Enquirer. Is it an intelligent law?

Theosophist. For the Materialist, who calls the law of periodicity which regulates the marshalling of the several bodies, and all the other laws in nature, blind forces and mechanical laws, no doubt Karma would be a law of chance and no more. For us, no adjective or qualification could describe that which is impersonal and no entity, but a universal operative law. If you question me about the causative intelligence in it, I must answer you I do not know. But if you ask me to define its effects and tell you what these are in our belief, I may say that the experience of thousands of ages has shown us that they are absolute and unerring equity, wisdom, and intelligence. For Karma in its effects is an unfailing redresser of human injustice, and of all the failures of nature; a stern adjuster of wrongs; a retributive law which rewards and punishes with equal impartiality. It is, in the strictest sense, "no respecter of persons," though, on the other hand, it can neither be propitiated, nor turned aside by prayer. This is a belief common to Hindus and Buddhists, who both believe in Karma.

Enquirer. In this Christian dogmas contradict both, and I doubt whether any Christian will accept the teaching.

Theosophist. No; and Inman gave the reason for it many years ago.

As he puts it, while "the Christians will accept any nonsense, if promulgated by the Church as a matter of faith . . . the Buddhists hold that nothing which is contradicted by sound reason can be a true doctrine of Buddha." They do not believe in any pardon for their sins, except after an adequate and just punishment for each evil deed or thought in a future incarnation, and a proportionate compensation to the parties injured.

Enquirer. Where is it so stated?

Theosophist. In most of their sacred works. In the "Wheel of the Law" (p. 57) you may find the following Theosophical tenet: - "Buddhists believe that every act, word or thought has its consequence, which will appear sooner or later in the present or in the future state. Evil acts will produce evil consequences, good acts will produce good consequences: prosperity in this world, or birth in heaven (Devachan). . . in the future state."

Enquirer. Christians believe the same thing, don't they?

Theosophist. Oh, no; they believe in the pardon and the remission of all sins. They are promised that if they only believe in the blood of Christ (an innocent victim!), in the blood offered by Him for the expiation of the sins of the whole of mankind, it will atone for every mortal sin. And we believe neither in vicarious atonement, nor in the possibility of the remission of the smallest sin by any god, not even by a "personal Absolute" or "Infinite," if such a thing could have any existence. What we believe in, is strict and impartial justice. Our idea of the unknown Universal Deity, represented by Karma, is that it is a Power which cannot fail, and can, therefore, have neither wrath nor mercy, only absolute Equity, which leaves every cause, great or small, to work out its inevitable effects. The saying of Jesus: "With what measure you mete it shall be measured to you again" (*Matthew* vii., 2), neither by expression nor implication points to any hope of future mercy or salvation by proxy. This is why, recognising as we do in our philosophy the justice of this statement, we cannot recommend too strongly mercy, charity, and forgiveness of mutual offences. Resist not evil, and render good for evil, are Buddhist precepts, and were first preached in view of the implacability of Karmic law. For man to take the law into his own hands is anyhow a sacrilegious presumption. Human Law may use restrictive not punitive measures; but a man who, believing in Karma, still revenges himself and refuses to forgive every injury, thereby rendering good for evil, is a criminal and only hurts himself. As Karma is sure to punish the man who wronged him, by seeking to inflict an additional punishment on his enemy, he, who instead of leaving that punishment to the great Law adds to it his own mite, only begets thereby a cause for the future reward of his own enemy and a future punishment for himself. The unfailing Regulator affects in each incarnation the quality of its successor; and the sum of the merit or demerit in preceding ones determines it.

Enquirer. Are we then to infer a man's past from his present?

Theosophist. Only so far as to believe that his present life is what it justly should be, to atone for the sins of the past life. Of course –

seers and great adepts excepted – we cannot as average mortals know what those sins were. From our paucity of data, it is impossible for us even to determine what an old man's youth must have been; neither can we, for like reasons, draw final conclusions merely from what we see in the life of some man, as to what his past life may have been.

H.P. Blavatsky
The Key to Theosophy, 197-201

THE BEACON LIGHT OF THE UNKNOWN

What does the world know of true Theosophy? How can it distinguish between that of a Plotinus, and that of the false brothers? And of the latter the Society possesses more than its share. The egoism, vanity and self-sufficiency of the majority of mortals is incredible. There are some for whom their little personality constitutes the whole universe, beyond which there is no salvation. Suggest to one of these that the alpha and omega of wisdom are not limited by the circumference of his or her head, that his or her judgment could not be considered quite equal to that of Solomon, and straight away he or she accuses you of anti-theosophy. You have been guilty of blasphemy against the spirit, which will not be pardoned in this century, nor in the next. These people say, "I am Theosophy," as Louis XIV said "I am the State." They speak of fraternity and of altruism and only care in reality for that for which no one else cares — themselves — in other words their little "me." Their egoism makes them fancy that it is they only who represent the temple of Theosophy, and that in proclaiming themselves to the world they are proclaiming Theosophy. Alas! the doors and windows of that "temple" are no better than so many channels through which enter, but very seldom depart, the vices and illusions characteristic of egoistical mediocrities.

These people are the white ants of the Theosophical Society, which eat away its foundations, and are a perpetual menace to it. It is only when they leave it that it is possible to breathe freely.

It is not such as these that can ever give a correct idea of practical Theosophy, still less of the transcendental Theosophy which occupies the minds of a little group of the elect. Every one of us possesses the faculty, the interior sense, that is known by the name of *intuition,* but how rare are those who know how to develop it! It is, however, only by the aid of this faculty that men can ever see things in their true colours. It is an *instinct of the soul,* which grows in us in proportion to the employment we give it, and which helps us to perceive and understand the realities of things with far more certainty than can the simple use of our senses and exercise of our reason. What are called good sense and logic enable us to see only the appearances of things, that which is evident to everyone. The *instinct* of which I speak, being a projection of our perceptive consciousness, a projection which acts from the subjective to the objective, and not *vice versa,* awakens in us spiritual senses and power to act; these senses assimilate to themselves the essence of the object or of the action under examination, and represent it to us as it really is, not as it appears to our physical senses and to our cold reason. "We begin with *instinct,* we end with omniscience" says Professor A. Wilder, our oldest colleague. Iamblicus has described this faculty, and certain Theosophists have been able to appreciate the truth of his description.

"There exists," he says, "a faculty in the human mind which is immeasurably superior to all those which are grafted or engendered in us. By it we can attain to union with superior intelligences, finding ourselves raised above the scenes of this earthly life, and partaking of the higher existence and superhuman powers of the inhabitants of the celestial spheres. By this faculty we find ourselves liberated finally from the dominion of destiny (Karma), and we become, as it were, the arbiters of our own fates. For, when the most excellent parts in us find themselves filled with energy; and when our soul is lifted up towards essences higher than science, it can separate itself from the conditions which hold it in the bondage of every-day life; it exchanges its ordinary existence for another one, it renounces the conventional habits which belong to the external order of things, to give itself up to and mix itself with another order of things which reigns in that most elevated state of existence."

Plato has expressed the same idea in two lines: "The light and spirit of the Divinity are the wings of the soul. They raise it to communion with the gods, above this earth, with which the spirit of man is too ready to soil itself. . . . To become like the gods, is to become holy, just and wise. That is the end for which man was created, and that ought to be his aim in the acquisition of knowledge."

This is true Theosophy, inner Theosophy, that of the soul. But followed with a selfish aim Theosophy changes its nature and becomes *demonosophy*. That is why Oriental wisdom teaches us that the Hindu Yogi who isolates himself in an impenetrable forest, like the Christian hermit who, as was common in former times, retires to the desert, are both of them nothing but accomplished egoists. The one acts with the sole idea of finding a nirvanic refuge against reincarnation; the other acts with the unique idea of saving his soul, — both of them think only of themselves. Their motive is altogether personal; for, even supposing they attain their end, are they not like cowardly soldiers, who desert from their regiment when it is going into action, in order to keep out of the way of the bullets? . . .

Gautama, the Buddha, only remained in solitude long enough to enable him to arrive at the truth, which he devoted himself from that time on to promulgate, begging his bread, and living for humanity. Jesus retired to the desert only for forty days, and died for this same humanity. Apollonius of Tyana, Plotinus, Iamblicus, while leading lives of singular abstinence, almost of asceticism, lived in the world and *for* the world. The greatest ascetics and *saints* of our days are not those who retire into inaccessible places, but those who pass their lives in travelling from place to place, doing good and trying to raise mankind; although, indeed, they may avoid Europe, and those civilized countries where no one has any eyes or ears except for himself, countries divided into two camps — of Cains and Abels.

Those who regard the human soul as an emanation of the Deity, as a particle or ray of the universal and ABSOLUTE soul, understand the parable of the *Talents* better than do the Christians. He who hides in the earth the *talent* which has been given him by his "Lord," will lose that talent, as the ascetic loses it, who takes it into his head to "save his soul" in egoistical solitude. The "good and faithful servant" who doubles his capital, by harvesting for *him who has not sown,* because he had not the means of doing so, and who reaps for the poor who have not scattered the grain, acts like a true altruist. He will receive his recompense, just because he has worked for another, without any idea of remuneration or reward. That man is the altruistic Theosophist, while the other is an egoist and a coward.

The Beacon-light upon which the eyes of all real Theosophists are fixed is the same towards which in all ages the imprisoned human soul has struggled. This Beacon, whose light shines upon no earthly seas, but which has mirrored itself in the sombre depths of the primordial waters of infinite space, is called by us, as by the earliest Theosophists, "Divine Wisdom." That is the last word of the esoteric doctrine; and, in antiquity, where was the country, having the right to call itself civilized, that did not possess a double system of WISDOM, of which one part was for the masses, and the other for the few, — the exoteric and the esoteric? This name, WISDOM, or, as we say sometimes, the "Wisdom Religion" or Theosophy, is as old as the human mind. The title of Sages — the priests of this worship of truth — was its first derivative. These names were afterwards transformed into philosophy, and philosophers — the "lovers of science" or of wisdom. It is to Pythagoras that we owe that name, as also that of gnosis, the system of ἡ γνῶσις τῶν ὄντων "the knowledge of things as they are," or of the essence that is hidden beneath the external appearances. Under that name, so noble and so correct in its definition, all the masters of antiquity designated the aggregate of our knowledge of things human and divine. The sages and Brachmanes of India, the magi of Chaldea and Persia, the hierophants of Egypt and Arabia, the prophets or Nabi of Judea and of Israel, as well as the philosophers of Greece and Rome, have always classified that science in two divisions — the esoteric, or the true, and the exoteric, disguised in symbols. To this day the Jewish Rabbis give the name of Mercabah to the body or vehicle of their religious system, that which contains within it the higher knowledge, accessible only to the initiates, and of which higher knowledge it is only the husk.

We are accused of mystery, and we are reproached with making a secret of the higher Theosophy. We confess that the doctrine which we call *gupta vidya* (secret science) is only for the few. But where were the masters in ancient times who did not keep their teachings secret, for fear they would be profaned? From Orpheus and Zoroaster, Pythagoras and Plato, down to the Rosicrucians, and to the more modern Free-Masons, it has been the invariable rule that the disciple must gain the confidence of the master before receiving from him the supreme and final word. The most ancient religions have always had their greater and lesser mysteries. The neophytes and catechumens took an inviolable oath before they were accepted. The Essenes of Judea and Mount Carmel required the same thing. The Nabi and the Nazars (the "separated ones" of Israel), like the lay Chelas and the Brahmacharyas of India, differed greatly from each other. The former could, and can, be married and remain in the world, while they are studying the sacred writings up to a certain point; the latter, the Nazars and the Brahmacharyas, have always been entirely vowed to the mysteries of initiation. The great schools of Esotericism were international, although exclusive, as is proved by the fact that Plato, Herodotus and others, went to Egypt to be initiated; while Pythagoras, after visiting the Brahmins of India, stopped at an Egyptian sanctuary, and finally was received, according to Iamblicus, at Mount Carmel. Jesus followed the traditional custom, and justified his reticence by quoting the well-known precept:

> Give not the sacred things to the dogs,
> Cast not your pearls before the swine,
> Lest these tread them under their feet,
> And lest the dogs turn and rend you.

H.P. Blavatsky
Le Phare De L'Inconnu, The Beacon Light of the Unknown
https://www.theosophytrust.org/462-le-phare-de-linconnu

THINGS COMMON TO CHRISTIANITY AND THEOSOPHY

Turning now to doctrine, we find again complete agreement with the dogmatic part of Christianity in these older religions. Salvation by faith is taught by some priests. That is the old Brahmanical theory, but with the difference that the Brahman one calls for faith in God as the means, the end, and the object of faith. The Christian adds faith in the son of God. A form of Japanese Buddhism said to be due to Amitabha says that one may be saved by complete faith in Amita Buddha, and that even if one prays but three times to Amita he will be saved in accordance with a vow made by that teacher. Immortality of soul has ever been taught by the Brahmans. Their whole system of religion and of cosmogony is founded on the idea of soul and of the spiritual nature of the universe. Jesus and St. Paul taught the unity of spiritual beings — or men — when they said that heaven and the spirit of God were in us, and the doctrine of Unity is one of the oldest and most important of the Brahmanical scheme. The possibility of arriving at perfection by means of religion and science combined so that a man becomes godlike — or the doctrine of Adepts and Mahatmas as found in Theosophy — is common to Buddhism and Brahmanism, and is not contrary to the teachings of Jesus. He said to his disciples that they could if they would do even greater works — or "miracles" — than he did. To do these works one has to have great knowledge and power. The doctrine assumes the perfectibility of humanity and destroys the theory of original sin; but far from being out of concordance with the religion of Jesus, it is in perfect accord. He directed his followers to be perfect even as the Father in heaven is. They could not come up to that command by any possibility unless man has the power to reach to that high state. The command is the same as is found in the ancient Aryan system. Hence, then, whether we look broadly over the field at mere ritual dogma or at ethics, we find the most complete accord between Theosophy and true Christianity.

But now taking up some important doctrines put forward by members of the Theosophical Society under their right of free investigation and free speech, what do we discover? Novelty, it is true, to the mind of the western man half-taught about his own religion, but nothing that is uncommon to Christianity. Those doctrines may be, for the present, such as Reincarnation or rebirth over and over again for the purpose of discipline and gain, for reward, for punishment, and for enlargement of character; next Karma, or exact justice or compensation for all thoughts and acts. These two are a part of Christianity, and may be found in the Bible.

Reincarnation has been regarded by some Christian ministers as essential to the Christian religion. Dr. Edward Beecher said he saw its necessity, and the Rev. Wm. Alger has recorded his view to the same effect. If a Christian insists upon belief in Jesus, who came only eighteen centuries ago after millenniums had passed and men had died out of the faith by millions, it will be unjust for them to be condemned for a failure to believe a doctrine they never heard of; hence the Christian may well say that under the law of reincarnation, which was upheld by Jesus, all those who never heard of Jesus will be reborn after his coming in A.D. I, so as to accept the plan of salvation.

In the Gospels we find Jesus referring to this doctrine as if a well established one. When it was broached by the disciples as the possible reason for the punishment by blindness from birth of a man of the time, Jesus did not controvert the doctrine, as he would have done did he see in his wisdom as Son of God that it was pernicious. But at another time he asserted that John the Baptist was the reincarnation of Elias the ancient prophet. This cannot be wiped out of the books, and is a doctrine as firmly fixed in Christianity, though just now out of favor, as is any other. The paper by Prof. Landsberg shows you what Origen, one of the greatest of the Christian Fathers, taught on preëxistence of souls. This theory naturally suggests reincarnation on this earth, for it is more natural to suppose the soul's wanderings to be here until all that life can give has been gained, rather than that the soul should wander among other planets or simply fall to this abruptly, to be as suddenly raised up to heaven or thrown down to hell.

The next great doctrine is Karma. This is the religion of salvation by works as opposed to faith devoid of works. It is one of the prime doctrines of Jesus. By "by their works ye shall know them," he must have meant that faith without works is dead. The meaning of Karma literally is "works," and the Hindus apply it not only to the operations of nature and of the great laws of nature in connection with man's reward and punishment, but also to all the different works that man can perform. St. James insists on the religion of works. He says that true religion is to visit the fatherless and the widows and to keep oneself unspotted from the world. St. Matthew says we shall be judged for every act, word, and thought. This alone is possible under the doctrine of Karma. The command of Jesus to refrain from judgment or we should ourselves be judged is a plain statement of Karma, as is, too, the rest of the verse saying that what we mete out shall be given back to us. St. Paul, following this, distinctly states the doctrine thus: "Brethren, be not deceived; God is not mocked; for whatsoever a man soweth, that also shall he reap." The word "whatsoever" includes every act and thought, and permits no escape from the consequences of any act. A clearer statement of the law of Karma as applied to daily life could hardly be made. Again, going to Revelations, the last words in the Christian book, we read all through it that the last judgment proceeds on the works — in other words, on the Karma — of men. It distinctly asserts that in the vision, as well as in the messages to the Churches, judgment passes for works.

We therefore must conclude that the religion of Jesus is in complete accord with the chief doctrines of Theosophy; it is fair to assume that even the most recondite of theosophical theories would not have been opposed by him. Our discussion must have led us to the conclusion that the religion of Karma, the practise of good works, is that in which the religion of Jesus agrees with Theosophy, and that alone thereby will arrive the longed-for day when the great ideal of

Universal Brotherhood will be realized, and will furnish the common ground on which all faiths may stand and from which every nation may work for the good and the perfection of the human family.

William Quan Judge
Paper read before the Aryan (New York) Theosophical Society, 1894
https://www.theosophytrust.org/200-things-common-to-christianity-and-theosophy

EVERY CELL AND ORGAN HAS MEMORY

Moreover, we, Theosophists, understand the terms "psychic" and "psychism" somewhat differently from the average public, science, and even theology, the latter giving it a significance which both science and Theosophy reject, and the public in general remaining with a very hazy conception of what is really meant by the terms. For many, there is little, if any, difference between "psychic" and "psychological", both words relating in some way to the *human* soul. Some modern metaphysicians have wisely agreed to disconnect the word Mind *(pneuma)* from Soul *(psyche)*, the one being the rational, spiritual part, the other – *psyche* – the living principle in man, the breath that *animates* him (from *anima,* soul). Yet, if this is so, how in this case refuse a soul to *animals?* These are, no less than man, informed with the same principle of sentient life, the *nephesh* of the 2nd chapter of *Genesis.* The Soul is by no means the Mind, nor can an idiot, bereft of the latter, be called a "soul-less" being. To describe, as the physiologists do, the human Soul in its relations to senses and appetites, desires and passions, common to man and the brute, and then endow it with God-like intellect, with spiritual and rational faculties which can take their source but in a *super-sensible* world – is to throw forever the veil of an impenetrable mystery over the subject. Yet in modern science, "psychology" and "psychism" relate only to conditions of the nervous system, mental phenomena being traced solely to molecular action. The higher *noetic* character of the Mind-Principle is entirely ignored, and even rejected, as a "superstition" by both physiologists and psychologists. Psychology, in fact, has become a synonym in many cases for the science of psychiatry. Therefore, students of Theosophy being compelled to differ from all these, have adopted the doctrine that underlies the time-honored philosophies of the East. What it is, may be found further on.

To better understand the foregoing arguments and those which follow, the reader is asked to turn to the editorial in the September

Lucifer ("The Dual Aspect of Wisdom," p. 3), and acquaint himself with the *double aspect* of that which is termed by St. James in his Third Epistle at once – the *devilish, terrestrial* wisdom and the "wisdom from above." In another editorial, "Kosmic Mind" (April, 1890), it is also stated, that the ancient Hindus endowed every cell in the human body with consciousness, giving each the name of a God or Goddess. Speaking of atoms in the name of science and philosophy, Professor Ladd calls them in his work *"supersensible beings."* Occultism regards every atom[1] as an "independent entity" and every cell as a "conscious unit." It explains that no sooner do such atoms group to form cells, than the latter become endowed with consciousness, each of its own kind, and with *free-will to act* within the limits of law. Nor are we entirely deprived of scientific evidence for such statements as the two above-named editorials well prove. More than one learned physiologist of the golden minority, in our own day, moreover, is rapidly coming to the conviction, that memory has no seat, no special organ of its own in the human brain, but that it has *seats* in every organ of the body.

"No good ground exists for speaking of any special organ, or seat of memory," writes Professor G. T. Ladd. "Every organ, indeed, every area, and every limit of the nervous system has its own memory" (loc. cit., p. 553).

The seat of memory, then, is assuredly neither here nor there, but everywhere throughout the human body. To locate its organ in the brain is to limit and dwarf the Universal Mind and its countless Rays (the *Manasaputra*) which inform every rational mortal. As we write for Theosophists, first of all, we care little for the psycho-phobian prejudices of the Materialists who may read this and sniff contemptuously at the mention of "Universal Mind" and the Higher *noetic* souls of men. But, what *is* memory, we ask. "Both presentation of sense and image of memory, are transitory phases of

---

[1] One of the names of Brahmā is *anu* or "atom".

consciousness," we are answered. But what is Consciousness itself? – we ask again. *"We cannot define Consciousness,"* Professor Ladd tells us. [2]

Thus, that which we are asked to do by physiological psychology is, to content ourselves with converting the various states of Consciousness by other people's private and unverifiable hypotheses; and this, on "questions of cerebral physiology *where experts and novices are alike ignorant,"* to use the pointed remark of the said author. Hypothesis for hypothesis, then, we may as well hold to the teachings of our Seers, as to the conjectures of those who deny both such Seers and their wisdom. The more so, as we are told by the same honest man of science, that "if metaphysics and ethics cannot properly dictate their facts and conclusions to the science of physiological psychology. . . in turn this science cannot properly dictate to metaphysics and ethics the conclusions which they shall draw from facts of Consciousness, by giving out its myths and fables in the garb of well ascertained history of the cerebral processes" (p. 544).

Now, since the metaphysics of Occult physiology and psychology postulate within mortal man an immortal entity, "divine mind," or *Nous*, whose pale and too often distorted reflection is that which we call "Mind" and intellect in men – virtually an entity apart from the former during the period of incarnation – we say that the two sources of "memory" are in these two "principles." These two we distinguish as the Higher *Manas* (Mind or Ego), and the *Kama-Manas, i.e.,* the rational, but earthly or physical intellect of man, incased in, and bound by, matter, therefore subject to the influence of the latter: the all-conscious SELF, that which reincarnates periodically – verily the WORD made flesh! – and which is always the same, while its reflected "Double," changing with every new incarnation and personality, is, therefore, conscious but for a life-period. The latter "principle" is the *Lower* Self, or that, which manifesting through our

---

[2] *Elements of Physiological Psychology.*

organic system, acting on this plane of illusion, imagines itself the *Ego Sum,* and thus falls into what Buddhist philosophy brands as the "heresy of separateness." The former, we term INDIVIDUALITY, the latter *Personality*. From the first proceeds all the *noetic* element, from the second, the *psychic, i.e.,* "terrestrial wisdom" at best, as it is influenced by all the chaotic stimuli of the human or rather *animal passions* of the living body.

The "Higher EGO" cannot act directly on the body, as its consciousness belongs to quite another plane and planes of ideation: the "lower" *Self* does: and its action and behavior *depend on its free will and choice* as to whether it will gravitate more towards its parent ("the Father in Heaven") or the "animal" which it informs, the man of flesh. The "Higher Ego," as part of the essence of the UNIVERSAL MIND, is unconditionally omniscient on its own plane, and only potentially so in our terrestrial sphere, as it has to act solely through its *alter ego* – the Personal Self. Now, although the former is the vehicle of all knowledge of the past, the present, and the future, and although it is from this fountainhead that its "double" catches occasional glimpses of that which is beyond the senses of man, and transmits them to certain brain cells (unknown to science in their function), thus making of man a *Seer,* a soothsayer, and a prophet; yet the memory of bygone events – especially of the earth earthy – has its seat in the Personal Ego alone. No memory of a purely daily-life function, of a physical, egotistical, or of a lower mental nature – such as, *e.g.,* eating and drinking, enjoying personal sensual pleasures, transacting business to the detriment of one's neighbor, etc., etc., has ought to do with the "Higher" Mind or EGO. Nor has it any direct dealings on this physical plane with either our brain or our heart – for these two are the organs of a power higher than the *Personality* – but only with our passional organs, such as the liver, the stomach, the spleen, etc. Thus it only stands to reason that the memory of such-like events must be first awakened in that organ which was the first to induce the action remembered afterwards, and conveyed it to our "sense-thought," which is entirely *distinct from the "supersensuous" thought*. It is only the higher forms of the latter, the *superconscious* mental experience, that can correlate with the cerebral and cardiac centres. The memories of physical and *selfish* (or personal) deeds, on the other hand, together with the mental experiences of a terrestrial nature, and of earthly biological functions, can, of necessity, only be correlated with the molecular constitution of various *Kamic* organs, and the "dynamic associations" of the elements of the nervous system in each particular organ.

Therefore, when Professor Ladd, after showing that every element of the nervous system has a memory of its own, adds: – "This view belongs to the very essence of every theory which considers conscious mental reproduction as only one form or phase of the biological fact of organic memory" – he must include among such theories the Occult teaching. For no Occultist could express such teaching more correctly than the Professor, who says, in winding up his argument: "We might properly speak, then, of the memory of the end-organ of vision or of hearing, of the memory of the spinal cord and of the different so-called 'centres' of reflex action belonging to the chords of the memory of the medulla oblongata, the cerebellum, etc." This is the essence of Occult teaching – even in the Tantra works. Indeed, every organ in our body *has its own memory.* For if it is endowed with a consciousness "of its own kind," every cell must of necessity have also a memory of its own kind, as likewise its own *psychic* and *noetic* action. Responding to the touch of both a physical and a *metaphysical* Force,[3] the impulse given by the *psychic* (or psycho-molecular) Force will act from *without* within; while that of the *noetic* (shall we call it Spiritual-dynamical?) Force works *from within without.* For, as our body is the covering of the inner "principles," soul, mind, life, etc., so the molecule or the cell is the body in which dwell its "principles," the (to our sense and comprehension) immaterial atoms which compose that cell. The

---

[3] We fondly trust this very *unscientific* term will throw no "Animalist" into hysterics *beyond* recovery.

cell's activity and behavior are determined by its being propelled either inwardly or outwardly, by the noetic or the psychic Force, the former having no relation to the *physical* cells proper. Therefore, while the latter act under the unavoidable law of the conservation and correlation of physical energy, the atoms – being psycho-spiritual, not *physical units – act under laws of their own,* just as Professor Ladd's "Unit-Being," which is our "Mind-Ego," does, in his very philosophical and scientific hypothesis. Every human organ and each cell in the latter has a key-board of its own, like that of a piano, only that it registers and emits sensations instead of sounds. Every key contains the potentiality of good or bad, of producing harmony or disharmony. This depends on the impulse given and the combinations produced; on the force of the touch of the artist at work, a "double-faced Unity," indeed. And it is the action of this or the other "Face" of the Unity that determines the nature and the dynamic character of the manifested phenomena as a resulting action, and this whether they be physical or mental. For the whole of man is guided by this double-faced Entity. If the impulse comes from the "Wisdom above," the Force applied being noetic or spiritual, the results will be actions worthy of the divine propeller; if from the "terrestrial, devilish wisdom" (psychic power), man's activities will be selfish, based solely on the exigencies of his physical, hence animal, nature. The above may sound to the average reader as pure nonsense; but every Theosophist must understand when told that there are *Manasic* as well as *Kamic* organs in him, although the cells of his body answer to both physical and spiritual impulses.

Verily that body, so desecrated by Materialism and man himself, is the temple of the Holy Grail, the *Adytum* of the grandest, nay, of all, the mysteries of nature in our solar universe. That body is an Æolian harp, chorded with two sets of strings, one made of pure silver, the other of catgut. When the breath from the divine Fiat brushes softly over the former, man becomes like unto *his* God – but the other set feels it not. It needs the breeze of a strong terrestrial wind, impregnated with animal effluvia, to set its animal chords vibrating. It is the function of the physical, lower mind to act upon the physical organs and their cells; but, it is the higher mind *alone* which can influence the atoms interacting in those cells, which interaction is alone capable of exciting the brain, *via the spinal "centre" cord*, to a mental representation of spiritual ideas far beyond any objects on this material plane. The phenomena of divine consciousness have to be regarded as activities of our mind on another and a higher plane, working through something less substantial than the moving molecules of the brain. They cannot be explained as the simple resultant of the cerebral physiological process, as indeed the latter only condition them or give them a final form for purposes of concrete manifestation. Occultism teaches that the liver and the spleen-cells are the most subservient to the action of our "personal" mind, the heart being the organ *par excellence* through which the "Higher" Ego acts – through the Lower Self.

Nor can the visions or memory of purely terrestrial events be transmitted directly through the mental perceptions of the brain – the direct recipient of the impressions of the heart. All such recollections have to be first stimulated by and awakened in the organs which were the originators, as already stated, of the various causes that led to the results, or, the direct recipients and participators of the latter. In other words, if what is called "association of *ideas*" has much to do with the awakening of memory, the mutual interaction and consistent inter-relation between the personal "Mind-Entity" and the organ of the human body have far more so. A hungry stomach evokes the vision of a past banquet, because its action is reflected and repeated in the *personal mind*. But even before the memory of the personal Self radiates the vision from the tablets wherein are stored the experiences of one's daily life – even to the minutest details – the memory of the stomach has already evoked the same. And so with all the organs of the body. It is they which originate according to their animal needs and desires the electro-vital sparks that illuminate the field of consciousness in the Lower Ego; and it is these sparks which in their turn awaken to function the reminiscences in it. The whole human body is, as said, a vast sounding board, in which each cell bears a long record of impressions connected with its parent organ, and each cell has a memory and a consciousness of its kind, or call it instinct if you will. These impressions are, according to the nature of the organ, physical, psychic, or mental, as they relate to this or another plane. They may be called "states of consciousness" only for the want of a better expression – as there are states of instinctual, mental, and purely abstract, or spiritual consciousness. If we trace all such "psychic" actions to brain-work, it is only because in that mansion called the human body the brain is the front-door, and the only one which opens out into Space. All the others are inner doors, openings in the private building, through which travel incessantly the transmitting agents of memory and sensation. The clearness, the vividness, and intensity of these depend on the state of health and the organic soundness of the transmitters. But their reality, in the sense of trueness or correctness, is due to the "principle" they originate from, and the preponderance in the Lower *Manas* of the *noetic* or of the phrenic ("*Kamic*," terrestrial) element.

H. P. Blavatsky
Lucifer, October & November 1890
https://www.theosophytrust.org/522-psychic-and-noetic-action

ON THE HIGHER MIND, KAMA-LOKA AND THE ASTRAL LIGHT

For, as Occultism teaches, if the Higher Mind-Entity – the permanent and the immortal – is of the divine homogeneous essence of "Alaya-Akasa," [1] or Mahat, – its reflection, the Personal Mind, is, as a temporary "Principle," of the Substance of the Astral Light. As a pure ray of the "Son of the Universal Mind," it could perform no functions in the body, and would remain powerless over the turbulent organs of Matter. Thus, while its inner constitution is Manasic, its "body," or rather functioning essence, is heterogeneous, and leavened with the Astral Light, the lowest element of Ether. It is a part of the mission of the Manasic Ray, to get gradually rid of the blind, deceptive element which, though it makes of it an active spiritual entity on this plane, still brings it into so close contact with matter as to entirely becloud its divine nature and stultify its intuitions.

This leads us to see the difference between the pure noetic and the terrestrial psychic visions of seership and mediumship. The former can be obtained by one of two means; *(a)* on the condition of paralysing at will the *memory* and the instinctual, independent action of all the material organs and even cells in the body of flesh, an act which, once that the light of the Higher Ego has consumed and subjected forever the passional nature of the personal, lower Ego, is easy, but requires an adept; and *(b)* of being a reincarnation of one, who, in a previous birth, had attained through extreme purity of life and efforts in the right direction almost to a *Yogi*-state of holiness and saintship. There is also a third possibility of reaching in mystic visions the plane of the higher Manas; but it is only occasional and does not depend on the will of the Seer, but on the extreme weakness and exhaustion of the material body through illness and suffering.

---

[1] Another name for the Universal Mind.

The Seeress of Prevorst was an instance of the latter case; and Jacob Boehme of our second category. In all other cases of abnormal seership, of so-called clairaudience, clairvoyance and trances, it is simply – *mediumship.*

Now what is a medium? The term medium, when not applied simply to things and objects, is supposed to be a person through whom the action of another person or being is either manifested or transmitted. Spiritualists believing in communications with disembodied spirits, and that these can manifest through, or impress sensitiveness to transmit "messages" from them, regard mediumship as a blessing and a great privilege. We Theosophists, on the other hand, who do not believe in the "communion of spirits" as Spiritualists do, regard the gift as one of the most dangerous of abnormal nervous diseases. A medium is simply one in whose personal Ego, or terrestrial mind, (psyche), the percentage of "astral" light so preponderates as to impregnate with it their whole physical constitution. Every organ and cell thereby is attuned, so to speak, and subjected to an enormous and abnormal tension. The mind is ever on the plane of, and quite immersed in, that deceptive light whose soul is divine, but whose body – the light waves on the lower planes, infernal; for they are but the black and disfigured reflections of the earth's memories. The untrained eye of the poor sensitive cannot pierce the dark mist, the dense fog of the terrestrial emanations, to see beyond in the radiant field of the eternal truths. His vision is out of focus. His senses, accustomed from his birth, like those of a native of the London slums, to stench and filth, to the unnatural distortions of sights and images tossed on the kaleidoscopic waves of the astral plane – are unable to discern the true from the false. And thus, the pale soulless corpses moving in the trackless fields of "Kama loka," appear to him the living images of the "dear departed" ones; the broken echoes of once human voices, passing through his mind, suggest to him well co-ordinated phrases, which he repeats, in ignorance that their final form and polish were received in the innermost depths of his own brain-factory. And hence the sight and the hearing of that which if seen in its true nature would have struck the medium's heart cold with horror, now fills him with a sense of beatitude and confidence. He really believes that the immeasurable vistas displayed before him are the real spiritual world, the abode of the blessed disembodied angels.

We describe the broad main features and facts of mediumship, there being no room in such an article for exceptional cases. We maintain – having unfortunately passed at one period of life *personally* through such experiences – that on the whole, mediumship is most dangerous; and *psychic* experiences when accepted indiscriminately lead only to honestly deceiving others, because the medium is the first self-deceived victim. Moreover, a too close association with the "Old Terrestrial Serpent" is infectious. The odic and magnetic currents of the Astral Light often incite to murder, drunkenness, immorality, and, as Eliphas Lévi expresses it, the not altogether pure natures "can be driven headlong by the blind forces set in motion in the *Light*" – by the errors and sins imposed on its waves.

And this is how the great Mage of the XIXth century corroborates the foregoing when speaking of the Astral Light:

> We have said that to acquire magical power, two things are necessary: to disengage the will from all servitude, and to exercise it in control.
>
> The sovereign will (of the adept) is represented in our symbols by the woman who crushes the serpent's head, and by the resplendent angel who represses the dragon, and holds him under his foot and spear; the great magical agent, the dual current of light, the living and astral *fire* of the earth, has been represented in the ancient theogonies by the serpent with the head of a bull, a ram, or a dog. It is the double serpent of the *caduceus*, it is the Old Serpent of *Genesis*, but it is also the *brazen serpent of Moses* entwined around the *tau*, that is to say, the

generative *lingha*. It is also the goat of the witch-sabbath, and the Baphomet of the Templars; it is the *Hylé* of the Gnostics; it is the double-tailed serpent which forms the legs of the solar cock of the Abraxas: finally, it is the Devil of M. Eudes de Mirville. But in very fact it is the blind force which souls (*i.e.*, the lower *Manas* or Nephesh) have to conquer to liberate themselves from the bonds of the earth; for if their will does not free 'them from this *fatal attraction,* they will be absorbed in the current by the force which has produced them, and *will return to the central and eternal fire'.*[2]

The "central and eternal fire" is that disintegrating Force, that gradually consumes and burns out the *Kama-rupa,* or "personality," in the Kama-loka, whither it goes after death. And verily, the Mediums are attracted by the astral light, it is the direct cause of their personal "souls" being absorbed "by the force which has produced" their terrestrial elements. And, therefore, as the same Occultist tells us:

> All the magical operations consist in freeing one's self from the coils of the Ancient Serpent; then to place the foot on its head, and lead it according to the operator's will. 'I will give unto thee,' says the Serpent, in the Gospel myth, 'all the kingdoms of the earth, if thou wilt fall down and worship me.' The initiated should reply to him, 'I will not fall down, but thou shalt crouch at my feet; thou wilt give me nothing, but I will make use of thee and take whatever I wish. For *I am thy Lord and Master!'*

And as such, the *Personal Ego,* becoming at one with its divine parent, shares in the immortality of the latter. Otherwise . . .

Enough, however. Blessed is he who has acquainted himself with the dual powers at work in the ASTRAL Light; thrice blessed he who has learned to discern the *Noetic* from the *Psychic* action of the "Double-Faced" God in him, and who knows the potency of his own

---

[2] *Dogme et Rituel de la Haute Magie,* quoted in *Isis Unveiled.*

Spirit – or "Soul Dynamics."

H. P. Blavatsky
Lucifer, October & November 1890
https://www.theosophytrust.org/522-psychic-and-noetic-action

THE CYCLIC PILGRIMAGE
OF THE MONAD

... the Secret Doctrine teaches:

(c) The fundamental identity of all Souls with the Universal Over-Soul, the latter being itself an aspect of the Unknown Root; and the obligatory pilgrimage for every Soul – a spark of the former – through the Cycle of Incarnation (or "Necessity") in accordance with Cyclic and Karmic law, during the whole term. In other words, no purely spiritual Buddhi (divine Soul) can have an independent (conscious) existence before the spark which issued from the pure Essence of the Universal Sixth principle, – or the OVER-SOUL, – has (a) passed through every elemental form of the phenomenal world of that Manvantara, and (b) acquired individuality, first by natural impulse, and then by self-induced and self-devised efforts (checked by its Karma), thus ascending through all the degrees of intelligence, from the lowest to the highest Manas, from mineral and plant, up to the holiest archangel (Dhyani-Buddha). The pivotal doctrine of the Esoteric philosophy admits no privileges or special gifts in man, save those won by his own Ego through personal effort and merit throughout a long series of metempsychoses and reincarnations. This is why the Hindus say that the Universe is Brahma and Brahmâ, for Brahma is in every atom of the universe, the six principles in Nature being all the outcome – the variously differentiated aspects – of the SEVENTH and ONE, the only reality in the Universe whether Cosmical or micro-cosmical; and also why the permutations (psychic, spiritual and physical), on the plane of manifestation and form, of the sixth (Brahmâ the vehicle of Brahma) are viewed by metaphysical antiphrasis as illusive and Mayavic. For although the root of every atom individually and of every form collectively, is that seventh principle or the one Reality, still, in its manifested phenomenal and temporary appearance, it is no better than an evanescent illusion of our senses. (See, for clearer definition, In Vol.

I of *The Secret Doctrine*, p. 610, Addendum "Gods, Monads and Atoms," and also "*Theophania*," "Bodhisatvas and Reincarnation," etc., etc.)

H.P. Blavatsky
The Secret Doctrine, i 14 - 18

GENIUS AND REINCARNATION

Genius! thou gift of Heaven, thou light divine!
Amid what dangers art thou doom'd to shine.
Oft will the body's weakness check thy force,
Oft damp thy vigour, and impede thy course;
And trembling nerves compel thee to restrain
Thy nobler efforts to contend with pain
Or want, sad guest! . . .

          Crabbe

Among many problems hitherto unsolved in the Mystery of Mind, stands prominent the question of Genius. Whence, and what is genius, its *raison d'être*, the causes of its excessive rarity? Is it indeed "a gift of Heaven"? And if so, why such gifts to one, and dullness of intellect, or even idiocy, the doom of another? To regard the appearance of men and women of genius as a mere accident, a prize of blind chance, or, as dependent on physical causes alone, is only thinkable to a materialist. As an author truly says, there remains then, only this alternative: to agree with the believer in a *personal* god "to refer the appearance of every single individual to a *special act of divine will and creative energy*," or "to recognize, in the whole succession of such individuals, one great act of some will, expressed in an eternal inviolable law."

Genius, as Coleridge defined it, is certainly – to every outward appearance, at least – "the faculty of growth"; yet to the inward intuition of man, it is a question whether it is genius – an abnormal aptitude of mind – that develops and grows, or the physical brain, *its vehicle*, which becomes through some mysterious process fitter to receive and manifest *from within outwardly* the innate and divine nature of man's over-soul. Perchance, in their unsophisticated wisdom, the philosophers of old were nearer truth than are our modern wiseacres, when they endowed man with a tutelar deity, a Spirit whom they called *genius*. The substance of this entity, to say nothing of its *essence* – observe the distinction, reader, – and the presence of both, manifests itself according to the organism of the person it informs. As Shakespeare says of the genius of great men – what we perceive of his substance "is not here" –

> For what you see is but the smallest part. . . .
> But were the whole frame here,
> It is of such a spacious, lofty pitch,
> Your roof were not sufficient to contain it. . . .

This is precisely what the Esoteric philosophy teaches. The flame of genius is lit by no anthropomorphic hand, save that of one's own Spirit. It is the very nature of the Spiritual Entity itself, of our *Ego*, which keeps on weaving new life-woofs into the web of reincarnation on the loom of time, from the beginnings to the ends of the great Life-Cycle. This it is that asserts itself stronger than in the average man, through its personality; so that what we call "the manifestations of genius" in a person, are only the more or less successful efforts of that EGO to assert itself on the outward plane of its objective form – the man of clay – in the matter-of-fact, daily life of the latter. The EGOS of a Newton, an Æschylus, or a Shakespeare, are of the same essence and substance as the Egos of a yokel, an ignoramus, a fool, or even an idiot; and the self-assertion of their informing *genii* depends on the physiological and material construction of the physical man. No Ego differs from another Ego, in its primordial or original essence and nature. That which makes one mortal a great man and of another a vulgar, silly person is, as said, the quality and make-up of the physical shell or casing, and the adequacy or inadequacy of brain and body to transmit and give expression to the light of the real, *Inner* man; and this aptness or in aptness is, in its turn, the result of Karma. Or, to use another simile, physical man is the musical instrument, and the Ego, the performing artist. The potentiality of perfect melody of sound, is in the former – the instrument – and no skill of the latter can awaken a faultless harmony out of a broken or badly made instrument. This harmony depends on the fidelity of transmission, by word or act, to the objective plane, of the unspoken divine thought in the very depths of man's subjective or inner nature. Physical man may – to follow our simile – be a priceless Stradivarius or a cheap and cracked fiddle, or again a mediocrity between the two, in the hands of the Paganini who ensouls him.

All ancient nations knew this. But though all had their Mysteries and their Hierophants, not all could be equally taught the great metaphysical doctrine; and while a few elect received such truths at their initiation, the masses were allowed to approach them with the greatest caution and only within the farthest limits of fact. "From the DIVINE ALL proceeded Amun, the Divine Wisdom . . . give it not to the unworthy," says a Book of Hermes. Paul, the "wise *Master-Builder,*" (I *Cor.* III, 10) but echoes Thoth-Hermes when telling the Corinthians "We speak Wisdom among them that are perfect (the initiated) . . . *divine* Wisdom in a MYSTERY, even the *hidden* Wisdom." *(Ibid.* II, 7.)

Yet, to this day the Ancients are accused of blasphemy and fetishism for their "hero worship." But have the modern historians ever fathomed the cause of such "worship"! We believe not. Otherwise they would be the first to become aware that that which was "worshipped," or rather that to which honours were rendered was neither the man of clay, nor the *personality* – the Hero or Saint So-and-So, which still prevails on the Roman Church, a church which beatifies the body rather than the soul – but the divine imprisoned Spirit, the *exiled* "god" *within* that personality. Who, in the profane world, is aware that even the majority of the magistrates (the *Archons* of Athens, mistranslated in the Bible as "Princes") – whose official duty it was to prepare the city for such processions, were ignorant of the true significance of the alleged "worship"?

Verily was Paul right in declaring that "we speak wisdom . . . not the wisdom of this world . . . which none of the *Archons* of this (profane) world knew," but the *hidden wisdom* of the MYSTERIES. For, as again the Epistle of the apostle implies, the language of the

Initiates and their secrets no *profane,* not even an "Archon" or ruler *outside the fane* of the sacred Mysteries, knoweth; none "save the Spirit of man (the *Ego*) which is *in him*." (Ibid. v, II.)

Were Chapters II and III of I *Corinthians* ever translated in the Spirit in which they were written – even their dead letter is now disfigured – the world might receive strange revelations. Among other things it would have a key to many hitherto unexplained rites of ancient Paganism, one of which is the mystery of this same Hero-worship. And it would learn that if the streets of the city that honoured one such man were strewn with roses for the passage of the Hero of the day, if every citizen was called to bow in reverence to him who was so feasted, and if both priest and poet vied in their zeal to immortalize the hero's name after his death – occult philosophy tells us the reason why this was done.

"Behold," it saith, "in every manifestation of genius – *when combined with virtue* – in the warrior or the Bard, the great painter, artist, statesman or man of Science, who soars high above the heads of the vulgar herd, the undeniable presence of the celestial exile, the divine *Ego* whose jailor thou art, Oh man of matter!" Thus, that which we call *deification* applied to the immortal God within, not to the dead walls of the human tabernacle that contained him. And this was done in tacit and silent recognition of the efforts made by the divine captive who, under the most adverse circumstances of incarnation, still succeeded in manifesting himself.

Occultism, therefore, teaches nothing new in asserting the above philosophical axiom. Enlarging upon the broad metaphysical truism, it only gives it a finishing touch by explaining certain details. It teaches, for instance, that the presence in man of various creative powers – called genius in their collection – is due to no blind chance, to no innate qualities through hereditary tendencies – though that which is known as atavism may often intensify these faculties – but to an accumulation of individual antecedent experiences of the *Ego* in its preceding life, and lives. For, though omniscient in its essence and nature, it still requires experience through its *personalities* of the things of earth, earthy on the objective plane, in order to apply the fruition of that abstract omniscience to them. And, adds our philosophy – the cultivation of certain aptitudes throughout a long series of past incarnations must finally culminate in some one life, in a blooming forth as *genius,* in one or another direction.

Great Genius, therefore, if true and innate, and not merely an abnormal expansion of our human intellect – can never copy or condescend to imitate, but will ever be original, *sui generis* in its creative impulses and realizations. Like those gigantic Indian lilies that shoot out from the clefts and fissures of the cloud-nursing, and bare rocks on the highest plateaux of the Nilgiri Hills, true Genius needs but an opportunity to spring forth into existence and blossom in the sight of all in the most arid soil, for its stamp is always unmistakable. To use a popular saying, innate genius, like murder, will out sooner or later, and the more it will have been suppressed and hidden, the greater will be the flood of light thrown by the sudden eruption. On the other hand artificial genius, so often confused with the former, and which, in truth, is but the outcome of long studies and training, will never be more than, so to say, the flame of a lamp burning outside the portal of the pane; it may throw a long trail of light across road, but it leaves the inside of the building in darkness. And, as every faculty and property in Nature is dual – *i.e.,* each may be made to serve two ends, evil as well as good – so will artificial genius *betray* itself. Born out of the chaos of terrestrial sensations, of perceptive and retentive faculties, yet of finite memory, it will ever remain the slave of its body; and that body, owing to its unreliability and the natural tendency of matter to confusion, will not fail to lead even the greatest *genius,* so called, back into its own primordial element, which is chaos again, or *evil,* or earth.

Thus between the true and the artificial genius, one born from the light of the immortal Ego, the other from the evanescent will-o'-the-wisp of the terrestrial or purely human intellect and the animal soul, there is a chasm, to be spanned only by him who aspires ever onward; who never loses sight, even when in the depths of matter, of that guiding star the Divine Soul and mind, or what we call *Buddhi-Manas*. The latter does not require, as does the former, cultivation. The words of the poet who asserts that the lamp of genius –

> If not protected, pruned, and fed with care,
> Soon dies, or runs to waste with fitful glare –

– can apply only to artificial genius, the outcome of cultural and of purely intellectual acuteness. It is not the direct light of the *Manasa putra*, the "Sons of Wisdom," for true genius lit at the flame of our higher nature, or the EGO, cannot die. This is why it is so very rare. Lavater calculated that "the proportion of genius (in general) to the vulgar, is like one to a million; but genius without tyranny, without pretension, that judges the weak with equity, the superior with humanity, and equals with justice, is like one in ten millions." This is indeed interesting, though not too complimentary to *human* nature, if, by "genius," Lavater had in mind only the higher sort of human intellect, unfolded by cultivation, "protected, pruned, and fed," and not the genius we speak of. Moreover such genius is always apt to lead to the extremes of weal or woe him through whom this artificial light of the terrestrial mind manifests. Like the good and bad genii of old with whom human genius is made so appropriately to share the name, it takes its helpless possessor by the hand and leads him, one day to the pinnacles of fame, fortune, and glory, but to plunge him on the following day into an abyss of shame, despair, often of crime.

But as, according to the great Physiognomist, there is more of the former than of the latter kind of genius in this our world, because, as Occultism teaches us, it is easier for the personality with its acute physical senses and *tatwas* to gravitate toward the lower quaternary than to soar to its triad – modern philosophy, though quite proficient in treating this lower place of genius, knows nothing of its higher spiritual form – the "one in ten millions." Thus it is only natural that confusing one with the other, the best modern writers should have failed to define *true* genius. As a consequence, we continually hear and read a good deal of that which to the Occultist seems quite paradoxical. "Genius requires cultivation," says one; "Genius is vain and self-sufficient" declares another; while a third will go on defining the *divine light* but to dwarf it on the Procrustean bed of his own intellectual narrow-mindedness. He will talk of the great eccentricity of genius, and allying it as a general rule with an "inflammable constitution," will even show it "a prey to every passion but seldom delicacy of taste!" (Lord Kaimes.) It is useless to argue with such, or tell them that, original, and great genius puts out the most dazzling rays of human intellectuality, as the sun quenches the flame-light of a fire in an open field; that it is never eccentric, though always *sui generis;* and that no man endowed with true genius can ever give way to his physical animal passions. In the view of an humble Occultist, only such a grand altruistic character as that of Buddha or Jesus, and of their few close imitators, can be regarded, in our historical cycle, as fully developed GENIUS.

Hence, true genius has small chance indeed of receiving its due in our age of conventionalities, hypocrisy and time-serving. As the world grows in civilization, it expands in fierce selfishness, and stones its true prophets and geniuses for the benefit of its aping shadows. Alone the surging masses of the ignorant millions, the great people's heart, are capable of sensing intuitively a true "great soul" full of divine love for mankind, of god-like compassion for suffering man. Hence the populace alone is still capable of recognizing a genius, as without such qualities no man has a right to the name. No genius can be now found in Church or State, and this is proven on their own admission. It seems a long time since in the XIII century the "Angelic Doctor" snubbed Pope Innocent IV who, boasting of the millions got by him from the sale of absolutions and indulgences, remarked to Aquinas that "the age of the Church is past in which she said 'Silver and gold have I none'!" "True," was the ready reply; "but the age is also past when she could say to a paralytic, 'Rise up and walk'." And yet from that time, and far, far earlier, to our own day the hourly crucifixion of their ideal Master both by Church and State has never ceased. While every Christian State breaks with its laws and customs, with every commandment given in the Sermon on the Mount, the Christian Church justifies and approves of this through her own Bishops who despairingly proclaim "A Christian State *impossible* on Christian Principles." Hence – no Christ-like (or "Buddha-like") way of life is possible in civilized States.

H.P. Blavatsky
"Genius", *Lucifer,* November, 1889
https://www.theosophytrust.org/425-genius

"ISIS UNVEILED" AND THE "THEOSOPHIST" ON REINCARNATION

IN Light (July 8) C.C.M. quotes from the THEOSOPHIST (June 1882) a sentence which appeared in the Editor's Note at the foot of an article headed "Seeming Discrepancies." Then, turning to the review of "The Perfect Way" in the same number, he quotes at length from "an authoritative teaching of the later period," as he adds rather sarcastically. Then, again, a long paragraph from Isis. The three quotations and the remarks of our friend run thus:

"There never was, nor can there be, any radical discrepancy between the teachings in 'Isis' ('Isis Unveiled') and those of this later period, as both proceed from one and the same source – the ADEPT BROTHERS. (Editor's Note in Seeming Discrepancies.")

Having drawn the attention of his readers to the above assertion C.C.M. proceeds to show – as he thinks – its fallacy:

> "To begin with, re-Incarnation – if other worlds besides this are taken into account – is the regular routine of nature. But re-Incarnation in the next higher objective world is one thing; re-Incarnation on this earth is another. *Even that takes place over and over again till the highest condition of humanity, as known on this earth, is attained,* but not afterwards, and here is the clue to the mystery.... But once let a man be as far perfected *by successive re-incarnations* as the present race will permit, and then his *next* re-incarnation will be among the early growths of the next higher world, where the earliest growths are far higher than the highest here. *The ghastly mistake that the modern re-incarnationists make is in supposing that there can be a return on this earth to lower bodily forms*"; not, therefore, that man is re-incarnated as man again and again upon this earth, for that is laid down as truth in the above cited passages in the most positive and explicit form." (Review of T.P.W. in the *Theosophist*.)

And now for "*Isis*":

> "We will now present a few fragments of this mysterious doctrine of re-Incarnation – as distinct from metempsychosis – which we have from an authority. Re-Incarnation, *i.e.*, the appearance of the same individual – or rather, of his astral monad – twice on the same planet is not a rule in nature; it is an exception, like the teratological phenomenon of a two-headed infant. It is preceded by a violation of the laws of harmony of nature and happens only when the latter, seeking to restore its disturbed equilibrium, violently throws back into earth-life the astral monad, which has been tossed out of the circle of necessity by crime or accident. Thus in cases of abortion, of infants dying before a certain age, and of congenital and incurable idiocy, nature's original design to produce a perfect human being has been interrupted. Therefore, while the gross matter of each of these several entities is suffered to disperse itself at death through the vast realm of being, the immortal Spirit and astral monad of the individual – the latter having been set apart to animate a frame, and the former to shed its divine light on the corporeal organization – must try a second time to carry out the purpose of the creative intelligence. *If reason has been so far developed as to become active and discriminative, there is no re-incarnation on, this earth,* for the three parts of the triune man have been united together, and he is capable of running the race. But when the new being has not passed beyond the condition of monad, or when, as in the idiot, the trinity has not been completed, the immortal spark which illuminates it has to re-enter on the earthly planet, as it was frustrated in its first attempt. . . . Further, the same occult doctrine recognizes another possibility, albeit so rare and so vague that it is really useless to mention it. Even the modern Occidental Occultists deny it, though it is universally accepted in Eastern countries." . . .

This is the occasional return of the terribly depraved human Spirits which have fallen to the eighth sphere – it is unnecessary to quote the passage at length. Exclusive of that rare and doubtful possibility, then "*Isis*" – I have quoted from volume I, 351-2 – allows only three cases – abortion, very early death, and idiocy – in which re-Incarnation on this earth occurs.

> I am a long-suffering student of the mysteries, more apt to accuse my own stupidity than to make "seeming discrepancies" an occasion for scoffing. But after all, two and three will not make just four; black is not white, nor, in reference to plain and definite statements, is "Yes" equivalent to "No." If there is one thing which I ardently desire to be taught, it is the truth about this same question of re-Incarnation. I hope I am not, as a dutiful Theosophist, expected to reconcile the statement of "*Isis*" with that of this authoritative Reviewer. But there is one consolation. The accomplished authoress of "*Isis*" cannot have totally forgotten the teaching on this subject therein contained. She, therefore, certainly did not dictate the statements of the Reviewer. If I may conjecture that Koot Hoomi stands close behind the latter, then assuredly Koot Hoomi is not, as has been maliciously suggested, an alias for Madame Blavatsky. – "C.C.M."

We hope not – for Koot Hoomi's sake. Mme. B. would become too vain and too proud, could she but dream of such an honour. But how true the remark of the French classic: *La critique est aisée, mais l'art est difficile* – though we feel more inclined to hang our diminished head in sincere sorrow and exclaim: *Et tu Brute!* – than to quote old truisms. Only, where that (even) "seeming discrepancy" is to be found between the two passages – except by those who are entirely ignorant of the occult doctrine – will be certainly a mystery to every Eastern Occultist who reads the above and who studies at the same school as the reviewer of "The Perfect Way." Nevertheless the latter is chosen as the weapon to break our head with. It is sufficient to read No. 1 of the *Fragments of Occult Truth,* and ponder over the septenary constitution of man into which the triple human entity is divided by the occultists, to perceive that the "astral" *monad is* not the "Spiritual" *monad* and *vice versa*. That there is no discrepancy whatsoever between the two statements, may be easily shown, and we hope will be shown, by our friend the "reviewer." The most that can be said of the passage quoted from *Isis* is, that it is incomplete, chaotic, vague, perhaps – clumsy, as many more passages in that work, the first literary production of a foreigner, who even now can hardly boast of her knowledge of the English language. Therefore, in the face of the statement from the very correct and excellent review of "The Perfect Way" – we say again that "Reincarnation, *i.e.,* the appearance of the same individual – or rather, of his *astral* monad (or the *personality* as claimed by the modern Reincarnationists) – twice on the same planet is not a rule in nature "and that it *is* an exception." Let us try once more to explain our meaning. The reviewer speaks of the "Spiritual Individuality" or the *Immortal Monad* as it is called, *i.e.* the 7th and 6th Principles in the *Fragments*. In *Isis* we refer to the *personality* or the *Finite* astral monad, a compound of imponderable elements composed of the 5th and 4th principles. The former as an emanation of the ONE absolute is indestructible; the latter as an elementary compound is finite and doomed sooner or later to destruction with the exception of the more spiritualized portions of the 5th principle (the *Manas* or mind) which are assimilated by the 6th principle when it follows the 7th to its "gestation state" to be reborn or not reborn, as the case may be, in the *Arupa Loka* (the Formless World). The seven principles, forming, so to say, a *triad* and a *Quaternary,* or, as some have it a "Compound Trinity" subdivided into a triad and two duads may be better understood in the following groups of Principles :

"ISIS UNVEILED" AND THE "THEOSOPHIST" ON REINCARNATION

Group I.	**Spirit.**
7. *Atma*—"Pure Spirit."	*Spiritual Monad* or "Individuality"—and its *vehicle*. Eternal and indestructible.
6. *Boddhi*—"Spiritual Soul or Intelligence."	
Group II.	**Soul.**
5. *Manas*—"Mind or Animal Soul."	*Astral Monad*—or the *personal Ego* and its vehicle. Survives Group III. and is destroyed after a time, unless, —*re-incarnated* as said under exceptional circumstances.
4. *Kama-rupa*—"Desire" or "Passion" Form.	
Group III.	**Body.**
3. *Linga-sarira*—"Astral or Vital Body."	Compound Physical, or the "Earthly *Ego*." The three die together *invariably*.
2. *Jiva*—"Life Principle."	
1. *Stool-sarira*—"Body."	

And now we ask, – where is the "discrepancy" or contradiction? Whether man was good, bad, or indifferent, Group II has to become either a "shell," or to be once or several times more reincarnated under "exceptional circumstances." There is a mighty difference in our Occult doctrine between an *impersonal* Individuality, and an individual *Personality*. C.C.M. will not be reincarnated; nor will he be in his next re-birth C.C.M., but quite a new being, born of the thoughts and deeds of C.C.M.: his own creation, the child and fruit of his present life, the effect of the *causes* he is now producing. Shall we say then with the Spiritists that C.C.M., the man, we know, will be re-born again? No; but that his divine Monad will be clothed thousands of times yet before the end of the Grand Cycle, in various human forms, every one of them a *new* personality. Like a mighty tree that clothes itself every spring with a new foliage, to see it wither and die towards autumn, so the eternal Monad prevails through the series of smaller cycles, ever the same, yet ever changing and putting on, at each birth, a new garment. The bud, that failed to open one year, will re-appear in the next; the leaf that reached its maturity and died a natural death – can never be re-born on the same tree again. While writing *Isis*, we were not permitted to enter into details; hence

– the vague generalities. We are told to do so now – and we do as we are commanded.

And thus, it seems, after all, that "two and three" will "make just four," if the "three" was only *mistaken* for that number. And, we have heard of cases when that, which was universally regarded and denounced as something *very* "black" – shockingly so – suddenly re-became "white," as soon as an additional light was permitted to shine upon it. Well, the day may yet come when even the much misunderstood occultists will appear in such a light. *Vaut mieux tard que jamais!*

Meanwhile we will wait and see whether C.C.M. will quote again from our present answer – in *Light*.

H.P. Blavatsky
Theosophist, August, 1882
https://www.theosophytrust.org/449-isis-unveiled-and-the-theosophist-on-reincarnation

KARMA REQUIRES REINCARNATION

We are now in a transition period, and in the approaching twentieth century there will be a revival of genuine philosophy, and the Secret Doctrine will be the basis of the "New Philosophy." Science today, in the persons of such advanced students as Keely, Crookes, Lodge, Richardson, and many others, already treads so close to the borders of occult philosophy that it will not be possible to prevent the new age from entering the occult realm. H. P. Blavatsky's *Secret Doctrine* is a storehouse of scientific facts, but this is not its chief value. These facts are placed, approximately at least, in such relation to the synthesis or philosophy of occultism as to render comparatively easy the task of the student who is in search of real knowledge, and to further his progress beyond all preconception, provided he is teachable, in earnest, and intelligent. Nowhere else in English literature is the Law of Evolution given such sweep and swing. It reminds one of the ceaseless under-tone of the deep sea, and seems to view our Earth in all its changes "from the birth of time to the crack of doom." It follows man in his triple evolution, physical, mental, and spiritual, throughout the perfect circle of his boundless life. Darwinism had reached its limits and a rebound. Man is indeed evolved from lower forms. But *which* man? the physical? the psychical? the intellectual? or the spiritual? The Secret Doctrine points where the lines of evolution and involution meet; where matter and spirit clasp hands; and where the rising animal stands face to face with the fallen god; for *all natures* meet and mingle in man.

Judge no proposition of the Secret Doctrine as though it stood alone, for not one stands alone. Not "independence" here more than with the units that constitute Humanity. It is *interdependence* everywhere; in nature, as in life.

Even members of the T.S. have often wondered why H.P.B. and others well known in the Society lay so much stress on doctrines like

Karma and Reincarnation. It is not alone because these doctrines are easily apprehended and beneficent to individuals, not only because they furnish, as they necessarily do, a solid foundation for ethics, or all human conduct, but because they are the very key-notes of the higher evolution of man. Without Karma and Reincarnation evolution is but a fragment; a process whose beginnings are unknown, and whose outcome cannot be discerned; a glimpse of what might be; a hope of what should be. But in the light of Karma and Reincarnation evolution becomes the logic of what *must* be. The links in the chain of being are all filled in, and the circles of reason and of life are complete. Karma gives the eternal law of action, and Reincarnation furnishes the boundless field for its display. Thousands of persons can understand these two principles, apply them as a basis of conduct, and weave them into the fabric of their lives, who may not be able to grasp the complete synthesis of that endless evolution of which these doctrines form so important a part. In thus affording even the superficial thinker and the weak or illogical reasoner a perfect basis for ethics and an unerring guide in life, Theosophy is building toward the future realization of the Universal Brotherhood and the higher evolution of man. But few in this generation realize the work that is thus undertaken, or how much has already been accomplished. The obscurity of the present age in regard to genuine philosophical thought is nowhere more apparent than in the manner in which opposition has been waged toward these doctrines of Karma and Reincarnation. In the seventeen years since the Theosophical movement has been before the world there has not appeared, from any source, a serious and logical attempt to discredit these doctrines from a philosophical basis. There have been denial, ridicule, and denunciation *ad nauseum.* There could be no discussion from such a basis, for from the very beginning these doctrines have been put forth and advocated from the logical and dispassionate plane of philosophy. Ridicule is both unanswerable and unworthy of answer. It is not the argument, but the atmosphere of weak minds, born of prejudice and ignorance.

The synthesis of occultism is therefore the philosophy of Nature and of Life; the full – or free – truth that apprehends every scientific fact in the light of the unerring process of Eternal Nature.

The time must presently come when the really advanced thinkers of the age will be compelled to lay by their indifference, and their scorn and conceit, and follow the lines of philosophical investigation laid down in The Secret Doctrine. Very few seem yet to have realized how ample are these resources, because it involves a process of thought almost unknown to the present age of empiricism and induction. It is a revelation from archaic ages, indestructible and eternal, yet capable of being obscured and lost; capable of being again and again reborn, or like man himself – reincarnated.

> He who lives in one color of the rainbow is blind to the rest. Live in the Light diffused through the entire arc, and you will know it all.
>
> *The Path*

> He who knows not the common things of life is a beast among men. He who knows only the common things of life is a man among beasts. He who knows all that can be learned by diligent inquiry is a god among men.
>
> Plato

W. Q. Judge
The Path, November 1891; February, March & May, 1892
The Gupta Vidya I, 442-443

KRIYASHAKTI AND REINCARNATION

The wings of ideation are typically weighted down through identification with the astral and physical form. One's capacities for meditation and creativity are clipped through attachment to that which is merely a mutable projection. The force of this attachment is increased by the activity of *kamamanas*, particularly through speech and cerebration. All of these cause the astral to bloat until it becomes quite heavy. It is significant that in hinting about the after-death states of consciousness, Plato in the *Phaedo* uses as the primary pair of opposites the heavy and the light. Those whose souls were weighted down in life are weighted down even in death. In contrast, those who lightened themselves in life experience, effortlessly, a degree of lightness after death. They are able to ascend to the higher planes of consciousness. To experience the ultimate in lightness and effortlessness combined with fearlessness, detachment and faith in creativity, one must transcend altogether the astral plane. One must develop an inward sense of being that can function freely through the *karana sharira*, the permanent vesture which is the basis of the permanent astral body.

A developed disciple of *Brahma Vach* can gestate such an astral body in any life, and continue to do so over succeeding lives. Thus he, like an Adept, will eventually be able to exercise some volitional control over incarnation and to conceive and contemplate a voluntary incarnation. This process, continuing through many lifetimes, involves the hatching out of astral matter of a particular kind of permanent astral vesture, which itself is emanated out of the *karana sharira*, out of the purest vesture which might be called "the meditation body". It is what is sometimes called in Buddhist literature the Buddha-nature or Buddha-body. Only through profound meditation can one gain a sense of the potential reality of that subtle vesture of meditation. And only then can one transcend without effort the seeming insufficiency and false sufficiency that belongs to the astral plane through the separation of the sexes.

Long before an individual attains to this advanced and deliberate state of self-evolution, he can gain a provisional and theoretical understanding of *Kriyashakti* arising out of meditation as the paradigm of creativity. Citing the mysterious role played by *Kriyashakti* in the evolution of humanity and the presence of this power as latent in every human being, H.P. Blavatsky characterized *Kriyashakti* as

> ... the mysterious *power of thought* which enables it to produce external, perceptible, phenomenal results by its own inherent energy. The ancients held that any idea will manifest itself *externally* if one's attention (and Will) is deeply concentrated upon it; similarly, an intense volition will be followed by the desired result. A Yogi generally performs his wonders by means of Itchasakti (Will-power) and Kriyasakti.
>
> *The Secret Doctrine* II, 173

Human beings in every walk of life have had intimations of the reality of such powers, and even realized that what the Inner Self truly wishes is what ultimately is handed down through justice. This is Kriyashakti at the simplest level. This relationship of intense volition to tangible result cannot be understood inductively or in terms of likes and dislikes. One cannot even begin to ponder the idea of what one's inner Self – the Ishwara within – chooses without attaining a high degree of detachment. According to Patanjali, vairagya, or detachment, is indifference to everything but the Supreme Soul, rooted in a sense of supreme fitness and inner moral necessity. To act for and as the Supreme Self is to embody both dharma and shraddha, moral necessity and spiritual conviction. Paradoxically, when the mind and heart are concentrated deeply upon that which is totally right, one no longer desires anything for oneself. Then one will reach one's goal. This process of mental and spiritual creativity through and on behalf of universal good is experienced through mystic meditation. In the perfected human being, permanently rooted in consciousness on the plane of Akasha,

Kriyashakti unfolds as the ceaseless capacity of compassionate ideation extended in protective benevolence over all beings.

This divine capacity of the perfected human being is derived from the creative heart of the Logos. Its exercise by Buddhas and Mahatmas is inseparable from the creative compassion in the primal germ of mind at the origin of the cosmos. All phenomenal matter is only a kind of appearance which, at the root, is in essence inseparable from Root Matter or Mulaprakriti. In that primordial matter, which is the invisible essence behind all phenomenal matter, there is Daiviprakriti, the primordial Divine Light which is also Life in the highest sense. That eternal Life is also Light and Electricity at the earliest precosmic level. All of these are reflected at the dawn of manifestation in cosmic electricity or in the Light of the Logos in manifestation. They are reflected in the life that then becomes the Fohatic energy, which maintains an entire set of worlds in manifestation. At the primordial level, Light and Life can be summoned out of the Mulaprakriti which is hidden in phenomenal matter. Kamadeva is this highest energy of the purest ideation awakened in the primal germ of mind through Kriyashakti on the plane of the Logos. It is through Kriyashakti that the Lords of Wisdom, the Kumaras, the eldest sons of Brahms born of the body of night, created progeny in the Third Root Race of humanity. That progeny was and is both a single wondrous Being and a radiant Host of beings,

> . . . the so-called SONS OF WILL AND YOGA, or the "ancestors" (the *spiritual* forefathers) of all the subsequent and present Arhats, or Mahatmas, [created] in a truly *immaculate* way. They were indeed *created,* not *begotten,* as were their brethren of the Fourth Race, who were generated sexually after the separation of sexes, the *Fall of man.* For creation is but the result of will acting on phenomenal matter, the calling forth out of it the primordial divine *Light* and eternal *Life.* They were the "holy seed-grain" of the future Saviours of Humanity.
>
> Ibid.

The gestation and emanation of a new nucleus of Mahatmas and Adepts set apart for the coming races of humanity arose out of the original meditation of the highest divine beings in the Third Root Race. This is *Kriyashakti* in its most exalted sense. It is intimately connected with the mysteries of initiation, whereby a Bodhisattva can, out of the light of the Dhyani Buddha which is within himself, project a Manushya Buddha and a Nirmanakaya. It is also possible, through *Kriyashakti*, to project a certain type of human being which becomes a model and a redemptive saviour for races to come. This, associated with Padmapani Bodhisattva, is the highest and most sacred form of creativity. Every human being has within himself the principle of Christos, Chenresi, Avalokiteshvara or Padmapani Buddha. Every human being has within the spiritual essence of the universal light of the universal Logos which is eternal Life, and which encompasses each and every form of divine creativity.

> Attempt, I entreat you, to mark what I say with as keen an observation as you can. He who has been disciplined to this point in Love, by contemplating beautiful objects gradually, and in their order, now arriving at the end of all that concerns Love, on a sudden beholds a beauty wonderful in its nature. This is it, O Socrates, for the sake of which all the former labours were endured. It is eternal, unproduced, indestructible; neither subject to increase nor decay; not, like other things, partly beautiful and partly deformed; not at one time beautiful and at another time not; not beautiful in relation to one thing and deformed in relation to another; not here beautiful and there deformed; not beautiful in the estimation of one person and deformed in that of another; nor can this supreme beauty be figured to the imagination like a beautiful face, or beautiful hands, or any portion of the body, nor like any discourse, nor any science. Nor does it subsist in any other that lives or is, either in earth, or in heaven, or in any other place; but it is eternally uniform and consistent, and monoeidic with itself. All other things are beautiful through a participation of it, with this condition, that although they are subject to production and

decay, it never becomes more or less, or endures any change. When anyone, ascending from a correct system of Love, begins to contemplate this supreme beauty, he already touches the consummation of his labour.

Plato
The Banquet

Raghavan Iyer
The Gupta Vidya III, essay "Kriyashakti", p. 201-203
https://www.theosophytrust.org/885-kriyashakti

REINCARNATION AND SELF-TRANSFORMATION

In the Aquarian Age in which many see the life-process as the continually enacted and essentially hidden interplay of harmony and disharmony, suffering always comes as a benevolent teacher of wisdom. Pain serves as a shock to one's sense of identity, illusory self-image and acquired or ancestral habits. It challenges one's pride and perversity. It compels one to pause for thought and radically reappraise the meaning of life, obligations, and potentials in oneself and others. When suffering comes, it plumbs below the surface of the psyche, touching depths of untrammeled consciousness. Noumenal and noetic awareness enters into everyday experience, and is saluted by remarkable constellations of poets, singers and seers. Incidents of life once taken for granted suddenly look very different, because one's sensibility has been sharpened. Were this not so, there would be little meaning to the mere succession of events and the mere recurrence of mechanical responses to the sensory stream of consciousness.

There is constant learning, and there is the ever-present possibility of deepening the cognitive basis of awareness, the operative level of self-actualization. This is part of the evolutionary and unending process of etherealization and refinement of life in the cycle of rapid descent and painful ascent. This is an exceedingly slow and subtle process — there is nothing automatic about it — but it is ubiquitous. Such a process of refinement must involve first of all an altered mode of awareness, which for most human beings means the conscious adoption of a radically different perspective on human life and cosmic evolution. But it must also transform the range and reach of one's sense-perceptions, through a better and finer use of the sensory powers of touch, taste, smell, sight and hearing. Further, this process of etherealization and refinement must proceed through a harmonious commingling of centres in the brain-mind and spiritual heart, through inward surrender to the Sovereign Self and the silent invocation of the Light of the Logos.

One may imagine the immortal Triad as overbrooding the head, though incompletely incarnated because its reflected intelligence must consciously ascend towards the level of proper harmonization. This could be expressed in terms of metaphysical truths about consciousness which operates under laws of expansion and contraction, implying continuous creation, preservation and regeneration through destruction. These archetypal modes have been traditionally symbolized in the Hindu pantheon by Nara-Nari, Agni, Varuna and Surya, and also by Brahmā, Vishnu and Shiva. This sacred teaching about cosmic and human consciousness could also be conveyed from the standpoint of matter. The essential axiom of Gupta Vidya is the affirmation that spirit and matter are really two facets of one and the same Substance-Principle. Objectivity and subjectivity are wholly relative to centres of perception, to degrees of differentiation, and to the coadunition and consubstantiality of objects with subjects upon overlapping planes of substance. Put entirely in terms of matter, this would imply that a person whose consciousness is deepened would experience a richer awareness of the invisible aspects and mathematical points of visible matter. There would be a heightened sensitivity to the gamut of invisible relations between life-atoms, corresponding to subtle colours and rarefied sounds.

One would also be replacing an angular view by a rounded view: the greater the depth, the greater the roundedness. The price people pay for the settled three-dimensionality of their conception of the world of phenomena is that the brain-mind becomes captive to angular views. If people are not truly self-conscious, they become extremely obtuse or are hopelessly caught within narrow angles and restricted orbits of perception. Whereas a person who can intensify the depth of perception and feeling, through private pain and unspoken suffering merged in effortless awareness of the vast suffering of all humanity, gains greater depth as a human being. This is continuously enriched by meditative experience of the Silence that surrounds the mystery of *Sat* and *Asat*, Being and Non-Being. The more this becomes a way of life, the more it is possible to have a profoundly balanced view of the world and a well-rounded conception of selfhood, alchemizing and elevating personal awareness and individual sensibility to the height and breadth of universal self-consciousness and the depths of boundless space, eternal motion and endless duration.

This process of self-transformation may be illustrated by an initially shadowy circle, a very narrow segment of which seems to be lit up. There is a seemingly central focus, but it is only central to that visible segment, whilst the centre of the whole circle, most of which is obscured, remains hidden. This is analogous to the relationship between the personal ego and the individual Self. A human being with a narrow sense of identity is living only segmentally, existing only at one sensory level with reference to an unduly restricted horizon of human experience. Such a person is not properly centering, not really trying to get as full and rounded a view of himself and the world as possible. Out of this roundedness he could begin to sense a sphere of light surrounding himself in which he lives, moves and has his being. This will loosen a great deal of the fixity of categories of thought and emotional responses which, if seen clairvoyantly, reveal a sad mutilated shadow of the true Self of a human being. Herein lies the rationale for recovery through meditation of that pristine and rounded conception of the Self which is more in harmony with the music of the spheres and the Golden Egg of Brahmā in the ocean of SPACE. This transformation is indeed the psychological equivalent to the Copernican revolution, in which the sun of the *Atman* is central to the solar system. For the *Atman* to become the centre of a luminous sphere of selfhood would require a firm displacement of the false centering of consciousness, through *kama manas*, within a distorting segment of separative identity which is trapped in a fragmented view of space, time and secondary causation. The dwarfing of one's true selfhood is the crucifixion of

Christos, the obscuration of the light, the plenitude, the potential and the richness within every human being on earth.

To convey this as a criterion of human stature, the greater the depth of one's inwardness, the broader, the vaster, the wider the range of one's sympathies, and the more one is able to appreciate a wider variety of experiences, situations, contexts and human beings. The more secure one's depth of consciousness, the more one is able to exercise the synthesizing gift of the Monad, capable of seeing in terms of any of the specific sub-colours, and also able to penetrate to the very centre of the white light, seeing beyond it, and benevolently using the entire range of the spectrum. What is true of colours applies equally to sounds, and ultimately to consciousness itself. This is the sacred prerogative of a human being. It is because human beings fall, owing to shared and inherited limitations, but also owing to self-created limitations, they forfeit or forget altogether this sovereign prerogative and fail to mend themselves through meditation and self-study. Hence, the healing and restorative property of sleep which Shakespeare so suggestively describes as Nature's second feast, man's great restorer. The average human being deprived of the benefit of *sushupti* or sleep would simply not survive for long. Sleep and death are Nature's modes of restoration of balance. In order to take full advantage of sleep, the seeker must initially experience the pain of forcing the mind to return to a point on which it is placed, to a chosen idea, bringing the heart back to the deepest, purest and most pristine feeling of devotion, warmth and love. If one did this again and again, then certainly one would not only become more deep in response to life but one would also become more of a spiritual benefactor to the human race, drawing freely from the infinite resources of Divine Thought and the Light of the Logos, Brahma Vach.

> Just as milliards of bright sparks dance on the waters of an ocean above which one and the same moon is shining, so our evanescent personalities — the illusive envelopes of the immortal MONAD-EGO — twinkle and dance on the waves of

> Maya. They last and appear, as the thousands of sparks produced by the moon-beams, only so long as the Queen of the Night radiates her lustre on the running waters of life: the period of a Manvantara; and then they disappear, the beams — symbols of our eternal Spiritual Egos — alone surviving, re-merged in, and being, as they were before, one with the Mother-Source.
>
> *The Secret Doctrine*, i 237

The Monad-Ego is the three-tongued flame, the *Atma-Buddhi-Manas* which overbroods throughout the *manvantara* myriads upon myriads of personalities, instruments and vehicles through which the great work of evolution proceeds. This is made possible by the fact that the three-tongued flame of the four wicks is connected with the myriads of sparks. Although in each life these sparks seemingly become entangled through the four derivative principles into a shallow sense of separative identity as a personal man or woman in that life, this is really an illusion. All the elements in all the personal lives throughout the *manvantara* represent the diffused intelligence which is here ascribed to a single source — the Queen of the Night — radiating her lustre on the running waters of life. Between the hidden source of the flames throughout evolution — the Central Spiritual Sun — and the manifest source of all the myriad sparks involved in the evanescent phenomena witnessed by personal consciousness in incarnated existence, there would be a causal relationship. One is like a necessary reflection of the other. This is true cosmically. It is also true of every single human being. The astral form is like a lunar reflection of a solar light-energy that belongs to the *Atma-Buddhi-Manas* which is like the sun overbrooding every single human temple. The profoundly mysterious relation between the two is intimated by the symbol of the thread of Fohat. A very fine thread connects the solar activity of the higher principles and the lunar activity involving the reflected and parasitic intelligence of personal consciousness.

Everything can be seen, as in the Platonic scheme, as a reflection of what is higher on a more homogeneous plane. The relative reality of every single entity and event in life is a shadowy reality that presupposes something more primordial and more homogeneous. In this way, all life would trace back to the one single field of homogeneous ideation, homogeneous substance. If this is what makes the universe a cosmos — a single system — then the solemn task of the human being is to integrate life consciously and cheerfully; to do this, one must first negate the false sense of identity that belongs on the lunar plane. One must perceive in depth all the elements of being that contribute to the seeming continuity of consciousness in and through the astral form, and then reach further inwards through deep meditation to the sacred source of all consciousness and life. This alchemical work is represented in many myths as the separation of what is food for the soul from what is not, before and during after-death states. This sifting takes place through all Nature and is the deliberate undertaking of those who are pledged to self-regeneration in the service of humanity. "'Great Sifter' is the name of the 'Heart Doctrine', O Disciple."

Raghavan Iyer
The Gupta Vidya II, essay "Self-Transformation", 287

INDEX

1

1975 Cycle 186

A

abstract space 91
acousticoi, those who listen 179
acting only for the sake of results is an indictment of modern education in Kali Yuga 167
Adept 67
Adepts, general sum-total of impulse given by thought to matter includes the laser-sharp contributions of legions of 147
Adhiyajna, universal sacrificial processes of the cosmos 130
Agathon 25, 119
ahankara 38, 70, 129, 130, 136
ahankara at the level of physical name and form 130
ahankara as universal self-consciousness, coordinate with *Mahat* or universal mind 129
ahankara, lower forms of related to an identification with a name and a form 129
ahimsa 219
Ain-Soph 55
Ain-Soph, first recognizable link between the, and the highest intelligence of man 55
Akasha 61, 119, 184, 191
Akasha, pristine sphere of noetic awareness 127
Alaya 184, 234
Alaya-Akasa 360
alienation of the individual from the universal is repeated within the individual in a body 136
allegorical umbrella, provides a measure of assured protection to the fallible aspirant 132
Allegory of the Cave 230
anahata 166
anahata, vibration in the spiritual heart 166
analogy and correspondence 61, 65, 101, 159

anamnesis 49, 51, 53, 61
anamnesis is true soul-memory 49
anasakti, selfless action and joyous service 52
antaskarana becomes a drawbridge to be extended at will in the service of universal welfare 192
antaskarana, the inward bridge between the impersonal and personal selves 190
Anugita 221
Apollonius of Tyana 345
Aquarian Age 108, 207, 211, 214, 216, 217, 389
Aquarian Age is typified by the concept of vertical ascent 216
Aquarian Age, Pythagorean teaching of the, of Universal Enlightenment 58
Arcane philosophy begins at that precise point where an abyss has been discovered between the mind and brain 79
Ariadne's thread 61, 66, 67, 74
Ariadne's thread represents unbroken continuity of consciousness in the One Life 61
Ariadne's thread, trace, across incarnations 67
Army of the Voice 224
Arupa Manas, subordination of the elements of the lower *rupa* existence to the spiritual ideation of 184
asatya, falsehood 38
Astral Light 126, 360, 362
Astral Light, region of psyche 126
astral vesture 70, 118
astral vesture, permanent, which itself is emanated out of the *karana sharira* 384
Atlantean sorcerers 124
Atlantis, destruction of 124
Atma is the Higher Self 310
Atma-Buddhi 87, 88, 112, 118, 136, 155, 214, 228, 259, 265, 267, 271, 286
Atma-Buddhi, overbroods incarnated *Manas* but only at a distance 136
Atma-Buddhi-Manas 118
Atma-Buddhi-Manas, the noetic individuality 87
Atman 210, 229
atom, each is at its core a monad, an expression of the highest self *(Atman)*.. 123
AUM, every baby enters the world voicing the 197
Aura 287
Avalokiteshwara, the Logos 55
Aversion 39
aversion is itself a form of attachment 39
avidya 54
avidya, basic origin of, or ignorance, is *tanha*, the will to live 38

avidya, congenital ignorance, a peculiar perversity of the modified consciousness 34
awareness relative to the particular plane of perception on which we function 36

B

bardo 42, 44, 45
bardo, an intermediate state between birth and death, a period of gestation, a
 period in which there can be no Karma 40
bardo, symbolic forty-nine days of the 44
bardo, what happens in the 43
Bhagavad Gita 21, 30, 31, 50, 51, 52, 85, 94, 115, 117, 191, 193
Bhagavatam 94
bhakti 52
birth and death, see, as connected forms or phases of a single stream of
 consciousness 34
Bodhisattva 226
Bodhisattva path of service 127
Bodhisattvas 24, 30, 45, 67, 117
Bodhisattvic ideal 130
body, human, so desecrated by Materialism and man himself, is the temple of
 the Holy Grail, the *Adytum* of the grandest, nay, of all, the mysteries of
 nature in our solar universe 357
Book of Judgment 43
Brahmā 65, 109, 111, 390, 391
Brahmā function of expansion 129
Brahma Vach 57, 112, 392
brahmacharya, a period of probation 179
Brotherhood of Bodhisattvas 59, 67, 202, 229
Brotherhood of Bodhisattvas, There would be no survival for the human race
 over eighteen million years but for the continuous compassion of the 232
Brothers Karamazov, The 198
Buddha 12, 40, 42, 47, 92, 94, 99, 102, 103, 164, 179, 221, 222, 232, 237, 345, 348
Buddha declared: "Know ye who suffer, ye suffer from yourselves 25
Buddha nature 34, 40, 47
Buddha taught, not escape into some celestial retreat, but the gaining of
 nirvana in *samsara*, progressive enlightenment in the company of one's
 fellows 237
Buddhas of Contemplation, self-luminous beings who are masters of
 compassion 133
Buddha's own exemplary life was the beautiful and lustrous realization of
 three paramount principles — the principle of regeneration, the principle of
 renunciation and the principal of reverence 237

Buddhi 61, 68, 88, 123, 136, 156, 365
Buddhi Yoga 52, 166
Buddhi, the irrational spiritual Soul 256
Buddhi, the spiritual soul 243, 270
Buddhi-*Manas* can neither die nor lose its compound self-consciousness in
 Eternity 247, 299
Buddhi-Manas, the Spiritual Ego, is not the HIGHER SELF 276
Buddhi-taijasi 303

C

carnal immortality, delusion of 150
cell, every, must of necessity have also a memory of its own kind, as likewise
 its own *psychic* and *noetic* action 356
certitude, certitude, there is no, to be attained anywhere in the realm of
 differentiation 174
Chaos 106, 175
Chaos, the primordial matter, in which is hidden the light that is the soundless
 sound 175
Chârvâka 324, 329
chitkala, the voice of the daimon which is infallibly and constantly available to
 the individual 155
Christ 152, 153, 172
City of Man 225
conatus 167
conatus, Spinoza's term for the urge or will to sustain rational and spiritual
 self-preservation 166
consciousness, internal refinement of, is the method of evolution itself 147
consciousness, radical reorientation of, away from the *persona* and towards the
 Divine 189
contemplation 55, 56, 180
contentment 57
contentment and joy in a more collective sense of human welfare and a more
 universal sense of progress 103
continuity of consciousness 70, 71, 72, 95, 97, 103, 113, 211, 218, 234, 394
continuity of consciousness is to be seen not as something individual but
 rather universal 98
continuity of consciousness, Authentic, consists of unbroken self-conscious
 experience of the universality of the life-process 74
continuity of consciousness, recovery of 67
continuity of consciousness, to assist in the recovery of universal, one must
 adopt a radically different approach, grounded in metaphysics 62

continuity of spiritual self-consciousness 197
Control of thought and speech is an essential ingredient of soul etiquette and spiritual discrimination 230
cosmic and human evolution 106
cosmic manifestation 129
cosmic plenum 123
cosmogony, immediate and evident implications of the Great Breath in regard to 78
cosmos is a radiant garment of the divine Self 51
cultures grow infatuated with telling their inflated history only after they have begun to decay 209

D

Daiviprakriti 53, 159
Dakshinamurti 212
Dakshinamurti, the Initiator of Initiates, responsible for the Mysteries in the Third, Fourth and Fifth RootRaces 171
Dalai Lama 45
Days and Nights of Brahmā, *manvantara* and *pralaya* 123
death and immortality in Tibetan thought 33
Death comes to our spiritual selves ever as a deliverer and friend 248
death consciousness, if we want to understand what happens after death, we must first grasp 40
death need not be viewed as something unnatural 37
delusion 47, 63, 170, 177, 182, 186
delusion, basic honesty will go far to clean out the cobwebs of 60
Devachan . 153, 199, 246, 254, 261, 273, 276, 282, 283, 288, 289, 290, 292, 294, 296, 301, 307, 309, 319, 340
devachan is a period of rest and assimilation between lives 126
Devachan, an idealized and subjective continuation of earth-life 296
devachan, basis of the popular mythology of heaven 126
Devachanee 288, 290, 291
devas and *devatas* 51
devotion, problem that if one is devoted one has set up some kind of claim upon the object of 164
dhyana 52
Dhyana, four degrees of 266
Dhyani Buddhas 117
Dhyanis 133, 154, 193, 227, 228
dialectic 181
Divine Darkness 56, 134, 193

divine dialectic, proceeds through progressive universalization, profound synthesis and playful integration 76
divine gift of sound 56
Divine Ground 56
Divine Prototype 227
Divine Wisdom, the only Jordan whose waters can baptize in the name of the Father in Heaven, the *Mahaguru* on earth, the God in man 228
Dnyaneshvari 52, 53
dreamless sleep 238
dugpa 85
dugpa or sorcerer works through coercive imposition of combative will 85
Dzyan 207

E

Eastern sources, one must revert to time-honoured, to make sense of what may be inferred from physical evidence 63
education 21, 167
Egyptian teachers of Sais, the great, next to whom the Greeks were as little children 208
Einstein, Albert, there are no hitching posts in the universe 176
elemental, Human beings can collectively engender a gigantic, oppressive, like the idea of a personal God, or the Leviathan of the State 59
Eliphas Lévi 126
enlightened man cannot be imagined in a totally disembodied state 35
enlightenment 204, 221, 236, 237
equinox, autumnal 200
equinox, vernal 200
eros 99, 125
esoteric 35, 65, 346
Esoteric philosophy, pivotal doctrine of, admits no privileges or special gifts in man 365
esoteric, or the true 346
eternal duration 96
eternal reward or eternal punishment, we positively refuse to accept the cruel and unphilosophical belief in 263
evolutionary pilgrimage 123
evolutionary tide on earth 123
exoteric, disguised in symbols 346

F

Fifth Sub-Race of the Fifth Root Race 68
form, Platonic conception of, not bound up with anything fixed 99
fourth globe in the Fourth Round, humanity has completed the involutionary
    arc of this process and is now engaged in the difficult push upwards and
    inwards towards the source of all life-energy 147
Fourth Round 68, 70
Fourth Round, midpoint of the, over eighteen million years ago 62
freedom from the false division of eternal duration into a past, a present
    and a future 95

G

Gandhi, tried to resuscitate the teaching of Buddha 38
Gautama Buddha 191
Gayatri 132
Genius, great, can never copy or condescend to imitate, but will ever be
    original 371
Genius, true, needs but an opportunity to spring forth into existence 371
God is a circle with its centre everywhere and circumference nowhere 176
Gods, Monads and Atoms 366
Golden Age 124, 127, 163, 174
Golden Age vibration can be inserted into an Iron Age 125
Golden Age, in the, humans showed spontaneous reverence to Magus-
    Teachers 206
Golden Age, when humans were spontaneously held together by an effortless
    sense of moral and spiritual solidarity with the whole of nature 164
golden thread of continuous life — periodically broken into active and passive
    cycles of sensuous existence on Earth 199
Golden Verses 181
Great Breath 70, 77, 78, 87, 88, 89, 123
Great Breath, preserves the cosmos 123
Great Teachers assist in the self-production of whole human beings by making
    a holistic teaching come alive 179
gupta vidya (secret science) is only for the few 347
Gupta Vidya, based upon a central conception of an immortal individuality
    capable of infinite perfectibility 76
Gupta Vidya, septenary Teachings of, have a general reference to all systems
    within the cosmos 68
Gupta Vidya, the arcane standpoint of, is integrative, and always sees the One
    in the many 89

Guruparampara 163
Guruparampara, the golden chain of transmission of a galaxy of known and
    unknown teachers 163

H

H.P. Blavatsky 2
Hegel's metaphysical theory of evolution 100
heredity 226
Hermes 200, 207, 228
Hermes is the paradigm of the oldest sacred tradition, going back a million
    years ago to India *(Bharata Dwipa)* 207
HermesBudha 118
Hero in Man 126
Herodotus, *Euterpe* 208
Higher EGO cannot act directly on the body 355
higher *Manas* 85, 86, 88
Higher Self is ATMA 310
higher Triad 70
himsa, violence 38
Hiranyagarbha, the pristine golden egg of immortal individuality 54
hosts of hierophants are beings involved in universal welfare and uplifting the
    whole of humanity 165
hotri 87
hotri or hierophant is an initiated alchemist able to send forth beneficent
    emanations through a mighty current of concentrated thought 192
human being can consciously transcend all behaviour patterns 82
human being, every, is a ray of a colourless universal light 91
*human being's basic level of self-consciousness is directly proportional to that Monad's
    evolution as an independent centre of primordial formless intelligence* 144
Human beings produce a false sense of self out of a series of intense
    particularizations of will, thought and feeling 90
human beings, not all live in the same dimension of space-time 144
human souls at the present time of metamorphosis, there is a growing recognition
    and widespread acknowledgement of a fresh opportunity for 217
humanity of the future 139
humanity, whole of, is now coming closer to what is called the moment of
    choice 100

I

I and thou are the greatest lies 178

Iamblicus 344, 345, 347
I-am-I, pure consciousness without any reference to being a subject separate from other subjects 137
ideals to children and pupils through example and through precept is both beneficent and constructive, Transmitting 236
ideation, utmost effort of, will terminate in the vault of a sphere 54
ignorance, what men call day is the night of 117
immortal soul 201, 212, 214
immortal soul can recover the most illuminating continuity of consciousness 61
immortal soul, there is an indestructible element in every, which enables a human being again and again to make a fresh start 214
immortal Triad 109, 125, 390
immortal Triad overbrooding every human being is aware like a Pythagorean spectator 107
immortality 9, 24, 25, 26, 29, 31, 44, 45, 46, 50, 87, 182
immortality is a fact for the indwelling soul, for the individual ray of the overbrooding *Atman* 13, 26
Immortality is nothing but another aspect of mortality 46
immortality, first steps toward conscious 39
immortality, for the personal consciousness there can be no 13, 26
immortality, intimations of immanent 193
immortality, secret of 190
individuality 28, 79, 80, 93, 188
individuality, noetic 84
individuals imagine that they are isolated in consciousness from each other 141
infinite and unconditioned, that which is, can have no form, and cannot be a being 260
Initiate 67, 98
Initiate, functionally, the definition of an enlightened being is a being who chooses every thought 103
initiation 209, 211
initiation is to be understood as individuation through the universalization of consciousness 211
initiation of any sacred sound-vibration, when based upon exact spiritual knowledge, can set the keynote of an entire epoch 232
inner life of man must also conform to universal laws 79
inner pilgrimage, fundamental problem is to generate a sufficient sense of reality for the 146
Inquisition burnt her "heretics" out of pure Christian kindness 322
Integrity resides in the ability to recognize the difference between what one knows and what one does not know 219
intuition is an *instinct of the soul* 343

involution of spirit into matter, point of maximum, represents the fullest development of physical consciousness ... 145
invulnerability ... 163
Iron Age ... 126, 167
Ishwara ... 104
Isis Unveiled ... 2
Isolation of the immortal soul, a painful period of withdrawal from lesser supports ... 133
Itchashakti, the power of desire ... 59

J

Jacob's Ladder of ideation, by constructing and using a, an individual can insert himself or herself into the evolutionary programme ... 218
Jesus and St. Paul taught the unity of spiritual beings ... 348
Jesus' doctrine assumes the perfectibility of humanity and destroys the theory of original sin ... 348
Jesus taught, either blow hot or blow cold, for the lukewarm are spewed forth ... 220
Jivatman ... 72, 73
Jivatman, the One Life ... 72
Jnanashakti ... 59
jnanis, highest, are also the purest *bhaktas*, responding in magical sympathy to the cosmic will of Krishna ... 219

K

Kalahansa stands for all the endless cycles (*Kalachakra*) ... 193
Kali Yuga began over 5,090 years ago ... 124
kama ... 70, 84, 85
Kama loka and *devachan* are objective resonances present everywhere and always ... 141
kama manas ... 73, 85, 111, 114, 117, 391
Kama-loka ... 286, 309, 363
kamaloka, the origin of theological dogmas concerning hell and purgatory ... 126
Kama-rupa ... 85, 286, 287, 313, 363
Karana ... 155, 158
karana sharira ... 68, 159, 160, 167, 203, 206
karana sharira is that it is the ground of the latent knowledge called to active potency by Hermes ... 207
karana sharira, permanent vesture of the monad ... 206

karana sharira, the permanent vesture which is the basis of the permanent astral body 384
karana sharira, the vast human inheritance of spiritual wisdom and scientific magic was assimilated into the 206
Karanopadhi 241, 268
Karma acts incessantly; we reap *in our after*-life only the fruit of that which we have ourselves sown 247
karma and memory, operation of across lifetimes 138
karma and rebirth, twin doctrines of responsibility and hope 125
Karma and Reincarnation are easily apprehended and beneficent to individuals 382
Karma compassionately reduces opportunities for protracted delusion until the individual is compelled to learn essential lessons, Through successive incarnations 235
Karma gives the eternal law of action, and Reincarnation furnishes the boundless field for its display 382
Karma is the child of the terrestrial Ego, the fruit of the acts of his visible personality 327
Karma is the religion of salvation by works as opposed to faith devoid of works 350
Karma not a providential means of divine retribution 125
Karma works on the soul's behalf 125
Karma Yoga, the yoga of works 166
karma, *prarabdha*, the karma with which one has begun life 83
karmic attachment and memory, relationship between 234
Karmic punishment reaches the Ego only in the next incarnation 247
Katha Upanishad 190
Katha Upanishad is not only a philosophical dialogue, but also an alchemical text, replete with deeply evocative, enigmatic and magical mantrams 191
Kekule's dream, critical in biology 97
King Karma 319
knower and the known, become one, fused in transcendent moments of compassionate revelation 52
knower and the known, necessary relation between the 51
Krishna 22, 30, 31, 34, 36, 59, 60, 94, 117, 134, 164, 167, 186, 193
Krishna, the Logos in the cosmos and the hidden god in every man 21
Krishna's medicinal method in the *Gita* 58
kriyashakti 186
Kriyashakti in its most exalted sense 387
Kriyashakti, the power of visualization 59
Kriyashakti, totally purified creative imagination 103
Kshetragna within the sun 221

kshetrajna, higher *Manas*, the silent Spectator, source of spiritual will 85
kundalini 186
kutastha 53
Kwan Yin 159

L

Ladd, George T. 81
lanoos, true neophytes on the Path 59
law of karma or justice signifies moral interdependence and human solidarity ... 125
Lemurian Race lived in an idyllic Golden Age 124
liberation 233
Light of the Logos 109, 112, 159, 390, 392
light that shines in the "inner chamber", analogy between, and the subtle creative light of the first twilight at the dawn of the *Maha-Manvantara*...... 158
lighting up of *Manas* over eighteen million years ago at the midpoint of the Fourth Round 62
linga sharira 166, 167, 191, 203
Logos 224, 225
love, true, is proportional to spiritual wakefulness 233
lower *Manas* 84, 85, 88

M

Maha Shiva, the Mahayogin, head of the host of virgin ascetics called the Kumaras 149
Mahamaya 175
Mahat 57, 72, 129, 136
Mahatmas 26, 57, 127, 133, 172, 348
Mahatmas and Adepts, new nucleus of, set apart for the coming races of humanity 386
Mahatmas or Hierophants and Bodhisattvas renounce everything for the sake of suffering humanity 127
Mahayana Buddhism, rejection of the desire for liberation 130
man and the universe, continuous connection between 32
Man is the universe writ small 32
man ought to be ever striving to help the divine evolution of ideas by becoming to the best of his ability a co-worker with Nature 154
Manas 68, 85, 87, 172, 188
Manas itself is noetic, and signifies what could be called the spiritual individuality 84
manas, Lower, must be brought into firm alignment with higher *Manas*,

especially through the use of silence and conscious control of speech 229
Manas, lower, when it is disconnected from *kama*, can exercise a limited free will 84
Manas, the light of, and human self-awareness 167
Manas, the power of noetic thought, ideation and imagination 177
Manas, the root of the word 'man,' from *man*, 'to think' 27
Manasaputra 57, 105
Manasaputras 118
Manasic humanity today is at a moment like the dawn of Venus, filled with the promise of a future wherein societies and civilizations founded upon the sacrificial love of wisdom will flourish 225
Manas-Taijasi 246, 326
manifestation of Cosmos, whole process of is re-enacted in the *bardo* state, between death and rebirth 47
Manushya, true man capable of thought, reflection and deliberate action 123
manvantara 68, 72, 112, 123, 129, 393
manvantara and *pralaya* 69
manvantara, governed by the law of periodicity 123
manvantara, period of manifestation covering trillions of years 123
Masters 60
material body is not the obstacle, but rather attachment and identification with it 41
maya 107, 128
maya – the element of illusion which enters into all finite things 128
maya and *moha*, illusion and delusion 49
meditate upon meditation itself 133
Meditate upon the great Masters of Meditation 133
meditate, to, on death is to meditate on life 31
meditation .. 9, 25, 29, 30, 31, 38, 39, 44, 46, 50, 52, 54, 59, 63, 65, 66, 68, 69, 71, 74, 81, 86, 87, 107, 111, 113, 115, 116, 118, 119, 164, 176, 189, 192, 193, 391, 392, 394
meditation and contemplation are neither episodic nor dependent upon any technique 218
meditation, false 186
medium 361, 362
medium is supposed to be a person through whom the action of another person or being is either manifested or transmitted 361
mediumship 360, 361, 362
mediumship is most dangerous; and *psychic* experiences when accepted indiscriminately lead only to honestly deceiving others 362
memory, personal is a fiction of the physiologist 142
memory, recollection, remembrance 142

memory, seat of, is assuredly neither here nor there, but everywhere throughout the human body 353
memory, two sources of, are in these two "principles."; the Higher *Manas* (Mind or Ego), and the *Kama-Manas, i.e.*, the rational, but earthly or physical intellect 354
Men of the Word 127
mental asceticism 67
mental emanations, individuals owe it to their neighbours and their descendants, as well as to themselves, to purify their 185
metanoia 8, 25
metaphysical basis of sacrifice 226
metaphysics 62, 71, 74
metempsychosis, natural impulse 123
moksha, seven paths to the bliss of 128
moment of choice 100, 101, 102, 103
Monad 111, 392
Monad-Ego is the three-tongued flame, the *Atma-BuddhiManas* 112, 393
Monads 208, 211, 227
Mulaprakriti 56
Mulaprakriti is the reverse of *Parabrahman*, but they are both one and the same ...333
Mysteries 1, 2, 1, 2, 171, 297, 369, 370
Mystery Schools 207
mystic meditation, acts as an eliminator 134

N

Nachiketas flame of discernment and daring, only through the Guru that the chela has the golden opportunity of lighting up the 190
namarupa 38
namarupa, name and form 191
nation's, a, spiritual decline accompanies its material ascent 207
natura naturans, a dynamic process constantly unleashing creative energies .153
Nature, secret code language of 57
nidanas, twelve causes of being – the concatenated chain of antecedent causes 128
Nirmanakaya 41, 46
Nirmanakayas 46, 292
nitya pralaya, perpetual dissolution 70
nitya sarga 70
nitya sarga, perpetual creation 70
noetic action works at the level of the atomic 69
noetic magic, a summoning from latency to active potency of arcane

knowledge that was originally impressed in the imperishable soul-memory of all humanity 206
Noetic understanding is, therefore, rooted in universal unity 88
nothing which is contradicted by sound reason can be a true doctrine of Buddha 340
nous as the matter-moving mind, Platonic idea of 214

O

obstructions arising in meditation have their origins in forgetfulness, indolence and cowardice 133
old age, in, those beset by a sense of failure, a fear of death and a feeling of audience deprivation seek refuge in reminiscence 209
One Form of Existence 130

P

Parabrahm 56, 72, 210
Parabrahm, cannot cognize, except as *Mulaprakriti* 56
Parabrahman 324, 333
Paramita Path is connected with *antaskarana* 190
Paranirvâna 333
particle physics 206
past lives, record or reflection of all the, must survive 274
Patanjali 86, 88
Patanjali, taught of meditative state called the condition of the Spectator without a spectacle 137
Path, the 227
perfected human being, permanently rooted in consciousness on the plane of Akasha 385
perfected sages, souls free from the illusion of time and able to witness vast periods of evolution as ordinary human beings watch moments 67
personal self 42, 192
personal self, most of what one views as oneself is merely a set of tendencies 157
pessimism – a sure sign of corruption of truly human consciousness 157
philosopher practises continual process of consciously dying 86
Philosophia Perennis 127
philosophical negation, deep meditation, calm reflection and Pythagorean self-examination 118
Philosophy of Perfection of Krishna 58
planetary evolution describes a spiral 124
Plato 25, 26, 27, 28, 42, 50, 70, 85, 188, 191, 208, 230, 235, 344, 347

Plato, in Phaedo, depicts continual practice of dying as central to the life of the true philosopher 70
Plotinus 343, 345
prajna 61
pralaya 56, 67, 68, 69, 70, 72, 73, 128
pralaya and *manvantara*, dissolution and creation 70
pralaya, corresponding period of rest equal to *manvantara* 123
Prana 242, 269, 272, 313
Prana, or "Life," is the radiating force or Energy of Atma 313
prarabdha karma, the karma with which one has begun life 83
probation 179
Prometheus 152, 153
prostration 219
psuche, a self-moving agent 214
psyche 101, 108, 172, 187, 389
psyche, One cannot infuse the potency of the noetic mind into the polluted 82
psychic action works at the level of the molecular and the structural 69
psychic individuality, that self-determining power which enables man to override circumstances 80
pure being, develop the capacity to give a sense of reality to 137
purification of the will is vital to the spiritual regeneration of humanity 185
Pythagoras 50, 179, 180, 181, 232, 346, 347
Pythagorean teaching of the Aquarian Age of Universal Enlightenment 58

Q

quantum mechanics 206

R

Race in turn witnesses the rise and fall of continents, civilizations and nations 124
rebirth of humanity, the global, mirrors the archetypal birth of humanity in the Third Root Race 197
recollection 49, 153
recollection, all learning is 180
reincarnation 9, 21, 25, 28, 29, 30, 185, 345, 349
Reincarnation 349
Reincarnation and Karma are a part of Christianity, and may be found in the Bible 349
reincarnation and the trinity of man were held by many of the early Christian Fathers 265
Reincarnation, the philosophy of palingenesis 180

reincarnation, to make, a vital truth in one's personal life is to treat each day as an incarnation, to greet every person as an immortal soul 24
Religion of Responsibility of the Buddha 58
religion of responsibility, self-negation is shown by the timeless 175
remembrance 152
renunciation 69, 85
responsibility, in a position of , yesterday's libertine becomes today's tyrant 139
Resurrection 322
Resurrection of the Dead, or of all flesh, on the great Judgment Day 322
reverence, without, nothing worthwhile is possible in human life 237
Rishis and Mahatmas, likened in Upanishadic metaphor to the ribs of an umbrella sheltering all beneath 132
Robert Crosbie 2
Round is a major evolutionary period lasting many millions of years 124
Rounds and Races allow Man to assimilate the knowledge of every plane of existence 124

S

samadhi 238
Samma-Sambuddha 249, 250
Samma-Sambuddha, the knowledge of the whole series of one's past incarnations 302
samsara 34, 38, 44, 47, 170
samsara and *nirvana* actually refer to the two tendencies of the involvement of consciousness in form 35
Samsara and *nirvana* spring from the same ultimate essence, the *Adi Buddha* ..34
samskaras 128
samvriti 61
Sattva 53
sattva, rajas and *tamas*, the three dynamic qualities of Nature 51
Science of Spirituality of Shankara 58
scope of man's affairs all dictated by the needs of the soul 125
Secret Doctrine 2
Secret Doctrine points out where the lines of evolution and involution meet; where matter and spirit clasp hands 381
Secret Doctrine will be the basis of the "New Philosophy." 381
Secret Doctrine, The, the time must presently come when the really advanced thinkers of the age will be compelled to follow the lines of philosophical investigation laid down in 383
self-consciousness, divine origin of one's 199
self-correction and self-education 49

selfhood, dwarfing of one's true, is the crucifixion of Christos 111, 392
self-measurement should be in favour of what is strong, what is true, what is
  noble and what is beautiful in oneself 201
self-purification 184
Self-respect, only possible through the acquisition of moral self-consciousness...139
self-study 29, 69, 74, 111, 392
separate identity for each human being, falsehood of a 163
Shakespeare 141
Shankara 177, 179, 232
Shankaracharya 174
shila virtue — the attunement of thought, will and feeling to the pulsation of
  divine harmony 184
Shiva 109, 169, 170, 171, 172, 173, 390
Shiva as a *yogin,* as the archetypal Man of Renunciation, the paradigm of the
  pilgrim soul who has been through every possible experience of every
  possible human being 169
Shiva as the supreme god Maheshvara who presides over and transcends the
  process of creation 171
Shiva represents the assured capacity to reduce delusions to ashes 172
Shiva, destroyer of passions and of the physical senses, which are constant
  impediments to the growth of the inner spiritual man 149
Shiva, the supreme principle of potent ideation and constructive imagination,
  bridging the unconditioned and the conditioned 169
Shravakas, listeners 179
shunyata, supreme Voidness 86
Siva 149
Skandhas 7, 274, 275, 277, 283, 294, 296
sleep, healing and restorative property of, which Shakespeare so suggestively
  describes as Nature's second feast 112, 392
solstice, summer & winter 200
Soma 211
sophrosyne, the subordination of the inferior element to the superior 184
soul becomes capable at death of perceiving for a very short time the pure
  body of *Dharmakaya* 12, 42
Soul is by no means the Mind, nor can an idiot, bereft of the latter, be called a
  "soul-less" being 352
soul, for Plato, soul as perpetual motion or as a self-moving agent 27
soul, the desire to make noetic discriminations becomes the basis for a
  functional definition of the 27
soul-memory 60, 61, 66
Soul-memory is essentially different from what is ordinarily called memory .50
soul-memory, reawakening of 67

soul-memory, reminiscence 141
Souls progress from the restraint of the lower self or personality by the divine
 Self or individuality to the restraint of the Self divine by the Eternal 234
spiritual discipline 69
spiritual Ego of man moves in Eternity like a pendulum between the hours of
 life and death 252
Spiritual Ego, Buddhi-Manas, is *not* the HIGHER SELF 276
spiritual knowledge, springing up suddenly, spontaneously within the very
 depths of his being 57
spiritual self-regeneration in the service of others 201
Spiritual Sun 222
Spiritual teachers think and speak in terms of millennia and of millions of
 beings, and in many a Buddhist text it is said that the Buddha taught all
 three worlds 232
spiritual will 85, 116, 118, 176, 185, 188, 233
Sramanas, men of action 179
standpoint of the immortal soul 154
Stanzas of Dzyan 128, 130
Sthitaprajna, the Self-Governed Sage, the Buddhas of Perfection 58
sthula sharira 167
Sthulopadhi 241, 268
Suffering 90
Suffering and ignorance are collective; enlightenment and spiritual creativity
 are universal 95
Suffering is intrinsic to the universal stream of conditioned existence 92
Sukshmopadhi 241, 268
sushupti 112, 166, 392
Sutratma-Buddhi 201, 252, 305
Sutratma-Buddhi thus becomes *Manas-Sutratman*, and both arise through the
 fiery, Fohatic energy of the *Mahat-Atman* 201
sutratman 227
sutratman, In every incarnation the, should become stronger between the
 Silent Watcher — the overbrooding Dhyani or Divine Prototype — and the
 lunar shadow at the lower rung 227
sutratman, the repository of the fragrant aroma of past learning 214
sutratmic continuity and present learning, relationship between, is likely to
 remain obscure unless one is ready to probe deeply into the simplest things
 of life 213
sutratmic thread 71, 212
sutratmic thread, It is the continuity of this, that enables individuals to learn
 and recollect in any lifetime 213
svadharma 198

T

tanha, the powerful force impelling beings into involuntary reincarnation ...149
tapas 116, 200
Taraka Raja Yoga 241, 268
tathata 42
tathata, the *sunyata* state of total voidness 42
tejas 183
Tetraktys is emanated by concentrating the energizing light shed by the Logos 56
The Crest Jewel of Wisdom 58, 175
The Hero in Man 153
theoria and *praxis*, contemplation and conduct 180
Theosophical Movement 27
Theosophical Society 343, 349, 351
Theosophist, true, is one who independently strikes out and godward finds a path 100
Theosophy is building toward the future realization of the Universal Brotherhood and the higher evolution of man 382
theurgic powers, Every human being has brought into the world some distinctive experience of the immortal soul and its 233
theurgy 206
Third Eye 151, 207
Third Root Race 68
Time may be seen in terms of eternal duration, which is prior to it, and hence there are golden moments 97
time, serial view of, can have practical convenience 96
torchbearers for the humanity of our time 124
transition from the Fifth to the Sixth Sub-Races of the Fifth Root Race 68
Trikaya doctrine, the doctrine of the three bodies — the *Dharmakaya*, the *Sambhogakaya*, and the *Nirmanakaya* 40
true Self or immortal Triad 126
Turiya 53
turiya, a profound awareness from a standpoint which transcends the greatest magnitudes of spacetime 94
Turpitude (moral), taking pride in what is vile and base and pleasure in what is shameful; it is bravado in the service of Satan 227
twilight, hour of, as a metaphor for that time when "the Mystic shall be at home", A.E. calls it "the hour for memory" 152

U

unconscious cerebration at odds with the quickening of the Race-mind that is

taking place in the present cycle	139
undifferentiated consciousness, reality of total, soul has opportunity to see after death	43
Universal Brotherhood	351
universal enlightenment	230
universal enlightenment, part of the programme of evolution, cosmic and human, that there should be	154
universal good	164
Universal Mind	353, 360
universal responsibility, universal causation and universal unity	143
universal Self, deep love for is the true source of all other loves	134
universe, the, is man magnified a million times	32

V

Vach	127, 159
Vedânta	324, 326, 328, 331
Venus	87
Verbum	60, 124
Verbum of the *Gospel According to St. John*	55
violence, separateness and falsehood are all rooted in the fierce craving for life, for personal existence	38
Vishnu	129, 149
Vishnu function in the universe itself	129
vision of the spiritual travail of humanity requires a universal vision of karma and human experience	140
viveka, faculty of divine discrimination	52
Voice of the Silence	140, 158
volatility is invariably symptomatic of a high degree of karmic bondage	235
vow	348
vow, to take a, is to assist in the divine evolution of ideas	154

W

what is real in oneself and can be realized in practice is the only element that truly counts	203
Whenever an individual makes a new beginning, such a commencement could signify the start of a new phase of learning	214
Who am I?	50, 54
Will itself is a pure colourless principle which cannot be dissociated from the energy of the *Atman* released through breathing	185
will, purification of the	185

wisdom of the soul can span the *pralayas,* the periods of obscuration between Races and Rounds 61
Wisdom Religion or Theosophy is as old as the human mind 346
withdraw from identification with name and form *(namarupa)* through meditation 137

X

xenoglossy 213

Y

yajna 116, 190
yog, Sanskrit root, 'to unite' 52
yugas, doctrine of is not deterministic 124
yugas, Golden, Silver, Bronze and Iron Ages 124
yugas, the cycle of four epochs through which every Race passes 124

Z

zodiacal ages indicate the alchemical transmutation of the meta-psychological elements underlying formative change 211
zodiacal transition from the Piscean to the Aquarian Age, the formative forces of the emerging cosmopolis may be glimpsed through contemplating the 211

Printed in Great Britain
by Amazon

63130617R10245